Guy St. Clair
Knowledge Services

Current Topics in Library and Information Practice

Guy St. Clair

Knowledge Services

A Strategic Framework for the 21st Century Organization

DE GRUYTER
SAUR

Also by Guy St. Clair
SLA at 100: From "Putting Knowledge to Work" to Building the Knowledge Culture: A Centennial History of SLA (Special Libraries Association) 1909–2009
Beyond Degrees: Professional Learning for Knowledge Services
Change Management in Action: The *InfoManage* Interviews
The Best of OPL II: Five Years of *The One-Person Library: A Newsletter for Librarians and Management, 1989–1994* (with Andrew Berner)
Entrepreneurial Librarianship: The Key to Effective Information Services Management
Power and Influence: Enhancing Information Services within the Organization
Customer Service in the Information Environment
Managing the *New* One-Person Library (with Joan Williamson)
A Venerable and Cherished Institution: The University Club of New York 1865–1990
The Best of OPL: *Five Years of The One-Person Library: A Newsletter for Librarians and Management, 1983–1988* (with Andrew Berner)
Managing the One-Person Library (with Joan Williamson)

ISBN 978-3-11-046296-8
e-ISBN (PDF) 978-3-11-046552-5
e-ISBN (EPUB) 978-3-11-046308-8
ISSN 2191-2742

Library of Congress Cataloging-in-Publication Data
A CIP catalog record for this book has been applied for at the Library of Congress.

Bibliographic information published by the Deutsche Nationalbibliothek
The Deutsche Nationalbibliothek lists this publication in the Deutsche Nationalbibliografie; detailed bibliographic data are available in the Internet at http://dnb.dnb.de.

© 2017 Walter de Gruyter GmbH, Berlin/Boston
Typesetting: Integra Software Services Pvt. Ltd.
Printing: CPI books GmbH, Leck, Germany
♾ Printed on acid free paper
Printed in Germany

www.degruyter.com

For Andrew Berner

Foreword

As Charlie Munger of Berkshire-Hathaway famously said, "If you know how to learn, you know enough."

One of the things I so admire about Guy St. Clair's *Knowledge Services* is its ability to teach anyone how to learn from knowledge and to share knowledge, building on St. Clair's own pioneering experience and tools.

Winning companies today are all about continually gaining new knowledge, and then applying that knowledge. Thus, great organizations continually learn, unlearn, and relearn. At the same time, they have formed cultures wherein people embrace collective knowledge and growth by working alongside one another, and – even more often these days – with collaborators from outside their organizations.

Knowledge Services explains to readers just what it takes for an organization to learn strategically. Or, as its author puts it, ". . . to enable those who develop knowledge to share it, for the benefit of everybody in the workplace and in the knowledge services framework associated with the organization."

In this book, Guy St. Clair brings together, in an accessible and useful way, not only enlightening ideas, but also practical procedures for framing, completing, owning, and sharing knowledge and defining success. across organizations. He brings this to life with telling stories, ranging from a UN project in Kenya to an initiative at Citicorp.

Thomas Edison said he "readily absorbed ideas from every source." Peter F. Drucker said that the greatest innovations are those that challenge assumptions, and apply ideas from one application to another. Organizations that are built with knowledge services consistently share knowledge strategically and apply that knowledge to innovation and growth.

I have recommended *Knowledge Services* to all my students because I believe it will help each of them contribute something more critical to organizations they join or launch. It will teach them how to bring more knowledge to their customers, to their organizations, and to the world. And I heartily recommend it to anyone who is interested in learning how to better absorb, share, and apply new ideas. In today's world especially, I can't think of anything more important.

Elizabeth Haas Edersheim
New York Consulting Partnership
Author, *The Definitive Drucker* and
McKinsey's Marvin Bower
Lecturer, Consulting Strategies
Program, New York University

Contents

Foreword —— VII

Preface: Enabling the Knowledge-Sharing Culture —— 1

Acknowledgements —— 9

1	Building the Knowledge Culture —— 11
1.1	The KM/Knowledge Services Continuum —— 11
1.2	Management and Knowledge Services —— 26
1.3	Leadership and Knowledge Leadership —— 51
1.4	The Knowledge Strategist —— 80
1.5	The Organization as a Knowledge Culture —— 101

2	Applied Knowledge Services —— 119
2.1	Collaboration in the Workplace —— 119
2.2	Critical Success Factors: The Knowledge Services Audit —— 148
2.3	Measures and Metrics for Knowledge Services —— 169
2.4	The Knowledge Services Strategic Framework: A Recommended Strategy ("A Strategy for a Strategy") —— 192
2.5	Knowledge Services in Context: Enterprise Content Management (ECM) and Knowledge Asset Management (with Barrie M. Schessler) —— 217

3	The Way Forward —— 250
3.1	Change Management and Change Implementation: The Fundamental Knowledge Services Competency (with Dale R. Stanley) —— 250
3.2	Knowledge Strategist to Knowledge Thought Leader —— 276

Epilogue: Knowledge Services. The Critical Management Discipline for the Twenty-First Century Organization —— 295

Works Cited —— 303

Index —— 309

About Guy St. Clair —— 317

Preface: Enabling the Knowledge-Sharing Culture

Knowledge services is an approach to the management of intellectual capital that converges information management, knowledge management, and strategic learning into a single enterprise-wide discipline. The purpose of knowledge services is to ensure the highest levels of knowledge sharing within the organization in which it is practiced, with leadership in knowledge sharing the responsibility of the knowledge strategist. This book is written to provide guidance for the knowledge strategist and to serve as a reference for that management employee.

The knowledge strategist uses knowledge services as a framework for creating (or strengthening) the organization as a knowledge culture. In the knowledge culture, the entire enterprise benefits from excellence in knowledge sharing, an outcome characterized as successful knowledge development, knowledge sharing, and knowledge utilization (often designated with the acronym "KD/KS/KU").

In establishing knowledge services as a strategic framework for the twenty-first century organization, successful knowledge sharing becomes the norm, the standard. With successful knowledge sharing in place, the organization prospers and its mission is more easily and readily achieved than it would be otherwise.

In the workplace, one issue increasingly challenges all knowledge workers: the management of *intellectual capital*. That is, the facts, truths, or principles the organization's people know. This challenge continues to be of concern to organizational managers and enterprise leaders. It represents an enormous and costly drain for organizational management, particularly with respect to what might be referred to as the intellectual elements of the workplace. In the modern workplace, the management of intellectual capital continues to frustrate the best intentions of those responsible for organizational success (however organizational success is defined).

In many organizations, knowledge is not shared as well as it should be, and that impeded sharing is a very expensive weakness in any organization's management structure. This corporate knowledge (in the classical sense of the word "corporate") is recognized as *collective knowledge*. It is developed, shared, and expected to be used for the benefit of the organization in support of the accomplishment of the corporate or organizational mission. When knowledge is not shared, the quest to accomplish that mission is seriously impaired or, at best, inhibited and delayed.

The challenge of managing organizational knowledge is not new. The need to give attention to managing information, knowledge, and strategic learning and to establishing a framework for knowledge sharing has been a problem for management thinkers for longer than any of us can remember, and we continue to struggle with seeking solutions for making knowledge sharing easier and – in organizational terms – more productive.

We seemed to have found a solution several decades ago, with the introduction of knowledge management into the information management function. Knowledge management promised much. While enterprise leaders were a little slow in accepting the value and purpose of knowledge management (soon given its own acronym and eventually referred to simply as "KM"), there was considerable interest among some who worked with information, knowledge, and strategic learning. There was even enthusiasm – to a limited degree – within the wider population of knowledge workers, those members of the workforce who undertake such activities as writing, analyzing, and advising. Or, as expressed more broadly, employees in the workplace whose duties require them to use their knowledge, to earn their living by – as the work is often described – thinking, not by doing.

When KM came on the scene, there was more than considerable interest among one group of knowledge workers, those whose work is especially defined as "thinking." These were the academic scholars and, in particular, members of the academy whose subject specialty was management science. This group embraced KM with enthusiasm, generally raising the interest of many of us with any connection to information management and strategic learning. We were just as pleased. We truly thought KM was going to lead us to that knowledge-sharing nirvana we were all seeking for our organizations.

It didn't work out that way, as we now know all too well. Many in the workplace, especially middle- and upper-management employees as we went through the final years of the twentieth century and into the twenty-first, simply could not focus – with any useful perspective – on how a concept such as *knowledge* could be "managed." This hindered, but didn't prevent KM from developing; further evolution of KM awaited. Corporate blogger Jim Hydock, writing in 2015 about vendors at a professional conference for specialist librarians, referred to KM as an "artifact" of the last two decades or so, noting that KM had been "often maligned" (which was the case). But Hydock also optimistically noted that KM was now looking "refreshed" and in many ways reflected "a more mature model" (Hydock, 2015).

Despite that optimistic observation about KM, the fact is that organizational managers still seem to find themselves in a difficult situation with respect to knowledge management. There continue to be problems with KM being accepted in the management community and the concept is indeed "often maligned." Those of us working with information management, KM, and strategic learning recognized that it wasn't being accepted within the management leadership community as we had expected. We (and many of our organizational leaders) were frustrated that it was not leading us to where we wanted to be, so we began to look for another solution for managing intellectual capital, for helping us meet the knowledge-sharing challenge.

I took up the challenge, and in 2000 and 2001 I began to put forth the concept of *knowledge services* (St. Clair, 2000 and St. Clair, 2001). Whether anyone else was working with the term, I never found out; in any case, what I called "knowledge services" was a very specific solution for organization management, put forward for the purpose of enabling better knowledge sharing within organizations. As it turned out, knowledge services was not that far removed from KM, and as the elements of knowledge services began to fall into place, it became clear that perhaps what we had now was closer to KM than we had expected. As we played with knowledge services and worked with this new approach, we were aware that we had included KM, even from the beginning as we struggled to find a successor or a discipline for working beyond KM. It was one of the three "legs" of the knowledge services "stool," along with information management and strategic learning. So perhaps knowledge services was a new solution for sharing knowledge, and one which still retained KM as an essential element.

Whatever the connection, it did not take long to come up with a definition, a way of thinking about – and speaking about – this new management discipline we were ready to put to work for strengthened knowledge sharing. We identified knowledge services as an approach to the management of intellectual capital that converges information management, KM, and strategic learning into a single enterprise-wide discipline for the benefit of the business or organization in which it is practiced. As a management discipline, knowledge services connects with organizational success as knowledge workers seek to improve knowledge sharing in the company or the organization. It enables (or strengthens) knowledge sharing as the parent enterprise moves forward in the achievement of its organizational or business mission, establishing the environment for that KD/KS/KU mentioned above. In this connection, it is important to note that knowledge services as a management methodology is spoken of as a single entity, a compound subject, as we refer to such parts of speech in English grammar. As such, we apply the singular verb when we speak of *knowledge services*. Knowledge services *is* . . . .

Thus my rationale for writing *Knowledge Services: A Strategic Framework for the 21st Century Organization*: I want to provide readers – especially managers and organizational leaders who know of but are not comfortable with KM as a management framework – with structure for the implementation of knowledge services as a management and service-delivery methodology. In my first book on knowledge services, *Beyond Degrees: Professional Learning for Knowledge Services*, I put forward a number of "directions" (as I had done with a number of journal articles, presentations, and learning activities prior to that book's publication) designed to aid managers and information professionals in their approach to knowledge services (St. Clair, 2003). As I will describe later, that book was designed for a very different readership than this book and its purpose was singularly different. Now it is time for another book, prepared for a wider readership (dare I say a more universal readership?).

With the present work, I offer a specific framework for enabling any organization – for-profit, non-profit, or not-for-profit – to benefit from applying management, leadership, and knowledge services principles to the management of information, knowledge, and strategic learning in and throughout the organization. It is my intention to demonstrate how these principles – when thus applied – will provide particular value to the organization. Within this framework I include not only prescriptive directions for applying knowledge services. I give attention to the philosophy and history of management and leadership and their connection with information and knowledge services, specifically as they affect one's performance as a manager and leader in the knowledge services workplace. It is with this background, when combined with management and leadership skills, knowledge sharing, and the value of developing a knowledge services strategy, that the organizational knowledge culture can be built, or strengthened if it already exists.

When I suggest that this framework and these principles are designed to enable any organization – for-profit, non-profit, or not-for-profit – to benefit from their application I am quite serious. That inclusive point of view is deliberate and willful, for it is my purpose in this book not only to describe and provide prescriptive direction for managing knowledge services. I also take this opportunity to use his own statement about organizations to introduce Peter F. Drucker, my long-time mentor (although he never knew it and he has been dead for ten years), referred to often in this book. I have long advocated that any organization – and particularly those which formed the organizational background for most of my career – must be managed in what I referred to as a "business-like" manner, very carefully noting every time I stated the idea that I was not advocating that all organizations are for-profit businesses. Not at all. I was simply recommending that business management can provide valuable and useful insight, tools, and techniques for the management of any entity, any organization, any enterprise, for-profit or otherwise.

It was from Drucker's 1978 *Adventurers of a Bystander* that I took my inspiration for this concept although – truth to tell – it had been part of my professional thinking since I started my career. In the 1978 book, Drucker describes how when he was thirty years old he had published his first major book. It was *The End of Economic Man – The Origins of Totalitarianism*, published in 1939, and in the book he attempted, as he described it, "to analyze the roots of Nazism and the decay of

Europe's liberal and humanist traditions." By the time the book was published, though, he had "for quite some time been thinking of, and working on, a book that would deal with the future rather than the past, a book that would tackle the political and social integration ahead, assuming that Hitler would ultimately be defeated."

It was in his description of the later book, his book that "would deal with the future rather than the past" that I found my inspiration for my work and my professional career:

This book – published three years later under the title *The Future of Industrial Man* – first discerned that society was moving toward a society of organizations – we now call it "post-industrial society" – and that the question of status, function, and citizenship in these organizations and of their governance, would become central questions of the post-World War II world. *The Future of Industrial Man* was the first book that saw what by now has become almost commonplace: that the business corporation – or indeed any organization – is as much a social organization, a community and society as it is an economic organ. This book also laid the foundations for my interest in the management of institutions, and made it possible for me to start on the study of management.

With regard to the intended readership for *Knowledge Services*, some background may be in order. In the years leading up to the publication of my earlier knowledge services book, most of my work had focused on a wide-ranging but essentially single profession or line of work. I had been educated in the library and information science field, and although in the early days of my career my work as a management consultant took me away from library and information science fairly quickly, the influence of that line of work continued quite naturally as part of my professional thinking when I researched and wrote *Beyond Degrees*.

As part of this strong connection with library and information science, Dale Stanley has been – and continues to be – a strong influence. As a scientist and as a librarian, and as my closest colleague in the development and continued exposition of my ideas about knowledge services, Dale has been a partner in the work of SMR International and together we have shared in the experiences of working with much of the content about knowledge services that is shared here (he is quite naturally referenced frequently throughout this book).

Probably because my career had taken me considerably beyond library and information science, I began to realize in the late 1990s that there were elements in the overall concepts of knowledge management that were inhibiting its broad acceptance. As noted, I had continued to maintain a certain connection with library and information science. Although I seemed to be thinking more about KM and its role in the organization than about library management, I was obviously continuing to have some affiliation with librarianship.

Indeed, in 2005 – just two years after that first book on knowledge services had been published – I was invited to write the preface for a collection of essays about current issues in library and information science studies. In that essay, I again referred to knowledge services and incorporated into my definition the information, knowledge, and strategic learning attributes embedded in library and information science (they were already there – they had always been there). It just seemed natural to connect knowledge services and library science:

> Library science [I wrote in 2005] has broadened to embrace information science, using many of the organizational principles developed earlier as library science and now concerned with gathering and manipulating and storing and retrieving and classifying any form of information that has been recorded, in any format. But that simple transition is not enough now, for the modern seeker of knowledge wants more, to identify not only what has been captured and recorded but how it has been (or can be) used. Such an expanded and anticipated objective has brought about an even further broadening, if you will, of library and information science. Today we speak of librarianship, information management, knowledge management, and their overarching connection with learning, and we gather this entire realm of knowledge seeking into the discipline of knowledge services. This new discipline – the convergence of librarianship, information management, knowledge management, and learning – builds on the basic foundations of library science – as a *science* for the organization of knowledge – to lead the user in his or her quest. (St. Clair, 2005)

So knowledge services began with this very natural connection with libraries and information science. Of course I hope the present book will be used in the management of libraries, particularly in specialized libraries. It has long been my belief that with few exceptions, the management principles that apply in the world of organizational management also apply in what some describe as the "softer" areas of academia, non-profits, and not-for-profit entities such as libraries, universities, research facilities, historical societies, membership organizations, and the like. Like all other organizations, these must be managed in a "business-like" manner if they are to be managed successfully – as must also be each of their internal sections or business units. So there is content in this book that will be of use to managers in any of these fields, and will continue to be of value to library managers and those with management responsibility and authority for research and other information management organizations.

Connected to these thoughts, *Knowledge Services* is being published for a relatively new De Gruyter Saur series, designed to include books for which the authors are chosen "to provide critical analysis of issues and to present solutions to selected challenges in libraries and related fields, including information management and industry, and education of information professionals." The series title is "Current Topics in Library and Information Practice," and – from my point of view – having the book published in this series makes much sense, considering the origin of knowledge services.

At the same time, we can assert that these "related fields" mentioned for the series connect with any organization, business, community, or institution in which people come together to achieve an agreed-upon objective and in which they share knowledge in the successful achievement of that objective. In my opinion, knowledge services is subject- and organization-agnostic, and it is of critical importance for us to recognize that the principles identified and offered in this book apply in any field; they can be studied and applied with success in any organizational setting.

One reason for this emphasis has to do with my own work and experience, particularly after I began to focus my career on a consulting practice created to advise about knowledge services for any organization and in any management environment. This work together with my writings and my teaching activities (in client workshops, seminars, and webinars and, particularly, at the graduate level in academia) have all demonstrated that there is wide-ranging applicability for knowledge services in every organization and in all subject specializations.

As it happens, this assertion is most effectively demonstrated by the wide variety of corporate and organizational clients who turn to knowledge services when they realize that knowledge management, in and of itself, is a difficult concept in many management environments. These organizational leaders require an enterprise-wide approach to knowledge strategy that is not limited to particular discrete "domains" that operate as exclusive management entities or silos. For these organizational leaders, the knowledge services strategic framework enables an enterprise-wide management direction for the development of knowledge strategy.

The overall structure of this book is based on lectures offered in courses I teach at Columbia University in the City of New York. In late 2010, I was invited to come to the university to work on the development of a new graduate program in a to-be-determined subject area having to do with information and knowledge services. Our work evolved into Columbia's Master of Science in Information and Knowledge Strategy (IKNS), and I am very proud to have been one of the founders of the program, developed under the leadership of Dean Kristine Billmyer of the School of Professional Studies. I was part of an engaged and committed team of program development staff and as an employee of the university, I was honored to participate in the creation process for IKNS, working in program and course development, marketing, promotion, research, and overall planning. The program received its first graduate students in the autumn of 2011, and of course I was expected to teach a course. "Management and Leadership in the Knowledge Domain" was decided upon as my contribution to the teaching effort, both in the

IKNS program and, as luck would have it, also as a stand-alone classroom course, presenting my subject content twice each year to graduate students in other programs at Columbia.

In early 2015 I moved from IKNS to work with the School of Professional Studies Postbaccalaureate Studies Program, giving me the opportunity to teach my course for an even wider range of graduate students, including of course students from different graduate programs in the university as well as international graduate students in exchange programs, all taking my course as an elective. The course is now re-titled "Managing Information and Knowledge: Applied Knowledge Services," and the content is generally the same as in the original course although, as with any academic course, small changes and points of emphasis are put in place each time the course is taught. It all leads to "spreading the word" about knowledge services as a strategic framework in organizational management to a much wider audience and, in this case, an extremely diverse audience. It is a very gratifying position, and one which strengthens my assertion noted above (and based upon the responses of the graduate students I teach) that there is wide-ranging applicability for knowledge services in every organization and in all subject specializations.

It is my goal in *Knowledge Services* to offer a practical approach to the application of this strategic framework in any environment. Certainly not all of what I write here is totally practical. I've mentioned earlier that I sometimes take a slightly theoretical approach to knowledge services, including some recognition of the historical and philosophical background of the management, leadership, and knowledge services principals we embrace for enabling our work. There is much value in learning about what has come before.

At the same time, though, there is a need for a certain level of prescriptive direction when we speak about knowledge services, since the topic is relatively new and since so much effort is put into dealing with knowledge-sharing in practically any organization, even those which are moving – with varying rates of success – into their structure and organizational role as a knowledge culture. Therefore, Chapter 2, Section 2.4 provides a knowledge services "road map" (the popular designation in today's management community for the steps required for innovative actions). It is my sincere hope that this strategic tool will provide the checklist for any organization, regardless of the subject focus of the organization or the management structure already in place. I want our readers to use this road map to guide them as they move forward into knowledge services, and to strengthen knowledge services if our three-legged stool is already part of the organizational structure. If they do so, they will achieve success as knowledge strategists.

Guy St. Clair
15 April 2016

Acknowledgements

During my own journey in knowledge services, a great many people have expressed interest in the topic and kindly provided advice, offered guidance, and in more ways than I can remember influenced my thinking about this new and somewhat different approach to dealing with knowledge sharing in the organization. I thank them all sincerely, and wish it were possible to list all their names here. Sadly, as is the situation with most authors, while I am happy and deeply honored to list the names of many of these people, I must recognize that I am probably omitting some people who should be acknowledged, and I deeply regret this.

Nevertheless, among the many friends, clients, students, fellow strategic learning instructors and academic faculty, and co-workers who have willingly and openly given me assistance as I came along this journey, I specifically wish to acknowledge the support of and thank Kristine Billmyer, Scott Brown, Nishan DeSilva, Michelle Dollinger, Elizabeth Haas Edersheim, Victoria Harriston, Susan Henczel, Frances Hesselbein, Melanie Hibbert, Cynthia (Cindy) Hill, Richard Huffine, Deborah (Deb) Hunt, Robin Jourdan, Claudia Juech, Nerisa Jepkorir Kamar, Shahzad Khokhar, Steven A. Lastres, Kristin McDonough, Tammy Magid, Kevin Manion, Maureen Manning, Meghan Marx, Russell Maulitz, Amy Miller, Lisa Minetti, Evelin Morgenstern, Christopher M. Mundy, Douglas Newcomb, Hellen Nyabera, Ramon Padilla, Mary Palmieri, Thomas Pellizzi, Mitzi Perdue, Kerri Anne Rosalia, Bruce Rosenstein, Tony Saadat, Mor Sela, Megan Smith, Carolyn Sosnowski, and Pamela Tripp-Melby. There is another group which in my opinion must be given special attention. I describe them in the book's epilogue. They are Andrew Berner, Lee Igel, Anne Kershaw, Tim Powell, Barrie Schessler, and Dale Stanley, my special group of knowledge services advisers and colleagues. I thank them very sincerely for their advice and encouragement. Our conversations about knowledge services (with me individually or as a group) are always enlightening and enrich my thinking about our subject.

Finally, I must give particular recognition to the support (and editorial skills) of my husband, Andrew Berner. It is my honor to acknowledge him and to thank him for what he does for me professionally. I feel privileged to be able to dedicate my work to Andrew.

1 Building the Knowledge Culture

1.1 The KM/Knowledge Services Continuum

It is now clear that the knowledge continuum which began early in the last century has brought a new understanding and a new respect for knowledge to our modern management community. Nevertheless, we are not yet in a position to state that an organization's information, knowledge, and strategic learning content are shared to the extent that organizational stakeholders and affiliates require. We know that most organizations can benefit from better knowledge sharing, not only enterprise-wide but also within (and between) individual departments and business units.

That time will come, and while we are not yet where we want to be with knowledge sharing, we have learned much about how companies, organizations, and all other organized functional entities (including non-profit and not-for-profit organizations, as well as businesses) benefit when methodologies are established for ensuring practical knowledge sharing.

Indeed, our history goes further than most of us think. By the early 1900s, business leaders were beginning to recognize that change was needed with respect to information management, knowledge management, and strategic learning (although these functions had not yet been given the names we use now), and they began to give attention to distinguishing "practical and utilitarian" information from that sought for personal edification, educational purposes, or entertainment. As a result, across the twentieth century we find many examples of how workers in the sciences, business, and research struggled to deal with the information, knowledge, and strategic learning required to support their work.

By mid-century, business management had begun to take a hard look at how information was managed. Following World War II, the management of information (particularly scientific information) had reached a crisis point, and the struggle to deal with overwhelming quantities of information was on-going. As attempts to find solutions were made, information science – as a new discipline for dealing with the situation – became a major undertaking.

The management of information and the move toward the much talked about "information age" provided many strong and lasting contributions to the overall management of businesses and organizations. Yet while many of these innovations and new ways of thinking about information management were identified in many fields (not just in business management, as is widely assumed), the problem continued to grow. More innovation was required, and more solutions, and by the last decade of the century, the evolution of knowledge management (KM) was well under way. Organizational managers had begun to recognize that operational success could be better and more efficiently realized when the company's knowledge could be harvested and retrieved for organizational purposes.

Information management to knowledge management. Managing knowledge had been anticipated by several management and enterprise leaders who gave attention to these matters, including the man now regarded as "the father of modern management" (and who had – as described later – come up with the term "knowledge worker"). Peter F. Drucker was not about to permit the *value* of knowledge in the management arena to be minimized and he was one of the earliest management leaders to understand and put forward the concept that knowledge in and of itself is intrinsically valued for how it is used:

> The search for knowledge, as well as the teaching thereof, has traditionally been disassociated from application. Both have been organized by subject, according to what appeared to be the logic of knowledge itself ... Now we are increasingly organizing knowledge around areas of application rather than around the subject areas of disciplines. Interdisciplinary work has grown everywhere.
>
> This is a symptom of the shift in the meaning of knowledge from an end in itself to a resource, that is, a means to some result. Knowledge as the central energy of modern society exists altogether in application and when it is put to work.... (Drucker, 1969)

So the quest for solutions for managing all the information we were trying to deal with continued, giving rise – in 1982 – to probably one of the most-quoted statements we had about the problem: "We are drowning in information but starved for knowledge" (Naisbitt, 1982). John Naisbitt spent his career thinking about the future, and how future generations would deal with the problems he was identifying. He put forward his many ideas about the subject in *Megatrends*, his most influential work. The book was the product of ten years of research and established Naisbitt as one of the most important thinkers in future studies.

And Naisbitt's influence was not surprising. By the decade of the 1980s, certain signs were leading organizational leaders to think seriously about the management of information and knowledge. For one thing, increased computer power had put many management leaders on guard that something important was happening. While some of the runes were misread (such as the prediction about the "paperless office" – remember that one?) there was no doubt that the new field of information management and information science would enable sophisticated information capture and retrieval. Lynne Brindley, later Chief Executive, The British Library, has described what happened:

> The concept of information strategy was emerging, whereby information and libraries were seen as important knowledge resources to be harnessed and increasingly treated as a strategic asset – to underpin teaching and learning, research and knowledge transfer activities – which needed to be valued and managed.

Information strategies emerged in the 1990s in universities, with more or less enthusiasm, and beyond universities the focus was on the discipline of knowledge management, the concept of knowledge exploitation for competitive edge. There was recognition of the increasing economic value of information – of knowledge, both tacit (in people's heads) and explicit (more formal), as a key element of the corporate assets of the business. (Brindley, 2009)

Brindley went on to note that a strong proponent in this recognition of the emerging knowledge-based economy was Thomas Stewart, who had defined intellectual capital as "intellectual material that is put to use to create wealth." In doing so, Stewart seems to have introduced the concept of KM (although it was not called "KM" at the time): "Intellectual capital," he said, "is the sum of everything everybody in a company knows that gives it a competitive edge" (Stewart, 1997).

And by 1999 we had Drucker again sharing words of wisdom for us, this time providing us with the perspective we needed for thinking about knowledge as that corporate asset Stewart had identified:

Knowledge workers own the means of production. It is the knowledge between their ears. And it is a totally portable and enormous capital asset. Because knowledge workers own their means of production, they are mobile....

Management's duty is to preserve the assets of the institution in its care. What does this mean when the knowledge of the individual knowledge worker becomes an asset and, in more and more cases, the *main* asset of an institution? What does this mean for personnel policy? What is needed to attract and to hold the highest-producing knowledge workers? What is needed to increase their productivity? (Drucker, 1999)

So the movement toward "knowledge management" now began to make sense, and KM began to gain attention among leaders in the management community. As management leaders made the connection between the electronic capture of KM elements with knowledge sharing, performance, and strategic learning, the advantages of KM started to fall into place (and, importantly, to be recognized as *corporate* advantages).

Managing intellectual capital. For several generations, management and enterprise leaders in organizations and institutions were aware of the work performed by knowledge workers. For much of that time though, while the connection between organizational success and the role of those knowledge workers was more or less recognized, little particular attention was focused on their work. That state of affairs began to change in the early 1990s when Stewart called attention to the organization's intellectual capital and since then, organizational management and enterprise leaders have made many efforts to incorporate the concept of knowledge management into the workplace.

Was that the beginning of KM? The need for a solution had been apparent for some time. After the information "glut" of the 1950s, following the enormous growth of scientific and technical information that began during World War II (and which moved quickly into the further focus on scientific and technical information during the Cold War), and following the "information wars" of the 1960s and 1970s when the many disparate players in the information science and research management communities were all seeking to establish management leadership and authority for all dealings having to do with information and knowledge (commercial, scholarly, governmental, and all other categories of information), it was a natural next step to attempt to come to some understanding of the role of knowledge in organizational management and mission-specific success. As it turned out, a great many specialists and scholars in different parts of the world were working on the problem of how to manage these enormous amounts of information, so it was not too much of a stretch to try to apply some of these same techniques and solutions to dealing with the knowledge generated as that information was used, or to seek new techniques and solutions to be applied to the knowledge development and knowledge transfer process. So for some KM historians, the interest in KM as a subject and as a discipline dates to the 1950s.

Whatever the reasons for the growth of KM, people like Drucker and Stewart certainly pointed organizational leaders in the right direction, and the growth of interest in dealing with knowledge – with "managing" knowledge – made a great deal of sense. Indeed, aside from the value to the organization in the accomplishment of the organizational mission, it seemed to be generally assumed that achieving an understanding of the role of knowledge in the workplace would enable better performance. And why not? One does not attempt to organize and manage knowledge simply because knowledge is inherently good, or because acquiring knowledge makes one a better person. Achieving an understanding of knowledge in one's life and being able to deal with knowledge come together to foster an independence of thought, for most people a state to be desired, and unquestionably a state to be desired in the workplace. So it would seem to follow that understanding the role of knowledge in the workplace would permit one to give the subject at hand a level of attention that would enable excellence in knowledge asset management, leading to improved high-level research, strengthened contextual decision-making, accelerated innovation, and excellence in knowledge asset management, the now-recognized benefits of knowledge services invoked when the subject is discussed.

Thus we recognize a connection between knowledge and the workplace. As managers and organizational leaders began to place value on knowledge and the role of knowledge developed within the organization (and the importance of encouraging an organizational culture in which knowledge is shared by all employees at all levels), it made sense to think about how the organization at large might deal with this elusive and hard-to-capture intellectual capital.

Not surprisingly, by the late 1990s KM had become a function for considerable attention in the management of the well-run enterprise. Michael Dempsey, a journalist with *The Financial Times*, noted that "the first iteration of knowledge management featured a predictable helping of hype and was embraced by large organizations eager to underline their credentials by appointing a chief knowledge officer to spread the KM gospel. That approach belonged to the late 1990s and today businesses are less voluble about the term KM while more of them practice the ideas that gave rise to it" (Dempsey, 2006).

One of the reasons for that "predictable helping of hype" and our enthusiasm for the ideas that led to the rise of KM was simply that the whole idea of dealing with knowledge and attempting to manage knowledge seemed to be something of a contradiction. Could knowledge even be managed? The question has been asked often, and it is answered most often in the negative. Yet there was something very positive about the idea, and despite the difficulties (intellectually speaking) of defining what we were dealing with, it somehow felt "right," like something we *should* be doing in the workplace. For many knowledge workers (especially those who would develop expertise in knowledge services and become knowledge strategists), that struggle with "managing" knowledge was put into focus when Larry Prusak – often credited (along with Tom Davenport) with creating the term "knowledge management" – was interviewed about the subject. He acknowledged that he regretted having used the term, and expressed a wish to "take it back." Knowledge management, he said, "is really working with knowledge. You can't manage knowledge, *per se*. It is not a thing that is manageable. You can't manage love or honor or patriotism or piety. It is clearly working with knowledge, but the words got out there and there it is" (De Cagna, 2001).

Defining KM. So "knowledge management" it is, and at this point in time, many of the concepts associated with KM have become almost commonplace in the management lexicon. How they are put together, though, seems to vary widely in different organizations and environments. So much so that attempting to define KM becomes almost fun, and a big part of the fun is the fact that there are so many definitions and approaches to KM. Indeed, it might even be suggested that there are as many definitions of KM as there are people seeking to define it. It is a situation that leads to a considerable amount of confusion in some circles but in most cases the confusion is made more palatable (and interesting) as those participating in the discussion realize that what they are trying to do makes a great deal of sense. In their conversations they learn very early on that KM is context specific, and that no organization's specific KD/KS/KU framework is going to be like that of any other organization. KM in any organization is going to relate to and seek to address the organization's specific needs. In attempting to define KM in their own context-specific formulation, knowledge strategists and others in the organization discussing the subject are able to open themselves to a rewarding and often very useful intellectual endeavor.

Approaching a definition for KM begins with recognizing that many words and phrases come up with some frequency: "creating business value," "competitive advantage," "a systematic process," "leveraged decision-making," "collaborative," "integrated," and so forth. Some definitions acknowledge the role of technology, as Amrit Tiwana did when he described KM: ". . . an effective knowledge management strategy is . . . a well-balanced mix of technology, cultural change, new systems, and business focus that is perfectly in step with the company's business strategy" (Tiwana, 2000). Some definitions identify KM as a process, and others describe the discipline as a methodology for managing intellectual assets (especially unstructured assets) to ensure the creation, capture, organization, access, and use of those assets.

For some knowledge workers (and/or their managers), the goal is to take those unstructured assets and identify how that information can be transitioned from "information" to "knowledge," as Bruce Dearstyne has suggested. Dearstyne, a leader in the records and information management field, defines knowledge management as "cultivating and drawing on tacit knowledge; fostering information sharing; finding new and better ways to make information available; applying knowledge for the strategic advantage of the organization" (Dearstyne, 1999). Other definitions are directly practical. Nigel Oxbrow and Angela Abell, for example, took such an approach when they put forward their definition of KM: "The ultimate corporate resource has become information – the ultimate competitive advantage is the ability to use it – the sum of the two is knowledge management" (Oxbrow and Abel, 1997).

In attempting to define KM, it soon becomes clear that the function of managing knowledge is to ensure that working with knowledge becomes part of the workplace experience for all workers. Thus the function of working with knowledge is basically what organizations and institutions are attempting to do when KM is talked about, as we seek to put in place a framework for supporting that function. If the organization is to succeed in achieving its organizational mission, using knowledge developed within the organization and shared among organizational stakeholders becomes a critical purpose (Prusak and Davenport, 1998).

Still, there are problems with the many and various definitions applied to KM, and no matter how much intellectual pleasure we have in trying to pursue the discussion, the pleasure cannot alter the fact that in the workplace the discussion must focus on the anticipated KM role in the successful achievement of the organizational mission. For one thing, many of the definitions are not, by and large, particularly practical. It is not unusual for knowledge workers and their managers to experience some difficulty moving from their pleasant intellectual discussions about KM to identifying exactly how the discipline can be used in their particular workplace. They want to move to KM, and they know it is the right thing to do – to get their arms around the great wealth of knowledge captured within the organization – but making the move does not happen easily.

There are several reasons why this is the case. One constraint comes into play when the discussion turns to the ambiguities built into the definitions. People begin to ask questions like, "Is KM appropriate for our organization and culture?" or, put another way, "Are we ready for KM?" In many environments, "knowledge" as a term is a little off-putting, leading some workers (and, indeed, some in supervisory or management positions) to wonder if moving into KM is the right approach, since they have the idea that attention to "knowledge" is too academic, or too intellectual, and not down-to-earth enough with respect to the work of the organization. These arguments are quickly refuted when the discussion moves on to include examples of the costs of wrong information, or of knowledge not shared, or of failing to meet a compliance regulation because a particular knowledge-transfer procedure was not in place.

Discussions about defining KM also get a little sticky when bad examples are put forward (often by workers with limited or pre-conceived ideas about knowledge or the advantages of knowledge development and knowledge sharing in the workplace). Typically based on poorly defined or ill-conceived KM experiences that have not been successful and are often the result of a misplaced or misapplied technology focus to the subject at hand, these kinds of failures can sour executives and organizational sponsors, resulting in a larger reticence about KM that prevents innovation and intellectual stretching the next time a KM opportunity comes along. Even when there is interest in moving to a KM solution, many knowledge workers and knowledge strategists can find themselves bogged down in discussions about databases, new tools, technological barriers, and the like. By the time they get back to thinking about their users' perspectives and the "big-picture" organizational needs that got them to thinking about KM in the first place, the idea of putting KM to work for their organization has become a monumental task.

Of course there are the more formalized and structured definitions of KM, and reviewing them and seeking how they apply in the immediate workplace is a valid and welcome exercise and – not coincidentally – a valuable strategic learning experience. These definitions are legion, and while some focus on the technology or the organizational structure or the codification of seemingly divergent and almost-overwhelming content volume (our notorious "big data" of recent years), others, when reduced to their most applicable elements, make sense and assuredly apply in the organizations for which they are developed. For many who wrestle with defining KM, Michael E.D. Koenig made the job much easier in the introductory paragraphs of "What is KM? Knowledge Management Explained," his May 4, 2012 article in *KMWorld*.

Koenig's paper offers a description many have since used when describing KM, especially when speaking with co-workers and management leaders who came into their management careers prior to 1990 or so. In the article Koenig states that "Knowledge Management (KM) is a concept and a term that arose approximately two decades ago, roughly in 1990. Quite simply one might say that it means organizing an organization's information and knowledge holistically . . . ."

Koenig goes on to note that:

> The operational origin of KM, as the term is understood today, arose within the consulting community . . . and from there the principles of KM were rather rapidly spread by the consulting organizations to other disciplines. The consulting firms quickly realized the potential of the Intranet flavor of the Internet for linking together their own geographically dispersed and knowledge-based organizations. Once having gained expertise in how to take advantage of intranets to connect across their organizations and to share and manage information and knowledge, they then understood that the expertise they had gained was a product that could be sold to other organizations. A new product of course needed a name, and the name chosen, or at least arrived at, was Knowledge Management. The timing was propitious, as the enthusiasm for intellectual capital in the 1980s had primed the pump for the recognition of information and knowledge as essential assets for any organization. (Koenig, 2012)

Concluding his thorough analysis of the background of KM, Koenig notes that "perhaps the most central thrust in KM is to capture and make available, so it can be used by others in the organization, the information and knowledge that is in people's heads as it were, and that has never been explicitly set down."

It is truly a noble aspiration, and certainly Koenig is to be commended for thinking in this direction. Many of us like to think of this ideal, yet it remains elusive. In truth, we are not yet at the point where tacit information ("in people's heads") is "explicitly set down" in quantities that would render it particularly useful.

Nevertheless, we hope for it, and we make many attempts to move toward that fine state. As we attempt to be realistic, all of us working with KM and knowledge services find ourselves playfully – and perhaps with a little frustration – commenting about how there seem to be as many definitions of KM as there are people attempting to define it, a situation that is not at all hard to understand since any such attempt will be colored by the specific needs of the employees, operational structure, and goals and objectives of the organization.

So each of us involved with KM and knowledge services finds very particular definitions of KM to throw into the conversation. We wrap the specifics of knowledge services – our convergence of information management, KM, and strategic learning – around whatever definition of KM matches the needs of the specific situation with which we are dealing. To use the same construct as when we think about information management, KM, too, is "powered." Just as information management is powered by information and communication technology, so is knowledge management powered by the knowledge development, knowledge sharing, and knowledge utilization (KD/KS/KU) structure to which we give so much attention in knowledge services. The connection between knowledge services and knowledge management, then, becomes quite natural as we learn how the two concepts are conjoined – along with strategic learning – in support of one another in the organizational workplace. For some of us, despite all our efforts to be as specific as we can when we write and speak about KM it can also be helpful to think a little differently. While we don't refute the usual and multitudinous definitions for knowledge management – for they lead to a general understanding about KM and how it can be beneficial to the company or organization – some of us prefer to think a little off course about KM, to think of KM as being not necessarily a *product* or a *thing*. We see KM as a management *practice* that is used to help an organization manage explicit, tacit, and cultural information, knowledge, and strategic learning content in ways that enable the organization to reuse this content for creating new knowledge. "More than anything else, KM is an established atmosphere or environment, a *culture* in which the development, sharing, and utilization of knowledge – at all levels within the organization and including all levels of knowledge – are accepted as the essential element for the achievement of the organizational mission" (St. Clair, 2003). So perhaps, as KM definitions seem elusive and/or problematic, there is another way of thinking about KM, and this might be the way of resolving the conundrum.

Knowledge management to knowledge services. So despite the best intentions, efforts to move forward with knowledge management did not seem to be enough. Why? Because managers, corporate executives, and even leaders in organizations and institutions that were not necessarily business-focused required a unified approach. For efficiency and for effectiveness, they needed an enterprise-wide knowledge strategy that applied to all strategic knowledge. They wanted a strategy would enable the enterprise to access and deliver any content connecting to any part of the organization and, not to be dismissed, to its success.

These management leaders wanted a practical approach to dealing with information, knowledge, and strategic learning across the enterprise. They knew their organizations were challenged and the challenge had to be met. They had already learned that enterprise-wide knowledge development, knowledge sharing, and knowledge utilization (that KD/KS/KU we refer to so often) could not take place through the outputs of discrete functional entities. While these many functional units, such as records management departments, for example, or specialized research libraries, corporate archives, staff training and learning units, information technology departments, database design units, or web development units, to name a few, had been created and were put in place as individual and separate operational entities, no one was looking after *enterprise-wide* KD/KS/KU. No thought was being given to an institutional or organizational knowledge culture, one that would engage not only the usual knowledge-focused units of the organization, but all functional units (since all units must develop, share, and use knowledge). The entire organization needed a practical way to deal with knowledge, to establish some sort of efficiency in each section and to be of benefit to the larger enterprise.

The challenge would be an enterprise-wide knowledge services strategic framework, a strategy supported by knowledge specialists who understood and championed the place of a knowledge strategy as part of the organization's structural framework. These knowledge strategists (we would call them) would be charged with developing a solution for better knowledge sharing. Their approach – which would become knowledge services – would be a way to work, a management and service delivery methodology merging information management, KM, and strategic learning into a single over-arching operational function, an approach to the management of intellectual capital. Its purpose would be to ensure the highest levels of knowledge sharing within the organization in which it is practiced.

As a methodology, knowledge services was based on the understanding and agreement of all organizational stakeholders that the most critical asset of any group or environment is what its people know, the knowledge, the intellectual capital, that is (as Stewart had characterized it), the organization's most

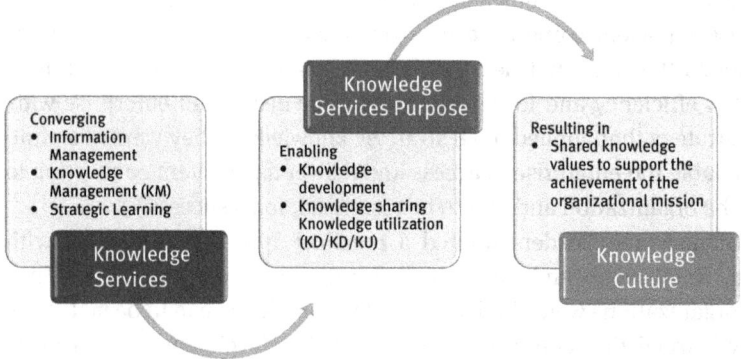

Figure 1.1: Knowledge services in the organization.

competitive (and arguably its most vital) asset. Knowledge services, and the knowledge services specialists to implement knowledge services, would provide the organization with the tools its people require for ensuring that the organization's intellectual assets are captured, organized, analyzed, interpreted, and customized for maximum return to the institution, a direction this author identified in what might have been the first published article on knowledge services (St. Clair, 2001).

Enter knowledge strategy. And the knowledge strategists to do the job. Knowledge strategists are management employees with responsibility for knowledge services, and they have a very specific role in the knowledge services workplace. It is their task to position themselves for developing knowledge services as the organization's strategic framework for managing its intellectual capital. In doing so, they use knowledge services as a technique, a tool for creating (or strengthening) the organization as a knowledge culture. They establish an operational environment for the organization in which the entire enterprise benefits from excellence in knowledge sharing, an outcome characterized as successful knowledge development, knowledge sharing, and knowledge utilization (KD/KS/KU).

So it turned out that for many employees in today's workplace, the solution dealing with the many problems relating to the management of intellectual capital is to combine KM with what is already being utilized and identified as productive, to move to knowledge services, the subject of this book. In doing so, they are then dealing with the three elements of knowledge services on an ongoing and connected basis. They establish information management as a workplace methodology concerned with the identification, acquisition, capture, organization and arrangement, storage, retrieval, analysis, interpretation, packaging, dissemination, and use of information. They recognize its value, and they recognize that knowledge services is powered by information and communication technology (ICT), as the term is phrased in Europe and other parts of the world or, as phrased in North America, by information technology (IT), with both abbreviations referring to any product or line of products that stores, retrieves, manipulates, transmits, or receives information electronically in a digital form.

They also have a clear understanding of the role of strategic learning in their work. These employees are strategic learning experts, for they long ago came to recognize that strategic learning is really nothing more than a fancy designation for any learning activity through which any employee becomes better qualified to do his or her job. It can be as sophisticated as leave time for pursuing an advanced degree in a subject that will strengthen workplace performance, or as uncomplicated as working with the colleague in the next cubicle to learn how to tweak an application to make it more relevant to one's work. Just as they understand information management, these knowledge workers understand strategic learning because it has always been part of their work, even if they don't use that term. And when called upon to do so, they embrace knowledge services because they understand that in converging information management and strategic learning with KM (however defined), they and other colleagues who work with information, knowledge and strategic learning become empowered to perform at a higher level. In doing so, they bring that enhanced performance into a workplace ambiance that acknowledges and supports KD/KS/KU, contributing to the success of enterprise as a knowledge culture.

It is a natural connection, this linking of information management, KM, and strategic learning. With these practices already connected in the minds of many knowledge workers, they are employees who, as we will see, are already qualified to become knowledge services leaders in their workplace. In their experience and in the excellence of their work with knowledge and in knowledge-related tasks, they become – in one way or another – knowledge specialists. In thinking about this natural connection, it is reasonable at this point to explore the arrangement of these parts and their connection with other terms and concepts being explored. Knowledge services, *per se*, is stated as the subject of this book, yet it is also a subject that is studied *along with* KM, with KD/KS/KU, with knowledge strategy, all leading up to the establishment – or strengthening if it already exists – of the knowledge culture as the primary contributing element to enterprise success. Yet no matter how delicately we move about this sextet of connecting parts in the management of the organization's intellectual capital, it is knowledge services that provides the foundation and enables the other parts of the process to move forward.

The organizational value of knowledge. When considering the role of knowledge services – regardless of the type of organization or enterprise – we generally begin with the organizational goal, its mission. Every enterprise has developed (or should have developed) an organizational vision statement, a mission statement, and a statement of the organization's values. While these are implicit and not spelled out in some organizations (a situation not recommended, as it leads inevitably to confusion and, in some cases, disarray in terms of customer and staff expectations), every organization has some goal or objective that states – however loosely – why it exists.

It is in the pursuit of the organizational mission that the catalytic property of knowledge services brings enterprise-wide value. As noted earlier, a basic tenet of knowledge services is that knowledge value is created when those who have knowledge and those who need to work with knowledge are able to share what they know, finding opportunities that produce tangible results. Thus knowledge services – as a management and service delivery methodology – is positioned to contribute to the organizational mission.

Making the connection between knowledge services and mission-critical success is not hard to describe (even though it is – depending on local circumstances – often hard to achieve). Obviously the goal is attainable (or chosen because it is thought to be attainable), or it would not have been chosen in the first place. It can even be achieved with excellence and high standards of quality service delivery if all stakeholders understand – as Peter Drucker has famously put it – that they give attention to three basic management elements. Managers and their direct reports must "focus on the mission, define the results we are after, and assess what we're doing and how we do it." The organization's management team and all participants in the effort must begin at the beginning, identifying and analyzing the parent organization's vision, mission, and values statements (Drucker, 1998).

A closely related next step is to identify, analyze, and compare the vision, mission, and values statements of the functional unit which has knowledge services management responsibility vis-à-vis the vision, mission, and values statements of the larger enterprise. These three actions, more than anything else, will ensure that all players in the process are aligned in their understanding of their larger goal and ensure that in the many discussions to follow, this goal will be the beacon that guides them in their work.

Of necessity, then, we speak much in the management community about the organization's vision, mission, and its values with respect to the workplace and its offerings to its market, and we do so also when thinking about the role of knowledge services in the larger enterprise. It is helpful to consider fundamental, agreed-upon definitions, and for our purposes we turn to Michael Allison and

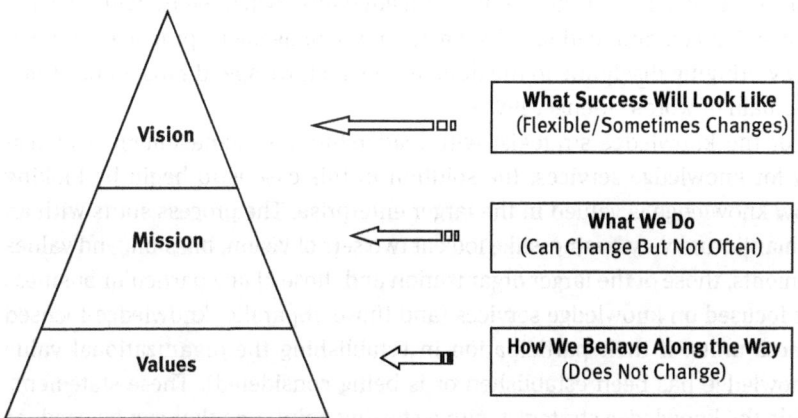

Figure 1.2: Vision, mission, values (Michael Allison and Jude Kaye: Strategic Planning for Non-Profit Organizations).

Jude Kaye, who write for the non-profit sector. Although they advise particularly for one environment, these specialists provide easy-to-articulate descriptions that can enable those with knowledge services responsibility in any environment to have themselves – and to be able to explain to others in the organization – a good idea of where the focus on knowledge services can begin. Allison and Kaye describe the vision statement as "an image in words of what success will look like," the mission statement as communicating "the essence of the organization, why it exists," and the values statement as a description of "principles or beliefs which guide stakeholders as they pursue the organization's purpose" (Allison and Kaye, 2005).

Deeper drilling is called for, though. Having an idea of what the enterprise vision, mission, and values are – as stated publicly – is one thing, but coming to grips with how they are incorporated into the organization's operations can be a challenge. Peter Senge captured the basics of this problem: "Peter Drucker has elegantly presented the three ingredients of the discipline of innovation: focus on mission, define significant results, and do rigorous assessment. But if it sounds so simple, why is it so difficult for institutions to innovate?" For Senge, the search begins with the mission: "It is very hard to focus on what you cannot define and my experience is that there can be some very fuzzy thinking about mission, vision, and values," Senge wrote. "Most organizations today have mission statements, purpose statements, official visions, and little cards with the organization's values. But precious few of us can say our organization's mission statement has transformed the enterprise. And there has grown an understandable cynicism about lofty ideals that don't match the realities of organization life." To move beyond the cynicism, Senge suggests, requires that managers recognize that the essence of leadership ("what we do with 98 % of our time") is communication: "To master any management practice, we must start by bringing discipline to the domain in which we spend most of our time, the domain of words" (Senge, 1998).

For the knowledge strategist with leadership and management responsibility for knowledge services, the solution in this case is to begin by looking at how knowledge is valued in the larger enterprise. The process starts with an unromantic and very businesslike look at two sets of vision, mission, and values statements, those of the larger organization and those of any particular business units focused on knowledge services (and those of parallel knowledge-focused business units, if their participation in establishing the organizational value of knowledge has been established or is being considered). These statements provide the knowledge strategist with a starting point, one that can be used, as noted above, to determine goals that the organization can be expected to meet as it pursues its specific purpose. It is in this activity that the particular strengths of the knowledge strategist come into play, for no one else in the organization has this knowledge worker's particular ability for linking the organization's knowledge services requirements with the requirements of the larger enterprise focus. In understanding the value of an organizational knowledge culture, this employee is well qualified to articulate how the implementation of KD/KS/KU through knowledge services can yield results that will benefit the entire organization.

We now understand that the organizational goal is to achieve success, however success is defined for the organization. To achieve that success requires the consideration of several specific elements in the organization's operational structure. First of all, we recognize that an enterprise-wide knowledge culture establishes a theoretical and intellectual atmosphere for actionable interactions with respect to information, knowledge, and strategic learning. In every organization, all transactions and intercourse among the various stakeholders require the sharing of information, knowledge, and strategic learning. When KD/KS/KU is carried out in a culture that recognizes and supports the highest standards of knowledge sharing, all parties reap the rewards. As an organizational and operational philosophy or ethos, the knowledge culture stands as a functional environment in which all parties seek to strengthen the relationship between technology and knowledge, with particular emphasis on strengthening the connection between technology and knowledge as developed and shared in the workplace.

The results of that connection are evident in organizations where knowledge services is taken seriously, for they lead to the optimal creation, use, and sharing of information, knowledge, and strategic learning across the entire enterprise. These knowledge-services focused organizations give priority to demonstrating the critical and strategic role of high-quality knowledge services for all organizational stakeholders, including leadership, staff, and affiliates. There is generally a central connection point or knowledge nexus for the organization, often with operational responsibility for the management of knowledge services delegated to this functional unit, ideally on a whole-of-enterprise basis. In these knowledge-centric organizations the elements – the different steps – of the knowledge services strategic framework are under the leadership and authority of the organization's knowledge strategist and shared by and respond to the requirements of the organization's employees. It is a useful and productive arrangement, with particular attention given to developing and implementing mission-specific and inclusive enterprise content management (ECM) and to the structuring of a knowledge-focused organization in which staff skills and competencies reflect the commitment to support the organization through strengthened relationships among all enterprise stakeholders.

1.2 Management and Knowledge Services

Management and leadership provide the foundation on which applied knowledge services is built. In this section and the next we explore a variety of techniques and tools for managing and leading the development of the knowledge services strategic framework. In doing so, our objective is to provide the background for ensuring that the organizational knowledge strategy – built on that strategic framework – matches the organizational mission or business strategy. Meeting the goal is required, whatever the subject or purpose of the enterprise.

There are those who assert that looking to the future means never referring to what has gone before. I am not one of them. There are also those who feel that a book such as this should offer only prescriptive advice, that is, it should simply tell the reader "how to do it right." Many people seeking to learn about a new field or profession are interested only in "tell me what I need to know to be able to work in this field so I can get a job." So much of what the learner comes to understand about a type of work boils down to that "how-to-do-it" construct, without much attention to how workplace applications came about or what different influences brought about the specifics of the work as now practiced.

On the contrary, I think it is important to recognize that management and leadership theory and practices did not spring full grown from contemporary business schools, but represent the present iteration of theories and practices dating further back than one might expect. A few examples will suffice.

For example, from the ancient days of China we learn that military leader Sun Tzu (sixth century BC) recommends understanding both strengths and weaknesses – in both the manager's (my term, not his) own organization and the organization's competitors. Nearly a thousand years later, Niccolò Machiavelli (1469–1527) in *The Prince* depicts the manager (again, my term) as harsh when necessary but – at the same time – understanding the value of the positive results of managing. In the classical management literature, both Adam Smith (1723–1790) – in *The Wealth of Nations* – and John Stuart Mill (1806–1873) were known for theories relating to management elements such as resource allocation, production, and pricing, and by the time we get to the nineteenth and early twentieth centuries, we have a solid list of the manager's tasks from Henri Fayol (1841–1925): "to manage is to forecast, plan, organize, command, coordinate, and control."

Somewhat parallel with Fayol's work is that of Mary Parker Follett (1868–1933), a very creative manager who started out as a social worker and through her work in that field became a management theorist. Now identified as one of the great pioneers in organization theory and organizational behavior, Follett was so successful in her work she was recognized for her advice and her intellectual contributions. Indeed, President Theodore Roosevelt was so impressed with Follett and her work that he named her his personal advisor for guidance about managing not-for-profit, non-governmental, and voluntary organizations. Surely an interesting contradiction to what most of us think about in terms of management and management development because – with Follett – the attention was not necessarily with financial affairs and the achievement of profit. She was interested in organizational management *per se*, without concern about whether her management advice would be applied in a business or non-profit organization.

Interestingly Follett's life coincided with that of another American president, Calvin Coolidge who, in speaking about the role of the press in democracies to the Society of American Newspaper Editors in 1925, used the phrase "the chief business of the American people is business" (most often misquoted as "The business of America is business"). Famously thought by later generations to have been so caught up in the great attention to business during this period (he was in the White House from 1923–1929), he was, in fact, merely suggesting in the speech that the press is likely to be "more reliable" if it pays attention to "business currents" than if it does not. In Follett's case, though, her focus was on any kind of management and organizational leadership and she was not promoting management solely as a business discipline. In fact, Follett is thought to have coined the term "transformational leadership," a phrase we will work with in the next section as we look at Frances Hesselbein's thoughts about transformational leadership.

One specific of the growth of management as an organizational function has had great impact, and that was the first appearance of salaried managers, probably in the late nineteenth century. That it came about is not surprising, as this was just about the time of Frederick Winslow Taylor's famous and very important *Principles of Scientific Management*. Taylor (1856–1915) was mostly interested in establishing efficiency and – as one of the earliest management consultants – is credited with having established the modern system of industrial management. Taylor, along with Chester Barnard (1886–1961) whose 1938 book *The Functions of the Executive* set out a famous theory of management and organizational studies, were to become two of the most influential theorists leading into the period between the two world wars and the immediate aftermath from the end of World War II.

Concurrently and taking those of us who want to become acquainted with the influential management and organizational theory leaders on into the mid-twentieth century and their connection with knowledge services, we come again to Peter Drucker, already discussed (and to be further discussed) in this book. In my opinion there is no greater influence for us as we think about the management connection with knowledge services and the development of organizational knowledge strategy. Drucker began this particular influential role in 1939 with the publication of *The End of Economic Man: The Origins of Totalitarianism*. He had started the book in 1933, a few weeks after Hitler came to power, and the book led the way to his assertion that society's leaders and enterprise managers must come to think of management as an alternative to tyranny. It was a pretty heady assertion in 1939, when the book was first published, and it wasn't ignored. Indeed, writing in the introduction to a later edition of the book, Drucker himself described the attention it had received, by noting that "Winston Churchill, then still out of office, wrote the first review, and it was a glowing one. When, a year later, after Dunkirk and the fall of France, he became prime minister he gave the order to include *The End of Economic Man* in the book kit issued to every graduate of a British Officers' Candidate School." Drucker also apparently had a little fun observing that the book was "appropriately enough packaged together with Lewis Carroll's *Alice in Wonderland* by someone in the War Department with a sense of humor."

The journey into management and the management/knowledge services connection holds up very well when we embark on one more element of management and organization development history, the ongoing "management-as-an-art-or-management-as-a-science" discussion (I won't distinguish it at this point as an argument because it's been going on far too long and no conclusion has been reached, or will be reached). Management can be (and is) considered a science when we go back to the work of such early management leaders as the aforementioned Frederick W. Taylor. With his 1911 *Principles of Scientific Management* Taylor called for managers to use standardized and systematic methods – a technique that became known as "scientific management" – for establishing work rules and organizing the work that employees were expected to carry out. He became famous, and Taylor is often considered the leader in the management-as-science school of thought. It is generally to Taylor that we allude when we think about basing managerial decisions on the precision of the facts and principles we attempt to apply in any given situation. In this connection, of course, it is in common perception that respected value judgements are to be made – whenever there is a financial consideration – using the famous "bottom line." Obviously this description for any kind of management is vastly oversimplified, but it does help to give us an idea of what the knowledge strategist, as a manager and as a leader, will be expected to deal with when functioning in a management position (which, ideally, is exactly where in the organizational management structure the knowledge strategist functions!).

At the other end of the spectrum, management (and leadership, as we shall see) can be considered an art when the practice of management incorporates and drives much of its managerial activity around soliciting and respectfully listening to the thoughts, ideas, constructs, and opinions of other people with whom the manager works. Going back to an earlier discussion on a different subject, thinking of management as an art takes us back to the "humanist" idea of working, a concept that depicts people coming together as colleagues and co-workers to accomplish some goal or achieve some mission. Among the leaders in this line of thinking were people like David E. Lilienthal (*Management: A Humanist Art*), who took what he specifically referred to as a more "humanist" look at managing. While his professional recognition was not particularly in the management arena, Lilienthal certainly knew about the place and role of management in society and developed considerable expertise and recognition as a manager and leader throughout his career as a successful public utilities attorney, a founding director of the Tennessee Valley Authority (its chairman from 1941 until 1946), and the chair of the Atomic Energy Commission. In 1966 he was invited to deliver the Benjamin F. Fairless Memorial Lectures at Carnegie Institute of Technology. In the lectures, which he titled *Management: A Humanist Art*, Lilienthal described his subject of management as "simply stated: the ability to get things done." Throughout his career (and in other writings), Lilienthal had made the point that most people recognize that "big business is or can be a vital and beneficial social force," and he stated at the beginning of the lectures that his purpose in the lectures was "to describe my concept of the manager's function of leadership in the crisis areas of the world's life today and tomorrow." His conception of the managerial function was that it is "a humanist art, with the development of the latent capabilities of people as its basic goal and purpose."

So Lilienthal – like so many others who connect the management function to leadership – referred to many critical societal matters as he spoke about the management function (he was particularly taken with President John F. Kennedy's referring to the sixties as the "Decade of Development"). He made it clear that the societal "driver" he followed in his thinking about management was indeed "to get things done" but to get things done in a way that will provide the greatest benefit to society:

> The heart of the modern managerial task is to close the gap between man's goals and the fulfillment of those goals; to make practical in man's daily lives the discoveries of the scientist and the techniques of the engineer; to translate into reality the visions and dreams of poets and artists; to bring to actual fruition in men's lives the aspirations of social reformers, the theories and concepts of scholars and economists, the stirrings in the hearts of the compassionate, the desperate need of the hungry, the shelterless, the sick and the heavy laden. (Lilienthal, 1967)

These are indeed the thoughts of a manager and leader, and as Lilienthal pursued his version of the managerial function his belief was well stated: "Management's primary skill, in my view, is human, not technical, and therefore the manager must be measured broadly in terms of human personality, the intangible qualities of leadership." With Lilienthal it wasn't just techniques and standards; successful managers, in Lillienthal's version of this line of work, not only work with their employees. When appropriate, the manager must undertake the role of motivator and facilitator, thus connecting management with leadership. With the success of the lectures, Lilienthal can be credited with establishing the legitimacy of the concept of management-as-an-art.

So how do we connect today's management and organizational theorists with others who recognized the connection I refer to above, the link between information management, knowledge management, and strategic learning and the teachings and influence of earlier theorists? From my point of view, we look for people in our own timeframe, people like Henry Mintzberg, who noted as recently as 2011 that "Managers' time is filled with interruption, but basically managing is about influencing actions, working through people and information. Managing can't be programmed or simulated," a point of view that contrasts directly with that of the scientific and standardized management methods we are speaking about, when we talk about management-as-science (Allio, 2011). We intentionally look for people who can guide us as we seek to combine management with the work of the knowledge strategist and identify those contemporary management (and leadership) theorists who "speak to us," the writers and speakers who help us personally as we make the journey from theory to the implementation of practical, everyday activities that enable successful knowledge sharing.

In my case, I've come up with several I turn to regularly. The two at the top of the list are James Gleick (*The Information – A History, a Theory, a Flood*) and Walter Isaacson (*The Innovators – How a Group of Hackers, Geniuses, and Geeks Created the Digital Revolution*). Both books are full of history *and* management theory and advice, ranging from the academic, graduate-level operational and functional direction to the sweetest, conversational discussion about how you – or someone you know – can do this or that thing better. And, more than anything else about these two authors and their work, both are very talented story tellers, a fitting and singularly useful characteristic in any book having to do with the development of a knowledge services strategic framework or an organizational knowledge strategy. Knowledge work is story telling (possibly the single fact on which all those who work in the knowledge domain agree!).

But with these two authors it is more than story telling. It is providing further insight into the "management-as-art and management-as-science" discussion, and both leave us with a very good understanding that it is not either-or; it is both. Gleick's "sweeping survey" (as his book has been admiringly described) is indeed full of stories, and the people who make up those stories. He brings to life such names as, from as far back as the early nineteenth century, Charles Babbage, the designer of the "analytical engine," remembered primarily for coming up with the concept of a programmable computer. Also on Gleick's long list is Augusta Ada King, Countess of Lovelace, Lord Byron's daughter who was herself a mathematician and writer who worked with Babbage (and – for modern theater audiences – the inspiration for Thomasina in Tom Stoppard's 1993 play *Arcadia*). Many, many other names are there to inspire the knowledge strategist, names ranging from Alan Turing, Claude Shannon, and John Archibald Wheeler to G.H. Hardy, Charles Bennett, Lewis Mumford, and Stephen Hawking, all worth an excursion to the reader's favorite biographical resource (Gleick, 2011).

Equally fascinating to the knowledge worker who wants to learn more about the history of his or her field is Isaacson's book. Obviously the popular names – such as Steve Jobs – are there (and it's been said that Isaacson interrupted his work on *The Innovators* to write the Jobs biography). There are plenty of nineteenth-century figures (including Charles Babbage, here as well) and many in the twentieth century, Vannevar Bush, Grace Hopper, and many others, all too numerous to list here. Ada Lovelace is in Isaacson's book as well, several times as a matter of fact and she – rightly so – inspires Isaacson's beautiful conclusion to his book, written to be a history and a tribute to the many people who worked so hard over the years to enable the digital society we now enjoy. Not only is his book written to honor past innovators, he deliberately chooses to honor those who will work as hard in the future. In fact, his final thoughts are worth repeating as we think about management-as-art or management-as-science:

> C.P. Snow was right about the need to respect both of "the two cultures," science and the humanities. But even more important today is understanding how they intersect. Those who helped lead the technology revolution were people in the tradition of Ada, who could combine science and the humanities. From her father came a poetic streak and from her mother a mathematical one, and it instilled in her a love for what she called "poetical science." (Isaacson, 2014)

Isaacson concludes with what, for me, stands as the perfect motivation to lead us as we go forward with knowledge services and the development of knowledge strategy in support of the organization as a knowledge culture. Those of us working in this field cannot help but be inspired when we read Walter Isaacson's final comments in *The Innovators*:

> The next phase of the Digital Revolution will bring even more new methods of marrying technology with the creative industries, such as media, fashion, music, entertainment, education, literature, and the arts. Much of the first round of innovation involved pouring old wine – books, newspapers, opinion pieces, journals, songs, television shows, movies – into new digital bottles. But new platforms, services, social networks are increasingly enabling fresh opportunities for individual imagination and collaborative creativity. . . . This innovation will come from people who are able to link beauty to engineering, humanity to

technology, and poetry to processes. In other words, it will come from the spiritual heirs of Ada Lovelace, creators who can flourish where the arts intersect with the sciences and who have a rebellious sense of wonder that opens them to the beauty of both.

Which brings us back to Drucker and our quest for the most appropriate management approach for what we want to achieve as we seek to structure a knowledge services strategic framework. And certainly surprising no one who has read this far, Peter Drucker's thinking about management puts him, too, in the humanist corner. Drucker's management directions connect very precisely with knowledge and leadership and the interactions of the people designated as leaders in the management of an activity or organization. Indeed, in the book of Drucker's which seems to put forward his most rewarding thoughts about management (*Management: Tasks, Responsibilities, Practices*), he defines management and management responsibilities clearly. Although he outlined these thoughts often, the description in this book is the one that resonates strongly with me and so many of my colleagues. Drucker's management definition comes in the second and third paragraphs of his Preface:

> Management is tasks. Management is a discipline. But management is also people. Every achievement of management is the achievement of a manager. Every failure is the failure of a manager. People manage, rather than 'forces' or 'facts.' The vision, dedication and integrity of managers determines whether there is management or mismanagement.
>
> This book therefore focuses on the manager as a person. It focuses on what people do and what people achieve. Yet it always tries to integrate people and tasks. For the tasks are objective and impersonal. It is 'managers' who perform. But it is 'management' that determines what is needed and what has to be achieved. (Drucker, 1973)

This manager-as-humanist construct is reflected even further in a filmed interview with Dr. Lee H. Igel, a Drucker expert and Associate Professor at New York University's School of Professional Studies. The purpose of the interview was to give Igel the opportunity to speak about Drucker's management and leadership principles and how they connect to success for knowledge strategists. Igel began the conversation with a direct reference to Drucker's intuition about knowledge strategy, noting that Drucker had anticipated that organizations (and society) would undergo major transformation as we moved to what Drucker called a "knowledge society."

"He made it very easy," Igel said. "He didn't think it would happen until 2010 or 2020, and now we know we didn't get to it in 2010 [the interview was filmed in 2011] – or at least completely to it – so we have 2020 to look forward to. But the timing doesn't matter. Drucker could see that we were moving to a 'new way' of managing, a new way of doing business."

We moved on to speak a little about Drucker's ideas about management, and Igel commented that Drucker was very insistent that the management principles he espoused were not about him, but about a bigger idea, about applying them in to workplace, oriented to action. And the bigger idea continued to kick in with his own thoughts about what happened after he had expressed an opinion; when he wrote something, he would then render it obsolete. He very much believed that once something has been done, it was only a matter of time until everybody took it up.

"What's interesting about Drucker's management ideas," Igel continued, "is that in the past we had been managing in terms of collections, numbers, and such. It was (and still is for some managers) the old way. In Peter Drucker's world management is about human beings, and in the shift from collections to management that focus moved on to the workers as human beings. It's not about people being interchangeable parts. What we're really doing is identifying the new order, the new way of doing business, a new way of managing."

"Look at what's happening as we look at the world today. Today we have all these old assumptions, old ways of doing things. But now we have new realities to deal with, and we find ourselves turning toward organizations and society built on knowledge. Economics, politics, different parts of society: always doing things that have been around too long, and they can't continue to do that any longer."

So we have to ask: Where are we going? How did Drucker anticipate what was going to be happening?

"This was a question he was often asked," Igel said, "about how he came up with the important ideas he anticipated and put forward for people he knew would be interested. And as it turned out they were important ideas he had, about things he saw, like the rise of Hitler, or – much later – the fall of the Berlin Wall. But he resisted any reference that he might have been 'predicting.' Indeed, in one of Drucker's most famous quotes, he said very simply: 'I don't predict. I look out the window and see the future that is already happening.' It became one of his most famous sayings."

And with the coming of the knowledge society, is there any way we can connect that "looking out the window" with the what's coming up for us? Can we define knowledge services so that the convergence we're advocating helps organizations and their workers move forward into the knowledge society?

"Perhaps you've already done that," Igel said, a big smile on his face. "Perhaps you looked out the window and you could 'see the future,' could see that knowledge work in all organizations will require a new way – a different way – for enabling better knowledge sharing, and that's why you came up with knowledge services, why you put the course together for your graduate students."

And when we speak about Drucker and how we apply his ideas to management, particularly to management in the knowledge services/knowledge strategy arena, how do we apply and respond to what we see out the window? How would

Drucker advise a knowledge strategist to deal with a need for better knowledge sharing in his or her organization?

"It's a decision the knowledge worker has to make for himself or herself," Igel said. "The knowledge worker can't count on management to figure it out and tell them what to do. When that strategist looks out the window, the question that has to be asked is: how do I get to it, how do I make it practical? And that relates to one of the fundamental issues of management in general. Most executives aren't involved in knowledge services and knowledge strategy development. They need the information, the knowledge. They aren't interested in how it's managed or how it gets to them – generally speaking. One of the big Drucker ideas, you might say, is taking something that is theoretical and asking 'OK. What are you going to do about it? What are you going to do to make it practical?'

It's a question every knowledge strategist needs to ask.

For many of us, we've come to almost count on Drucker's humanist point of view for inspiration as we pursue our management tasks as knowledge strategists. Already we see that the knowledge strategist has the opportunity to approach the Drucker philosophy of management with a certain level of confidence, since we and the philosophy of knowledge sharing that has come down to us from him are in agreement and we can connect with what he offers. The first "direction" (we might call it) from Drucker notes that management has mostly to do with people and their engagement. With respect to the knowledge strategist's situation, the engagement he or she is looking for is engagement with other knowledge workers and their co-workers about the development, sharing, and utilization of knowledge. It is an activity knowledge strategists are involved in all the time.

Thus the knowledge strategist can consider and expect to encounter two types of management, management as an art and management as a science, with the two having enormous similarities and great differences. As the knowledge strategist moves into working with both "sides" (we might say) of the management spectrum, possibly the most important consideration must be a full and – as much as possible – unbiased understanding that in most workplace situations, both management types are going to be in play in any organization.

Many pages can be devoted to defining management, but that is not our purpose here. We have our informal definition at the beginning of the chapter, and additional informal definitions will fall into place as we move through our studies and experiences with knowledge services. Certainly we have Drucker's very direct description of management above. We have established that the knowledge strategist is going to have management responsibilities and authority with respect to enterprise-wide knowledge sharing, and will – not to be dismissed too quickly – be held accountable for the organization's knowledge sharing, for the success for knowledge services throughout the organization.

1.2 Management and Knowledge Services — 35

As for what those responsibilities will be and what the manager will do, this topic has been described so often that it seems almost excessive to try to come up with yet another definition of management. Before he offered his own definition (one of the best, in my opinion), Donald Hislop noted that "There is a vast academic literature concerned with explaining and understanding the role of senior and middle managers in organizations, with whole books being devoted to the topic" (Hislop, 2009). We can accept his word for that, although it's likely before this chapter is finished we will have been provided with a few more favorite definitions of management. In the meantime, though, hear Hislop's own definition for what we do as managers:

> Management as a term can be used as both a noun and an adjective. The term management, used as a noun, refers to a group of people who have responsibility for managing people and other organizational resources. Used as an adjective, management refers to the process by which people and organizational resources are controlled and coordinated with the intention of achieving particular objectives.

The definition can with good success be applied to the work of the knowledge strategist, as can a look at what Peter Drucker thought about management. An initial connection is described in Elizabeth Haas Edersheim's *The Definitive Drucker: Challenges for Tomorrow's Executives – Final Advice from the Father of Modern Management*. Under an expected header Edersheim gives us Drucker's philosophy on money, management, knowledge, and on the individual. As we anticipate the role of the knowledge strategist in building the knowledge services strategic framework for the enterprise, his words about management seem to match exactly what we are anxious to consider:

DRUCKER PHILOSOPHY
Efficiency is doing things right.
Effectiveness is doing the right things.

On Management
Management has mostly to do with people, not techniques and procedures. Their engagement is what matters.
The effective decision maker makes actually few decisions.
The three most important questions are:
- What is our business?
- Who is the customer?
- What does the customer consider value?

(Edersheim, 2007)

But the words mean much more than they appear to mean in this short list, and especially for those of us who work with knowledge services. For us, these are the phrases we begin with. Then we let them take us forward as we move into our work as knowledge strategists. One of the most impressive of Drucker's principles is that, as noted in our first section, knowledge workers are assets for the organization, and "management's duty is to preserve the assets of the institution in its care" (Drucker, 1999). Edersheim provides further guidance for us, for a full chapter of her book is devoted to Drucker's commitment to the role of knowledge workers as human beings (or more succinctly, as he said to Edersheim in one of their meetings, "Management is about human beings"). They are workers, of course, but they are workers whose value to the organization builds not so much on what the organization's leaders expect of the organization but what they expect – and support – in the value the workers bring to the organization. Edersheim refers often to Drucker's "human orientation" and from where I sit, that is the overarching secret (if there are any secrets in the management of the knowledge domain) to the success of any effort relating to the development of the knowledge services strategic framework – the enterprise-wide knowledge strategy – and the elevation of the organization to its functioning as a knowledge culture. The organization is going to rise or fall as its people are given the opportunity to do their best work as assets to the organization. Effectiveness is, of course, the standard we seek, and through knowledge services the organization positions itself for effectiveness because its leaders, its workers and their relationships (both internal and external), and its support of different and better methodologies all come together in the knowledge-centric environment. Or, in developing the knowledge services strategic framework, we find guidance in one of Drucker's most well-known ideas (Edersheim notes that he stated it often). He strongly encouraged what we refer to in knowledge services as strategic learning, creating opportunities for helping people learn and develop: "Every knowledge organization is a learning and teaching institution. Knowledge can't be taught, but it can be learned" (Edersheim, 2007).

Drucker doesn't stop with strategic learning, though. He takes knowledge-sharing "to the floor," as we would often describe it, by asking managers and – from our perspective – asking knowledge strategists if knowledge is built into:
1. customer connections (meaning, for the knowledge services team, their interactions with organizational staff for whom the knowledge services team provides guidance)
2. the innovation process (meaning, for the knowledge services team, how information, knowledge, and strategic learning can be used to accelerate innovation and provide a speedier solution for a problem for which an innovative approach is required)

3. collaborations (meaning, for the knowledge services team, how they and organizational working groups and communities of practice accomplish what they set out to accomplish)
4. the knowledge services team itself (meaning that the knowledge-sharing need is recognized as such and will be managed to ensure that knowledge relating to any specific project or activity will – now and in the future – be accessible when it is needed).

In my own knowledge-centric world, because I feel so strongly that all applications of knowledge services, knowledge strategy, and the organizational knowledge culture fit any organization (regardless of the subject matter or focus of the organization, and are not necessarily limited to the business world), Edersheim's chapter on "People and Knowledge" resonates strongly. Throughout the book, the emphasis is on Drucker's attention to the person, to people we – knowledge strategists or organizational managers – are working with; not surprisingly, that focus for us is even stronger in Edersheim's "People and Knowledge" chapter. And since the earlier "On Management" section of the Drucker Philosophy opens with "management has mostly to do with people, not techniques and procedures – their engagement is what matters," we now have laid out for us exactly what the knowledge strategist has before himself or herself, exactly what is needed for success in building the knowledge culture. Taking this idea in its logical direction I find much inspiration at the end of the chapter and happily quote Edersheim's final reflections about respecting employees and investing in them, and – as must surely have been made clear by this point – applying these thoughts to the work of the knowledge strategist:

1. People are much more than employees. They embody the knowledge, the capabilities, and the relationship that your company takes to the market. The organization is more dependent on its people than its people are on the organization. People *are* the most important investment a company makes.
2. Enabling people to live up to their potential, achieve their maximum effectiveness, and contribute to the organization's performance is what makes the difference between success and failure. That enabling is the role of management. In an organization of self-managing knowledge workers, "command and control" is obsolete. "Trust and support" is key.
3. Successful teams generally dissolve at the end of a project, but the knowledge organization must create and deploy them again and again.
4. Business survival requires applying and integrating knowledge continuously to create value all the time. (Edersheim, 2007)

For me this direction continues, and I am particularly impressed with what Edersheim offers us, especially as we might "translate" these ideas into knowledge services principles. In particular, I advocate the third, which in a single line accurately supports our goal for our knowledge culture, that in the knowledge culture the successful teams of the knowledge organization "must create and deploy them again and again."

These principles and others I have acquired about knowledge services and knowledge strategy match well what I've learned so far, and particularly with respect to the work of Peter Drucker. I have been – and probably will be for as long as I live – a great fan of two Drucker titles, books which I "swear by" (to use the popular cliché) and which I share with anyone who offers the slightest inkling of being interested in our work with knowledge services and knowledge strategy development. I refer to *The Daily Drucker* which, just as the title says, offers a day's worth of good thinking on each page, and *The Five Most Important Questions You Will Ever Ask About Your Organization.*

In this section, as we think about management and a management philosophy to take us forward as knowledge strategists, the latter turns out to be a particularly helpful guide, especially to complement the questions put forward in Edersheim's book (and, of course, her further explication on Drucker's approach to management conveyed throughout her book). The questions raised in *The Five Most Important Questions . . .* relate specifically to the idea that management has to do with people, with their engagement, just as we have been discussing. I submit that those of us seeking to influence an organization's acceptance – or growth – of its role as a knowledge culture would do well to bring the concepts in this book into our conversations with co-workers, affiliates, senior managers, and all others connected with us and our work in the organization. The book is all about engaging these colleagues and – we hope – potential knowledge services advocates in the organization, and the sections of this small reader can provide inspiration and practical guidance as the organization's knowledge strategist seeks to take the knowledge services strategic framework forward.

Yet in introducing these books to our management readers, there is another nagging question from some who work with strategy, including knowledge strategists. This concern comes into play as these strategists think about how management theory and practical implementation are combined, particularly those who – as I described earlier – are not particularly interested in learning about (or from) those who have come before. It is very easy to turn away from the Druckers and the Lilienthals and treat them and their ideas with some disdain. After all, they are gone now, and there are plenty of people who work in management who think of ideas about a more humanist approach to management as "old-fashioned" (the term I hear most applied by the uninitiated to Drucker's management philosophy) or "no longer relevant" (as with those who hear about Lilienthal's work and offer their opinion about his ideas of management as a humanist art). In my view, the philosophies offered by Drucker and Lilienthal and people like them – and many others, some of whom I've named earlier – are not old-fashioned or irrelevant. Their thinking is classic, in the opinion of Timothy Powell, to be heard from further in another part of this book. In Powell's way of thinking – and I am in total agreement with him – *classic* is the perfect word to describe the philosophy and principles given down to us from many of our earlier leaders. While their thinking might have come into the management language in an earlier time, nothing they or their colleagues have given us is anything less than a standard or model for moving forward with the practical implementation of management theory. We are honored to stand on their shoulders and learn from them.

The knowledge strategist as manager (1). The development of knowledge strategy – like the development of any business or management strategy – is nothing more that an attempt to decide upon a group of actions or activities that will produce an agreed-upon goal (which phrase itself might be another succinct way for describing the management function). Managers strategize all the time, and most managers are happy to do so. Developing strategy (regardless of the organization's subject matter, the workplace focus, or even the management structure of the institutions or firms that employ the managers) is based on the idea that with a strategy in place, the organization can accomplish what it has chosen to accomplish. And an added benefit of developing strategy is that the very act forces managers and their staffs to give thought to whatever organizational vision, mission, and values are in place. Basically these managers and their staffs are developing a road map for action, including (built into every strategy) a framework for monitoring what is accomplished and assessing the results. The steps to be taken are all summed up neatly in a precise little package of directions from Allison and Kaye (they call it "the value of planning"), referenced earlier when we considered the role of organizational vision, mission, and values. For Allison and Kaye the value of planning is that it:

- Forces all stakeholders to focus on the organization's purpose, business, and values.
- Provides a blueprint for action.
- Identifies milestones which can be used to monitor achievements and assess results.
- Provides information that can be used to market the organization.

Allison and Kaye wrap up their notes with their own definition of strategic planning, noting that the purpose of the strategic plan is prescriptive, to "help the organization do a better job by setting up an organizational framework that is both strategic and systematic" (Allison and Kaye, 2005).

As it happens – and it's the beauty of knowledge strategy – all activities, at every level, require KD/KS/KU. The principles of whatever line of work for which knowledge is developed and shared can be applied to the management of all of the organization's intellectual capital. At the same time, the knowledge strategy, built on the knowledge services strategic framework, ensures that knowledge sharing rises to the highest levels possible.

The experienced knowledge strategist's management activities require that he or she be multi-talented. Yet when we speak with these managers about their work, most of the talk seems to be about dealing with finances and cost situations or working with others in the organization who are not necessarily attuned with the knowledge services situation but who have a solid understanding of the organization's business needs. When the problem to be solved is one that relates to finding the best tool for searching for information, for example, or dealing with vendors who are not familiar with the specifics of an organization requiring a customized solution, a disconnect comes into play.

It is this kind of financial challenge – and especially from a "big-picture" strategic planning point of view – that the knowledge strategist as manager must frequently deal with. When is the best time to decide whether an overall records management solution, for example, can be acquired? Is it better to wait until there is a need – as happens in some large organizations – and attempt to go "back" to fix problems that could have been prevented earlier? Or does the KD/KS/KU planning team attempt to deal with starting with a totally new solution, bringing in all the disruption that such a solution brings into the organization. These are not easy questions to answer, and they put knowledge strategists to the test frequently as these they seek to carry out their management responsibilities.

In a similar test the knowledge strategist as a manager has a very specific responsibility to take the KD/KS/KU message out to the larger organization, particularly in guiding established working groups and administrative staff (to say nothing of the organization's technology management team) in understanding that knowledge services implementation success depends on a solid infrastructure. It's a management duty that seems to call for the unique qualifications of the knowledge strategist and one that, in many organizations, does not get resolved until later in the planning process. By that time, with the knowledge strategist finding himself or herself "running in circles" trying to keep track of groups and planning teams that had already been making decisions without the input of the knowledge strategist, the solution becomes more and more difficult to find and leads to disappointment all around until the solution is found and agreed upon.

Which thought leads to one of the most important attributes we find in people working with knowledge strategy. One of the knowledge strategist's most important responsibilities is communication. These managers must be able to convey to organizational leaders – as well as to all planning and administrative teams working with knowledge services – the realities and limitations of what can be done within the framework of the organization's technical infrastructure and the organization's corporate culture. These often pose challenges that require collaboration and on-going communication, and knowledge strategists must have expert skills in these areas.

There are other responsibilities, too, that strongly support the knowledge strategist's work as the knowledge authority – the "go-to" executive, perhaps – in the enterprise. Cynthia A. Montgomery, who specializes in connecting leadership with business management, finds three connected pursuits for business strategists, and I would argue that they are particularly appropriate for the knowledge strategist; these concepts need to be noted and available for quick reference in the knowledge strategist's management toolbox. In "How Strategists Lead," a journal article, Montgomery builds on the thesis of her book, *The Strategist: Be the Leader Your Business Needs* and describes the strategist as a meaning maker for companies, as a voice of reason, and as an operator. It is my opinion that these three management roles – strategy roles – are particularly required for the knowledge strategist.

Montgomery describes how ". . . it is the leader – the strategist as meaning maker – who must make vital choices that determine a company's very identity." Surely this is a management determination that, in the case of the knowledge strategist, can be argued to take up a critical place in the establishment of organization as a knowledge culture, an assignment that – it is becoming clear – senior management and enterprise leadership expect of the knowledge strategist.

And the knowledge strategist as a voice of reason? Absolutely. If there is any one function that the organization's stakeholders must be given the opportunity to understand, it is the ongoing quest for success with KD/KS/KU. Yet most people – even people who self-identify as "knowledge workers" – don't think about knowledge development, knowledge sharing, and knowledge utilization. It is just "something we do." Or not, as is often the case, which is why the knowledge strategist not only must assume responsibility for ensuring that KD/KS/KU is embraced as a normal part of the working life of the organization's employees and clients. When called upon (as happens often, or which should happen often), the knowledge strategist must also lead the way in setting up – or working with the people who set up – the organization's change management processes and activities. This, as much as anything connected with knowledge strategy, is a continuing challenge. The knowledge strategist – as the organization's voice of reason in matters having to do with the management of enterprise intellectual capital – has an obligation and the opportunity to see that KD/KS/KU succeeds. If change is required – as it will be – it is the responsibility of the knowledge strategist to ensure that change management principles are followed and that the change management function is undertaken for implementing the identified and necessary changes.

In the third role of the general strategist, Montgomery also makes a strong case for the knowledge strategist when she writes of the strategist as an operator:

> A great strategy, in short, is not a dream or a lofty idea, but rather the bridge between the economics of a market, the ideas at the core of a business, and action. To be sound, that bridge must rest on a foundation of clarity and realism, and it also needs a real operating sensibility.

A critical task of the knowledge strategist is to ensure that the practical, everyday realities of knowledge services and successful KD/KS/KU are designed into any knowledge strategy being developed. Whether the strategy is expected to provide guidelines for an enterprise-wide knowledge activity, or whether the focus is on a narrower and immediate short-term quick win, the knowledge strategist as operator continually keeps in mind the "distance" (it might be called) between theory and application. In its simplest and perhaps most reasonable framework, the whole purpose of knowledge development, knowledge sharing, and knowledge utilization is to establish a connection between what is developed and shared and how it is applied in the workplace. That application can, of course, be rooted (and often is so rooted) in the mundane day-to-day work that we just have to get done, and with a strong KD/KS/KU structure, all stakeholders are able to perform those tasks as well as they can be performed.

At the same time, though, there is the great goal of seeking and accelerating innovation, getting beyond the mundane, and it is in this role that the knowledge strategist as operator flourishes.

Responsible management. In the interview described above, Dr. Igel and I concluded by discussing what we understand to be two of the most important

Figure 1.3: The knowledge domain workplace.

requirements for managers, particularly as management principles are undertaken in support of successful, enterprise-wide knowledge-sharing. Considering the subject of the filmed interview, it is not surprising that these requirements emanate from Peter Drucker and what we've come to know about his own personal approach to management. Both Igel and I are impressed with the fact that throughout his work and his writings, Drucker (sometimes explicitly and sometimes by implication) spoke of the two requirements with equal attention. The first requirement is, of course, managing the organization, establishing the organization's effectiveness. The second is perhaps more subtle and alludes to a larger role for the well-managed organization, its role in supporting the "greater good." In the business world, the topic has become known as corporate social responsibility (and I suppose the terminology could be put to use in any organization, using the classical meaning of "corporate"). The subject (usually abbreviated in the management literature as CSR) is given much attention in the modern management community and it seems an appropriate concept for discussion with respect to knowledge services, knowledge strategy, and the organizational knowledge culture, since the whole idea behind knowledge sharing is to look away from one's self and to identify opportunities for situations in which colleagues and other affiliates can benefit from KD/KS/KU. In our conversation, Igel and I discussed how the knowledge strategist determines how CSR matches and gets built into his or her work as a knowledge strategist? "The organization is an organ of society," Igel says, sharing one of Drucker's most famous statements. "It exists as part of something bigger. You can't do harm in one area and do something socially responsible in another. The two responsibilities must work in concert. Social responsibility must work with the first requirement; the two requirements don't work separately. There is a need for management to incorporate social responsibility into the management plan, to make the decision to ensure that the organization contributes to society and is not causing harm."

And I quickly find a Drucker statement to support the point Igel and I were making in our conversation. In the same Preface referred to, the one in which Drucker offered the definition of management quoted above, he also had something to say about this larger role for organizations and their managers. As Drucker put it, in management the emphasis is not on management skills, tools, and techniques. It is not even on the work of management. It is on the tasks. Here is Drucker's take on responsible management:

> For management is the organ, the life-giving, acting, dynamic organ of the institution it manages. Without the institution, e.g., the business enterprise, there would be no management. But without management there would also be only a mob rather than an institution.

> The institution, in turn, is itself an organ of society and exists only to contribute a needed result to society, the economy, and the individual. Organs, however, are never defined by what they do, let alone by how they do it. They are defined by their contribution. (Drucker, 1973)

In our consideration of how we develop the knowledge services strategic framework and how the knowledge strategist will work as a manager, it is important to recognize and to understand that we must be careful about one seeming assertion of the modern management community. There seems to be one line of reasoning among modern business leaders that establishes management as "business administration," a way of thinking about management that implies that management doesn't have anything to do with entities outside commerce, such as, for example, organizations like charities and activities in the pubic sector. I strongly believe that is not the case, and in my opinion – especially as we seek to strengthen knowledge sharing within the organization – it is the responsibility of the knowledge strategist to follow Drucker's lead, to recognize that every organization must manage its work, people, processes, technology, and knowledge services to maximize effectiveness, and that effectiveness includes efforts to contribute "a needed result to society, the economy, and the individual."

It is a point well made in a newspaper article in which HSBC Chairman Stephen Green was quoted.

> Milton Friedman was wrong to assert that companies should focus on shareholder value above all other considerations. Of course you need a profit, but it is a by-product, a hallmark of success. It is not the *raison d'être* of business. . . . Businesses have to earn a satisfactory return on your risk capital, but they also need to form lasting and sustainable relationships with other stakeholders. Friedman said corporate philanthropy has no place. I think there is a very real place for corporate philanthropy. (Cave, 2010)

But CSR is not limited to external social responsibility. What happens to workers within the organization is equally (if not more) important, especially in terms of the role of knowledge services as an organizational management and service delivery methodology. Another article in the popular media had James Surowiecki commenting about a news item in which a leader in a major corporation decided to give attention to his company's own workers, bringing the idea of corporate responsibility home:

"So it is big news when, last month," Surowiecki wrote in *The New Yorker*, "Aetna's C.E.O. Mark Bertolini, announced that the company's lowest-paid workers would get a substantial raise – from twelve to sixteen dollars an hour, in some cases – as well as improved medical coverage."

Bertolini didn't stop there. He said that it was not "fair" for employees of a Fortune 50 company to be struggling to make ends meet. He explicitly linked the decision to the broader debate about inequality, mentioning that he [Bertolini] had given copies of Thomas Piketty's *Capital in the Twenty-First Century* to all his executives.

Surowiecki continued with the story:

> Companies are not just money-making machines [Bertolini said]. For the good of the social order, these are the kinds of investments we should be willing to make. . . . The fact that the benefits of economic growth in the postwar era were widely shared had a lot of do with the assumption that companies were responsible not only to their shareholders but also to their workers. That's why someone like Peter Drucker, the dean of management theorists, could argue that no company's C.E.O. should be paid more than twenty times what its average employee earned. (Suroweicki, 2015)

So managers are required to perform responsible management. How do we – as knowledge strategists – deal with what Drucker referred to as the "Responsibility Gap," when that level of responsibility is not being practiced? For one thing, we recognize in our role as knowledge strategists that we have an influential role to play in the organization, specifically as that role relates to the KD/KS/KU process. And as management employees, we understand that management is important to societal health and, not to be minimized, to the intellectual health and well-being of the participants who, with us, are seeking to improve knowledge-sharing within the organization through the knowledge services strategic framework we are building. For our purposes, we must look to the larger enterprise, the institution, the organ of society, and identify how we can use our influence within the organization to define the contribution the enterprise can (and hopefully, will) make to society. As knowledge strategists, there are specific steps we can take, and for our purposes I choose to return to the the approach Elizabeth Edersheim took in *The Definitive Drucker*. Some of these ideas do, of course, come through in the little book I've referred to before, *The Five Most Important Questions You Will Ever Ask About Your Organization*. But there is more to the management of knowledge services and the development of the knowledge services strategic framework than is discussed in that book (as valuable as it is). I find that I'm impressed not only with the title of the chapter of the book in which Edersheim "drills down" into Drucker's management philosophy (the chapter called "People and Knowledge"), which I mentioned earlier, but also the early section in which she specifically asks hard "Drucker questions" (she calls them). The section, like the chapter title, pulls no punches about the connection between the people who work in the organization and how knowledge is considered in the organization. In fact, the title of the section ("Investing in People and Knowledge: Five Drucker Questions") makes it easy for us to identify what we want to know (Edersheim, 2007).

The challenge now is going to be how, as knowledge strategists, the questions are answered and, as we move toward the conclusion of this chapter on

the management of knowledge services, I have a few thoughts to share with the organization's knowledge strategist:
1. Who are the right people for your organization?

    As the knowledge strategist, your primary responsibility is to develop the organization's knowledge services strategic framework and, in doing so, to influence to success of the organization as it moves toward structuring itself as a knowledge culture. The knowledge workers and strategic knowledge professionals who work with you in this endeavor are chosen (of course) for their understanding of the KD/KS/KU process and the connection between and convergence of information management, KM, and strategic learning, the three foundational elements of knowledge services. These are the tools of the trade for the knowledge domain.

    At the same time, and in some cases perhaps equally important, these employees will bring certain intangibles to their work, qualities such as their understanding of the role of knowledge in the particular organizational environment (that is, whether the organization functions as a for-profit or non-profit entity, its subject specialty, its management structure, etc.). Another important element in the skill set of the knowledge workers has to do with their ability to converse – in user-friendly and easily comprehended language (no knowledge services jargon, please!) to colleagues in the organization who do not have their professional expertise with KD/KS/KU and need to be given to understand the role of knowledge in the organization and the importance in which its application at all employee levels contributes to the success of the organization. These are delicate areas, and the knowledge workers and strategic knowledge professionals – together with the knowledge strategists – must take great care to ensure that their own expertise and experience do not work against them as they engage with colleagues. The answers to these kinds of questions and the comfort-level of fellow employees about the role of knowledge in the organization are basic to the "rightness" of the employees for the work they are called upon to perform in the organization's knowledge domain.

2. Are you providing your people with the means to achieve their maximum effectiveness and contribute to the organization's success?

    The response to this question begins with the organization's vision, mission, and values. These are given much attention in the workplace, and they are established clearly enough that after a certain amount of time working with the organization's KD/KS/KU process, each employee is aware of and – without thinking about it – understands and can articulate the organization's knowledge services philosophy and its relationship with the success of the organization in its achievement of the organizational mission. This understanding does not necessarily, of course, come with quick mottos thrown out in team meetings or notes posted on the walls. What this means is that there is an ambiance, an environment that speaks to why the organization and its knowledge services staff are there and their own understanding of their role in the organization's success.

A part of the story and a part that requires considerable attention is that every manager, including the knowledge strategist, must struggle with the age-old conflict between allowing employees to set their own workflow schedule and pushing those employees to meet certain performance criteria, standards often established by the organization's managers. What we are describing here are elementary workplace expectations, and how the knowledge strategist defines and describes those expectations for his or her employees. Of course certain levels of trust are built in, and both the knowledge strategist – as the manager – and the knowledge workers and strategic knowledge professionals who report to the knowledge strategist have an obligation to go beyond personal inhibitions and performance styles to meet what is required for the organization. As tasks are developed and assigned, that trust ensures that key performance indicators are established at the beginning of the development of the task and adhered to as the work of the task proceeds and the work is completed.

3. Do your structure and processes institutionalize respect for people and investment in human capital?

In the knowledge domain, this respect for people and investment in human capital is epitomized in the assignments given to the knowledge workers and the strategic knowledge professionals. If they are going to succeed as knowledge services specialists (another title in some environments for the strategic knowledge professionals) the focus – as Drucker and Edersheim describe – must be on their strengths as each assignment proceeds, on the feedback provided to them as they work through the task. If, for example, a task of the knowledge services team (typical in the development and implementation of the knowledge services strategic framework) is to interview certain senior workers about how they obtain the information they require for use in making their decisions, framing the interview questions with one another before the interviews take place gives team members the opportunity to think about and anticipate what some of the responses might be and how the team then can provide useful commentary for the senior staff as they respond. As the team meets to plan its interview questions, they and their knowledge strategist can work together on how to determine the best questions, with the knowledge strategist providing guidance based on his or her background and experience and, as the discussion continues, providing feedback that will reflect that expertise and, at the same time, encourage the staff members as they move toward the assignment.

4. Are knowledge and access to knowledge built into your way of doing business?

As we speak about the work of knowledge workers, strategic knowledge professionals, and knowledge strategists, the answer to this question is one we all think about, and love to debate. It is our *raison d'être* and very probably the explanation for why the pursuit and sharing of knowledge led us into our profession. In every organization, enabling those affiliated with the organization to develop, share, and utilize the knowledge they require in order to be successful in their work is a very high calling, and those of us in this work are very aware of how important this work is. And to respond to the question posed here in Peter Drucker's exercise, we are truly fortunate not only to be able to understand how important this work is but to be professionally situated to act on that good fortune. The job of the knowledge strategist is to be the manager, leader, and all-around knowledge guru in the organization, to "go-to person" (in the organizational vernacular) known to everyone in the organization when any questions having to do with KD/KS/KU come up; the knowledge strategist is recognized as the person to go to when an answer is needed.

5. What is your strategy for investing in people and knowledge?

On the other side of the coin, slightly removed from the optimistic response to the previous question, the knowledge strategist must also give considerable thought to how the workers in the knowledge domain will be chosen: who will be employed in the knowledge domain, what qualifications for success as a knowledge worker or strategic knowledge professional are required, what performance expectations there will be, and how these workers – focusing on the organization's knowledge domain and its contribution to the organization's continuing success – will know their work is recognized and appreciated.

One critical criterion for determining the success of the organization with respect to its investment in people and knowledge can be seen in a repeat of the last sentence of the response to the previous question: the extent to which the organization becomes positioned – with all the attendant benefits – as a knowledge culture. Throughout society there are positive signs that knowledge services, knowledge strategy, and the structuring of the organization as a knowledge culture are becoming increasingly recognized as attributes of the successful organization. At the same time, though, there continue to be management leaders in all types of organizations for whom attention to their organization's knowledge domain is considered something "soft," an approach to management that, if required, they will discuss as important and useful to the success of the organization but one to which they do not give much attention. They see it as "too academic" or interfering with the "real work" of the organization, and it is an attitude that affects the hiring of people with responsibility for knowledge services. And incidentally, this is not a charge – as often happens – to be laid against business and business management, where some of the most innovative and creative work in knowledge services has been accomplished. It happens in all fields of work, and it probably is no one's fault; it is simply the result of the "newness" – we might call it – of our attention to knowledge and its role and value in our institutions and our universal acceptance of that role and value is not yet complete.

Management essentials. Are there conclusions to be drawn about management and management principles as we apply them in building a knowledge services strategic framework? I think so, and to demonstrate I share another personal story, this one with no particular allusion (by name) to either of the parties, by request.

Noting that we often speak about our work as knowledge strategists with responsibility for managing the KD/KS/KU process in our employing organizations, we understand that most of the time we're required to deal with standard management functions. Once in a while, though, a real opportunity comes along (perhaps as a result of some version of responsible management as we have just described), and we find ourselves positioned to move the organization forward in terms of structuring the knowledge services strategic framework. Two recent queries from colleagues asked about how we prepare ourselves and our working groups for such an occasion.

One colleague asks what essentials he should have in his basket "as he floats through the knowledge services cloud on a balloon" (as he charmingly puts it). Another colleague notes that she may likely be presented with the opportunity to restructure the law firm's legal library into the firm's research and knowledge services center, a knowledge nexus for all knowledge services-related transactions and functions. She is a managing director in the firm, and she, too, is asking for essentials. Both want to know what they should be thinking about as they embark on their individual, organization-specific ventures.

If I were either of these professional colleagues, these are the "essentials" I would aim for:
1. *Extremely high visibility in the organization.* Make it your business to ensure that everyone understands what strategic knowledge is and what is available through the research functions for which you are responsible. Make sure all staff and affiliates know that if they have any exercise, task, product

development idea, project, database development, enterprise content, or even something as seemingly simple as a document management issue to deal with or choose from, you – as knowledge strategist for the organization – and your team have KD/KS/KU skills and expertise that make you the people to consult in the organization.
2. *Structural "fit."* Position any knowledge services functional units (research department, specialized library, records management/organizational archives, etc.) to ensure that they support units and programs where the action is. You and your staff want to be known for taking on the tough tasks, the hard stuff that no one else – even the subject experts – can figure out for themselves (or when they try to figure it out for themselves get it wrong). Stay away from the kid stuff. And when you and your team are part of a successful strategic knowledge sharing scenario, promote the hell out of it. Let anybody who gets within ten feet of you know how tough the job was and how great it was to pull it off (and how proud you and your team members are for the success of the effort). And be sure to give credit to the people from outside your unit who worked with your team to make it a successful.
3. *Build your troops.* Within every department or functional unit in the organization, identify someone to be that unit's designated person who – while focusing on the specific subject or functionality of the unit – has responsibility as the knowledge services point person for the unit. This person doesn't have to be an information, knowledge, or strategic learning "professional" *per se*, but it should be someone who is assigned when hired to "help" the unit in terms of knowledge services (and the person doesn't have to have top-heavy qualifications – just an interest in helping people find what they need to know). Once you've identified the point person for each of the units, you and your team take responsibility for and work with unit management in mentoring, advising, and coaching the point person so they learn to direct people to your knowledge services center, research center (or whatever the organizational knowledge nexus is called) for any query having to do with finding and learning what they need to know

Leading to . . .

4. *Knowledge leadership.* Establish yourself and your team as the strategic learning specialists for the organization. Your goal is to make sure the knowledge development, knowledge sharing, and knowledge utilization process is built in to the organizational culture. Talk about what Dale Stanley refers to as the "catalytic" quality of knowledge services, about how KD/KS/KU enables you and the people you come in contact with to create knowledge value through KD/KS/KU. Use the language. Get people to talking about strategic knowledge

and what strategic knowledge is for each person's workplace. Create the KD/KS/KU buzz in your organization.
5. *Go holistic.* Take whatever steps are necessary to see that you and your team support the entire organization. There's been a lot of Peter Drucker in this book so far, and one of the attributes so often ascribed to Drucker is that his real contribution lies in his "integrative, holistic thinking." Integrative, holistic thinking works in managing strategic knowledge services, too. Make it enterprise-wide. Don't allow yourself and your staff to become the intellectual "pets" of this or that research unit or function. If that's what's needed, get yourself or a staff member embedded in that unit's projects, on a case-by-case basis. Your job is to be the KD/KS/KU process managers, knowledge strategists for the entire organization.

Our next step is to develop further that link between management and leadership, so clearly established as we think about the people and ideas put forward here, in order to come up with specific directions for how we employ that link for building the knowledge services strategic framework for the organizations that employ us.

1.3 Leadership and Knowledge Leadership

A trend I have observed is that of approaching management and leadership as two separate concepts, two separate ways of thinking about how to "get things done" (management) and how to "inspire the best performance" (leadership) – the two ideas usually associated with management and leadership. There is probably a good reason why we tend to separate the two and as we review the subject of leadership in this chapter, we can expect to find well-articulated differences between leadership and management.

I question the separation and wonder if it is justified (despite the fact that I've done just that with these two sections). It seems to me that as we think about organizational effectiveness – and in particular about knowledge services and the knowledge strategist's role in the organization – what we're looking for is more of a combined approach to leadership and management (and perhaps in other lines of work as well, although that is not our purpose here).

As a manager, the knowledge strategist has a critical function in the organization, and going further, the manager-as-leader construct could almost have been designed with the knowledge strategist in mind, particularly as he or she works with developing the knowledge services strategic framework. As noted earlier, Montgomery is quick to focus on the leadership role of managers, particularly in terms of the manager's role as "meaning maker" for the organization. Could there be a better affirmation of the leadership role for the knowledge strategist? Certainly being the organization's meaning maker for any discussion having to do with the organization's knowledge domain is one of the strongest requirements (perhaps *the* strongest) for the knowledge strategist.

This claim can be supported from what we have already discussed about management. Drucker, for example, seemed to be emphasizing throughout his long career the "higher" role of the leader/manager, and his advice about integrity in leadership (". . . it is character through which leadership is exercised; it is character that sets the example and is imitated.") makes sense for the knowledge strategist (Drucker, 1973). In dealing with the information- and knowledge-related elements of the organization, the leader-manager's work is two-fold: to manage the successful deployment of knowledge strategy in order to ensure the continuing success of the organization's KD/KS/KU process, and to maintain (or to establish, if it is not already in place) the organization as a knowledge culture. It is in this latter role that the knowledge strategist excels (and in which Drucker's direction comes to its highest fruition). The knowledge strategist is working with all elements of the organization to establish (and monitor) that beliefs and values relating to information, knowledge, and strategic learning build on and connect with an understanding of the value of those disciplines and, in particular, that they converge for the benefit of the organization. The result – the firm belief of all of us in this game – is the organization as a knowledge culture.

When there is a corporate knowledge culture, the knowledge strategist is positioned to move knowledge-related programs forward. The point was made by Nishan DeSilva, Director, Information and General Management Compliance, Microsoft Legal Operations Group, when he described how – in looking at the overall environmental ambiance for success with KD/KS/KU – the company's culture plays an influential role in the success of the knowledge strategist's work:

> In almost every company or organization, there are wide variations in awareness about the value and the importance of the knowledge-sharing function. At the same time, the company's structure as a knowledge culture has great influence in policy development, and when the knowledge strategist is experienced in such activities as conducting the knowledge services audit or working with the knowledge strategy development team, that influence comes into play. (DeSilva, 2012)

Knowledge leadership: Our knowledge services landscape. It is that influential role that brings us to knowledge leadership. What is being presented here is nothing less than a knowledge leadership opportunity for the knowledge strategist. This management employee, recognized as the senior leader for building the organization's knowledge services strategic framework, is given an opportunity supported by a group of factors that enable success in building and sustaining the knowledge culture. Closely matching the attributes of the knowledge culture described in Section 1.5, these determinants stand firmly on two inviolable pillars, leadership and collaboration. Without either leadership or collaboration (this latter to be discussed in Chapter 2, Section 2.1), the knowledge culture cannot come into being or, if it already exists, it cannot survive.

Leadership is the quality that stands at the forefront of the many talents, skills, and abilities that combine to enable excellence in organizational effectiveness. Leadership also affects management and service delivery in any organization's various business units, including those relating to the management of information, knowledge, and strategic learning where, as we now recognize, the knowledge culture connects with the leadership skills of the knowledge strategist. Working with his or her team of strategic knowledge professionals and similarly connected employees throughout the organization, the knowledge strategist seeks to develop a knowledge services strategic framework in which "adaptive work," as Ronald A. Heifetz and Donald L. Laurie have described it, is undertaken (Heifetz and Laurie, 1997). This, they contend, is *the work* of leadership, to direct the workforce to respond to changes in society and in the workplace by developing new strategies, learning new ways of operating, and, significantly, reviewing and clarifying workplace values. Connecting the idea of adaptive work with the environment in which knowledge services is managed and delivered could constitute an almost classic description of the challenge enterprise leadership faces. As the organization struggles with changes taking place at almost every level and in almost every job – with economic dislocations, with mergers and acquisitions and bankruptcies, with new and unsettling HR and human capital regulations, with continually improving technology, and with new approaches to knowledge access evolving at a rate of change unimagined just five years earlier – managers must constantly observe and make judgments about the effectiveness of knowledge services and the success of the KD/KS/KU process.

In taking that challenge to the next level, to direct our attention to the role of leadership in developing and sustaining the knowledge culture, it is helpful to understand that how leadership is defined and succeeds is connected directly to the particular situation for which leadership is required. It was Edgar H. Schein in his classic *Organizational Culture and Leadership* who determined that the leader as a "creator of culture" succeeds in doing so by transferring "beliefs, values, and basic assumptions" to subordinates (Schein, 1992). Schein identified three ways in which the process of building culture occurs. As the knowledge strategist seeks direction for building the enterprise-wide knowledge culture, these can be used

to establish a customized and dedicated "knowledge culture-building" context (as we might call it) for the knowledge strategist's employing organization:
1. The knowledge strategist and the culture building team (that is, the people who share the same knowledge values and ambitions as the knowledge strategist) think and feel the same way about the purpose and value of the organization functioning as a knowledge culture.
2. Through knowledge-sharing and strategic learning, the culture building team indoctrinates and socializes others in the organization – especially others in positions of authority or influence (or both) – to their way of thinking and feeling.
3. Likewise, through knowledge-sharing and strategic learning, the knowledge building team and these other knowledge-focused employees serve as role models, with their behavior inspiring others affiliated with the enterprise to identify with them and to accept the beliefs, values, and assumptions of these fellow employees.

In sustaining the knowledge culture, similar forces drive the knowledge strategist and those associated with the creation of the knowledge culture (which, it should be acknowledged, is in many cases nothing more than the discovery, codification, and restructuring of an intellectual infrastructure that is already in place). For the task of sustaining or maintaining the knowledge culture, the challenge is one of ensuring that the components of knowledge services – the tools as well as the knowledge sharing and the strategic learning – are designed to "fold in" to the usual, daily, and non-exceptional elements of the workplace. At the same time, those with responsibility for and interest in the ongoing success of the organization as a knowledge culture take it upon themselves to mentor, train, and otherwise encourage continuing interest in knowledge services and the KD/KS/KU process as a workplace standard. Finally, above all else, the knowledge strategist and the team that has developed or overseen the recognition of the enterprise-wide knowledge culture must do all they can to prevent the growth of organizational processes that would impede interest in sustaining the knowledge culture; every effort must be made to ensure that all affiliated staff – and most particularly younger staff – are given every opportunity to be part of sustaining an organizational environment in which knowledge services and KD/KS/KU thrive.

Which means that leadership required for maintaining and sustaining the knowledge culture must have a different focus, one which – as in most leadership roles – combines leadership and management but in this case also has a specific direction. It is a type of leadership we characterize as "knowledge leadership," for its primary purpose is to ensure that knowledge services and the KD/KS/KU process are managed for the benefit of knowledge *use* in the organization and that knowledge *value* is conveyed back to all enterprise stakeholders. Thus the usual distinctions of leadership and management (which Abraham Zaleznik adroitly characterizes as "the same only different") become less about contrast and more about similarities, and we see the knowledge strategist exhibiting characteristics of both the leader and the manager.

Zaleznik, for example, suggested as early as 1992 that management is power *by position* (Zaleznik, 1992). Of course, the manager of any business unit focused on knowledge services and knowledge strategy is in place to manage. At the same time, Zaleznik also posited that leadership is power *by influence* and we cannot lose sight of the fact – in particular with respect to the work of the knowledge strategist – it is the influential role of those working with knowledge services to provide guidance and direction not only in assisting organizational colleagues as they deal with their day-to-day knowledge services needs, but to take control, indeed even take ownership, of the organizational knowledge strategy and assure its implementation.

The twinned elements of knowledge leadership can be seen in another iteration, one that seems almost unique in the general organizational management and leadership picture but is the accepted standard in the management and delivery of knowledge services. In Zaleznik's dichotomy, managers are planners and focus on process. Leaders are "inspiring visionaries who focus on substance." Combining these, could there be a better description of the work of the knowledge strategist? This leader's primary responsibility – a two-part responsibility – is to define the knowledge culture for the larger enterprise and to pave the way for restructuring the enterprise as a knowledge culture (or strengthening it, if it already exists). In doing so, the knowledge strategist – as noted in Section 1.4 – is challenged to identify and master the two types of knowledge required in the workplace, which Hatten and Rosenthal have written are the knowledge to boost performance when organizational objectives are known and understood and the knowledge to help define new objectives and identify the strategies to pursue them (Hatten and Rosenthal, 2001). Both are the domain of the knowledge strategist and both require planning and a focus on process, the manager's tasks, and vision and a focus on substance, the leader's tasks. The knowledge strategist combines them in knowledge leadership.

It is the job of the knowledge strategist (working with his or her knowledge team, the knowledge workers and the strategic knowledge professionals described earlier) to provide knowledge leadership, to smooth and accelerate the progress of KD/KS/KU in the organization. In doing so, and especially through providing a knowledge services strategic framework for the company or organization, permitting improved contextual decision making, accelerated innovation, higher-level research, and excellence in knowledge asset management, knowledge strategists ensure the continuation of organizational success. The organization's knowledge strategists have a responsibility to their organizations to provide knowledge leadership. Certainly by the time they are positioned as knowledge strategists, they have the ability, the knowledge of concepts, and the skills, and that's where knowledge leadership comes into play. It's a role the knowledge strategist is obliged to play, whether there is a management expectation that they practice knowledge leadership or whether they – innovative and receptive professionals that they are – take it on themselves. It's in the workplace that we see – and the knowledge strategist acts on – the connection between the management of the organization's intellectual capital and the organization's success.

At the same time, knowledge leadership can also lead to knowledge services ambition, a positive form of ambition that is rooted in ensuring that all parties have the tools, services, and consultations they require as they seek to manage their contribution to the success of the organizational mission. Victoria Harriston, who manages the Research Center of the National Academies of Science, Engineering and Medicine in Washington, DC, is absolutely certain that the more knowledge services as a management discipline can be moved *across* the larger enterprise, the better.

"I want to embed knowledge services in every part of the organization," Harriston said in a conversation with me. "That's my goal. And I particularly want knowledge services to be a critical component in the high-profile parts of the organization. I want the knowledge services staff to partner and collaborate everywhere we're needed. That's the strategic direction I've chosen and it's what I'm trying to bring to the National Academies" (Harriston, 2006).

For knowledge strategists and the people who have agreed to come along with them in building and then sustaining the knowledge culture for the organization, the path is clear. There is the recognition and an acknowledgement of the value of enhancing a knowledge leadership role, one that combines the planning and process-orientation skills of the manager with the visionary focus of the leader.

So with little deviation from our quest for a strategic direction for building and sustaining an organizational knowledge culture, we can continue to address the roles of the knowledge strategist and the strategic knowledge professionals who work with the strategist in the KD/KS/KU environment. These have in fact four functions, serving as a knowledge services authority for all organizational affiliates, acting as a knowledge facilitator or consultant for those who require guidance beyond "good enough" research and data-gathering; providing in-house expertise on all matters relating to the management of information, knowledge, and strategic learning, particularly in terms of how those disciplines converge in the delivery of knowledge services; and performing as a knowledge coach for people for whom the development and sharing of knowledge are not necessarily high-performance criteria as they consider the work they do.

In the knowledge culture, the strategic position of the knowledge strategist and his or her knowledge-connected colleagues is simply to lead KD/KS/KU. Naturally that work relates to the roles listed above, and builds on basic core responsibilities: to identify knowledge needs, to analyze, synthesize, and interpret knowledge content, and to facilitate client utilization.

In working with the knowledge strategist in the development of the knowledge culture, the knowledge services professional is particularly well qualified but there are others, as noted before, who possess these same qualifications and they, too, can be conscripted to join the knowledge culture building team. Why? Because much of what brings success, when a group of people are called together to perform a task, are basic KD/KS/KU sharing skills, skills that many people share. I have identified the following:
- trust
- collaboration (with no disincentives for collaboration)
- collegiality
- concentration on relationship building.

Connected with this list is another consideration. While there is the expressly rewarding assumption that the work being done is important work, the goal now is to make it part of the everyday work life of every employee in the organization. Once the enterprise is functioning as a knowledge culture, KD/KS/KU and the elements of the knowledge culture are incorporated into the usual habits of all workers. In the knowledge culture, knowledge development, knowledge sharing, and knowledge utilization are not something "extra" to be given attention in addition to one's "regular" work; it becomes integrated into the daily workflow of each employee having any employment connection with knowledge services or knowledge strategy. Or, as one colleague asserts, KD/KS/KU is simply "part of your desktop."

Understanding the leadership dynamic. Leadership in the management community continues to be, as it has been for many decades, that elusive but much sought-after quality which has the power to enable an organization, enterprise, company, or institution to succeed. When we pull back a little from the big picture, though, we recognize that there are leadership qualities that are directly responsible for the success of knowledge services in the organization, whether limited to one or a group of knowledge-focused parallel functional units or established to ensure the highest levels of quality in KD/KS/KU enterprise wide. Whatever the service sphere, the first criterion for success for the knowledge strategist is his or her leadership ability, and among the many guidelines and techniques put

forward for success in leadership, James Kouzes and Barry Posner's five "practices" of good leadership resonate in knowledge services:
1. Model the way.
2. Inspire a shared vision.
3. Challenge the process.
4. Enable others to act.
5. Encourage the heart (Kouzes and Posner, 2002).

Examples abound. In modeling the way, a knowledge strategist in a large and fast-paced organization who takes times from his or her management routine to "work the desk" is sending all staff a message that services provided will only be successful when the staff works together as a team, with the strategist as part of that team. We see this scenario in the New York office of a multinational investment bank, where the strategic knowledge services staff provides data to the company's analysts on a 24-hour basis, with professional staff providing knowledge services delivery in three eight-hour shifts each day, and the knowledge strategist making it her business to work with the query staff on each of the shifts at least once a month (and more often, of course, during the regular daytime shift, when she tries to put in at least two half-days a week at the query desk).

Another example comes from a large public research library environment, where the knowledge strategist and the strategic knowledge professionals have what they refer to as their "information and advice" role. Similar to the services-participation attitude of the knowledge strategist at the investment bank, the entire team recognizes its entrepreneurial/intrapreneurial role and they all participate in the larger activity themselves, scheduling their own activities to work with the knowledge "customers" (the staff uses that term) and to serve as advisors to them and other staff members who require internal consultation with respect to knowledge-related matters.

That example also supports Kouzes and Posner's second leadership practice, that of inspiring a shared vision. An even more striking example can be found in a medium-sized company in which management's focus in recent years has been on developing organizational effectiveness. As it happens, this company is involved in a business in which the ideas generally associated with "nurturing" – as we might characterize it – are strong, so the idea of inspiring a shared vision is appropriate and easily incorporated into the environment of such an organization. This company provides a "train-the-trainers" program for developing countries, a program in which native trainers in agricultural development are taught to work with local farmers to teach them how to increase crop yield and thus their own profits or, at least, be be able to contribute to the better feeding of the people for whom they have responsibility. In seeking to advance the success of the company's KD/KS/KU and to raise the level of commitment to internal sharing among all staff, management invited department heads of several business units with records, report generation, publication, and other research-related activities to come together. Their brief was to develop a vision for KD/KS/KU that would incorporate the perspectives and values of each of the functional units and at the same time establish a corporate-wide operational standard and perspective that would create an almost automatic KD/KS/KU framework. As a result, the team seeking to create the shared vision were by definition establishing a collaboration base, and team members were able to incorporate a variety of requirements and goals into the development of a KD/KS/KU process and structure.

Kouzes and Posner's leadership mandate to challenge the process offers a slightly different way for using collaboration to move toward the knowledge culture. When there are established procedures that clearly impede or slow the transfer of information, knowledge, and strategic learning content in place, does not the knowledge services director have a mandate or "charge" to challenge the process, to remove the impediments to good service and make the whole process work better? That was the driver for one colleague who recognized at her organization that in today's workplace, the old paradigms don't always work. Managing an information resources center for a consumer products service company in the American southwest, she saw the value of moving toward a management framework that builds on innovation and connections, with a focus on realignment, that critical element in the modern management picture that recognizes that the old ways of doing things have to be re-shaped and re-focused to meet new demands and new responsibilities.

Sometimes the leadership role simply requires a "defining moment" (to use the term often associated with this type of recognition in the workplace, when a manager – in the case the company's knowledge strategist – identifies a situation that has clear potential for quick improvement). In realigning a unit's knowledge-related work, the knowledge strategist is simply recognizing that today's workplace requires new tools and new techniques. Often, many of these situations call for what we think of as "quick wins" – an easy-to-implement solution that is at hand but has just not been thought about before. But even if the management solution isn't a quick win and requires further study and analysis, the serious knowledge strategist puts it in place. The leadership role is to understand that if something still works, fine, but if it needs to be re-thought, or re-framed, or even dropped from the larger scheme of things, the knowledge strategist must take that action.

More often than not, networking is the solution. It is a critically important approach to studying issues in an organization's knowledge domain, and since it is something all organizational workers do all the time, in their personal lives, in the groups and organizations in which they participate, it is (or should be) a natural way to think about knowledge-related issues. So the knowledge strategist makes every effort at the workplace to interact with every group, with HR, with quality teams, with technology management. And it is an activity that goes two ways: if there is a section or department of the organization that requires the expertise of the knowledge strategists, that expertise is shared, just as their expertise is shared with the strategic knowledge team when needed.

There are occasions when challenging the process simply means setting up a workplace environment that enables others to act. An old management adage goes something like this: *Decide what has to be done, hire the best people, and let them do it.* Obviously what we have here is an idealized scenario because the knowledge strategist sometimes finds that the people he or she has hired (or who have been assigned) to work in the knowledge services unit are not the best people. There are times when – for various political or bureaucratic reasons – employees with limited experience, expertise, and even sometimes familiarity are assigned to the business unit with responsibility for knowledge services, and much energy is spent dealing with performance standards (oftentimes as much effort as spent providing services to the unit's clients). On the other hand, when the knowledge services business unit is staffed with the best people, there is an environment that could be thought of as almost competitive, since the work produced is of such high quality and the unit's staff members are so well qualified and enthusiastic about their work. In these nearly perfect situations, the move toward collaboration is not an effort. In fact, it is usually built in, part of the fabric or ambiance of the unit as it moves forward to identify and provide newer and better methods for service delivery. In this environment, collaboration succeeds, and much of the knowledge strategist's management effort focuses on providing oversight while new products are developed, new arrangements are studied, and relationships between delivery staff and users grow into professional collegiality.

A variation on collaboration and cooperation in the knowledge services arena can be found in some operations which have responsibility for management and service delivery functions that are not necessarily thought of as "knowledge-focused" but which are, in reality, knowledge functions. As such, they enable a high level of collaboration and inter-departmental cooperation. For example, since the early days of assigning journalists with the American military in 2003, the term "embedded" has become well recognized. While used in that context to describe journalists who go to (or near) front lines with the troops, the term has become somewhat fashionable in other lines of work as well. In knowledge services, the term is used to describe a situation wherein a project management group or product development team has a member of the organization's strategic knowledge services team "embedded" with the group as its work begins. The purpose of the embedded information professional (or "insourced" knowledge professional, as the concept was described when it first appeared in information and knowledge services work a few generations earlier) is to have an information/knowledge/learning specialist attached to the team, to be the knowledge services "guru," so to speak, from the beginning of the project, to ensure that the management and delivery of knowledge services matches and is specifically customized for the work at hand. The situation matches Kouzes and Posner's leadership practice of enabling others to act, because the knowledge strategist – aware of and with a good understanding of the quality of the skills, professionalism, and performance ability of the embedded knowledge services professional – can have that person work with the project group with confidence that the employee will be an integral element of the group's success.

To encourage the heart, which is the fifth of Kouzes and Posner's leadership practices, the knowledge strategist has only to recognize that leadership is about relationships, and be willing to put himself or herself in a position to look at the workplace through the eyes of the people who are employed in the knowledge services functional unit. One way of "encouraging" the heart is well established among managers: to devise plans and workable schemes for recognition and celebration, so that all employees know that their contributions are seen for what they are, and that those contributions are acknowledged as critical to the success of the unit in meeting its obligations and serving its users. On the other hand, recognition and celebration are important, but another element of the encourage-the-heart leadership practice – particularly applicable in the knowledge services environment – is to bring all employees into the management picture. As the knowledge strategist seeks to meet the demands of enterprise leadership and establish practices for measuring impact, delivering metrics, and providing the required reports and compliance documentation, it becomes important to allow employees in the department to know that their contribution is equally as valuable as that of the knowledge strategist.

A fail-proof methodology practiced in many organizations is to provide knowledge workers, strategic knowledge professionals, and knowledge strategists with opportunities for conference and convention attendance, participation in professional development and specialized training activities, participation in professional associations and societies, and similar "rewards" that provide employees with tangible recognition that their workplace performance is important. In one large multi-national manufacturing company, the head of the enterprise-wide division for managing knowledge services (which incorporates both IT and research services) must travel several times a year to company sites in different parts of the world. When financially feasible (and when she can make a case for the presence of the employee), she takes a member of the headquarters knowledge services team with her, having assigned that employee specific duties and responsibilities. For other trips, she will arrange for one of the knowledge services staff from another site to meet up with her at the meeting destination. Finally (since the company is successful and enterprise leadership long ago recognized the critical KD/KS/KU role), an annual meeting of all knowledge services staff takes place, usually before or following another professional conference, and all employees working in the field are invited (and expected) to attend. When this level of support is provided to staff, the parent organization benefitting from the knowledge services functional unit clearly appreciates and "encourages the heart" of its employees, providing good opportunities for collaboration and expecting useful results from the collaboration and cooperation that is incorporated into the company's business model.

For most of us, the transition to the high level of leadership referred to in these descriptions requires only a slight "push," an understanding of how we will approach the combination of knowledge services expertise with the requirements of the workplace. We know that in every organization our management abilities enable us to ensure that specific steps are taken to accomplish what we and our co-workers seek to accomplish. At the same time, though – as suggested at the opening of this section – we need to combine management skill with something less tangible. As I think about knowledge services, it is the leadership dynamic that affects how we develop a knowledge-sharing "whole" for the organization that employs us, including the workplace where we and our colleagues demonstrate our commitment to the development of the knowledge services strategic framework.

We recognize that leadership comes in a wide variety of concepts, ideas, and points of view, and many organizational management theorists make it clear that no one type or style of leadership will work for all workplace situations. Indeed, many management advisers and consultants recommend understanding as much about leadership and its many varieties as one can, in order to ensure the application of whichever style or type of leadership works in any given situation. While such a broad-based approach might seem to be a bit of "overkill" in many workplace situations, there's no question that the knowledge strategist will – almost by definition – be presented with opportunities for taking advantage of the manager-as-leader construct mentioned earlier. For that employee, no single description of the leadership role will suffice. There are many, and the knowledge strategist will spend most of his or her employment moving among the many approaches to leadership available for application in the KD/KS/KU workplace.

Attempting to list and describe all the varieties of leadership is not our purpose here, but such an attempt does not distract us too much from considering some of the styles and types we often hear about (and whether these terms refer to leadership "styles" or "types" continues to be a topic for discussion; to me that argument seems simply semantic). Certainly the range of leadership studies over the past few decades has given the broader topic of leadership much attention, and there was a period when some of the larger universities were investing great sums in leadership "institutes" and such, together with efforts in some of academic institutions to construct free-standing buildings and functional units for leadership studies not necessarily connected with any single department or program. That "specialty" seems to have subsided to some degree, and much of the attention to leadership now appears to be focused on the application of leadership attributes by enterprise leaders and middle managers as they seek to develop their employees and motivate them to undertake actionable tasks that will support the mission of the larger organization.

Such is the case with knowledge services and the development of knowledge strategy to meet the knowledge-sharing requirements of the organization. As a result, many different approaches to leadership come up, including (almost always) the name of Warren Bennis. As one of the most recognized pioneers in leadership studies, Bennis is perhaps best known for his "table" (it might be called) specifying the differences between management and leadership, describing succinctly and in an easy-to-follow style what management is and when it is not leadership, and vice versa (Bennis, 2009). A selection will suffice:

1. A manager administers; a leader innovates.
2. A manager's focus is on systems and structure; a leader's focus is on people.
3. A manager relies on control; a leader inspires trust.
4. A manager asks: "how?" "what?"; a leader asks "why?"
5. A manager does things right; a leader does the right thing (similar to Peter Drucker's statement on efficiency and effectiveness).

For each of these diverging characteristics, the knowledge strategist can find plenty of opportunities for application, and one of my favorites is the third, which takes us back to the engagement scenario, the focus on people which is clearly representative of the manager-as-leader/leader-as-manager construct. A special example comes from one of the most respected leaders in specialized librarianship, Deborah Hunt. Hunt is Library Director of the Mechanics Institute, San Francisco, founded in 1854 and one of the world's most famous subscription libraries. She is also a consultant (Principal, Information Edge in San Leandro, CA) and a past-president of the Special Libraries Association. When asked about her own opinions and experiences with leadership, she immediately described situations in which the leader makes an impact and helps others understand what their potential is and then helps them make plans for reaching that potential.

Hunt focuses much of her professional advising and mentoring on working with others in her profession. "I expect you to step up and become the leader" is an oft-stated admonition from Hunt. At the same time, she is quick to assure any colleague she's working with that "leadership is about leading by serving, not in the sense of being subservient, but rather by bringing others along, setting the example that it isn't just about the leader but also about those he or she leads."

When asked why she is particularly drawn to working with people as what might be described as a "sharing" leader, she lets her visitor hear one of her favorite quotations, from Oliver Wendell Holmes, Jr.: "A mind that has been stretched by a new experience can never go back to its original dimension." Hunt even has an example, a story that describes a specific two-way leadership experience (we might call it) in which she not only learned about leading but about being a participant in a leadership situation in which she was led:

> Engagement is really a leadership skill, and it is through engagement that management and leadership merge. Earlier in my career, I was invited to come to work on a project for the Exploratorium (San Francisco's famous "public learning laboratory"). I had little experience with the subject of the project, and even less knowledge about how the project would be undertaken at the Exploratorium. When I spoke with the person directing the program, she made it clear that she, too, has some experiential and knowledge "gaps" with respect to the work but, as she put it, "we will learn together." It was an eye-opening experience for me because it demonstrated an unexpected approach to leadership that was new to me. We would learn together, and that's exactly what we did. (Hunt, 2016)

Hunt's example matches what one of the more notable of the knowledge domain leaders writes about. Art Murray, CEO at Applied Knowledge Sciences, Inc. always says and writes interesting commentary about what's happening in our field, and I was impressed when he once noted the value of learning in the knowledge-sharing process, a comment that certainly fits what Hunt was experiencing (and refers back to our earlier content about strategic learning): "Be a source of learning for others, by coaching and mentoring," Murray said, "and seek out others to help you grow in the same way. Never, ever, stop learning, innovating, growing and creating value" (Murray, 2008). Hunt has obviously taken his advice.

At the same time, Hunt's example also probably falls into one of Daniel Goleman's several leadership categories, probably what he calls "visionary" and/or "coaching" leadership. Best known for his work in emotional intelligence, Goleman and his co-authors in their *Primal Leadership* came up with the list of leadership traits that most organizational leaders refer to: visionary, coaching, affiliative, democratic, pacesetting, and commanding (Goleman, Boyatzis, and McKee, 2001). As

Hunt's experience demonstrates, though (and an opportunity that must be kept in mind for the knowledge strategist), there are probably few single leadership styles that work in every situation, or as a single, individual type.

Nevertheless, these leadership types, along with those of Bennis, and Kurt Lewin (the latter known primarily for his work in social psychology) all merge together to give us a useful overall list of leadership attributes that support the work of the knowledge strategist. Lewin, a scholar and also a management expert, dealt with leadership attributes. He defined them in terms of work environments – the authoritarian leader, the democratic leader, and the laissez-faire leader. For our purposes, it seems – this early in the knowledge services strategic framework development process – that the democratic leadership type is the one which best matches what the knowledge strategist must apply.

Transformational leadership. So it becomes clear, as noted above, that like many other concepts and principles put forward in the knowledge domain, leadership, too, has its wide range of descriptions, perspectives, and activities. All of these, when undertaken, can be offered as examples of leadership and most people working with knowledge services (myself included) have a few favorites which they invoke from time to time. In my case, I like to think about what we call "transformational leadership," a type of leadership whose elements are quickly evident from its name. There are many examples, more than we need to describe here, but they are quickly identified in the workplace. One example that often comes up is the employee who never thought of himself as having very good writing skills and was often self-deprecating about his writing ability. But when asked by the knowledge strategist to conduct research and prepare a brief written document describing his findings relating to a particular research project, he produced a praiseworthy report and received much attention for the excellence of his work. The knowledge strategist, in her position as a transformational leader, enabled the employee to *transform* himself from an employee who avoided writing assignments to one who came to excel in such assignments.

So transformational leadership doesn't have to be complicated and, as noted in the example from Deb Hunt above, often builds on learning opportunities, sometimes only for the employee being led but most often with learning taking place for both the leader and the person being led.

Hislop, introduced in the last section, also has his own ideas about transformational leadership and provides us with a useful and more formal definition, as well as good background: "a mode or style of leadership focused on the development of long term visions, values, and goals which also involves persuading workers to become attached to them and to work towards achieving them" (Hislop, 2009). I'm not so sure this is exactly what happens with knowledge strategists because they do not have the luxury of adhering to a single context for their leadership applications. More often, the knowledge strategist's chosen leadership approach must be the one (and probably the only one) which fits the specific context of the situation at hand. It can, indeed, be focused on Hislop's "long-term visions, values, and goals" but it can also – not to be too simplistic in our description – apply in a situation in which an employee is transformed by a new way of looking at one of the many workplace activities in which he or she participates.

Another approach to transformational leadership comes from Frances Hesselbein, who might easily be referred to as the dean of American leadership development, particularly in her identification with transformational leadership. Recognized as one of the most highly respected experts in the field, Hesselbein was awarded the Presidential Medal of Freedom by President Bill Clinton in 1998 and in April, 2015, she was named one of the world's "50 Greatest Leaders" in *Fortune* magazine. For 26 years, Hesselbein has been and continues as President and CEO of The Frances Hesselbein Leadership Institute (formerly The Peter F. Drucker Foundation for Nonprofit Management, renamed in her honor in 2012).

In her contribution in the Drucker "five questions" book, Hesselbein describes how she came up with her theory of transformational leadership. Always a great story teller, Hesselbein talks about how she often saw transformational leadership in practice when she was CEO of the Girl Scouts of the U.S.A. Her first experience with transformational leadership in that organization actually occurred before she came to work there, for having been invited to meet with the search committee for the position, she had a good idea of what she would say when asked the inevitable interview question: "If you come to work for the Girl Scouts, what will you do?"

Hesselbein had done her homework and she was aware that the organization needed to be transformed. She told the search committee so, saying that she would bring a "total transformation" to the Girl Scouts, the largest organization for girls and young women in North America. She wanted diversity among the members, for she knew the organization was made up mostly of white, middle-class members focusing on subjects like homemaking and storytelling. She felt the girls and young women of the Girl Scouts could aspire to different roles in society, but about the demographics of the membership, when she asked for statistics about the racial and mix of social classes in the membership, she was told that information was not available. "It is discrimination to collect that kind of information," she was told.

Hesselbein's response?

"No it isn't," she said. "It is discrimination *not* to collect that kind of information." Then she went on to describe for the search committee how she would manage the organization differently, giving the girls and young women who were its members skills and learning activities to teach them how to be leaders, to be entrepreneurs, and how to contribute to society.

When the interview finished, she was politely thanked for her time and with her husband drove back to Western Pennsylvania, not expecting to hear any more from the Girl Scouts Search Committee.

She was wrong. She had a call the next day, offering her the job, and she moved to New York to take up her new work.

Transformational? Absolutely, for under Hesselbein's leadership, the Girl Scouts of the U.S.A. grew to become the largest organization for girls and young women in the world. It was totally transformed into a multi-cultural organization open to all racial and societal groups, and the transformation took place not only in the membership. Transformational change came to the organization's leadership, to its national leadership (its board of directors), and at the local levels as well, among its 335 local councils. And, not to be ignored, there was the transformational change of which Hesselbein is particularly proud, and it took place right in the offices of the Girl Scouts of the U.S.A. as the organization's staff became completely diversified (Hesselbein, 2016).

Not surprisingly, Hesselbein's commitment to transformational leadership continued. In her essay on transformational leadership in the *Five Questions . . .* book she writes about another example, a situation when she was sent to China for a particular knowledge-sharing activity. On the trip, she recognized that – regardless of the environment or geographic location – the power of discussing "vision, mission, and goals," even in different languages, enabled people "in every sector, in every culture, to have dialogues of great meaning that help transform organizations."

In her theory of transformational leadership, Hesselbein identifies a series of what she refers to as "milestones," eight steps that enable organizations to "meet their destination." Hesselbein's milestones provide a valuable list of generalized directives that can be used to connect knowledge strategy leadership to the organizational mission, with each of them contributing to the development of the knowledge services strategic framework.

Frances Hesselbein's milestones to the knowledge-sharing destination, which Hesselbein identifies as "an inspired, relevant, viable, effective organization" are these:
1. Scan the environment.
2. Revisit the mission.
3. Ban the hierarchy.
4. Challenge the gospel.
5. Employ the power of language.
6. Disperse leadership across the organization.
7. Lead from the front; don't push from the rear.
8. Assess performance (Hesselbein, 2015).

Two of Hesselbein's milestones (the first two, in fact) can be very well put to work by the knowledge strategist as he or she contemplates the knowledge services strategic framework. Certainly the first milestone, scanning the environment, provides a good example, for the environmental scan can be an informal way of conducting what is more seriously undertaken with the knowledge services audit (described in detail in Chapter 2, Section 2.2). The knowledge services audit combines the methodologies of the standard *needs analysis* (asking what knowledge resources and services community of practice participants require to do their work), the *information audit* (which determines how knowledge assets are actually used), and the *knowledge audit* (which looks at knowledge assets, how they are produced, and by whom). Whether conducted as a formal procedure (the audit) or as a less formal environmental scan, the information collected provides a "snapshot" of the knowledge culture, the quality of knowledge developed and shared in the organization, and the organization's knowledge-sharing "health."

The second of Hesselbein's milestones – revisiting the mission – can also be adapted for the benefit of the knowledge services strategic framework, to be used to provide an analysis of the relationship between the organization's knowledge domain and the organization as a whole. The task of revisiting the mission is basically a two-part activity, with the knowledge-sharing mission established (or being established as the knowledge services strategic framework is developed). The knowledge-sharing mission is constantly under review, either by the knowledge strategist and members of his or her team or by others throughout the enterprise with an interest in and an understanding of the value of a well-framed knowledge strategy. Concurrently, though, in the second part of this activity, the knowledge strategist and the knowledge services team are continually thinking about and reviewing the organization's enterprise-wide mission, in order not only to keep up with what the organization's C-suite leaders are doing and saying but to be always "on top" of the connection between the knowledge services strategic framework and the mission of the organization or company.

Both of these "milestones," as well as the other six, provide a useful checklist as the knowledge strategist and the knowledge services strategic framework team move forward in their planning. In fact, using this as a checklist for one or two simple operational reviews can provide enough background for a short-term "quick win" report that can then be used for a larger review. Hesselbein's methodology is sound and can yield important benefits as the knowledge strategist and the knowledge services strategic framework team move forward in their efforts.

Visionary leadership. I referred to two types of leadership that are particularly attractive to me, types of leadership that from my experience have been extremely enlightening when I've observed them in my work with clients seeking to develop a knowledge services strategic framework. Certainly, as described above, transformational leadership has much to recommend itself for the knowledge strategist. And it is a natural step to connect transformational leadership with visionary leadership. For describing the visionary leadership/knowledge strategy connection, Elizabeth Haas Edersheim's work comes into the picture again. This time, though, we are not looking at Drucker and Edersheim's descriptions of his advice, as she wrote about in *The Definitive Drucker*. Before she undertook that study, Edersheim wrote *McKinsey's Marvin Bower: Vision, Leadership, and the Creation of Management Consulting*. There are, of course, major differences in the two efforts. For one thing, *Knowledge Services* – this book – is not necessarily about management consulting. Although Marvin Bower is recognized as the "father of the management consulting profession," a profession he himself brought into being, his influence and his inspiration for the knowledge strategist might be limited (by scale if for no other reason, for Bower's work and that of McKinsey's consultants was generally focused on the work of CEOs of large companies and businesses).

Nevertheless, there are good leadership concepts that apply in both efforts and, as we shall see, Bower's work was extremely focused on visionary leadership. In much of their work, knowledge strategists do indeed take on an entrepreneurial role, interacting throughout the organization with all affiliates and stakeholders and, in most cases, identifying more as intrapreneurs (in Gifford Pinchot's phraseology from 1978). We can refer with success to much of their work as "internal management consulting," a consulting specialization that obviously addresses the subjects connected with the knowledge domain. Certainly what Edersheim writes about Bower and his work in the management consulting profession can provide us with useful guidance as we approach our own management consulting work for knowledge services.

At the same time, I continue to be impressed with one of the most memorable of Bower's contributions. While it might be a bit of a stretch to suggest this connection, when Edersheim writes about Bower's "defining, building, and syndicating the right firm personality" I can't help but be reminded about what we in our field think of as the enterprise-wide knowledge culture. Is it possible, I wonder, to take some of the ideas Bower put forward in defining and establishing McKinsey's "firm personality" and apply these ideas in the knowledge strategist's quest for the organizational knowledge culture? Surely the development of the characteristics that define the firm personality (which Edersheim asserts was the "absolute cornerstone" of Bower's vision of the institution) can connect to our efforts

(Edersheim, 2004). Certainly, as Edersheim writes that "the 'personality' of a professional firm – like that of an individual – can be roughly defined as the total impression the firm makes on those who come in contact with it or who hear or read about it" applies in similar ways to that organizational knowledge culture the knowledge strategist seeks for the organization with which he or she is affiliated.

Can we not use that same term (or the same idea) to define the organizational knowledge culture, as it is achieved? I would like to think so. As I say, based on my experience with knowledge work in organizations, I see the application of the idea of a firm personality matching that of the concept of the knowledge culture, as we describe in Section 1.5. When we do that, what happens is that both the firm personality and the knowledge culture come together with both (and probably with other structural descriptions) as part of the overall, larger firm's or organization's management strategy. It then makes sense that this "joining together" contributes to "the total impression the firm makes on those who come in contact with it or who hear or read about it."

This idea might be supported by the following, for at the same time, two of the characteristics Edersheim identifies as defining the firm personality lead us nicely into our subject, addressing leadership in the knowledge domain. They can, with no change in meaning, be applied to the work of the knowledge strategist. A first characteristic of the firm personality which applies is "professional-value-based leadership by all," with no authoritarian role for the knowledge strategist and a shared commitment by the knowledge strategist and all knowledge workers employed in the knowledge services unit to excellence in the work of the knowledge domain. The second is "a common problem-solving approach designed to rapidly get to the heart of the matter and spawn insightful, powerful solutions." Again, we almost have a definition of the approach that the knowledge strategist must take as he or she undertakes to develop the knowledge services strategic framework. The framework will, indeed, provide solutions that "get to the heart of the matter and spawn insightful, powerful solutions." It cannot be allowed to do any less; the organization requires insightful knowledge services, producing powerful KD/KS/KU solutions if its intellectual capital is going to succeed in matching the organization's mission and contribute to the successful achievement of that mission.

As we think about how Bower's visionary leadership inspired McKinsey to achieve what it became, Edersheim has identified several leadership specifics. In the chapter she titles "The Bower Reach" she introduces these specifics with attention to how he thought about the company and its work: "Marvin Bower was directly responsible for this rich legacy of leadership because he lived the attributes he believed were critical to good leadership and encouraged those he worked with to reach a new level of consciousness and behavior incorporating these qualities."

The list is impressive, and the value of incorporating each of these qualities into the development of the knowledge services strategic framework – the organization's knowledge strategy – seems clear to me. "The Bower Reach" – Marvin Bower's visionary leadership – builds on:
1. integrity/trustworthiness;
2. fact-based visioning and a pragmatic "Monday morning" path to turn vision into reality;
3. adherence to principles/values;
4. humility and unassuming respect for others;
5. strong communications/personal persuasiveness;
6. personal involvement/demonstrated commitment (Edersheim, 2004).

It is Bower's work in leadership – especially in what has come to be known as visionary leadership – that truly connects with the work of the knowledge strategist. For me, following on the experiences and observations of my career as a knowledge services management consultant, there is a certain sense of satisfaction when I find that I am able to relate the Bower attributes to the work done by the knowledge strategist, particularly as this management employee is embarking on the development of the knowledge services strategic framework for the organization.

From my perspective, making that connection between visionary leadership and the management/leadership professionalism of the knowledge strategist is best accomplished when we look at knowledge services and how knowledge services contributes to organizational success. Knowledge services is made up of three converged elements: information management, knowledge management, and strategic learning. When converged, the combination leads to – as noted throughout this book – strengthened research, contextual decision-making, accelerated innovation, and successful knowledge asset management. It is a combination that works, proven time and again in many organizations, regardless of the type of organization. The reason it works has to do with four constituent parts (we could use the word "elements" again, if we chose, to describe these constituent parts):
- interactive planning;
- network-based partnerships;
- cross-functional communication;
- shared learning and training.

These are the foundation, we might say, of the knowledge services construct that supports the organizational knowledge strategy and the organization as it develops (or strengthens) itself as a knowledge culture.

At the same time, these four constituent elements are connected by attributes of their own, for they are held together and work together based on what I like to refer to as the basis of visionary leadership for any organization in which knowledge services is practiced (or expected to be practiced), the organizational commitment to transparency, collaboration, and collegiality. What is being put together in knowledge services is a vision – going back to management as a humanist art as described in the previous section – that the knowledge strategist will use as the foundation for visionary leadership, all coming together (and required) in the capacities Marvin Bower believed were critical for good leadership.

In my opinion there is probably no more important management task having to do with the achievement of the organizational mission than functioning under the encompassing capacity of a well-prepared and well-understood knowledge services strategic framework. It is a point I make often. I feel this way because the work we do with knowledge services is new; our line of work (do we call it our "profession" yet?) has not been around as an organized and codified workplace activity for very long; many people are still not aware of the value of knowledge services (or of knowledge) and its contribution to organizational success. So it is important work we are doing (and even the word "important" probably understates by some degree what I mean to say) and since it is a relatively new undertaking, we cannot succumb to any "easy-way-out" or less than honest descriptions and expectations about what knowledge services brings to the organizations in which knowledge strategists are employed, or organizations that should be practicing knowledge services. If we are going to succeed with having knowledge services, knowledge strategy, and the structuring of the organization as a knowledge culture become part of our management and leadership "toolbox" we must also adopt the highest standards for how we practice KD/KS/KU. Those highest standards include, with no exception, the adoption of integrity and trustworthiness as fundamental virtues in how we manage and how we lead.

When the idea of integrity comes to mind, I have always had a way of thinking about the concept, and while it might not match the usual dictionary definition (which is usually something along the lines of following high standards or "adhering to moral and ethical principles," as integrity is described in one definition) it does not veer far. It builds in honesty and trustworthiness of course, just as Edersheim clearly identified as two of Bower's requirements for visionary leadership. And it seems to me that integrity also goes beyond that. Early in life I came to the conclusion – probably from observing other people (for that's always been one of my favorite learning methods) – that the people who have integrity are people who do what they say they will do. So of course trustworthiness and integrity come into the picture, and become important components – often not even specified but just "built in" – when a knowledge strategist takes the lead in building the knowledge services strategic framework.

Core leadership principles. In many situations in the knowledge strategist's work, leadership principles from other types of work or industries can transition very usefully into the knowledge domain. I am a firm believer in the value of reviewing (and learning from) what happens in other lines of work and how any principles or guiding insights can be applied in knowledge services. Lee Igel, for example, has identified six leadership principles and they match well some of our thoughts in the conversation with Igel described earlier. He refers to his ideas about leadership as "six core principles" and they are, in my opinion, appropriate for any manager/leader. Certainly they work as well for knowledge strategists as they do for physician executives, the original target readers (in the *Physician Executive Journal*). These leadership action principles Igel identifies are:

1. Focus on what needs to be done.
2. Focus on values as the dominant chord.
3. Identify and respond to your professional "defining moment".
4. Emphasize learning over metrics.
5. Embrace continuous learning and how it mobilizes multiple knowledges.
6. Conserve what works and abandon what doesn't (Igel, 2012).

The items on Igel's list can, indeed, be characterized as essential attributes for knowledge strategists seeking to bring KD/KS/KU success into their employing organizations. Here's why. Igel's leadership principles provide the structure the knowledge strategist needs to follow in order to take charge of the enterprise-wide information, knowledge, and strategic learning function in the organization. As I think about how some of these principles can be applied, I find myself recalling experiences and observations from my work as a consultant with organizations seeking to build a knowledge strategy.

A first example – connecting with Igel's leadership principle that we should focus on what needs to be done – comes up in this kind of situation. When the knowledge strategist gets wind of an up-coming knowledge initiative – or better yet if the knowledge strategist is chosen by management to lead the knowledge initiative – the first determination must be, as Igel puts it, "what the situation requires and the results that need to be achieved to make a difference." The question then becomes simple. What is the organizational need driving the development of the initiative? Is it, for example, some gap between funding the information and knowledge requirements for a project and real project costs? If that's the case, all the knowledge strategist needs to do is follow the Harriston example at the National Academies of Sciences, Engineering and Medicine and convince project managers to include costs for information and knowledge services – research costs – in the project budget *before* the decision is made to move forward with the project. While that advice seems natural and effective, it comes as something of a surprise to learn that funding estimates for research and knowledge services are not always included in project planning. When it is – once those amounts are clearly established – the gap between financial requirements that are real (and realistically arrived at) and those identified through guesswork activity-related "estimates" becomes a non-issue.

A second leadership principle from Igel states that the leader should focus on values as the dominant chord. The knowledge strategist must ask what KD/KS/KU values drive the organization's work. It so happens that I have worked with a knowledge strategist in a healthcare organization who, in her work, is participating in the development of a multi-element, global mHealth (mobile health) program connected with women's health in rural Africa. The program seeks to identify in-depth research and KD/KS/KU practices currently in place, and the effort has little to do with the parent company's primary product line. The activity simply fits into the company's – and the knowledge strategist's – value proposition that in addition to performing its normal business activities, the company is committed to contributing to the common good. In this particular situation, women's health needs are frequently impeded because in some communities any interaction with the women – even by healthcare workers who are themselves women – is forbidden unless a male member of the family is present and even then, the interaction often is not permitted to take place. For this knowledge strategist, she has her team work with residents of local villages who are able to use their mobile telephones for receiving private healthcare instructions. The use of mobile telephones as a "work-around" benefits the patients as well as the healthcare professionals who are providing the medications and enabling the patients to receive advice they would otherwise not have available to them.

When Igel writes about his third leadership principle – that leaders identify and respond to their professional "defining moment" – he makes it clear that achieving purpose is critical for leadership success. As Igel writes, "unless the right people are in the right positions, no one will be effective in achieving anything." Here's another Africa example: At one of the many non-governmental organizations in Nairobi – where a large number of NGOs are headquartered – I had the opportunity to became familiar with a situation in which the research library of one of the large NGOs was not making much of a contribution to organizational effectiveness. In fact, just the opposite. Much research was being conducted throughout the organization, research undertaken by the many professional specialists and scholars working for the NGO, but little research was being conducted using the facilities, staff, and resources of the research library. In fact, several of the various divisions of the organization had their own dedicated research units, with staff (with varying levels of research expertise) employed as research workers. They did not seem to understand the benefits of taking advantage of the services offered by the research library.

As it happened, the organization hired a dynamic knowledge strategist to manage the research library, a step that proved to be remarkably prescient for addressing the needs of the larger organization since the design and development of a knowledge strategy was already in progress, having been organized some months before the library management position was filled. Coincidentally (or perhaps not), the knowledge strategist engaged to manage the research library found herself uniquely positioned to bring continuous upgrades to the overall knowledge services delivery picture. She knew, from her own experience in similar research organizations and in academic institutions and from her understanding of the importance of an enterprise-wide approach to research management, that a new direction for the management of research in the organization was required. She took it upon herself (even speaking about it as she was being considered for the position) to bring up the idea of a knowledge services audit, in order to capture a "snapshot" of the organization's research management situation. Once hired, she went forward with the knowledge services audit, for she had created a considerable level of enthusiasm amongst her managers and, not to put too fine a point on it, amongst her own direct reports. She moved forward, she adapted her findings into recommendations, she exploited (in the positive sense of that word) the enthusiasm she had engendered, and she was successful in bringing major improvements to the organization's KD/KS/KU process. She was the right person in the right place at the right time, and it was a defining moment for the organization (and for the knowledge strategist, I might add).

Igel's fourth principle is simply stated (although perhaps not so simple to follow), to "put the emphasis on learning over metrics." Of course we don't ignore metrics. No one would ever suggest that and later in this book considerable attention is give to measurements and metrics for knowledge services. Quantification continues to play a large role in the management of knowledge services. Yet there are occasions when what is measured does not seem to have much to do with organizational effectiveness, and Igel's advice stands up when the knowledge strategist is seeking to establish the knowledge services strategic framework for the organization. Indeed, again quoting Igel, "What is needed are measurements that relate current performance to future effectiveness." So the knowledge strategist asks, "What metrics are we using? Transactions? Effectiveness measures? ROI?"

Although it could probably happen in the merger of any two or more separate organizations, in the American Mid-West I had an experience in which our team of consultants worked with two merging historical societies seeking to combine knowledge services operations. Both organizations – located in adjacent communities, neither of which had resources for supporting historical archives for two separately managed organizations – were dealing with archives management from the histories of their respective communities, and a considerable body of literature, artifacts, and assorted memorabilia had been collected in several locations. It was important material relating to history of the communities, going back into the late eighteenth century, and no one in authority in the community wanted to see any items accidentally lost or misplaced since scholars referred to the materials with frequency and would be expected to use them more and to better result once they were combined and re-organized. What impressed me most about the assignment was the willingness of knowledge strategists in both societies to assess and learn how to make use of the best metrics formats from both institutions, discarding metrics from which no future effectiveness would be realized (such as, for example, counting the number of visitors to the individual archives collections without measuring how or for what purpose the materials were used). So the knowledge workers participating in the process changed their metrics, focusing on who would be receiving the information, on who would be making decisions based on the metrics, and on what these people wanted (or needed) to know.

In Igel's fifth leadership principle (straight out of Drucker, of course, and any number of other leadership advisers), Igel invites knowledge strategists to embrace continuous learning and connect with how continuous learning (what we call "strategic learning" and what in some organizations is referred to as "organizational learning") mobilizes multiple knowledges. One of the toughest challenges for the knowledge strategist is the management of a wide variety of formats and media, and then managing what is learned from dealing with that challenge. In one situation with which I'm familiar, the knowledge strategist for a commercial magazine publisher has devised a splendid KD/KS/KU structure for the design, maintenance, usage, and availability processes having to do with reader content. At the same time, he has worked with his staff to create ease-of-use, format-agnostic, desktop-available records of all content relating to stories, layout and design, advertising, sales, and proprietary information. He got the idea from conversations with other executives in the company. In these conversations he learned about how much staff time was continually being devoted to preparing and customizing report formats for different target readers who – not surprisingly – were continually challenged in obtaining required information relating to different information-management situations. Prior to coming into the publishing company, he had developed knowledge strategy and knowledge-sharing frameworks for two very different types of organizations. One of his jobs had been in records and information management (RIM) in a financial services company, and the other had been in an international development organization in which he had responsibility for (and was accountable for) long-range planning for the development of an organization-wide knowledge strategy. In the publishing company, he was able to build on his prior experience and his expertise, becoming a *de facto* internal consultant for format management. It was a phenomenal undertaking for the publishing company and actually required several years to implement, but once in place, the critical relationships among multiple constituencies established the publisher as a model for other firms doing similar work.

Finally, we come to Igel's sixth leadership principle, that we conserve what works and abandon what doesn't (again, having come down to us from a great many advisers in the leadership realm). Igel writes about how "continuous learning increases the yield of what is known," noting that "as a consequence, it is increasingly clear which methods are worth continuing and which should be dispatched." One critical duty of the knowledge strategist is making these judgments. Working in an environment in which shared learning and teaching – a hallmark of the enterprise-wide knowledge culture – is understood and expected, the knowledge strategist finds himself or herself positioned for taking actions that might be awkward in other situations. For the knowledge strategist, providing analysis, insight, and interpretation for a wide range of content-seeking clients is part of the job, and "letting go" is recognized simply as being part of the picture. The specifics can be as basic as working with the company's records management and archives professionals to determine an enterprise-wide approach for digitizing corporate archives. Or it can be as sophisticated as determining whether – in a company in which there is a vibrant and well-managed research operation – supporting a stand-alone specialized library or research department is feasible as information, knowledge, and strategic learning requirements transition from "what was" or "what is" to "what will be." As Director Pamela Tripp-Melby of the United States National Library of Education has pointed out:

> As it turns out, in those organizations and companies where the knowledge strategist's position and accomplishments are recognized as contributing to organizational effectiveness, the larger enterprise gets double benefits. It is not only a situation in which the knowledge strategist influences the success of the company in how it does business. Simply with the authority and the responsibility for managing strategy as it relates to the company's pursuit of excellence in KD/KS/KU, the knowledge strategist also ensures that information, knowledge, and strategic learning are better organized for knowledge development, knowledge sharing, and knowledge utilization when any one (or all) of these actions are required. (Tripp-Melby, 2012)

As the knowledge strategist – the organizational knowledge domain's manager-leader – moves forward with the development of the knowledge services strategic framework for the twenty-first-century organization in which the knowledge services team is employed, a comfortable understanding of the leader-manager role in the activity begins to fall into place. By the time we get to the leadership and management activities *per se*, they are not necessarily thought about a great deal because they are – as characteristics of the knowledge strategist's work – no longer "special" or given any particular attention. They are just there, workplace attributes to be used by the knowledge strategist as the leader-manager goes about his or her work.

Yet they are – no matter how unspoken or unacknowledged these attributes are in the daily activities of the workplace – never far from us. The professional media seems to be almost consumed with attention to management and leadership. On these subjects we never run out of books and articles to read, Internet sites to explore, blogs (both professional and personal) to linger over, lectures to attend, courses to take, professional development and strategic learning opportunities to consider (and sign up for and pay for, with our or our employer's money). Management and leadership as subjects to think about continue to be ubiquitous in our lives and try as we might, we still find ourselves trapped (usually pleasantly so) when we can gain a little more insight in these subjects. Of course the history and background of both subjects has been with us for a long time, changing and growing as societal and workplace needs changed and grew, and I continue to be fascinated by the attention I – and most of the people I know in our line of work – give to management and leadership. It's not an unnatural fascination, not by any means, because as we explore changing attitudes and gain new insights in leadership and management, we become better leader-managers (and hopefully better people and better citizens).

In our work as knowledge strategists we learn from what others have to share with us about these topics and since leadership and management are so much a part of our work with knowledge services, as we conclude these two sections on these subjects, I find we are taken on a rewarding and pleasant journey by Joshua Rothman. He gives us plenty of history and background, of course, and while he is ostensibly writing about the "leadership industry" (as he calls it), possibly with a slightly pejorative slant, and while he is describing an incredibly wide range of books on leadership, it soon becomes clear that the management/leadership dichotomy is almost as much his topic as leadership alone. And Rothman's essay is a handsome gift to us as we incorporate – often without thinking about it – the attributes of leadership and management into our work in the organization's knowledge domain. I was intrigued by Rothman's noting that "many of today's challenges are too complex to yield to the exercise of leadership alone" and that even so "our faith in the value of leadership is durable – it survives, again and again, our disappointment with actual leaders."

I would take an opposing stance. In my work – and especially in my work with knowledge services – leadership survives "again and again" because our management and knowledge leaders (as described in this and the preceding section) get results, results that can be calculated and identified as supporting the organization as it moves to success in achieving its mission. We don't embark on a knowledge services strategic framework because it's the right thing to do; we do it because it will provide rewards in the organization structured as a knowledge culture and with an knowledge-sharing "personality" (thank you, Marvin Bower) that supports the achievement of that mission. So it's no surprise, as Rothman points out (I gather reproachfully) that one study – done by McKinsey coincidentally – found out that "two-thirds of executives say that 'leadership development and succession management constitute their No. 1 'human capital priority'; another study found that American companies spend almost fourteen billion dollars annually on leadership training seminars." Of course they do, and they should, for if the achievement of knowledge-sharing excellence through the management and leadership in the KD/KS/KU process achieves mission success, it is a very worthwhile activity. I like that Rothman describes a group of scholars who introduced the concept (and term) for what happens with leadership: "the romance of leadership." If leadership – together with excellence in management – results in mission success, and if, in one of the cited examples, perceptions about an organization's well being were higher when external judgments "attributed the boost in the company's performance to good leadership," it is a good thing. It's OK to refer to it as "the romance of leadership." And I would suggest that it's OK to refer to "the romance of management." Certainly there is a "romance" with leadership and management when these disciplines are applied to knowledge management and knowledge services. I like that Rothman describes leadership as a narrative device. Of course. The successful management of intellectual capital – KM – together with knowledge services, its practical "side," has always been thought of as story-telling. And if, as Rothman puts it

> To some extent leaders are storytellers; really, though, they are characters in stories. They play leading roles, but in dramas they can't predict and don't always understand. Because the serialized drama of history is bigger than any one character's arc, leaders can't guarantee our ultimate narrative satisfaction. (Rothman, 2016)

Our "ultimate" satisfaction? Perhaps not but what leaders can do – and what they do – is to present us with opportunities to align our own quest for satisfaction with their own experiences – pro and con – and allow us (especially those of us working with knowledge services) to aim for satisfaction. If we are not always successful, we do not give up and drop knowledge services or let go our work in developing and then implementing our knowledge services strategic framework. And we certainly do not, once we have that knowledge strategy in place, push it aside and permit the organizational commitment to knowledge value slip away. That's a negative perspective, and that's not the way the knowledge strategist works.

1.4 The Knowledge Strategist

The knowledge strategist is critical to successful knowledge sharing in the organization. The organization's effectiveness begins with an enterprise-wide knowledge culture, built on a knowledge strategy supported by successful KD/KS/KU, the operational result of the knowledge services strategic framework. The knowledge strategy matches the company's management strategy, and to achieve KD/KS/KU success and ensure the development of a meaningful knowledge strategy, enterprise leaders turn to knowledge strategists.

As we review the attributes and requirements for success as a knowledge strategist, we recognize that this manager's responsibilities will be to deal with the main objectives of the knowledge strategy and then to proceed forward with designing implementation plans for how these objectives are to be achieved. In our review, we of course attempt to provide for ourselves an honest response to the "why-do-we-need-a-knowledge-strategist?" question (inevitably brought up), and in doing so we return to the "why?" for the knowledge strategy itself.

From my perspective and based on my experience and observations in my work, I respond with the following. We need a knowledge strategy:
- To empower staff and increase organizational efficiency, effectiveness, and accountability by providing easy access to accurate, timely, and relevant information, knowledge, and strategic learning content, including procedures that enable all organizational stakeholders to carry out their work effectively, make informed decisions, and promote an organizational culture of learning.
- To strengthen internal collaboration and harness the organizational network in order to document and synthesize knowledge, experiences, best practices, and lessons learned.
- To establish cost-effective organizational frameworks and systems to support priority knowledge needs, in order to support evidence-based KD/KS/KU.

Organizational success – however defined – requires an established environment for managing intellectual capital (and defining – yet once again – the knowledge domain as the environment in which intellectual capital is managed).

The knowledge services strategic framework – designed and developed through the leadership and management expertise of the knowledge strategist – provides the blueprint and guidelines for its management. With these tools, the knowledge strategist enables all stakeholders and affiliates to understand the data/information/knowledge/learning sequence and its role in enabling collaboration and the application of knowledge for organizational success (organizational effectiveness). In doing so, the knowledge strategist establishes the knowledge services/knowledge strategy operational function as one critical element of the enterprise-wide organizational structure and through his or her relationships with the organization's highest-level management creates an environment that is favorable to (and indeed requires) knowledge sharing.

Knowledge services and knowledge strategy. The search for a solution for better knowledge sharing has been recognized for a long time, and with new urgency during and since the last two decades of the previous century. Now, with a knowledge services approach and new attention to the benefits of knowledge services as a critical management framework for the organization, many knowledge workers whose workplace activities involve challenges with knowledge sharing are qualified to perform as the organization's knowledge strategists, whether those employees are recognized as such or not. That recognition is forthcoming if the organization's leaders are inclined – or persuaded – to understand the value of knowledge in organizational success and to give these employees the management and leadership authority that their work as knowledge strategists requires. These knowledge strategists enhance the organization's relationship with its information, its knowledge, and its strategic learning, bringing the organization to a new place and affirming the organization as a knowledge culture, ensuring the highest standards of enterprise-wide knowledge sharing.

With knowledge services on the scene and acknowledged in many organizations as "the practical side of knowledge management" (as the effort has been characterized by Dale Stanley), enterprise leaders have been able to "put KM to work" – another popular characterization of knowledge services. It wasn't that long ago that enterprise leaders came to understand that with knowledge services, the value of this management discipline lay in its very practicality. Indeed, with this practical approach to the management of information, knowledge, and strategic learning, managers have been able to understand that the organization has the advantages of higher-level research, strengthened contextual decision-making, accelerated innovation, and – especially for those organizations in which knowledge sharing is recognized for its value – excellence in knowledge asset management.

In the management community, the development of knowledge services as a different kind of management framework was part of the new emphasis on the role of knowledge in the operational environment, an emphasis that turned out to be a different way of looking at the organization's intellectual assets and its collective knowledge. This emphasis has continued, with the result that KD/KS/KU as a benefit of working with the knowledge services strategy framework is now clearly expected (and desired) in the modern, well-managed organization. Enterprise leaders recognize that the knowledge-*centric* organization is one in which success at all levels is supported by a willingness to share information, knowledge, and strategic learning developed within and for the organization. A beneficial side effect has been that transparency (that is, openness and a lack of "hoarding" in transactions having to do with information, knowledge, and strategic learning) is now understood to be for the common good, and the old days of "information power" seem to be gone. Thus for many with management authority, KD/KS/KU becomes a necessary organizational ambition.

If, as is generally understood to be the case, the larger goal of the organization is to achieve success (however success is defined in the specific operational environment), understanding that the data-information-knowledge-learning-sharing construct can be directly applied in the KD/KS/KU process becomes a critical component in enterprise success. The whole effort results in enabling quality management with respect to the organization's information, its knowledge assets, and the arrangement and implementation of its strategic learning programs (both formal and informal).

Why knowledge services in addition to KM? From the perspective of some who work with KM and knowledge services (and this author is one of that group), the strength of knowledge services is that it exemplifies what has been referred to in some quarters as the "humanist wing" of KM, indeed to the humanist wing – we might say – of any organizational management methodology, just as described in Chapter 1, Sections 1.2 and 1.3. We have heard allusions to this "side" of KM for several years, with the case usually being made – and well made – that it is through KM that the content of any given search is captured. With knowledge services, that content and the knowledge associated with it are developed and, in most cases, made available for sharing for its potential utilization by other people. These could be fellow workers, members of a working group or community of practice dealing with a single subject, or simply another person who is seeking to learn how to work better and be more productive (strategic learning). The machine – the technology – for a long time was thought of as the "pipeline" through which the content – the knowledge – would pass to the human beings who would use it for whatever purpose was required. That idea has now changed, with both KM and technology management recognized as seeking the same goal. The long assumed conflict between the engineers and the content advocates seems to be over (or almost over), and the two practitioner camps are no longer fighting about which is more important, the technology (the pipeline) or the content (the knowledge) that is captured and made available through the technology. A good example of this positive development has been the recent decision in several organizations to re-name the intranet portal for their internal workers as the organization's "knowledge management" or "knowledge services" portal.

This natural coming together of technology and content is another sign that knowledge services characterizes a more humanistic or person-to-person approach to knowledge sharing than that experienced (or expected) in the strictly KM-focused sharing of information or knowledge. Particularly when the activity is limited to a technological process or restricted to a jargon-laced subject-specific attempt at knowledge sharing (or worse, in a situation that combines both), we often find that the KD/KS/KU expertise and skills of the participants are not given appropriate consideration, and the end-product is not as good as it could have been. In the opinion of some knowledge strategists, the ease and almost normal broad application of the three elements of knowledge services to any group interaction will result in a more effective and efficient achievement of the group's agreed-upon objective. Supported by knowledge services, the group engenders – even unwittingly sometimes – an ambiance in which relationships among the people involved (whether as a working group, CoP, or any other gathering of colleagues expecting to achieve a specific goal) depend upon and benefit from the collegial and collaborative personal contact among the participants in the activity.

It is a good place to be, and it has, in its way, opened the door to that third element of knowledge services, what we refer to as strategic learning. We now think of strategic learning (sometimes still referred to as "organizational learning") as the successful achievement of skills, competencies, knowledge, behaviors, and/or other outcomes required for excellence in workplace performance. The purpose of strategic learning is to enable those who develop knowledge to share it, for the benefit of everybody in the workplace and in the knowledge services framework associated with the organization. When we cut through the many layers that come up whenever we speak about any of the three elements of knowledge services, we find that simplification seems to help and nowhere is that more evident than with strategic learning. Simply said, strategic learning is anything anybody does to learn how to work better, to work smarter.

This assertion leads quite comfortably to my explanation as to why we choose to think in terms of knowledge services and not in terms of KM as usual. As noted earlier, the popular definition of knowledge services incorporates knowledge management, placing it alongside two other equally important disciplines, information management and strategic learning. These three elements do not completely lose their individual identities the way coffee, sugar, and milk converge to produce a pleasant breakfast drink. Each retains its own characteristics and when converged creates an enhanced management framework, knowledge services.

When the three are thus converged in this important management methodology, when they come together, each takes pride of place in establishing knowledge services as the strategic framework for managing intellectual capital. The converged elements then operate as a single enterprise-wide discipline that functions to ensure the highest levels of knowledge sharing within the organization.

We understand now that it is through the convergence of these three disciplines – information management, KM, and strategic learning – that we create knowledge services, the underlying foundation for the knowledge culture. So naturally we're asked: cannot knowledge management do the job? Why must KM converge with information management and strategic learning to support enterprise success?

There are two reasons. The first is that in today's organizations, the management of information, knowledge, and strategic learning as unconnected activities (even when these activities are recognized as related) is insufficient. The problem has to do with the standard "silo" or "stovepipe" issues we hear so much about. For several years, leaders in the three disciplines (and, we're discovering, in other disciplines as well) have been doing a good job of establishing their credentials and proving the viability of providing an organizational focus in their particular area of expertise. But they were working alone, or each in their own performance environment. Information management, KM, and strategic learning – as organizational functions – were not working together.

With these three lines of work, we've now for several decades been able to see the engineers and technical professionals making great progress in resolving the issues connected with managing information (with no small assistance from many, many intellectual leaders in other disciplines, it must be noted). KM, too, when it came into the picture as intellectual capital, created its own body of practitioners although, as we've thought about often, it was at times a confused and amorphous coterie of people doing their best to bring some level of order out of the KM chaos.

It was hoped that throughout many professions, the development and provision of strategic learning as an operational function would be given attention. Very successful tools and techniques for managing strategic learning were created and implemented, all with one goal in mind, the development of an enterprise-wide framework for supporting excellence in the management of intellectual capital.

In reality, exactly the opposite happened. With functional units such as records management departments, specialized libraries, organizational archives, staff training and learning units, even information technology departments being created and put into place as separate operational entities, no one was looking after enterprise-wide knowledge development and knowledge sharing. That need for an institution-wide knowledge culture, one that would engage not only the usual information-focused units of the organization but all functional units as well, was not being met. Indeed, even some operational functions and such critical administrative operations as executive services, financial management, human resources/human capital, research and development, marketing, sales, legal services, and even facilities management needed to be participating in the implementation of an organizational knowledge sharing system, and it was not happening. The knowledge workers who were employed in these activities (and their managers, we must not forget) all needed a practical way to develop and share knowledge for the benefit of the organization that employed them. Aware of this, as noted earlier I first introduced the concept of knowledge services in 2000 and 2001 and knowledge services came on the scene to meet the needs of these knowledge workers and their managers. The premise was direct and to the point: by converging information management, KM, and strategic learning as an enterprise-wide management methodology, knowledge services enables knowledge sharing among all knowledge-related activities.

As acceptance has grown for knowledge services and with the inclusion of KM as one of its three constituent elements, it has become clear that the focus in knowledge services is on human capital, on how people work together and how the parent enterprise benefits from that cooperative environment. How it all comes together – this sequence of human beings moving forward with a strategy for knowledge sharing – is a question we ask ourselves often, as we think about and observe knowledge services as a management approach for knowledge sharing in the organization. We recognize, almost immediately as we begin our deliberations, that the effort succeeds based on the work of the knowledge strategist and his or her understanding of that knowledge-sharing sequence. It is the progression of knowledge services as the foundation or basis of a knowledge-sharing framework that supports the organizational knowledge strategy which, in turn, enables the functioning of the organization as a knowledge culture.

Establishing responsibility and authority. As in every change management or organizational re-structuring activity, serious effort must be made to avoid confusion and to ensure effectiveness as the planning process for the knowledge strategic framework moves forward. And, as is usually commented upon in almost every situation in which change or some re-structuring is undertaken, the opportunity for finding an exact model (even in the same organization or community) is very limited, since – as all of us observe often – each organization is unique and has its own operational structure and culture. These are very powerful elements in the move toward a knowledge services strategic framework and they cannot be overlooked; they must be given serious attention early in the process.

To state the challenge simply, staff members engaged in each of the organization's various operational functions are unlikely to understand the role of knowledge services in the same way. Each employee or group of employees sees and understands knowledge services differently, and even when they become aware of knowledge services and its importance to the successful achievement of the organizational mission, employees at all levels will look at knowledge and the value of organizational knowledge in terms of how these affect (or do not affect) their own individual work situations.

It is in bringing together employees of all functional levels that we ensure success for those starting out on the journey toward the development of the knowledge services strategic framework. The idea will come from somewhere. There is some reason – the "why?" – for thinking about "how-we-can-do-better" or "what-should-we-be-doing-differently?" in terms of knowledge sharing, and those reasons must be articulated to ensure that all participants in the planning process are in tune with one another. There might be a specific knowledge-sharing problem that must be addressed or there might be a new way of sharing knowledge in a particular situation that someone hears about and – in hearing about it – recognizes it as an opportunity for development in his or her particular situation.

Yet even considering these probable variations in the introduction of knowledge services in organizations (and of variations within the organizations themselves), two important considerations, if given attention early in the process, will influence how we structure the knowledge services strategic framework. These have to do with the work that each of the employees does (that is, what his or her job duties are), and the organizational affiliation of each of the employees involved in the strategic planning effort. Our goal is to establish – early on – who "owns" the strategy being developed, who has implementation responsibility and oversight, and – in terms of their other responsibilities in the department with which that person is affiliated – how they can proceed with knowledge services and what their expectations for success might be. Or, in simpler terms, where they work, what their work is, and how that work connects with knowledge services. As these questions are answered, we make use of what we learn in order to seek some elaboration of their interest (required or voluntary) in knowledge services and try to get some understanding of how they will be able to participate in strategic planning for the knowledge services strategic framework.

At the same time, and of almost equal importance to these two considerations, we give attention to who is thinking about knowledge services and to their possible connection with the present situation. In other words, the individuals who might – perhaps very informally at this point – be staff members who are likely candidates to constitute an early discussion group or planning group.

On the other hand, in some organizations we have top-down situations in which one (or more) of the enterprise leaders has done work, including studying and probably engaging in discussions with others in similar management or leadership positions – either in the organization at hand or with colleagues in external organizations – and has decided to explore KM and knowledge services for the organization. Whatever the genesis or the motivation for the interest might be, there is seldom any movement toward further exploration from only one interested employee, unless that employee happens to be at or very near the apex of the management structure. While the concept of knowledge services for the organization might not yet have reached the "community-of-practice" stage, the interest of at least a small group of potential conversationalists is required.

When there is a group of workers interested in talking about knowledge sharing and the introduction of a knowledge services strategic framework for the organization (and the group can be as informal as two people who work well together and in their mutual activities notice a need for or opportunities for better knowledge sharing), these people begin with thinking about who they are and what their work entails. For those of us who specialize in knowledge services and have worked for the last two decades or so with our topic as a specific management methodology, our general experience has been that three types of employees give attention to knowledge services. They can be considered knowledge services practitioners or strategic knowledge services professionals, as this latter designation is sometimes applied if they are employed in an organization which recognizes the enterprise-wide value of knowledge services in organizational success. On the other hand, many people are "practitioners," although they may not be so designated; for them it is just that their "practice" is not linked

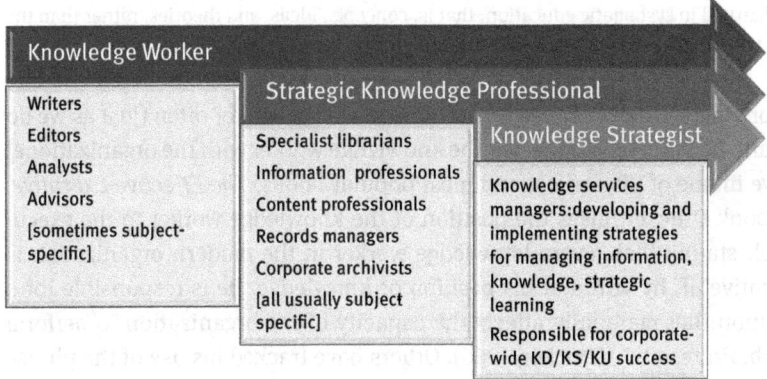

Figure 1.4: Managing and supporting the knowledge domain.

to any formal sort of recognition, any specific tasks related to their job description, or specifically involved in the implementation of knowledge services.

Of the three groups of employees usually identified as working in the knowledge domain and in positions specifically connected with the organization's knowledge services strategic framework, the first group are those who are generally (and by this time in history almost ubiquitously) known simply as "knowledge workers." With the other two groups (who are, of course, themselves "knowledge workers"), both are concerned with the three elements that make up the construct of knowledge services, leading to KD/KS/KU, the product of high-quality knowledge services. We categorize knowledge workers in the second group as "strategic knowledge professionals" and those of the third as "knowledge strategists." Of the three groups, though, it is the knowledge workers, *per se*, the first group, who draw our attention in almost every line of work having anything to do with the development of the knowledge services strategic framework.

The "knowledge worker" term as an employee designation comes up often, for we have indeed moved into an age in which most white-collar workers are knowledge workers. Even industrial workers, agricultural workers, and service employees are now using advanced management techniques and tools for dealing with the information and knowledge sharing (and even strategic learning, we recognize) required for their work, yet certainly many of these workers are not dealing with what we would think of as knowledge services.

So naturally we bring Peter Drucker's famous term – *the knowledge worker* – now into the picture. Drucker described it best in 1973:

> A primary task of management in the developed countries in the decades ahead will be to make knowledge productive. The manual worker is yesterday – and all we can fight on that front is a rearguard action. The basic capital resource, the fundamental investment, but also the cost center of a developed economy, is the knowledge worker who puts to work what he has learned in systematic education, that is, concepts, ideas, and theories, rather than the man who puts to work manual skill or muscle. (Drucker, 1973)

Not surprisingly, Drucker spoke about the knowledge worker often (just as we do today), and he had even connected the knowledge worker with the organizational executive in one of his earliest and most popular books, *The Effective Executive*. In that book Drucker raises the position of the knowledge worker to the executive level, stating that "every knowledge worker in the modern organization is an 'executive' if, by virtue of his position or knowledge, he is responsible for a contribution that materially affects the capacity of the organization to perform and to obtain results" (Drucker, 1966). Others have tracked his use of the phrase to as early as 1959, in *The Landmarks of Tomorrow*, the date many who study the subject use as the first appearance of the term in the management literature

(Drucker, 1959). And we continue to use the term with its specific meaning, as journalist Evan Rosen did in an article about collaboration. In his article, Rosen continued Drucker's earlier contrast of the knowledge worker with the manual worker (although Rosen dates the term to ten years later): "Management guru Peter Drucker coined the term 'knowledge worker.' In his 1969 book, *The Age of Discontinuity*, Drucker differentiates knowledge workers from manual workers and insists that new industries will employ mostly knowledge workers." Rosen then goes on to note – and all of us working in knowledge services would agree – that "Drucker was clearly prescient about the expanding role of knowledge in an information-based economy" (Rosen, 2011).

So the term – now universally attributed to Peter Drucker – seems to show up all over the place, and the generally accepted meaning for the term would seem to describe these workers as employees who are valued for their ability to act and communicate with knowledge, who undertake such activities as writing, analyzing, and advising. In other words – as we focus on knowledge, knowledge sharing, and knowledge services – these are the organization's employees who are most likely to participate in any effort in this direction.

But not necessarily, for many employees are workers who *utilize* information, knowledge, and strategic learning content, and they are employed for that purpose. They make up the large number of organizational and institutional knowledge workers – in the traditional meaning of the term and probably including the great majority of people so designated – and they are not what we would call knowledge professionals, *per se* (not that we would so designate them). They work with knowledge, and on the knowledge services spectrum they are certainly at some level involved in KD/KS/KU but they are not specifically working with the *management* of these activities. Many of them, naturally in the course of their workplace duties, perform work that is subject specific and that qualification alone positions them at a certain "specialist" level. For these workers, doing their work as subject-matter specialists in a wide range of organizational functions qualifies them as knowledge experts in their subject. And it is this practice which leads, in some organizations, to the assignment of these individuals – people who act and communicate with knowledge within a specific subject area – to a larger or broader organizational role as "knowledge manager." In this case, though, the connection with a more formal role in the development of a knowledge services strategic framework would probably be limited, or if undertaken, self-driven. Generally speaking, whether these people are thought of as "knowledge workers" or are knowledge "specialists" because of their particular expertise in the subject of the work they do, they have little to do with planning for and/or strategizing about knowledge services or, for that matter, any of the other activities we so casually label as part of "the knowledge domain."

The strategic knowledge professionals are the employees who are specifically engaged in the classical knowledge services tasks. They identify, develop, classify, retrieve, interpret, and disseminate and share both internal and external information, knowledge, and strategic learning content. They, when required, use their own expertise and professional skills to enable the analysis and implementation of the content they have provided. These strategic knowledge professionals, called in some fields "knowledge services specialists," are often thought of as information professionals, content professionals, records managers, organizational archivists, specialist librarians, and others working in related roles supporting the management of the organization's knowledge domain (which in its own right is defined as that part of an organization's structure that incorporates knowledge development, knowledge sharing, and knowledge utilization – KD/KS/KU – at any level to ensure success in whatever workplace activities are taking place). One of the largest groups of this category of strategic knowledge professionals is made up of the many people who work in research. Of these, there are three types: managers of large research and development operations, research "associates" who do the actual searching and deliver the results of their work to other organizational employees, or research "specialists" who undertake research projects that cross organizational boundaries.

These strategic knowledge professionals can usually be counted on to contribute to an enterprise-wide understanding of a subject or group of subjects through focused analysis, design and/or development, and discussion in and with project-focused communities of practice. They use their research skills to define problems and to identify alternatives. They generally connect with professionals in other disciplines and work with captured knowledge – tangible information – in physical and/or electronic repositories, with the distinction being understood that the knowledge these professionals manage is strategic, directly connected to organizational or corporate effectiveness (hence their descriptor: *strategic* knowledge professionals). Fueled by their expertise and their insight, these strategic knowledge professionals work to solve problems in order to influence organizational decisions and priorities. We refer to them as "strategic" knowledge professionals because the information, knowledge, and learning they provide, is *strategic* knowledge and it is limited to the subject at hand for which the organization is responsible. It is knowledge which contributes to the success of the organization, and the strategic knowledge professional knows how to "dig it out." The knowledge may be in a particular place and the strategic knowledge professionals can be counted on to understand a subject or a group of subjects in order to provide what it required.

As it happens, this last thought leads to the recognition of a possible fourth group of employees who can claim attention, as we work toward a knowledge services strategic framework for the organization (the knowledge strategist – the third group – will be described below). These are people who can be referred to as "non-knowledge focused workers," for they are not, in most cases, particularly concerned with the practice of KM, the development of a knowledge services strategic framework or a knowledge strategy, nor do they have much interest in the organization functioning as a knowledge culture. They are people in the workplace – throughout the enterprise – who think of themselves as employees with a job to do. They don't give much attention to how much knowledge (or whether *any* knowledge) is required for the completion of their tasks. But we cannot dismiss these employees as having no association with knowledge services or with our organization's knowledge strategy. All of them have been involved in one of the primary components of knowledge services, since all of them had to be taught some of the elements that enable them to complete their work. They had to experience strategic learning from the people who were doing the work and were showing them – teaching them – how the work would be done by them. So everybody in one way or another is connected with knowledge and knowledge services. Some people just don't see themselves in this way, or think of themselves as employees who should focus on how knowledge is shared in the organization.

The knowledge strategist. While strategy has been part of management for decades, knowledge strategy is a new management discipline. It is the discipline that organizations are using to capture and understand knowledge and using to make knowledge work. It's all about knowledge management and knowledge services, and the work that is done in this new discipline is the work of knowledge strategists. Our attention to the knowledge strategist – the third of the three groups of knowledge workers who work with knowledge services – begins with what we might call the "people-to-people" focus of knowledge services, the humanist side of working with knowledge alluded to earlier. The knowledge strategist is the manager whose work is to curate (in the classic sense of that word, that is, to *take care of* or to *have oversight* for) information, knowledge, and strategic learning content as acquired, captured, and made available for retrieval for re-use as required. We have defined knowledge services as an approach to the management of intellectual capital that converges information management, KM, and strategic learning into a single enterprise-wide discipline; or, if put another way, *developing and implementing strategies for managing information, knowledge, or organizational learning.* These activities provide focus for the knowledge strategist for matching the organization's knowledge strategy with its management strategy or mission.

Understanding knowledge strategy and the role of the organizational knowledge strategist – in particular the management and leadership purpose of that role – requires first that we come to a good understanding of strategy itself. Doing so is not a complicated process, since all organizational management requires some familiarity with strategy and strategy development. And since the primary audience for this book can be described with some confidence as organizational employees who are people either currently working as knowledge strategists or – more likely – people who aspire to learn more about developing a knowledge services strategic framework for their employing organization and in the process to become knowledge strategists, regardless of current work, we offer here a few thoughts about strategy and strategy development itself. For most of us, strategy (despite the term's many definitions, probably as many as for KM!) is recognized simply as a set of actions or activities that will produce an agreed-upon goal. In our line of work, it was Shawn Callahan who offered a useful two-part perspective about management strategy that has become popular in the knowledge services workplace:

> Strategy should be viewed as a combination of (i) the actions that are *intended* to result in anticipated business outcomes; and (ii) the actions that *emerge* as a result of the many complex activities that are undertaken within an organization. (Callahan, 2002)

Just three years earlier, Michael Zack had pulled knowledge into the management arena by incorporating corporate knowledge into the larger organizational mission. As Zack put it, knowledge strategy is "the organization's business strategy that takes into account its intellectual resources and capabilities" (Zack, 1999).

Some knowledge services professionals, though, take a slightly different approach, thinking about knowledge strategy as a separate managerial entity and methodology. While incorporating Zack's idea of "taking into account . . . intellectual resources and capabilities," we also – going back to Drucker – can enlarge Zack's definition to bring three additional elements into the picture, understanding knowledge strategy as a management function that:
1. looks at both opportunities and results;
2. supports an enterprise-wide focus on knowledge needs and service-delivery successes for the larger organization;
3. enables decision-making about KD/KS/KU that balances objectives and needs against potential returns for the larger organization.

Using these thoughts, we can now begin to think more specifically (and perhaps a little more simply) about knowledge strategists as management professionals who:
1. implement knowledge strategy;
2. re-conceptualize, transform, and support new ways of managing intellectual capital as a corporate asset;
3. lead enterprise-wide KD/KS/KU, enabling and sustaining the organizational knowledge culture.

As employees, knowledge strategists are expected to design and plan knowledge-related activities and, most important, to establish policy, to work with enterprise-wide leadership in designing and framing knowledge policy for the organization. In particular, knowledge strategists are expected to give attention to future knowledge-related roles and activities that will affect organizational success. Despite the obvious importance of such a role in an organization, there are not yet a great many jobs with the exact title of "knowledge strategist" being described, probably because knowledge services and knowledge strategy development continue – probably for another few years or so – to represent a management methodology that is still considered in some organization to be an emerging methodology. Certainly we can expect to see them listed in the future but even without specific job descriptions now, the work of the knowledge strategist – or would-be knowledge strategist – is required in all organizations. Employers today are seeking knowledge professionals for a wide range of responsibilities in knowledge work, and they all incorporate much – if not all – of the elements built into information and knowledge strategy development as a workplace function.

Those who work (or will work) as knowledge strategists reflect many different prior professional experiences. Many people moving into this work are mid-career job changers seeking to take their work to a different level. Some of us who work with these mid-career students and job changers on a regular basis have come to refer to them as our "step-up" colleagues. They are all employed in good jobs, and most of them are somewhere 35 to 50 years of age. They like their work, but something is nagging at them. They feel the need to do something else, and they have learned (or intuit) that all organizations require – sooner rather than later – expertise in managing information, knowledge, and strategic learning. These "step-up" career changers understand that their work and their careers will be more interesting and rewarding if they can, indeed, step-up to managerial work in knowledge strategy.

As for their backgrounds, as mentioned earlier many would-be knowledge strategists (perhaps most, at the present time) seem to migrate to information- and knowledge- and strategic learning-focused work through their earlier experiences as subject-matter experts in the fields in which they are employed. At the same time, it is becoming more and more apparent that there are certain professionals who – through expertise learned on the job or through their formal education – are naturally positioned for success as knowledge strategists. Pamela Tripp-Melby, introduced earlier, points to the value of the many contributions of varying professionals working in knowledge-related positions can make as knowledge strategists, particularly in providing solutions to the knowledge sharing challenges of the organization.

> It's important to recognize the contributions different kinds of information and knowledge professionals can make to the organizations or institutions where they are employed. In my work, I frequently come across specialist librarians, records managers, archivists, and enterprise metadata specialists – among others – who have important skills to contribute to the larger knowledge strategy development process and, in particular, to the implementation of the organization's knowledge strategy once it has been agreed upon. These knowledge workers are already "ahead of the game" and can be especially valuable for companies moving seriously into knowledge services. (Tripp-Melby, 2012)

Certainly these workers "ahead of the game" are moving into highly valued and rewarding positions as they bring their prior experience and expertise into their work as knowledge strategists. Other fields, too, provide a "natural" sort of connection for information, knowledge, and strategic learning professionals to consider, as they look to move into work as a knowledge strategist (professional workers such as research managers, directors of healthcare organizations, management consultants, professional services, non-profits and development organizations, or any other organization dealing with information-, knowledge- or human-capital intensive activities all come to mind).

At the same time, it is important to recognize that success in working with knowledge services and knowledge strategy development can also be successfully undertaken by interested management employees who do not have background and expertise in what is usually thought of as "knowledge-related work." Indeed, for the knowledge strategist there is often no connection with any of the other discrete disciplines that make up what we usually think of as the components of the knowledge domain. These are all important disciplines, but they are primarily about collections, including of course modern digital collections. As Andrew Berner has pointed out, one of the most distinguishing characteristics of knowledge strategy – the discipline in which the knowledge strategist is employed – is that it is not a collection-based approach to KD/KS/KU (Berner, 2010). Knowledge strategy – as a discipline – is a management-based approach to knowledge development, knowledge sharing, and knowledge utilization. Going even further, Dale Stanley, my colleague at SMR International, says the information and knowledge strategy approach goes even beyond a management approach to KD/KS/KU, to a cultural or organizational-effectiveness perspective about how to deal with knowledge (Stanley, 2011).

So the knowledge strategist does not necessarily work with collections, although the work of those who do work with discrete disciplines – when it is part of their background – informs the work of the knowledge strategist. These functional and often separate departments of the organization, such as the research and development unit, the specialized library, the human capital/human resources department, IT and technology management, public relations and communications departments, legal services, and/or executive office files and collections (and many similar functions) all collect and are required to manage great bodies of content, and once we get to that level and start thinking about the management- or cultural- or effectiveness-approach to knowledge and knowledge value, we discover something about what corporate and organizational management needs.

While understanding the role and value of these discrete disciplines, what the enterprise really requires is qualified leadership and management staff to pull these – and other – disciplines together, to provide an enterprise-wide approach to knowledge strategy. In taking on this role, the knowledge strategist is then positioned to link the corporate knowledge strategy with the organizational management strategy, thus ensuring organizational effectiveness.

So in these early days of knowledge strategy, jobs being advertised for these management employees working *with* knowledge strategy do not make reference, generally speaking, to the need for a "knowledge strategist." At the present time these jobs require the expertise, education, and management and leadership skills identified by corporate management for people who will perform what are – under a variety of descriptions – tasks and responsibilities leading to the development and implementation of solid knowledge strategy. This type of work draws an amazingly wide variety of people to knowledge strategy, and the graduate program and the single graduate course on the subject alluded to in this book's Preface (at Columbia University in New York) brings in students from 18, 20, or as many as 30 different industries for each arriving cohort. Once they have finished their studies – whether in the graduate program or in the completion of the course in knowledge services which they take as an elective as part of other graduate studies – they take their degrees from Columbia University expecting to become leaders in these emerging fields relating to information and knowledge strategy, often (in fact, usually) working in the same industries where they had been employed prior to their graduate studies.

Coming from a broad range of industries and professions, knowledge strategists are found to be working under many job titles: "content management and knowledge strategist," "knowledge consultant," "knowledge architect," "content records manager," "knowledge analyst," "knowledge process engineer," "knowledge specialist," "collaboration specialist," and "KM systems manager" are a few. As these are just the beginning stages of this important new line of work, most people involved in knowledge strategy as a discipline feel safe in predicting that in the not-too-distant future there will be senior executive positions at the C-suite level, beyond the current CIOs, CTOs, CKOs, and CLOs, with titles like the "Chief Knowledge Strategist" or "Chief Research Management Strategist."

The knowledge strategist as manager (2). In this fast-approaching future world of KM, knowledge services, and knowledge strategy, roles and responsibilities are going to vary according to the category in which the knowledge worker, strategic knowledge professional, or knowledge strategist works. One description heard at a KM conference referred to these roles as "above the line" and "below the line." The work might be service-based (that is, providing a service that is knowledge-focused) or it might be a managerial or leadership role, perhaps departmental or having to do with one or more functional unit or, in an ideal situation, connecting to an enterprise-wide knowledge function or activity. Depending upon the managerial structure of the organization (and its size), there is a wide variety of arrangements for how knowledge strategy as a discipline is shaped. In a small organization, probably with fewer than 250 or so total staff, the knowledge strategist – as a management level employee – is in charge of a functional unit (I like to call it the knowledge services unit). And again depending on the size and requirements of the parent organization and activities undertaken in the unit, the knowledge services unit might be part of a larger research management function or some other unit in the organization. As for staff, the knowledge strategist will supervise at a minimum one or two knowledge workers (in the classic definition, with some understanding of knowledge-related work and probably some subject expertise) and certainly one or more strategic knowledge professionals, with specific expertise in KD/KS/KU.

At the other end of the spectrum, again depending on the size of the parent organization, the knowledge strategist might be one of several employees working in similar knowledge services units in different divisions. Eventually, probably the ultimate goal of any knowledge strategist is to undertake the enterprise-wide role of Chief Knowledge Strategist or Chief Knowledge Services Officer, as noted earlier. And we must stop and recognize, as in all cases having to do with organizational management and knowledge services, that the structure and arrangement for the work that might be associated with a knowledge services unit will

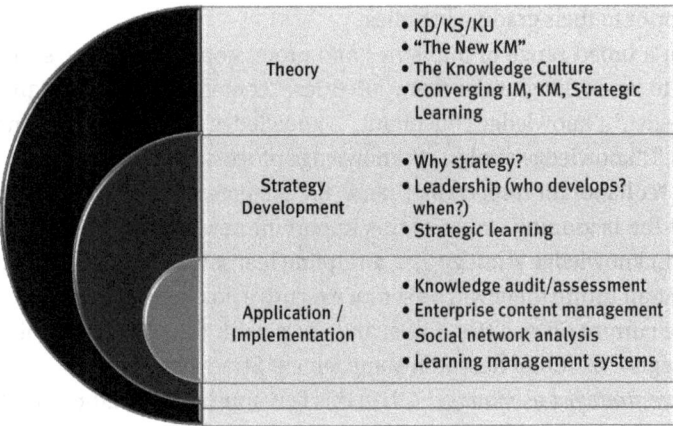

Figure 1.5: The knowledge services overview.

relate strictly to the variations to be found in the the parent organization's management and operational structure.

In all cases, though, the operational structure within which the knowledge strategist works has been identified and described by Dale Stanley, who notes that the KM, knowledge services, knowledge strategy relationship requires knowledge strategists who can work in three related frameworks:
1. In the discipline of knowledge services (the theoretical, where the people working in the discipline deal with defining – and often teaching about – information management, KM, and strategic learning).
2. In the strategy area (that is, strategy development), with people who will be knowledgeable about the discipline and principles of modern KM and knowledge services and be able to turn knowledge services theory into strategies that are relevant to their organizations.
3. In application and implementation (that is, people who will possess skills in specific techniques and applications for implementing the strategies) (Stanley, 2009).

With this last, we have also identified enabling skills, ways of working that are not necessarily inherent or exclusive to KD/KS/KU but are, nevertheless, activities we consider "enablers" in helping organizations create and implement their strategies. These are things like change management, the knowledge services audit, measurement and metrics, content portfolio review, and oversight for other specific management tools and tactics that help support the knowledge services strategic framework in the organization. As we move into the knowledge strategy realm, we recognize almost immediately that knowledge services is linked to an enterprise-wide knowledge strategy, an organizational management strategy that, as noted earlier, "takes into account the company's intellectual resources and capabilities" (Zack, 1999).

The various disciplines that support knowledge sharing – regardless of the specific role of the individual knowledge services unit or function – can be thought of as connected under one strategic knowledge "umbrella," bringing together different perspectives that affect the organizational KD/KS/KU process. Or, if not literally "connected" yet, the company or the organization is striving to make the connection, to ensure that all organizational knowledge is accessible, preferably via a single, user-friendly platform. In doing so, organizational management recognizes and follows the lead of its knowledge strategists, the people who play a significant role in integrating the knowledge-sharing function into the organization's day-to-day operations.

This understanding of the knowledge services management and leadership role is described throughout this book (and addressed specifically in

Chapter 2, Section 2.4 as we look in particular at the development of the knowledge services strategic framework). In anticipation of what will be conveyed later, we recognize a variety of considerations about what is required of the successful knowledge strategist, who plays such an important part in the development and sustaining of the corporate knowledge culture. A good place to begin is to think about what I've called here "the knowledge strategist as manager (2)." Here we think about the knowledge strategist's operational responsibilities just as – with "knowledge strategist as manager (1)" in Section 1.2 we gave attention to the knowledge strategist's more theoretical responsibilities, relating to the role of the knowledge services strategic framework in support of knowledge sharing throughout the organization.

Now we think about the workplace, how it functions, and its operational arrangement with respect to the larger organization. Of course we begin with our definition of the knowledge domain, since that is the focus of the employees who have responsibility for "looking after" (in the classical sense of the word *curate* as I used it earlier) the issues, planning and implementing enterprise-wide activities pertaining to knowledge services, to information management, knowledge management, and strategic learning. These employees, also described earlier, are the organization's knowledge workers – that is the knowledge workers who are assigned specifically to work with the knowledge strategist as part of his or her team – and the strategic knowledge professionals. When we refer to "enterprise-wide," of course, we are talking about the size of the organization and whether there is one functional unit responsible for this work or whether, in a larger organization, the work is scaled up to meet the requirements of the larger organization. There are, in my experience, small organizations with a single knowledge strategist and few professional workers reporting to this management, as noted above, but these situations are few and far between. Generally speaking, a dedicated business unit specifically focused on knowledge sharing and the organization's knowledge services will be established to work for an entire organization (the knowledge services unit mentioned earlier), if the organization is not too large, or, if part of a larger, multi-national entity, designed to serve a single department or group of departments. The knowledge services unit will be often designated, if it is a stand-alone unit or part of a not-too-large organization with a unique descriptor, such as "Knowledge Services" or "Research and Knowledge Services" or a similar departmental or unit title (and even, sometimes, with a bit of grandeur, like the "Knowledge Nexus" of one medium-size company I heard about). Scale is important for the successful implementation of a knowledge services strategic framework, and a business unit or organizational function that is too small is unlikely to be in a position to provide much support.

So the knowledge strategist has specific "office-management" responsibilities and he or she will have his or her direct reports. In most cases, though – unless the knowledge services business unit is very large with many staff and several knowledge strategists are required – the single knowledge strategist will be in charge. The position is one of both manager and leader, as described in Sections 1.2 and 1.3, and the work of the knowledge services unit will be accomplished by the unit's knowledge workers and its strategic knowledge professionals all engaged as a team, working with the knowledge strategist. And while these are some of the considerations for describing the very general work of the knowledge strategist, as with all things relating to knowledge services the usual caveat is in place: all descriptions of the work and the team are subject to the individual considerations of the particular organization of which they are a part. One company's knowledge domain and knowledge services employees will not necessarily match those of another company or organization.

The same can be said about the duties which the knowledge strategist is expected to perform, and another consideration is the job description for the management employee who will be (or is) working as a knowledge strategist, whether the position is so designated or not. We all want to know what the knowledge strategist does, what the job description for the position looks like. After being involved with the development of a number of job descriptions for clients who were seeking to engage one or more knowledge strategists, and combining a few real-time descriptions devised for clients with observed (and perhaps slightly "idealized") management expectations about the work of the knowledge strategist, I offer the following. As usual, the normal caveat is included here as well, that what is presented is only one perspective about the work of the knowledge strategist, and each such description will have its own particular point of view reflecting the philosophy, needs, and workplace focus of the employing organization.

The prospective knowledge strategist who meets these qualifications is assured success in preparing a knowledge services strategic framework in support of the knowledge culture in the employing organization:

Job Description: Knowledge Strategist

Purpose: The Knowledge Strategist will serve as a trusted advisor to the organization's management by leading and overseeing the development of collaboration and implementation solutions for information and knowledge sharing within various corporate groups. As Knowledge Strategist, you will have the opportunity to combine your technical skills, creativity, and customer focus to define and improve management processes and deliver great technical solutions that ensure your colleagues within your immediate department and our customers have access to and get the best out of the company's collected knowledge.

Your Role as Our Knowledge Strategist

Responsible for helping to develop and move forward the department's operations strategy to support the overall management objectives for the organization and ensuring it is delivered on time

- Lead the identification, capture, categorization, and sharing of tacit and explicit information and knowledge for all stakeholders (internal and – as required – external), including highly visible company-wide efforts to introduce new strategies, processes, and tools to ensure the successful flow of information, knowledge, and strategic learning content to all affected stakeholders.
- Work across the operational unit to drive and evangelize management consulting and solutions capabilities by communicating the value of reusable solutions to departmental professionals across multiple divisions from senior executives and down.
- Work with the department's managers and web strategists to champion a culture of adopting information, knowledge, and strategic learning content and services on the web consulting services and process solutions.
- Evaluate, assess, measure, and restructure the department's solutions portfolio to diagnose strengths and weaknesses and identify ways to maximize operational value creation for sections, communities of practice (CoPs), and specific-focus working groups.
- Discover ways to better leverage departmental and industry best practices or practice-level assets and capabilities for greater department-wide synergy and competitive impact.
- Identify, assess, and develop operational process improvement opportunities and technology solution recommendations for mitigating and managing potential legal risks in the development of legal services that could impact our clients.
- Collaborate with the solutions team to identify and drive opportunities for the use of new technologies to improve operational processes in key practice groups.
- Lead ongoing knowledge services audit and opportunity assessment activities, including gap analysis undertaken for knowledge services delivery, and direct strategic learning activities required for ensuring staff understanding and participation.
- Through interviews, research, benchmarking, and forecasting, assess current or departmental practice solutions and offer recommendations for functional process and technology automation improvements.

Based on the details conveyed in the sample job description offered above, we now turn to that management employee's primary task. Having determined that the organization and its stakeholders and affiliates will benefit from operating in an environment that functions as a knowledge culture supported by a well thought-out and well-prepared knowledge strategy, they are ready to move forward. They will embrace what is probably the knowledge strategist's most critical responsibility (and an ongoing one): to develop the knowledge services strategic framework, an organizational knowledge strategy that will ensure that the organization is structured to function as a knowledge culture.

1.5 The Organization as a Knowledge Culture

The knowledge-centric organization. The previous pages have described a wide range of topics for us to consider as we think about how knowledge is shared within the organization, topics and examples that help guide us as we pursue excellence in knowledge sharing for the common good and related to the organization's well-being. All of these knowledge-focused elements come together in knowledge services, the convergence of information management, KM, and strategic learning. With this convergence, the enterprise moves to what we recognize as a knowledge culture. It is a much desired state of affairs, this knowledge culture, if the comments and aspirations of many in the management community are taken at face value. It is not unusual in situations in which an organization is conducting a knowledge services audit or developing a knowledge services strategic framework for there to be reference to a knowledge culture, as in "What we need in this company is a culture that helps us use what we know," or "How can we change the culture of the organization so our workers understand the value of sharing the knowledge they develop?"

The obvious response to comments like these is knowledge development, knowledge sharing, and knowledge utilization but as is pointed out by many leaders in the field, KD/KS/KU does not happen automatically. In fact, some managers are reticent about KD/KS/KU and demonstrate a certain skepticism about the idea of a knowledge culture, asserting that KD/KS/KU cannot be directed but must evolve from a willingness on the part of all players to share the knowledge they bring to the process.

Of course. The whole point of knowledge management, knowledge services, and building and sustaining the knowledge culture is to move away from the command-and-control management framework. It can be safely asserted (certainly it is my belief) that the purpose of knowledge services is to create an environment for a knowledge culture in which the willingness of all enterprise stakeholders to share knowledge is fundamental and a given.

It is not such a stretch, this quest for a knowledge culture. For many years, organization leaders have lamented the fact that much information, knowledge, and strategic learning is not shared, and that this lack of sharing inhibits good workplace performance. At the same time (particularly since the growth of KM and management's interest in KM over the past several decades), the informal sharing of information, knowledge, and learning – the famous "water-cooler" or "elevator" conversations – has led to great efforts to identify elements of these sharing activities that can be developed into management principles. Adding to the interest in knowledge services has been the development and acceptance of a management style that recognizes the value of conversation, that collaboration and interactive cooperation are all basic building blocks in the knowledge-centric organization and contribute to the successful deployment of knowledge services as a practical and utilitarian methodology supporting the development of a knowledge culture.

The knowledge culture has been defined and its attributes listed. Just as culture itself is an accumulation of shared beliefs and values within a particular population, so, too, is the knowledge culture an accumulation of shared beliefs and values – most often within an organization or other group of people – about knowledge and the application of knowledge for that organization or group's success. Within the knowledge culture, specific attributes apply. These are:

1. Strength in collaboration (with no disincentives to collaborate).
2. Respect for and support of the integrity of the knowledge process, with an emphasis on transparency (except in clearly defined situations requiring proprietary discretion or security), honesty, and trust.
3. Focus on the larger organizational role and the benefits for the larger organization (not on individuals or individual departments).
4. Professional allegiance to the organization or enterprise; allegiance to an external influence, such as a profession or a school of thought or a political, religious, or social philosophy, is secondary.
5. Enthusiasm for information technology and communication in the knowledge development, knowledge sharing, and knowledge utilization (KD/KS/KU) process.
6. Respect and enthusiasm for knowledge services as a management and service-delivery methodology.
7. Respect for the intellectual foundation of the effort; the intellectual quest is not disdained.
8. The recognition that intellectual capital is an essential and critical organizational asset and that KM – however defined – is a legitimate functional operation in the organization (St. Clair, 2009).

The knowledge strategist in the knowledge culture. As we have seen, for the knowledge strategist – the management employee with responsibility for knowledge services – there is a very specific role in the organizational knowledge culture. That employee (usually in a management or supervisory position) maintains beliefs and values about knowledge that build on and connect with an understanding of the organization of information, knowledge, and strategic learning and of how those disciplines function together for enterprise-wide benefit. The knowledge strategist also has a clear understanding of the relationship between knowledge and technology. He or she is eminently qualified (probably better than any other workers in the organization) to make the connection between strategy and the planning, design, and implementation of information, knowledge, and strategic learning systems. This employee is thus positioned, this knowledge strategist, for playing a leading role in delivering knowledge services, the practical side of KM, and for putting knowledge management to work in support of the larger organizational mission.

It is an important distinction, this knowledge services leadership role for the knowledge strategist. This manager's workplace, especially if it is a single information or knowledge service center, is positioned to be the organizational knowledge nexus, if that is what enterprise leaders want for the organization. And the knowledge strategist takes seriously his or her own leadership role in bringing knowledge integration to the organization and carefully distinguishes between knowledge management and knowledge services. The knowledge strategist understands that "knowledge management" is sometimes an inappropriate descriptor, and recognizes that knowledge *per se* cannot be managed, although – as is often described (and noted earlier in this book) – KM can be characterized as working with knowledge, for example, or as managing the knowledge eco-structure. For Dale Stanley, the most practical approach for dealing with the knowledge *management* conundrum is to focus on knowledge services. Instead of attempting to define KM, Stanley advises organizational management to move to knowledge services:

> Knowledge services can be considered knowledge catalysis. Once knowledge has been developed, value is created by facilitating an interaction (knowledge sharing) among those who have knowledge and those who need to work with knowledge. It is the creation of knowledge value through KD/KS/KU, finding and leveraging opportunities that produce tangible results. (Stanley, 2008)

The knowledge strategist is the natural employee for creating knowledge value for knowledge strategists are, if nothing else, true knowledge, information, and strategic learning catalysts. They clearly understand the place of positive change in the workplace and they express no doubts about their role in the creation of knowledge value. Indeed, knowledge strategists – regardless of the other job titles applied to them as knowledge workers – have long distinguished themselves in providing added value to the information, knowledge, and strategic learning delivery process.

Like Stanley, Alvin L. Jacobson and JoAnne Sparks recognize the value creation objective. They demonstrate that it is through the successful management

of the "strategy-focused" knowledge services department or functional unit that creating knowledge value is realized. Jacobson and Sparks take the position that to begin the process – whether for knowledge services or any other KM or knowledge sharing objectives – knowledge strategists and the knowledge workers who provide knowledge services must identify and give attention to four essential actions in the process. The knowledge strategist must:
1. Determine the central value proposition and objectives of the plan.
2. Conduct an opportunity assessment of existing services, projects, technologies, and skill sets against the value proposition.
3. Build strategic maps that show how you plan to get the organization from where it is today to where you want it to be tomorrow.
4. Design and implement a measurement system that will monitor ongoing performance to plan and enable "mid-stream" corrections (Jacobson and Sparks, 2001).

The key element, of course, has to do with change, and the importance of embracing change for the good of the larger enterprise. As became evident during the last years of the twentieth century – when information management was evolving into KM and then into knowledge services – and as knowledge services moved into supporting the development of the knowledge culture for organizations, the ability to move fast and generate tangible returns becomes critical to organizational success. These qualities – speed of delivery and ROI – are no less true for knowledge services than for any other management tool, and it is through the application of change management principles that speed of delivery and ROI are achieved.

While the term "change management" has become something of a cliché during the past few years – perhaps from overuse but just as likely from its characterization as something few managers want to deal with – the concepts that underlie change management continue to be valid and important in organizational management. For every knowledge strategist interested in leading the organization into knowledge integration as the organization transitions to a knowledge culture (or for the knowledge workers or strategic knowledge professionals who are the knowledge strategist's direct reports), mastering change management becomes, in and of itself, an essential management responsibility. As long ago as 1991, it was being asserted by David S. Ferriero and Thomas L. Wilding that organizations must be in a constant state of openness to change if they are going to maintain a high degree of relevance (Ferraro and Wilding, 1991). Thus change aimed at maintaining corporate relevance was seen by them (and can still be seen) as both desirable and inevitable, an idea that has probably contributed to the acceptance that has come to guide knowledge strategists in many companies and organizations. Indeed, recognizing the desirability and inevitability of change and developing skills (or employing skills already developed) for building a foundation for change, for managing resistance, for encouraging participation, and for creating methods for rewarding and recognizing enterprise stakeholders who successfully embrace KD/KS/KU have become major factors in determining knowledge services success. They lead directly to KD/KS/KU. They bring attention and credibility to the importance of understanding and utilizing change management (however the activity is designated in the workplace) into the development of the knowledge culture, and they should not be underestimated.

Thus as we look to the development of a knowledge services focus for the organization, we consider a number of underlying themes:

1. the extent to which the enterprise is perceived and enabled as a knowledge culture by all its stakeholders (and in particular the organization's managers and leaders, exemplified by their participation as sponsors in the management of an enterprise-wide knowledge services strategic framework);
2. perceptions of value with respect to knowledge and the role of knowledge services in the creation of value for the work of the organization;
3. elements of organizational success at play in the larger enterprise and how these are monitored and measured;
4. change management and change implementation as an operational construct.

When these themes are recognized as part of the organization's functional structure and all enterprise affiliates understand how they affect organizational success, attention to a strengthened knowledge services focus can begin and the knowledge culture – elusive until now, and thought, perhaps, not to be possible – is at hand.

Building the knowledge culture. The greater or "higher" effort, of course, is to structure the organization as a knowledge culture (or strengthen it, if it is already functioning at least in part, as a knowledge culture). As all readers recognize from what they have seen so far, in the modern organization – in my opinion – this move toward the knowledge culture begins with knowledge services. The transfer of information and knowledge and the application of strategic learning are fundamental in any workplace activity in which success is expected. Whether that success is related to an individual employee's performance in the accomplishment of a single task, attaches to the success of the performance and contribution of the department with which that employee is affiliated, or combines with enterprise-wide activities in support of the organization-wide mission, it is in the bringing together and mutual interaction of all activities having to do with information management, knowledge management, and strategic learning – the usual formula for describing knowledge services – that success is realized. Connected with workplace efforts that evolve through KD/KS/KU, knowledge services functions as the underpinning of the organization's larger operational focus.

As such, knowledge services forms the basis of an agreeable operational scenario. As the practical side of KM, and supporting as it does KD/KS/KU at all functional levels of the enterprise, the benefits of knowledge services result in the ongoing functioning of an enterprise in which organization development and organizational effectiveness are by definition structured around the development, sharing, and utilization of enterprise-related knowledge. In this very idealized circumstance, the effect is a very particular one: the organization performs as an environment or an ambience in which KD/KS/KU is the "normal" functional methodology. The transfer of knowledge, information, and strategic learning content is integrated into the successful management of the organization and supports its operational structure, with attention to the organization's intellectual resources and capabilities incorporated into the enterprise management strategy. The daily lives of all people affiliated with the organization are affected by how well knowledge services is managed, and when knowledge services is well managed, the enterprise functions as a knowledge culture.

But that idealized description must be tempered with a heavy dose of reality. The knowledge culture – even if such a culture is already in place – does not happen automatically or from some higher altruistic motivation. Developing a knowledge culture (where one is not already in place) and sustaining that knowledge culture require the confluence of a number of different elements, none more important than the standard of leadership in place in the larger enterprise and the collaborative ambiance that characterizes the knowledge-focused organization. Another critical factor affecting the existence of an organizational knowledge culture is that most people affiliated with the enterprise do not spend much – if any – time thinking about the role of knowledge in the success of their efforts. Indeed, at some times there appears to have been in some sections of society an almost avoidance of consideration in this direction. Any attention to the role of knowledge in the achievement of success, whether in the workplace in any other element of society was avoided and, sadly, sometimes disdained.

As we move forward into the now-comforting familiarities of the twenty-first century, the tide is turning, thanks to the efforts of many who work with intellectual capital and who have for the last generation or so given much attention to educating enterprise leaders about the importance of incorporating attention to knowledge management into the overall management structure. And, as noted earlier, much of the attention to KM and its role in the workplace has emanated from the academic community, connecting excellence in the management of intellectual capital to organization development and organizational effectiveness, with a particular emphasis on information management, technology management, and similar fields of endeavor in which information science – as the medium for delivery – links to enterprise success.

Without being too optimistic, it is even beginning to appear that within the organizational management community the emphasis on organizational effectiveness is influencing the way knowledge workers (and other organizational affiliates) think about knowledge, perhaps ushering in a new day for these workers. Might this be the dawn of a new era, a new "golden age" of knowledge development, knowledge sharing, and knowledge utilization in a new society in which excellence in KD/KS/KU becomes recognized as a driver of success? Might we now be seeing signs that what we used to refer to as "the information age" is transitioning to a new "knowledge age"? Is, perhaps, a new way of thinking about the *value* of knowledge taking hold?

If this is the case (and there are those of us who assert that it is), it would be a natural fit – in this time and at this particular place in history – for knowledge workers to take on the responsibilities of building and sustaining the knowledge culture for their employing organizations. Indeed, in today's workplace the working environment is one in which information and knowledge workers (whether they are identified as knowledge strategists or not) are ideally positioned to lead this effort. In very specific terms, they have the opportunity to bring their own management and professional expertise into the larger organization, moving from individual departments to take on a wide-ranging level of responsibility within the organization. They do this by moving into enterprise-wide knowledge asset management, the methodology that takes its roots from asset management, knowledge management, and systems thinking. With this effort, knowledge services advances into a functional area that has not been embraced before, curating and managing content across the organization. It is a workplace activity which knowledge strategists are particularly qualified to initiate and implement, as we shall see in Chapter 2, Section 2.5. In many respects, the critical knowledge services function now is to take ownership of the organization's knowledge assets and provide management and service delivery from an enterprise-wide perspective. The limited points of view of the past – when information, knowledge, and strategic learning were managed from the perspective of a particular department or section of the organization, an external professional allegiance, or other limiting point of view – are fast falling out of favor.

Nevertheless, the reality that must now be addressed is how to take advantage of this new thinking about knowledge and how, specifically, to match the company or organization's management strategy with a knowledge strategy that acknowledges and incorporates the components of the knowledge culture. Yet before the organization as a knowledge culture can be considered, we must give thought to the enterprise-wide culture *per se* and the wider "place" of information, knowledge, and strategic learning within the organization, stepping back to consider just what the organizational culture is, with respect to knowledge services. We ask about the KD/KS/KU process in the overall organization, and the current and (perhaps) more ordinary knowledge-sharing activities, the incentives and, possibly, any disincentives for KD/KS/KU in the organization, and perhaps even some history of KD/KS/KU in the enterprise as it has functioned and operated up to now.

At the same time, we seek to determine if there is an expressed desire from leadership for improved knowledge development, knowledge sharing, and knowledge utilization and, equally important, if there is leadership interest in any tangible modeling or reinforcement in this direction. A critical consideration at this point is whether there is strong political ownership for a knowledge culture (or at least for planning strategy for building a knowledge culture) in place. If not, can such ownership be developed?

Related to the idea of leaders involved in – or at least cognizant of and supporting – a move toward a knowledge culture, we need to determine key players – either current or potential – who would be recruited if there is a move toward a knowledge culture. We are likely to discover, probably with not very much effort, interest in the idea of an enterprise-wide and cross-functional knowledge culture, but then we would have to ask if the interest is tangible? And on what is that interest founded? Who in authority (the ownership question again) is able to ensure the success of re-focusing the organization as a knowledge culture?

And taking into consideration a "bigger" picture, we try to determine who the key players are when it comes to determining organizational success. We try to determine if there is an organizational strategy development functional unit in place, or an organizational department focused on organizational effectiveness. These people – both managers and employees – should be aware of the role of knowledge services in enterprise success, and if they are not, their awareness must be raised. They need to be asked if it would make any difference to them – and to the success of the functional units with which they are affiliated – if the organization were restructured to function as a knowledge culture.

And not to put too fine a point on the effort, we look around and try to identify (if we do not already know about) any serious management or organizational problem that can be resolved through a new way of thinking about information, knowledge, and strategic learning. Are there activities that are not monitored, controlled, or developed adequately because of knowledge-sharing issues? If so, what are they and how could an enterprise-wide knowledge services strategic framework, as part of an enterprise-wide knowledge culture, provide a solution?

With all these ideas now circulating in our minds and the minds of our colleagues with whom we work, we move on to thinking about what we want the knowledge culture to be, starting with our vision of the knowledge culture for the organization with which we are affiliated. In doing so, we move into an almost formalized knowledge leadership role within the organization in which we are employed, and we are not reticent about embracing knowledge leadership in the workplace.

Leadership is about vision, about having an idea of what you want to achieve. For those in the organization who think about the role of knowledge and how the implementation of quality services impacts organizational success, as well as those responsible for providing enterprise-wide leadership (including for information management, KM, and strategic learning), building and then sustaining a knowledge culture is based on vision. It is a vision that begins with thinking about just how good knowledge services can be, how successful the knowledge culture could be in supporting the organization as it achieves the organizational mission. Obviously these judgments can be determined only after the fact. But to move toward that success requires having a strong vision, a direction to pursue, and a sense of purpose that moving in that direction is best for the organization and its affiliates and stakeholders.

It is the vision of the knowledge culture that provides support from organizational leaders. Management wants to know, and rightly so, the central value proposition for building and, once built, for sustaining an enterprise-wide knowledge culture? What are the objectives? What will be achieved? Who will be the players? How do those responsible for managing and delivering knowledge services (and those in agreement about the need for a knowledge culture) begin their work? In the beginning, these questions are not easy to answer without considerable research and – as important as anything else – extended conversation and discussion. There are steps that must be taken, directions to follow, and they must be considered early in any consideration of knowledge services and the structuring of the organization as a knowledge culture. The following tasks are required.

Establish the value proposition. When we speak about the value proposition in knowledge services, and particularly as we seek to assign a value proposition to building and sustaining a knowledge culture, we have a definite goal in mind. We are attempting to articulate the benefits stakeholders and others connected with the enterprise will receive as a result of their affiliation with organizational management and the delivery of knowledge services.

While most people in almost every environment can find what they require and "get by," so to speak, it is not the most effective way to pursue and apply information, knowledge, and strategic learning content. It can be a very costly method if results are merely "good enough" and that level of KD/KS/KU becomes some sort of standard or takes place on a continuing basis. Assigning a value proposition to knowledge services and to the development of the knowledge culture is an expression of added value, enabling knowledge workers to recognize that the quality of work they perform in knowledge-seeking activities is an added benefit of their membership in the community (regardless of whether that community is defined as the larger organization or an individual group within it).

To determine the value proposition for the development of a knowledge culture is a major undertaking, particularly since the activity in itself will bring about a major restructuring. Making that determination will ultimately enable those affiliated with the organization to think about information management, knowledge management, and strategic learning in a very different way, requiring us to begin the process by asking a very direct question: What will happen if we lead the way in making the organization a knowledge culture? Do we have leadership authority for restructuring the organization as a knowledge culture? What will be the benefit to the organization? And to answer those questions we must consider a more basic idea: what is the motivation for considering such a major change in the organizational culture? Have any of the following drivers influenced the move in this direction (and there are probably more than one of these now at play in the discussions about the knowledge culture)?

1. interest and direction from senior management;
2. industry practices and awareness (through benchmarking studies or similar activities) of strengthened KD/KS/KU in external organizations and competing industries, leading to a desire to move that strength into the organization;
3. concern about the lack of knowledge and misunderstandings about the value of knowledge as related to organizational success;
4. conversations with colleagues and other knowledge workers.

Obviously we identify strategic opportunities for demonstrating how the knowledge culture can ensure higher-level research, improved KD/KS/KU, and final application of the identified knowledge in the solution required. Articulating those results is almost a given, and in a knowledge culture any activity involving knowledge search will provide benefits that would not have been available otherwise. We support this activity by identifying the bottom-line impact of the knowledge culture, asking such questions as: what outsourcing can be avoided? what costly project staff can be reduced? what reductions in travel, meeting arrangements, and other related expenses will be eliminated, expenses that would otherwise be charged to the knowledge delivery process?

The next step is to focus on projects that will achieve notice, to establish that any activity undertaken as part of knowledge services management – especially activity with a short-term payoff – can be talked about, in order to refer to the success of a well-managed KD/KS/KU process for the organization. Related, of course, is the use of meaningful measures of progress and demonstrated results, and it is here that we make use of what is probably the most important phrase in the whole knowledge culture-building process: Make it relevant. Whatever savings are being demonstrated or products proven to be worthwhile, they must relate *exactly* to the successful achievement of the parent organization's mission. If that direct connection is made, the validity of the change is proven and those driving the knowledge services activity are positioned to demonstrate that the proposed recommendations are viable. In making the point, the value proposition is strengthened as discussions and demonstrations about future opportunities are carried out in terms of how, in the knowledge culture, they will impact performance and organizational effectiveness.

Here is an example: at one large multinational organization, the development of the value proposition for moving to a knowledge culture was achieved through specific strategic objectives:
1. Build a leadership team for managing the program.
2. Establish an organization-wide KD/KS/KU culture.
3. Build a knowledge-centric strategic learning framework for the agency, in cooperation with Human Resources (HR) and any other functional departments involved in strategic learning, professional development, and training.
4. Deliver knowledge services through a program the combines the values of the digital format with the strengths of collaboration and cooperation.
5. Manage the knowledge services department or section with an on-going emphasis on opportunity-focused and results-focused efforts.[1]

Identify partners and sponsors. As is made clear in practically every discussion related to knowledge services, the work of developing and then sustaining the knowledge culture cannot be done by any one person or group of people, no matter how well-respected and how successful they are in the management and delivery of knowledge services. For the knowledge culture to move from thinking about desired effect to become a reality, the organization's knowledge strategist (and others to be recruited to participate in developing the knowledge services

---

[1] Taking into account that such a process – especially in an organization operating within the international community – requires serious consideration of other cultures and environments and how workplace performance in the larger organization is influenced by these. Of particular importance is the question of how knowledge services competes with or collaborates with these cultural and environmental influences in the process of building and sustaining the knowledge culture. What level of collaboration and cooperation, for example, is required to ensure that these are integrated into the knowledge culture?

strategic framework) must turn his or her attention to identifying partners and sponsors who will work with them. Dale Stanley and I give considerable attention to the role of sponsors in Chapter 3, Section 3.1, when we write about change management, but a few comments can be useful in this context. For example, knowledge services sponsors will include a variety of people located at various levels throughout the organization, and three come immediately to mind: the knowledge strategist themselves and their like-minded colleagues (who may or may not have "professional" qualifications in knowledge services management), people in other departments who are recognized for innovative leadership, and sponsors recruited from senior management. While some employees may display initial reticence about taking on a responsibility of such great consequence, as they learn about the opportunities for success and the importance of their work in advancing knowledge services in the larger organization, they will want to be part of it. Becoming characterized as a knowledge services "sponsor" and building up a reputation as an employee who supports knowledge services can play a big role in attracting employees to this activity.

Finding sponsors and partners becomes especially fruitful for the knowledge strategists, simply because they are already recognized as networkers within the organization, or at least in the departments in which they spend most time engaging in most of their activities. Knowledge strategists are already comfortable speaking with others about information, knowledge, and strategic learning, and it would not be unusual for them – using their networking skills – to have contacts with other knowledge workers throughout the company or organization. Through their networking, these employees will have identified people in other departments already recognized for their innovative leadership, innovative "thinking" that can be put to use in conversations about knowledge work. They are thus in a good position to bring these other knowledge workers and colleagues into the picture as knowledge services sponsors. While some of these people may not necessarily be active with respect to knowledge development, knowledge sharing, and knowledge utilization, or think of themselves as such, as knowledge leaders in their departments they participate at some level in KD/KS/KU. Indeed, it is often the case that "professional" information and knowledge workers – such as research associates, database development staff, specialist librarians, and such – are not the only qualified people to serve as knowledge services sponsors for the larger enterprise. As the organization moves in the direction of a knowledge culture, the activity provides a very good opportunity for the networking to continue, moving to an advantageous result for all affiliates.

Perform an opportunity assessment/knowledge services audit. In knowledge services, this step (described in detail in Chapter 2, Section 2.2) is most often referred to as a knowledge services audit or evaluation, but how it is designated is not nearly as important as the clear understanding of this activity's purpose or value. Moving toward an enterprise-wide knowledge culture includes a thorough assessment of the larger culture, in order to determine the organization's overall maturity level. It is extremely important to have an understanding or even an inventory of existing services, projects, technologies, and skill sets against which the proposals for the knowledge culture can be matched. At the same time, and equally important, an "ambiance" or culture assessment is in line, since a basic decision must be made early as to whether the organization is one that would benefit from a knowledge culture, or even if there is interest about the possible advantages of an enterprise-wide knowledge culture. If the organization is one in which the *status quo ante* is the norm, there is little reason to pursue the effort (but, truth to tell, with strong examples regarding the value proposition for the knowledge culture laid out for any interested parties, there are hardly any organizations that would not benefit from a more knowledge-focused environment).

Build the business case for knowledge services. Of course, we are not discussing here the business case recommended for standard management situations, with its requirement that it be a formal written argument to convince a decision maker to approve this or that proposed activity. The knowledge strategist and his or her team have already done that by conducting the knowledge services audit and then turning the audit findings into their recommendations for the knowledge services strategic framework, the proposed organizational knowledge strategy. The business case for the knowledge domain does, however, take on some of the concepts incorporated into the usual business case (depending on the requirements of the organization and how much formality goes into this sort of workplace activity in the particular organization or institution). Much of this will already have been incorporated into the content of the knowledge services audit, the measurement and metrics plan for knowledge services, and the knowledge strategy document, particularly in the executive summary of each of these documents. If, however, these are long documents (and lack the executive summary), a statement document – a business case for knowledge services – can be put together in order to permit the articulation and capture of primary requirements for improved knowledge sharing and for taking steps to structure and, when built, for sustaining the organization as an enterprise-wide knowledge culture. This business case, if required, begins (and, again, this content might have been incorporated into the knowledge services audit and/or the knowledge strategy strategic framework document) with a statement of need and the development of a knowledge services charter describing the vision, mission, and values statements for the effort. Once the charter or statement of purpose has been prepared (called in some organizations the "terms of reference" document), the knowledge

strategist and other members of the knowledge services team or working group move on to developing a framework for implementing the process:
1. Identify necessary operational objectives and prepare a statement describing how these objectives are reached in an organization that is built and functions as a knowledge culture. Match these more general objectives to the specifics of the present organization and the findings and recommendations of the knowledge services audit and the knowledge strategy.
2. Identify specific projects/initiatives, in priority order, and provide justification for same.
3. Plan for technology implementations that support these initiatives.
4. Describe the roles of the knowledge strategist, other strategic knowledge professionals and specialists, other affiliated participants, and sponsors, advocates, and champions who have committed to supporting the work of the knowledge services business unit.
5. Prepare review and monitoring metrics, and include in the design of these instruments a measurement system for monitoring not only ongoing performance but a flexible structure that will permit "mid-stream" corrections.
6. Prepare a change management plan.
7. Prepare a strategic learning/training plan.
8. Prepare a communications plan for both internal and external targets, with a commitment to transparency and knowledge sharing.

Why, at this point, a business case for knowledge services?

For two very good reasons that will become very apparent once the business case (formal or otherwise) begins to be inculcated into the work of the internal or employee communications staff and, by using every available medium, will take the knowledge services "message" to the organization. The business case is by definition a tool for describing the reasons why an initiative is undertaken (and while it is usually thought of as a written document, it can be – especially if the documentation of the knowledge services audit and the knowledge services strategic framework are readily available to all relevant staff and management – a presentation or series of presentations, or even a verbal agreement, again depending of the culture of the organization and the experiences of its employees in similar situations). And there is logic behind the construct of the business case, whether it is used as a "real" business case in a company or whether it is adapted, as here, for a different kind of organization. It's a simple logic, simply building on the idea that whenever resources (money, effort, staff time) are going to be consumed for any activity within the organization, they must support a business or organizational need. That is the case with the development of the knowledge strategy and the structuring of the organization as a knowledge culture.

Pursue the ideal. As the development of a strategic framework for the transitioning of the organization into a knowledge culture begins to come to fruition and as early successes are recorded and communicated, the envisioned knowledge-centric organization takes shape. There are signs that the organization is moving toward an environment or ambiance in which the organization itself is recognized for its knowledge focus, and at this point, some consideration of the transition from what earlier was referred to as knowledge management to knowledge services is in order. For example, such a framework can be established beginning with Mark Clare and Arthur Detore's definition of KM as "a set of management activities designed to leverage the knowledge the organization holds in order to create value for employees, customers, and shareholders/stakeholders" (Clare and Detore, 2000). Acknowledging that it is in the practical and actionable tasks described in the definition ("leverage," "create value," etc.) that we see KM transition into knowledge services, we see the practical side of KM used and now acknowledged to "put KM to work." These activities then become services, products, and consultations for supporting the enterprise-wide mission of the company or organization.

The transition resonates particularly well with another KM definition, that of Karen Reczek. Describing how specialized librarianship can be seen as integrating into KM (and vice versa), Reczek raises points that make me think about what could be an intriguing question: can the two disciplines combine into a new profession?

> Knowledge management refers to strategies and structures for maximizing the return on intellectual and information resources. Because intellectual capital resides both in tacit form (human education, experience, and expertise) and explicit form (documents and data), KM depends on both the cultural and technological process of creation, collection, sharing, recombination, and reuse. The goal is to create new value by improving the efficiency and effectiveness of individual and collaborative knowledge work while increasing innovation and sharpening decision-making. (Reczek, 2008)

Again, by giving attention to the actionable items in the definition, we see a natural situation for converging KM with information management and strategic learning into knowledge services. As with Clare and Detore, the action terms included in Reczek's phraseology (creating new value, improving efficiency, improving effectiveness, collaboration in knowledge work, increased innovation, sharpened decision-making) all combine to move the theoretical of KM to the practical of knowledge services.

Doing so shapes a management situation that is best described through the lens of viability, in response to the following question: can the organization function and be sustained as a knowledge culture if the advice in these pages is accepted and built upon? The answer can be a positive one, depending on how the following criteria match the review of the organization as a knowledge culture:

1. The potential of the organization as a knowledge culture connects specifically with its "primary" value – that is, its mission (why the organization exists). A strong example is the work of Megan Smith, Research Specialist at the American Physical Therapy Association. Early in her work at APTA, she found herself in the fortunate position of being part of an enterprise-wide restructuring. Being so positioned, Megan was able immediately to begin thinking of the restructuring as an "opportunity to rethink the delivery of information and knowledge services." Making a natural connection, she was also positioned to define a new role for herself, as she had been moved from APTA's library into a new position, with responsibility for providing customized knowledge services to the association's Public Policy, Practice, and Professional Affairs Unit. Her first steps were pretty obvious (although – sad to say – steps often neglected in some organizations): she started with drafting a value statement for what the results of the new embedded information and knowledge services structure would be, and she stated those expected results succinctly and clearly: "more informed decisions for the organization" (Smith, 2014).

2. Organizational characteristics support the acceptance of knowledge services as a strategic framework, and while this is true in many lines of work, Dr. Russell Maulitz's definition of medical informatics makes it clear that in modern healthcare the route to knowledge services is becoming clearer all the time. Dr. Maulitz, Chief Medical Officer at Starship Health Technologies LLC and a professor in the Department of Family, Community, and Preventive Medicine at Drexel University's College of Medicine in Philadelphia, speaks about the "informaticist" (in knowledge services we might call this employee the knowledge strategist, since the qualifications and responsibilities seems to be the same for both). This person, he says "is going to do the information science, and informatics is really where computer science and healthcare and information science come together and overlap. Information is the science and health IT is the technology, including getting down into the weeds and rolling out electronic health records and all of the technological realities of the modern world."

Since knowledge services is all about the practical side of KM it is not difficult to connect medical informatics and knowledge services. "Not at all," Dr. Maulitz says. He talks about how when he first became interested in the larger subject of medical informatics, that practical side was more "aspirational" since at that time medical informatics had a way to go. (As indeed, he insists, it still does.) Yet with this aspirational focus medical informatics evolved into a reach for something better than just technology, something

that – in medicine – would benefit the larger society and contribute to the greater good, positioning that line of work for knowledge "where the pain points are when it comes to knowledge sharing," a situation Dr. Maulitz characterizes as one of the "sweet problems" that influence his approach to his work (Maulitz, 2015).
3. Knowledge sharing and strategic learning in the enterprise is recognized as a cultural and organizational advantage and encouraged, not thwarted. Mitzi Perdue, who has written about Perdue Farms and its founder the late Frank Perdue, makes a point that knowledge sharing was part of the company's management and operational structure. Part of it, of course, had to do with Frank Perdue's personality – he loved conversation (more the listening part than the talking part but the overall art of conversation was very important to him). "Frank was known for his egalitarian ways, possibly from his background of growing up on a farm," Mitzi Perdue said in an interview. "For Frank it wasn't a case of 'I'm the boss and you'll do what I tell you to.' Even when he knew how to get from here to there, he wanted to hear what other people had to say, what they thought about whatever was being talked about. And listening was his way for conveying that. Everyone was important to him, and no matter how big the company became, he engaged in conversation. With other executives of course, but also with people on the line, truck drivers, distributors . . . . With whoever needed to speak with him. And in these conversations he was teaching as well. One of his big ideas was what came to be known as the 'Perdue model' for education: teaching people while they are working" (Perdue, 2015).

All of which brings us to our concluding vision for those responsible for knowledge services, an ideal but achievable effect of knowledge services and its role in building and sustaining the knowledge culture. In an organization structured as a knowledge culture, the ownership responsibility for knowledge services includes management responsibility for the organization's internal knowledge-sharing and innovation practice, probably led by a senior-level management employee, the knowledge strategist to whom we give so much attention. In some organizations, that role may very well be taken by a C-suite manager employed for the purpose (a Chief Strategy Officer, for example, or a Chief Knowledge Strategist). Whether a member of the C-suite or not, the work of the organization's knowledge strategist has specific responsibility, authority, and accountability, all of which connect with his or her ability to guide the organization in converging the three knowledge services elements into an actionable, opportunity-focused, and results-focused operational framework. It is a knowledge services strategic framework that moves the organization forward toward excellence in knowledge sharing and success in the achievement of the organizational mission. By including knowledge services in the organizational structure (alluding to the accepted description of knowledge strategy as organizational management strategy – supported by knowledge services – that incorporates attention to intellectual resources and capabilities), enterprise leadership emphasizes the critical connection between the organization's overall management strategy and its knowledge strategy.

2 Applied Knowledge Services

2.1 Collaboration in the Workplace

Collaboration is natural in the knowledge culture. If the organization's knowledge culture has developed from a knowledge services strategic framework designed to support the organization's knowledge strategy, collaboration will be fixed in the organizational management structure.

With collaboration, the knowledge strategist – the management employee recognized as the organization's knowledge services leader – now moves forward to develop the organizational knowledge services strategic framework. With that strategy in place, enterprise leaders (including the organization's knowledge strategist) are able to position the organization for excellence in knowledge sharing, and specifically for moving to the four achievements we identify as the benefits of excellence in knowledge services management: enhanced contextual decision making, accelerated innovation, strengthened knowledge asset management, and – if the organization is research-focused in any of its activities – higher-level research. As knowledge services enables knowledge development, knowledge sharing, and knowledge utilization (KD/KS/KU), collaboration stands out as the operational driver for success. It provides managers with a straightforward frame of reference for ensuring that knowledge services supports and makes possible the results the larger enterprise is seeking. In this section we give attention to collaboration as a management methodology, to collaborative leadership (including shared ownership), to the collaborative workplace, and to their combined effect on the development of the knowledge services strategic framework.

The Collaborative Workplace. From what I've observed in my work and my interactions with others in our field, I can affirm that the collaborative impulse is alive and well and understood by most people. Indeed, collaboration is recognized as a critical and fundamental component of knowledge services and our planning and administrative efforts with knowledge services in the workplace. On a larger scale, however, as human beings, we collaborate all the time, usually not even thinking about the act as a "collaborative" one. And as far as collaboration in the workplace is concerned, there, too, we have a long history. When we speak about *collaborative methods* in organization development and their effect on the management of the organization we are recognizing that this basic human activity can be encouraged, supported, and even manipulated to support the achievement of organizational goals. In doing so, we bring this most fundamental of knowledge services attributes into the management picture, ensuring that the processes, behaviors, and conversations that take place between individuals and in groups result in an approach to problem solving that benefits all workplace stakeholders.

The KD/KS/KU collaboration pulls from three approaches to human interaction:
1. Horizontal. Involving interactions among employees at the same management level within the organization.
2. Vertical. Involving employees at different levels, though this has the inherent problem of deference to those at higher levels, even when such deference may not best serve the collaborative effort.
3. Random. Involving collaborative efforts that arise on an "as needed" basis, and may end as soon as the specific need is met.

As we know from both experience in the wider society and uniquely from work in knowledge services, collaboration is a constantly shifting mix, and may involve combinations of the above. Any or all of these forms of collaboration work best if one brings into the process as many people as possible. The goal is to get to a collaboration that recognizes and benefits from the fact that, in the most popular phraseology associated with the experience, "none of us is as smart as all of us."

It is a subject James Surowiecki, financial columnist for *The New Yorker* and the author of *The Wisdom of Crowds*, has taken up on several occasions. Surowiecki, introduced earlier, has very clear ideas about how the value of diversity and the commonalities of the people involved affect the relationships between the organization's knowledge workers and those with management and delivery responsibility for knowledge services are worth thinking about. Surowiecki writes:

> You want diversity among the entrepreneurs who are coming up with ideas, so you end up with meaningful differences among those ideas rather than minor variations on the same concept. ... [In studies,] a group made up of some smart agents and some not-so-smart agents almost always did better than a group made up of just smart agents ... so putting together only people who all do the same thing [*e.g.*, information/knowledge managers in this case] means that as a whole the group knows less than it otherwise might. Adding in a few people who know less but have different skills actually improves the group's performance. (Surowiecki, 2005)

Surowiecki is talking about "the difference difference makes," as he puts it, and we can adapt his insights to make a strong case that knowledge strategists make use of the "role" of differences as they seek to move the cooperative cross-functional knowledge services strategic framework to the collaborative stage. To his way of thinking (and I agree with Surowiecki) grouping together only people who are alike does not always work because the people who are alike tend to resemble each other in what they can do and how they think about – in this case – the role of knowledge in the larger organization. Adding a few people who know less – or, to put it another way, who know "else" – improves the collaborative performance. These people may, in fact, know more, but about something else. As Surowiecki puts it:

> It seems like an eccentric conclusion, and it is. It just happens to be true. The legendary organizational theorist James G. March, in fact, put it like this: "The development of knowledge may depend on maintaining an influx of the naïve and the ignorant, and ... competitive victory does not reliably go to the properly educated." The reason, March suggested, is that groups that are too much alike find it harder to keep learning, because each member is bringing less and less new information to the table. Homogeneous groups are great at doing what they do well, but they become progressively less able to investigate alternatives. Or, as March has famously argued, they spend too much time exploiting and not enough time exploring. Bringing new members into the organization, even if they're less experienced and less capable, actually makes the group smarter simply because what little the new members do know is not redundant with what everyone else knows. As March wrote, "[The] effect does not come from the superior knowledge of the average new recruit. Recruits are, on average, less knowledgeable than the individuals they replace. The gains come from their diversity."

Surowiecki continues his argument and I'm not sure I could say it any better:

> But if you can assemble a diverse group of people who possess varying degrees of knowledge and insight, you're better off entrusting it with major decisions rather than leaving them in the hands of one or two people no matter how smart those people are. This doesn't mean that well-informed, sophisticated analysts are of no use in making good decisions. (And it certainly doesn't mean that you want crowds of amateurs trying to collectively perform surgery or fly planes.) It does mean that however well-informed and sophisticated an expert is, his advice and predictions should be pooled with those of others to get the most out of him. The larger the group, the more reliable its judgment will be.

The specifics of this level of success with knowledge services are provided by Geert van der Linden, Vice-President for Knowledge Management and Sustainable Development at the Asian Development Bank, who provides a useful paradigm as he describes his goal for transforming organizational knowledge into organizational effectiveness. He notes that the bank's efforts to put knowledge to work and to create value from knowledge for ADB's member countries an effort that requires significant changes and attention to change management and in fact demands nothing less than "a change in corporate culture." To this end, the focus is on making the connection between technology and knowledge, to ensure that the collaboration between technology and KM/knowledge services works. Since, as van der Linden puts it, the knowledge economy is about "grasping the opportunities and capitalizing on the access technology provides," it is also about "understanding and accepting the proposition that 'none of us is as smart as all of us'" (van der Linden, 2004).

That the collaborative environment is one in which all stakeholders participate as equal peers and in which diverse points of view are built into the collaborative process is a point of view now accepted as a desirable general management structure for knowledge services, particularly emphasized with the management and delivery of knowledge services and of particular value to the knowledge services strategic framework development team. If the knowledge stakeholders are clever, they will give attention to one of the best examples, coming from the United States Army in its "Knowledge Management Principles":

Principle 1 – Train and educate KM leaders, managers, and champions.

Principle 2 – Reward knowledge sharing and make a knowledge management career rewarding.

Principle 3 – Establish a doctrine of collaboration.

Principle 4 – Use every interaction whether face-to-face or virtual as an opportunity to acquire and share knowledge.

Principle 5 – Prevent knowledge loss.

Principle 6 – Protect and secure information and knowledge assets.

Principle 7 – Embed knowledge assets (links, podcasts, videos, documents, simulations, wikis...) in standard business processes and provide access to those who need to know.

Principle 8 – Use legal and standard business rules and processes across the enterprise.

Principle 9 – Use standardized collaborative tool sets.

Principle 10 – Use Open Architectures to permit access and searching across boundaries.

Principle 11 – Use a robust search capability to access contextual knowledge and store content for discovery.

Principle 12 – Use portals that permit single sign-on and authentication across the global enterprise including partners. (U.S. Army, 2008)

These U.S. Army principles support a stated objective, "to connect those who know with those who need to know (know-why, know-what, know-who, and know-how) by leveraging knowledge transfers from one-to-many across the Global Army Enterprise." Of the twelve principles, it is the third which resonates strongly with the management and delivery of organizational knowledge services and which can comfortably be moved over into and be adapted by organizations in the civilian workplace. This principle recognizes the value of collaboration to the extent of recommending that the knowledge services effort be built on a "doctrine of collaboration." It is based on the rationale that "a collaborative environment fosters new ideas, understanding, and ways to execute the commander's intent"

with the implication that leaders must "incorporate the Core Principles of Collaboration into their business procedures and human resources practices" and those core principles, too, are clearly stated:
1. Responsibility to Provide – "need-to-share" should be replaced by "responsibility to provide".
2. Empowered to Participate – Soldiers and civilians are empowered to participate and share insight in virtual collaborative communities without seeking prior permission.
3. User-driven – Collaborative communities are self-defining, self creating, and adaptable. Users own the collaborative community, not IT providers.

The comprehensiveness of this group of principles and the thoroughness of the KD/KS/KU qualities that seem to be built into them indicate that they can be successfully transferred into the general organization development/organizational effectiveness environment. For knowledge strategists seeking to integrate collaboration into the development and maintenance of an enterprise-wide knowledge culture, the obvious level of respect for the individual contribution of each member of the collaborative group is of particular interest. This element in the process wisely creates an intellectual and knowledge-focused environment that connects to the very foundations of the organizational knowledge culture, whether already in place or in some stage of its initiation.

Another fruitful example comes from the U.S. Federal Government, in which a group of employees published its "Federal Knowledge Management Initiative Roadmap" (U.S. KM Working Group, 2008). There, too, the "exchange of knowledge and resources to better apportion effort," as the committee defines collaboration, opens the discussion to diverse and varied points of view. The group's guidelines recognize that collaboration in today's workplace not only permits but probably requires virtual (online) systems, since "we now have the capabilities of 'virtual collaboration,' 'virtual communities' and even 'virtual organizations'" and distributed networks which the committee describes as "a staple knowledge management interest."

These are valuable protocols, in my opinion, and their value is considerably strengthened when we return to the lessons of Chapter 1, Section 1.2 (on management for knowledge services) and Chapter 1, Section 1.3 (on leadership) following these as rules and responsibilities for inculcating knowledge services into the organizational culture or – as with McKinsey – linking them to the organizational "personality." From my point of view and based on what I've observed in the management of organizations (of any type) the best match seems to go back to what we learned from David Lilienthal's recommendations about the manager-leader and how they apply to the development of a knowledge services strategic framework. I am aware of the great time difference between when he was presenting his lectures at the Carnegie Institute of Technology (1967) and our present-day concerns with the management of intellectual capital; at the same time, I do not feel the need to defend his suggestions. Including an additional few paragraphs from Lilienthal's remarks brings our attention to the collaborative effort in the modern organization's quest for strengthening its knowledge culture. Lilienthal's guidelines provide what for me is a perfect transition for working with knowledge services (and in this context I cannot paraphrase Lilienthal's eloquent prose and must therefore provide the full quotation):

> The managerial function – whether in private business or public affairs – is too often defined and practiced as solely that of administration – that is, of unifying and weaving together the separate skills and knowledge of technicians and professionals. Only rarely is there recognition of dynamic management's chief art – providing the understanding and the inspiration by which men are moved to action. Management's primary skill, in my view, is human, not technical, and therefore the manager must be measured broadly in terms of human personality, the intangible qualities of leadership.
>
> What is the heart of the broad management process? I might put it in these words: management requires a humanist outlook on life rather than merely mastery of technique. It is based on the capacity for understanding of individuals and their motivations, their fears, their hopes, what they love and what they hate, the ugly and the good side of human nature. It is an ability to move these individuals, to help them define their wants, to help them discover, step by step, how to achieve them.
>
> The art of management in these terms is a high form of leadership, for it seeks to combine the act – the getting of something done – with the meaning behind that act. The manager-leader would combine in one personality the robust, realistic quality of the man of action with the insight of the artist, the religious leader, the poet, who explains man to himself, who inspires man to great deeds and incredible stamina. The man of action alone, nor the man of contemplation alone, will not be enough in the situations we now confront; these two qualities together are required to meet the world's need for leadership. (Lilienthal, 1967)

In understanding these special considerations and connecting them to enterprise goals, the knowledge strategist finds himself or herself positioned to set up a collaborative relationship that can – with the right team and incorporating the active involvement of sponsors from senior management – lead to the highest levels of excellence in the management and delivery of knowledge services. Just how high those levels can go is demonstrated in the response of a colleague to a query about the future of research management in the knowledge culture. With the development of sponsors and champions (and with the cooperation of managers with responsibility for other knowledge-focused functional units), the knowledge strategist can seek cross-functional programs and projects that will establish a mutually beneficial framework: "We need," this colleague writes, "to take ownership of institutional knowledge and provide access to information across the organization. Instead of asking departments to share, we need to manage their information for them so that it is inherently shared with those who need to have access to it. Integrating contact databases, records management, commercial databases, and library holdings will provide a rich picture of what an organization knows today, and what organizational staff need to learn for tomorrow" (St. Clair, "Prospects").

Collaboration vs. Hierarchy. It was Edward M. Marshall who codified a new way of thinking about how people work, and especially how they work together. In his book, *Transforming the Way We Work: The Power of the Collaborative Workplace*, Marshall succinctly and carefully put forward a set of guidelines for bringing collaboration to the workplace, particularly for companies in which collaboration is not established as part of the working environment (Marshall, 1995). The purpose of the guidelines is to provide managers with direction for ensuring that employees are motivated as the company achieves its organizational mission.

Designed for all organizations and any institution or enterprise in which serious attention to management principles is applied, Marshall's thoughts and recommendations were particularly attractive to employers of knowledge workers and information professionals looking at the evolving transition from knowledge management to knowledge services. Since knowledge services, as a management methodology, is built on the foundation of the collaborative experience (and essentially is doomed to fail if the organizational environment is not a collaborative one), the framework Marshall proposed can be something of a management handbook for knowledge strategist, giving them a framework for achieving success with the KD/KS/KU process. As this framework was incorporated into the idea of developing and sustaining the knowledge culture in the larger

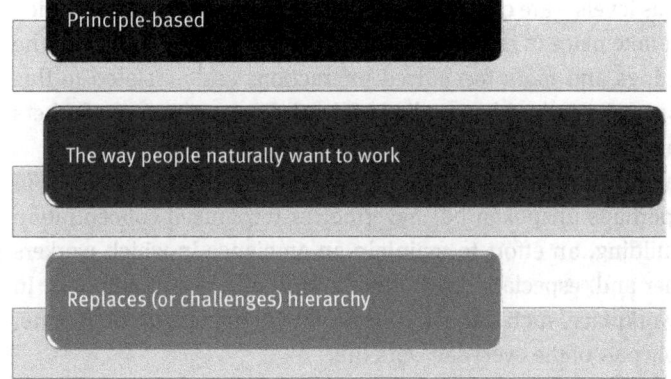

Figure 2.1: Knowledge services = collaboration (Edward W. Marshall: Transforming the Way We Work).

organization, the principles and criteria presented in Marshall's book became and continue to be recognized as essential criteria in the effort to move knowledge services forward in the larger enterprise.

Building on Marshall's work, we now recognize that the attributes of the collaborative workplace are well established. Sometimes referred to as "critical factors" for establishing a collaborative environment, the list begins with trust, and moves on to include institutional and interpersonal willingness to trust one's co-workers, one's direct reports (as well as the senior managers "up the corporate ladder" to whom one reports), enterprise leadership, and the other stakeholders. All of these people make up the large universe of people affiliated with the organization, people who will benefit, either directly or indirectly, in well-managed knowledge services. In some organizations, this reference to truth as a critical part of workplace success might seem overstated or given too much weight. In point of fact, however, it has long been established that when trust is betrayed (or, worse yet, when some employees – for whatever reason – choose cynicism to avoid participating in trusting relationships with their organizational colleagues), the "recovery time" to get the institution or group back to the point where co-workers trust one another and begin again to work together toward success is a difficult and often unfruitful period.

In the collaborative workplace, conscious effort is made to remove disincentives for collaboration, and there have been notable changes in behavior in recent years – even in organizations that were already characterized as collaborative – as social networking tools have become available and staff begins to use them. Removing disincentives for collaboration is not limited to new tools, though, for even before workers (particularly knowledge workers) had access to such electronic enhancements, collegiality had long been a much-noticed attribute of the collaborative workplace. In the collegial office, staff interactions – at and between various levels – are quickly recognized in such specifics as the quick conversations that take place in random meetings, a lack of complaint about the necessity for meetings and more formalized interactions and – related to this latter – a clear respect for and understanding of the time commitments of others who must be engaged in such meetings.

What it all amounts to, it seems, is that the collaborative workplace is one in which there is a perhaps unspoken but nevertheless recognized concentration on relationship building, an effort to maintain an ambiance in which workers respect one another and, especially, each other's work efforts and opinions. In the collaborative workplace, such respect, collegiality, willingness to collaborate, and trust are simply part of the everyday work life.

For Marshall, the point is that collaboration is the way people *want* to work. Even as he provides his own list of core values in the collaborative workplace,

it is clear that as workers (and, again, especially with knowledge workers), the people Marshall finds working collaboratively do so from a highly unselfish point of view, with their workplace behavior characterized by:
1. respect for people
2. honor and integrity
3. ownership and alignment
4. consensus
5. trust-based relationships
6. full responsibility and accountability
7. recognition and growth.

Using these seven core values as the foundation for the collaborative workplace, Marshall contends that this will be the cultural framework for management in the twenty-first century. For Marshall, collaboration is defined as "a principle-based process of working together [resulting in] trust, integrity, and breakthrough results by building true consensus, ownership, and alignment in all aspects of the organization." Since collaboration, he asserts, is the way people naturally want to work Marshall proposes that "collaboration is the premier candidate to replace hierarchy as the organizing principle for leading and managing in the twenty-first century." Whether that will be the case remains to be seen, for the elementary structure for organizational management (perhaps connected to a very reasonable attempt to "humanize" the management process) continues to adhere to the hierarchy. Obviously some environments can be nothing less, and while much attention is given to the "flattening" of the organizational structure and important attempts are made – often symbolic – to provide a more open and transparent management ambiance – most organizations require having a person or group of senior people at the top of a hierarchy, with the leadership and responsibility that such a pyramid structure requires. Even an effort as ambitious as that of a New York mayor to locate the mayor's desk at the center of a group of offices (as happened in one administration in New York) cannot change the fact that the mayor is the senior management employee for the city, and he is looked up to as the responsible leader in that position.

Still, even the most hierarchical of organizations is moving *toward* (if not able to embrace totally) the collaborative model. The jury is still out on whether such efforts will result in a dramatic transfer of authoritative responsibility in the larger management community. Nevertheless, as the twenty-first century moves forward there are clear signs that enterprise leaders expect, if not a total transition to collaboration as an organizing principle, at least attention to and some re-evaluation and re-structuring of the "command-and-control" methodologies previously employed. Certainly as exemplified by the U.S. Army KM principles described earlier, and the many other approaches to KD/KS/KU found in today's modern organization (far too many to list here), it has become clear that openness, shared responsibility, and consensus with respect to organizational management are now expected.

We must remember, though, as a cautionary note, that all organizations do not subscribe to the concept of the collaborative workplace, and there are environments in which collaboration and the KD/KS/KU approach are not appropriate (companies working on highly sensitive defense operations, for example, or certain levels of management in such fields as finance, executive search, law, or some government agencies). In these situations structural and operational success are understandably responsible for much of the resistance to collaboration although – even at the senior management level – that resistance can often be attributed to a semantic confusion, with organizational leaders concerned that *collaboration* necessarily implies *transparency*. While transparency is an attribute of the collaborative mindset, as we have seen above, it is not necessarily required and can indeed be excluded or limited, still permitting situations in which a collaborative interaction between peers and colleagues can take place without the disclosure of restricted information. In any case, we can look beyond that slight caveat and advise that collaboration and cooperation have a positive impact on the management and delivery of knowledge services and enable the successful achievement of the organizational mission. Even in those organizations requiring the highest levels of confidentiality and privacy, developing and sustaining a knowledge culture that incorporates KD/KS/KU for internal operations enables enterprise-wide success as the organization moves toward the achievement of its mission.

So the war has not been won. Or even some of the battles, for there continue to be situations in which there simply is not a clear understanding among an organization's employees and stakeholders about the value of KD/KS/KU, about what it can bring to the organization, and why knowledge must be shared if the organization is to succeed. Certainly the reasons for moving in this direction run the gamut of what might be called the "success principles" of organization development and organizational effectiveness, yet there continue to be barriers to the development of the collaborative workplace, barriers that seriously impede the organization as its leaders and managers and intrapreneurial thinkers try to move forward.

One of the barriers, it must be recognized, is ignorance. For most people, regardless of the kind of work they do, thinking about knowledge and the KD/KS/KU process is not very high on their list of concerns. Indeed, as has been proven many times and in many well-documented cases, people think about information, knowledge, and strategic learning *when they need to*, when some force outside their "usual" way of thinking about their work brings to their attention that they must look beyond their usual resources and seek elsewhere for what they require. With these workers – especially if they are knowledge workers – there is clearly a need to explain and thus establish why it is important to share knowledge.

Most knowledge strategists have a good idea why knowledge should be shared, but whether those reasons have been conveyed to the knowledge workers and other information professionals under their supervision and, especially, to colleagues and knowledge services clients affiliated with other parts of the enterprise, is a matter of conjecture. At the risk of stating the obvious, staff with responsibility for the management and delivery of knowledge services would do well to establish the following ten reasons for KD/KS/KU as drivers for their approach to establishing and sustaining a collaborative environment:

1. to provide situation management expertise and advice;
2. to identify and disseminate knowledge about best practices;
3. to provide for the development of a growing body of knowledge about agreed-upon subjects;
4. to support high quality analysis;
5. to enable near real-time collaboration and the exchange of pertinent information and knowledge among participants;
6. to comply with any existing legal knowledge-sharing requirements/regulations;
7. to ensure protection of critical information;
8. to establish rational analysis of activities reported in a consistent manner, through the use of a standard reporting process;
9. to "level the playing field," so that all participants are describing the same types of activity, using the same language;
10. to simplify and reduce bureaucratic impediments to planning for success (for projects, clients etc.).

Still, there continue to be impediments and barriers to the development of the collaborative workplace, and two that seem to be most powerful in organizations where leadership is wrestling with managing and delivering knowledge services are the much-discussed silos dilemma and the unwillingness of some people to share. There is no question – at this time in the history of management science and its role in organizational effectiveness – that seemingly ever-present attention to the silo "mentality" of some workers is detrimental to organizational health. Yet attempts to engage in cross-functional problem solving or knowledge sharing frequently become bogged down in departmental- and functional unit-related priorities, making the attempt to ascertain the effects of the silo effect ineffective.

We know the origin of the concept. In the information technology environment, a silo is simply a system that cannot easily integrate with any other system, so there will be more than one version of the same data captured in different technology products. Often thought of as "islands of automation" in this context, the problem of the silo as a management impediment is obvious: if a group in one department is approaching a problem from that department's specific point of view, groups in other departments approaching the same problem will not benefit from the diversity and broader perspectives. Duplicate or even multiple decisions will be made, often decisions that contradict one another when folded into the larger organizational management picture.

Of course, silos can also be mindset driven. They sometimes originate with the primal urge for self-preservation. The problem is exacerbated by the fact that silos are sometimes encouraged (hopefully unintentionally) by organizations and leaders who think specialization equals efficiency and/or effectiveness.

The silo-type situation (also referred to as "smokestacks" or "stovepipes," particularly in the military) can be a grave one for the knowledge strategist, for within the organization there might be any number of functional units that have knowledge asset management issues that relate to or perhaps have some connection with the management and delivery of knowledge services as performed in the functional unit with that responsibility. When units such as corporate archives, records management, and project reports management are all dealing with the same issues but dealing with them in their own silo-ed environment ("we don't do it that way in our department"), the values and benefits of the collaborative workplace have eluded incorporation into the organization's work environment and progress is seriously inhibited. It is this lack of interest in common solutions that seems to most effectively inhibit knowledge services management, leaving the silo or smokestack management structure as a serious impediment to collaboration.

At the same time, it is important to recognize that impediments to successful knowledge services are not necessarily structural, and the organization is not always to blame when collaboration becomes difficult and people resist KD/KS/KU. Human nature comes into the picture, and in many cases, there seems to be some connection to what Stephen Covey characterizes as a "scarcity" mentality, held by people who "tend to see everything in terms of win-lose. There is only so much; and if someone else has it, that means there will be less for me" (Covey, 2004). For these people, resisting the collaborative instinct or awkwardly "pushing back" against the organization's collaborative environment seems to be something of a survival technique, since they have not yet learned that, as Covey puts it, "the more we develop an abundance mentality, the more we are genuinely happy for the successes, well-being, achievements, recognition, and good fortune of other people." If the resisters can be convinced, their – and the organization's – success is achieved in the same communal framework.

Yet there are other barriers to the collaborative workplace that must be considered and resolved for the process to succeed. These often include what might be thought of as "access issues," to borrow phraseology often used in another context when speaking about knowledge services. We find these when employees do not know where to find what they need to move the KD/KS/KU process forward. In many cases, knowledge services and knowledge asset management have not necessarily been taught to neophyte management practitioners, and the value of KD/KS/KU as a management technique must be determined for them, usually through the mentoring and leadership of knowledge services sponsors or through their own readings and learning activities.

Yet even these situations seem to be less daunting when compared to what many have come to consider the greatest impediment to knowledge sharing in the organization. For many organizational employees, the seemingly lofty nature of the thinking about and attempting to deal with knowledge, knowledge services, and knowledge sharing serves as a major barrier, often inhibiting success with KD/KS/KU. While the concepts of knowledge services and KD/KS/KU are intuitively appealing, they are hard to define in understandable and meaningful terms and many managers and other enterprise leaders have difficulty, as one colleague puts it, "getting their arms around KM and knowledge services." As a result, at the senior management levels of the organization there is often a sort of uncomfortable awkwardness about working with the knowledge strategist, with many managers responding, quite correctly (and as noted earlier), that knowledge cannot be managed and even when the concept is characterized as attempting to work *with* knowledge, it is sometimes difficult for enterprise leaders to make the connection between knowledge services and the successful accomplishment of the organizational mission.

Similarly, while knowledge services as an organizational management and service delivery methodology is conceptually not a difficult concept for strategic knowledge professionals and others with workplace experience in the management of information, knowledge, and strategic learning, such is not always the case for many other workers in the organization, even though we refer to most of them as knowledge workers. Connecting the role of and the value of knowledge services in the workplace to their daily activities is a daunting task for many people, and even some knowledge services professionals find themselves becoming so entrenched in the routine of their jobs that they simply are not motivated to make the connection. Nor is there the additional motivation, as with some other management-related methodologies, for these employees to recognize knowledge services and its development in the workplace as a mechanism for advancing their own careers because, truth to tell, the exposure they have been given to knowledge services and the "management" of knowledge services in the larger enterprise scheme does not, from their own perspective, seem to relate to them and their own career ambitions. Thus, like many senior managers, we have employees working in activities that could be described as knowledge related but the employees do not recognize that, or they feel that what they are doing is more related to technology management. The two are – or usually are – different, even if they are similar.

Thus, proposed changes or moves to consider or initiate a knowledge services strategic framework must be explained, with explanations that make sense both to managers and to staff. The development of a collaborative workplace wherein KD/KS/KU is built in to every interaction is part of that picture and as such often suffers from the same lack of understanding and resistance to the "lofty nature" of the process. One solution, a technique adopted by a number of organizations in the last ten years or so, is to change the phraseology. It has now been pretty well established that organizations using the term "knowledge services" instead of "knowledge management" find a more receptive audience to the concepts usually associated with KM. While there are probably several reasons for explaining this shift, the simplest would seem to be that "knowledge services" as an operational focus is easier to deal with than "knowledge management," since services are by definition tangible and can be bought, sold, and the quality of service delivery measured. As noted, the concepts related to "managing" knowledge are difficult to describe and for many present a confusing and tangled array of choices that lead away from the workplace needs associated with information, knowledge, and strategic learning.

For any initiative, these and the typical impediments of internal politics, internal and intra-departmental competition for time and resources, and, particularly, the lack of financial support, all play a limiting role when the knowledge strategist and other management staff are seeking to move toward a more collaborative workplace. And as we speak about internal politics, even if we do not like the idea of giving attention to such topics, we have to remember another particularly insidious impediment to collaboration in the workplace, one that seems to come up with a certain frequency. I call it anti-collaboration or, perhaps using a better designation, *faux*-collaboration. Why it comes up can be based on any number of reasons, although this activity seems to show up more often among knowledge workers who have – without seeking it – been given a certain level of responsibility with respect to knowledge services, the development of knowledge strategy, and the move toward (or enhancement of) the organization as a knowledge culture. For these management employees, despite having limited qualifications, expertise, or experience with knowledge work, are attracted by the same "lofty nature" of knowledge work (exactly the opposite of the workers described above, for these knowledge strategists like and attach themselves to the idea of some sort of organizational or divisional superiority from working in the knowledge domain). They use their limited background to work at establishing knowledge-sharing procedures and management policies that often do not match (or do not match very well) the goals and objectives of the parent organization. They are not skilled enough to recognize that what they are seeking to do – or have their employees do – is not necessarily moving the intellectual capital management effort forward. They do know, however (having learned or perhaps having observed) that collaboration as a management methodology is a critical component of the knowledge sharing process, so they create their own version of collaboration. Sadly, some of these knowledge strategists cannot move away from established management methodologies that they have used throughout their careers; they give a great deal of "lip service" to collaboration. What they are using, however, as their particular management framework – totally opposed to the manager-leader construct so required for success as a knowledge strategist – is their own variation on the old-fashioned command-and-control management style. For them, the approach to collaboration is their own definition of collaboration (not often stated as such or even thought about, but in fact representing the management style these knowledge strategists follow) summarized as something along the lines of: "We'll collaborate, and here's how we will collaborate: I'll tell you what to do and then you'll do it, and then when we describe it to others, I'll say that you and I have decided to do this." Not a good situation, and certainly an approach – or lack of an approach – that is opposed to or, probably even more realistically, anathema to collaboration in the knowledge services workplace.

For companies and organizations that have been able to move beyond these types of limitations, and are successful and not obliged to deal with impediments and barriers to KD/KS/KU, collaboration and cooperation can be seen to thrive when three critical elements are in place, all supporting (either in tandem or individually) the knowledge-sharing structure:
- the commitment of sponsors who speak about, model, and reward employees and fellow executives who embrace KD/KS/KU in the successful accomplishment of the organization's work
- formal or mandated collaboration designed to support the development and continuation of a knowledge-centric environment – a knowledge culture – building on the highest principles of teaching, learning, and sharing
- the leadership role of the person (or group of people) with management and delivery responsibility for knowledge services

The role of sponsors in KD/KS/KU success is critical but it is not, as any experienced knowledge strategist will describe, a simple or casual exercise (as Dale

Stanley and I describe in more detail in Chapter 3, Section 3.1). In the first place, distinctions must be made between the role of a sponsor (as opposed, say, to that of a champion or advocate). In most cases, we tend to think of champions and advocates as people in the organization who make use of the services provided through the knowledge services functional unit, or have some experience in this area, but they are generally not in a position to "do" anything about the management and delivery of knowledge services, or provide any authority for assuring or enhancing their success. That work is the responsibility of the knowledge strategist and his or her staff, with approval and resource allocation provided by the people to whom the knowledge strategist reports, generally up the management chain in a hierarchically managed organization. But as has been established in organizational management for many decades, the active interest of a member of the organizational management team or enterprise leadership is high on the list of criteria for success, a fact no less true in knowledge asset management than in any other functional activity in the organization.

With knowledge services, we generally refer to sponsors as enterprise leaders who make it their business to "say, model, and reward" (as this activity is usually described) the value of KD/KS/KU to the successful accomplishment of the organization's work. It is easy enough, through conversations with various leaders and by taking advantage of standard communications media used to convey information throughout the organization, to identify champions and advocates willing to express their approval and support of any particular facet of KD/KS/KU. An example can be found in a typical research operation in Washington, DC, say, a "think tank" studying a particular public policy. In the organization, a team of knowledge workers is seeking to identify and standardize contact information about experts consulted by various departments in the organization as program staff seek advice. There is no problem in having senior management support for the project and, in fact, the working group will welcome the approval of senior management and those managers' comments about the project. Particularly if conveyed throughout the organization, that support will make the study group's work easier, since the project's credibility will have been established as management's support is established. These senior managers are obviously champions and advocates of the work being undertaken.

It is a much different matter when that expression of interest from the senior manager is one element of the three-part construct required for sponsorship (to "say" that he or she supports the effort). Of course the generous recognition provided by champions and advocates is valuable for, as noted, establishing credibility or for ensuring that any antithetical response to the project is checked. In most cases, though, more is needed, and that is when the role of the champion or advocate must be advanced to that of sponsor, with the other two elements of management commitment brought into the picture. The advantages of having managers or enterprise leaders model and reward the KD/KS/KU activity can be quickly stated. If the virtue of the project is brought to their attention, especially at the beginning of the project, not only is their participation valuable for the credibility provided. They also have the opportunity to learn how to make use of the service being established (to "model" its effectiveness) and to demonstrate to the larger organization that they, as sponsors, recognize its value and that they expect others to learn to do the same (to "reward" its adoptions, a particularly useful circumstance if the management sponsor or sponsors are recognized as early adapters in the organization). In the development of the experts database described above, the value of the sponsors' role becomes clear when one of the senior management team who is obliged to, say, provide a presentation to a Congressional hearing is able not only to utilize the newly established database himself, he is able to do so with such success that he makes it clear that the tool is a valuable knowledge asset for the organization and he expects others in the organization to make use of it as well. The collaboration between the sponsor and the responsible knowledge strategist in these types of situations is an invaluable asset in moving the organization forward in meeting its objectives and can possibly be characterized as the most effective of all collaborative efforts.

Related to this level of collaboration, the place of formal or mandated collaboration as practiced in some organizations should not be overlooked. Over the past decade or so, we have seen the growth of considerable attention to the role of collaboration, particularly in the field of organization development and possibly linked to the burgeoning interest in organizational effectiveness as a part of organization development. Indeed, the subject has become so prevalent that collaboration-management technology has been developed to manage collaboration processes in both traditional and virtual enterprises. In dealing with the former, it is not unusual to see an organization's management team establish a collaboration or collaboration-like environment, a situation that can be informal (using word-of-mouth and other communications media commonly applied within the organization) or formal, in which organizational management seeks to restructure and brand the organization with a collaborative framework. In both cases, the role of strategic learning, the principles of the learning organization and its matching methodology, the teaching organization, and other knowledge-sharing techniques and practices are linked to KD/KS/KU success.

So far, there seem to have been varying levels of success with mandated collaboration. If understood by all employees as part of a larger enterprise effort to move toward enhanced organizational effectiveness, together with attention to a less hierarchical management structure, the effort can be successful and benefits will be recognized by employees, particularly knowledge workers as their attention to collaboration and cooperation enables tangible and measurable results. There are some delays, of course, and circumstances might mean that the effort does not move forward as quickly as some organizational managers or the knowledge strategist might like, since some people will – as noted – not relish the thought of being required to adjust their behavior and perform differently. In these cases, it is not unusual for the management agenda to be clear and to the point, but some of the typical barriers can prevent adoption as early as expected.

On the other hand, some companies build collaboration into their business model. This situation is particularly noticeable with new companies, while others introduce the collaborative model as re-structuring is considered and implemented. In both situations, management finds the benefits associated with collaboration and cooperation recognized and accepted with little dissent. At one large research organization, famous for the seriousness of its published studies in a wide variety of scientific, technical, and medical specialties, concern about the quantity of duplicated effort and lost time in program development – from basic decision-making about whether to move ahead with the program on through research, study, and results publication – led to much discussion about how the situation could be alleviated. The efforts of a concerned team of strategic planners resulted in the development of a group of strategic research liaisons established specifically to collaborate with program planners from early conversations about program initiatives, an example of the embedded strategic knowledge professional method described earlier. In another organization, also a large research-focused company, initiatives are undertaken with a "single-site" base of operations, with one member of a specific functional unit assigned oversight responsibility as project lead, but the actual work of the group of collaborating employees is "location neutral" and is expected to be performed with participants from throughout the world (it is an international company), taking advantage of the value of electronic networking tools.

In addition to these examples, there is another in which incorporating collaboration into an organization's business model has proved to be remarkably useful in large organizations. During my career our company has performed more than one knowledge services strategy development project that resulted in the appointment of knowledge services focal points. In these companies and institutions the knowledge strategist and his or her team confer with department heads and other management leaders in identifying talented employees to serve as what we called each department's "critical knowledge services custodians." It is a remarkably successful management technique for supporting collaboration, since it establishes a network or community of practice that gives enterprise employees and, especially, knowledge workers, strategic knowledge professionals, and the knowledge strategist someone to turn to when a knowledge-sharing issue comes up for discussion and when a solution to a knowledge-focused problem is required.

For the knowledge strategist and management colleagues considering such a "built in" collaboration technique, a first step is to define the role. In organization development, the term "focal point" describes any center of activity or attention, and in business and organizational management, we go a little further, applying the term to the person within a business unit or department who is responsible for coordinating actions and tasks relating to a specific operational function (in this case knowledge services). The employee designated the "knowledge services focal point" has ownership responsibility for the function within the unit and practical authority for bringing that activity into play in the particular business unit. Thus the knowledge services focal point also has a certain level of oversight responsibility (or custodial responsibility, as I like to think of this role) and is positioned to coordinate planning and implementation of knowledge services activities within the business unit, including service delivery.

In the business unit, the knowledge services focal point is a critical employee, a vital link between knowledge services – as a management practice or discipline – and other members of the department. The point person is usually a specifically identified employee, with knowledge services focal point responsibilities built into the job description. In some workplace environments this can be a current employee who is also assigned to carry out the work of the knowledge services focal point. This "assignment" arrangement, though, is not usually as successful as that in which focal point responsibilities are built into the job description from the time the employee is hired or is promoted into the job.

The work of the knowledge services focal point is fairly clear cut, although the employee's responsibilities will vary somewhat, as determined in the organization's management structure and culture. A primary responsibility is to serve as the chief advocate for monitoring and improving the status of knowledge services across the business unit and, as knowledge-sharing success grows within the unit, he or she will continue to function in this role. Typical activities include advocating and assisting in knowledge services policy formulation within the specific business unit in which he or she is employed, sharing and showcasing good knowledge services practices, and collaborating in the development of recruitment and promotion mechanisms.

In a particularly significant exercise, the knowledge services focal point participates in and supports a network of knowledge services focal points in different entities throughout the larger organization, providing guidance and advocacy for all knowledge workers employed in the company. As a result, this broader-based network of business unit or departmental focal points specializing in knowledge services takes on a significant role in the larger organization. This group of employees includes workers not formally associated with knowledge services or the KD/KS/KU business unit although they do, probably informally but also formally, work in its support. Thus each focal point is positioned not only to provide critical support to his or her own business unit or departmental management; he or she is also positioned to collaborate with other knowledge services focal points within their network for problem solving beyond the individual business unit. As a network of identified knowledge workers, the group can – in this very important role – influence the development of knowledge services policies for the larger organization and serve on working groups for studying and developing specific innovations, bringing a knowledge services perspective to those studies. Equally important – as a discipline-specific community of practice – the company's knowledge services focal points can monitor the status of knowledge services not only in their individual business units and departments. They can, when appropriate, lead in the development of new and higher-functioning knowledge services delivery for the entire organization.

As organization management contemplates the move from a hierarchical to a collaborative management framework, even when doing so with some sense of hesitancy and recognizing that there is seldom going to be a "one-or-the-other" final definition of the process, the result is good. This is certainly the best approach for the knowledge strategist as he or she moves forward with the knowledge services strategic framework. As he or she is brought into the process, the education, background, and traditions associated with that person's experience are liable to include a positive point of view about the value of collaboration, networking, and social interaction as a way of doing work. The results, in most cases, are impressive. The work environment seems to take on a healthy, more enabling character as the attitudes of the employees move from competition to collaboration. The old-fashioned ideas associated with "information is power" ("I have power over you because I have the information you require and you have to come to me to get it") begin to change. In this good situation, "information power" moves to something along the lines of "relationship power," with knowledge workers recognizing that they can do their work more successfully if they think about how they can help one another instead of working alone, with the accompanying lowering of stress in situations that had been stressful in the past. The collaborative, partnering workplace brings with it a different, more modern, and certainly more respectful perspective for managing KD/KS/KU, one that matches exactly the very practices knowledge services professionals pride themselves on bringing to the workplace.

Collaborative Tools and Techniques. A wide variety of collaborative tools and techniques is available for bringing knowledge workers into a workplace ambiance that includes – or in some cases is based on – collaboration, cooperation, and the willingness of all participants to incorporate "sharing" concepts into the management and delivery of knowledge services. As a society, we have now moved into a period of social networking, and with the presidential elections of 2008 and 2012 now recognized as the first American elections in which the power and influence of the Internet were used to actually influence the outcome of the election, it is clear that networking, collaboration, and cooperative endeavors will be incorporated into the workplace much faster (and, it is hoped) more profitably than had been imagined.

Therefore, such management practices as communities of practice (CoPs), network analysis (and enhancements to network analysis, such as Value Network Analysis), and the rapidly evolving Web 2.0 social networking tools are all now regularly associated with knowledge services delivery, and will continue to expand almost exponentially as knowledge workers recognize and take up the tools of social networking to apply in the workplace. CoPs, for example, probably represent the oldest form of knowledge transfer, learning by observation, going back to the days when an apprentice would be positioned to learn from a more experienced worker (the Army's "right hand ride" is an interesting example of this kind of learning). Etienne Wenger-Trayner, one of the first to write about "communities of practice," began his work by looking at this type of learning. He realized that the knowledge exchanges of apprentice and master are often embedded in a larger group (such as a craft guild or professional group) which he dubbed a "community of practice." To Wenger and others in the field like Hubert St. Onge, a CoP is a group of people who share a common interest in one area of knowledge, a community that allows the less experienced members to learn, while the more experienced impart knowledge and gain in expertise. Such an activity is recognized as an ancient, naturally occurring group phenomenon which – as the elementary structure of the organization becomes a knowledge culture – can be harnessed by the larger organization for its benefit. Wenger has provided his own definition of the CoP:

> A "community of practice" is a group of people who share an interest in a domain of knowledge, for instance, how to do open-heart surgery or how to write children's books. Together they develop a set of approaches that allow them to deal with this domain successfully.
>
> More formally, I would say that a community of practice really must have three elements in it: domain, community, and practice. (Wenger et al., 2002)

Wenger expanded on the three elements – of particular connection with the development of the knowledge services strategic framework – in a later paper.

While I delightedly make the claim that CoPs are indeed a relevant and viable collaboration vehicle for the knowledge strategist and the knowledge services staff, I'm not sure I love the analogy with youth gangs and gang members as communities of practice (although I do – with much pleasure – accept that our knowledge strategist, knowledge workers, strategic knowledge professionals, and all our supportive colleagues in the organization can be analogous with the Impressionists):

1. *The domain:* A community of practice is not merely a club of friends or a network of connections between people. It has an identity defined by a shared domain of interest. Membership therefore implies a commitment to the domain, and therefore a shared competence that distinguishes members from other people. (You could belong to the same network as someone and never know it.) The domain is not necessarily something recognized as "expertise" outside the community. A youth gang may have developed all sorts of ways of dealing with their domain: surviving on the street and maintaining some kind of identity they can live with. They value their collective competence and learn from each other, even though few people outside the group may value or even recognize their expertise.

2. *The community:* In pursuing their interest in their domain, members engage in joint activities and discussions, help each other, and share information. They build relationships that enable them to learn from each other; they care about their standing with each other. A website in itself is not a community of practice. Having the same job or the same title does not make for a community of practice unless members interact and learn together. The claims processors in a large insurance company or students in American high schools may have much in common, yet unless they interact and learn together, they do not form a community of practice. But members of a community of practice do not necessarily work together on a daily basis. The Impressionists, for instance, used to meet in cafes and studios to discuss the style of painting they were inventing together. These interactions were essential to making them a community of practice even though they often painted alone.

3. *The practice:* A community of practice is not merely a community of interest – people who like certain kinds of movies, for instance. Members of a community of practice are practitioners. They develop a shared repertoire of resources: experiences, stories, tools, ways of addressing recurring problems – in short a shared practice. This takes time and sustained interaction. A good conversation with a stranger on an airplane may give you all sorts of interesting insights, but it does not in itself make for a community of practice. The

development of a shared practice may be more or less self-conscious. The "windshield wipers" engineers at an auto manufacturer make a concerted effort to collect and document the tricks and lessons they have learned into a knowledge base. By contrast, nurses who meet regularly for lunch in a hospital cafeteria may not realize that their lunch discussions are one of their main sources of knowledge about how to care for patients. Still, in the course of all these conversations, they have developed a set of stories and cases that have become a shared repertoire for their practice.

It is the combination of these three elements that constitutes a community of practice. And it is by developing these three elements in parallel that one cultivates such a community (Wenger-Trayner, 2015).

Thus the link between CoPs and KD/KS/KU can be quickly established, for in order to achieve KD/KS/KU as a culture the organization must identify and understand what knowledge domains are essential to enterprise success, a connection that emerges as one of the most important attributes of the community of practice. At its most fundamental, the CoP is an activity of social learning in which practices emerge and evolve as people with common goals interact and seek to achieve those goals, a point which Wenger makes when he says "CoPs are very rich sets of relationships and responsibilities around learning and knowledge that really are the cornerstone of the KM initiative in an organization," connecting the management of the knowledge in the domain to the relationships among the various members.

Journalist Alex Cohen identifies further attributes for CoPs, noting that community membership is static, that content is formed over time as individuals associate with others who face similar issues and challenges, that research groups may not be formally recognized by the organization, and that, typically, there is no hierarchy (or there should not be any hierarchy). With respect to the latter, Cohen (2001) notes that a leader usually (but not always) emerges. In any case, Cohen notes, it is the free flow of ideas among all the participants that keeps the CoP alive and vibrant, an idea that led some early leaders in KM/knowledge services to think about CoPs as an implementation tool for KD/KS/KU. Certainly the link is there, for the attributes Cohen identifies, as it happens, are the very characteristics and commonalities that match the work of strategic knowledge professionals as they engage in their work with the organization or the community's knowledge assets. These in turn contribute to the development of social and organizational intellectual capital, a necessary ingredient in the establishment of a KD/KS/KU framework for the larger enterprise. Was the development of communities of practice the foundation of KD/KS/KU? Probably not, since much attention from the earliest day of KM and knowledge services was being given to the whole idea of sharing knowledge as soon as it was developed (or even as it was being developed, in many cases). Nevertheless, there were efforts to characterize CoPs as an approach or a perspective for dealing with KM and the management of intellectual capital.

Care should be taken, though, when considering CoPs in this context of collaboration for KD/KS/KU. It might be wise to give attention to the differences between a community of practice and a team, just as we distinguish between collaboration and team management. A CoP is not necessarily a team, since a team is defined by a task (e.g., "task force," "task group," etc.) and teams are usually functional and not necessarily strategic in their goals and execution. Also, teams generally reflect the management philosophy and goals of senior leaders (sponsors), require ongoing development, and produce quality results only when they are functioning well. Like CoPs, though, teams predate formal knowledge management and knowledge services theory, and ideas about teams and team management are deeply entrenched in human experience, leading to the application of much that springs from team management to communities of practice.

Thus CoPs, teams, and other networks become a staple tool for knowledge services and, through strategic learning, play a critical role in the KD/KS/KU process. Related to these tools is the larger picture of social networks and social network analysis as a sociological methodology that comfortably fits into knowledge services. Mapping the relationships and exchanges of various members of a group, social network analysis is a tool used by business to help with decision making and, in managing a project, for calculating the project's critical path and activity times, also sometimes referred to as "critical path analysis." Utilizing social network analysis provides a structure for identifying and reviewing collaborative relationships, and determining how to react to consequences brought about through the social connections provided by networks for collaboration.

From the knowledge asset management perspective, a social network seeks to connect relevant links between and among the various points of intersection of the network, often presented as a social network diagram. When connecting social network analysis to collaboration for knowledge services success, a number of characteristics emerge, including the fact that members of the network can have personal and, especially with knowledge services, professional relationships (although, to be fair, it should be noted that the professional actually incorporates personal relationships as they occur in the workplace). Such networks can also be technological, as among Web sites, and the emphasis in all of these networks as they relate to knowledge asset management is on how the links of the network affects individuals and their relationships, including such critical concerns as workflow and performance. Of course, the effectiveness builds on the structure and the make-up of the group. Whether the group of participants is "open or small," as some describe these groups, or "loose or tight," as others put it, affects the success of the network.

Moving beyond social network analysis, some experts in knowledge services look to value network analysis, reflecting on how VNA focuses on the most critical, essential intangible exchanges that support the work. The emphasis here is on the seriousness of the effort, as Verna Allee, one of the experts in VNA, puts it, not just the "nice to do" stuff or some vague encouragement to "share knowledge." With VNA, knowledge services professionals are required to spell out specific deliverables and behaviors that they need and expect from each other to work effectively and to build good relationships. The effort includes the specific admonition, as Allee describes it, that knowledge is not a deliverable. Knowledge is an asset, and as such requires a strategic knowledge professional or knowledge strategist to convert the knowledge asset to some negotiable form of value. Thus all the players in the knowledge services scenario are forced "to negotiate around intangibles such as various forms of knowledge in a very clear, specific direct way" (Allee, 2008).

The results of moving toward collaboration in the knowledge services workplace are not hard to quantify as we return to Marshall's assertion that collaboration is the management framework for organizational effectiveness and connect it to Allee's value network analysis. For a useful starting point, the characteristics that Marshall ascribes to the collaborative leader will be in place before VNA begins. Connecting the analysis of core values, skills assessment, a well-formulated and clearly understood statement of the operational vision, mission, and values (personal but within the context of the workplace), an equal understanding of the leadership and management philosophy in the organization, and an ability to make choices, set measures, and make commitments to success (however defined) all come into play. With this picture of the value network captured, the knowledge strategist – not surprisingly – takes on a collaborative leadership role for the larger enterprise. The benefits of the effort then become apparent and transition to useful tools that establish strengthened collaboration in knowledge asset management:
- Internal collaboration enables organizations to compete externally.
- Decisions are faster, of higher quality, and customer-driven.
- Decisions are made on the basis of principle rather than power or personality (resulting in greater buy-in and impact).
- The energy of the workforce is focused away from internal conflicts.

- Cycle time is substantially reduced.
- Strategic alliances that might have failed not only succeed, but build trust and produce extraordinary results.
- Return-on-investment increases dramatically.
- Workforce takes on full accountability for enterprise success.
- Reduced conflict. (Marshall, 1995)

With these benefits in place, the partnership workplace is a desirable and reasonable goal and I agree with Marshall, Allee, and others that the harmonies of the collaborative workplace lead to higher-level accomplishments in the achievement of the enterprise mission. Having in hand a clear understanding of the circumstances that support and reinforce the collaborative management framework, we can move toward a recommended strategy for identifying and taking the next steps in its development. We begin with reiterating the value of sponsors in the initial stages of any effort designed to develop a collaborative, partnership-focused environment. The essential role of sponsors is (or should be) clearly understood in the workplace, and the lack of a sponsorship relationship, particularly with an objective as critical as that of creating a collaborative and cooperative management framework, will only result in eventual failure. As a useful step, all interested parties can review the U.S. Army KM principle # 3, discussed earlier, and seek to develop an understanding of how workplace performance and innovation can only succeed under the aegis of an interested and committed sponsor. Putting together a "doctrine of collaboration" or, at the very least, talking points for such a doctrine can now be determined. Without this review, taken up with the full understanding that a doctrine cannot exist without authority supporting the legality and viability of the doctrine, even one as directed to success as a doctrine of collaboration, or without the commitment of an enthusiastic sponsor as part of the process, the desired value networking analysis and collaboration will not happen.

Once sponsorship has been established and the value of a collaborative organizational effectiveness structure agreed to, the knowledge strategist can move to building the development team, identifying and soliciting interest (and agreement to participate, when appropriate) among people within the parent organization. These will be colleagues and fellow workers who connect with and can are willing to be part of a collaboration management team, one that will ideally include staff from HR, Legal, and IT as well as knowledge workers known as such. While seeking partners, I also recommend that some consideration be given to looking externally, bringing in people who work in organizations where collaboration is an integral part of the management model. If their advice and interest can be solicited without compromising security or other corporate restrictions relating to knowledge sharing, there can be value in hearing the opinions of experienced external colleagues who have been successful in establishing a partnership workplace.

A knowledge services collaborative success. At an architectural firm in the American northwest, a knowledge strategist was successful in moving forward with the company's knowledge services strategic framework. She did it by putting collaboration directly into the picture. As she worked on the knowledge services strategic framework for the firm, she had several senior managers (as well as her own staff) sharing in its success, And even with some 300 staff in the company – architects, designers, and a strong contingent of research specialists – the "tone" of the company's knowledge-sharing environment was well known, both throughout the company and amongst other organizations in the community. This company was truly functioning as a knowledge culture.

So we might ask: why was the company's knowledge domain so successful? There is a very simple answer: the knowledge strategist for the company – the management employee with responsibility, authority, and, not to be dismissed, accountability for the company's knowledge-sharing success – made an important early decision. With the support of her planning team, she asked to have the knowledge services staff located in the very center of the floor where most of the company's research activities took place. When the request was granted, she specifically designed an open space for herself and her staff (no enclosed carrels or cubicles, but including several glass-walled conference rooms for private conversation available throughout the floor). The Research and Knowledge Services Center was truly "in the center of everything," she said. It was known to everyone in the company (usually by its informal name, the company's "knowledge nexus" since that was how everybody thought of it), and ultimately the center became a popular place for collaboration as well as for research and knowledge sharing.

When we spoke about her experience in developing the center, she made it clear that she had a very specific reason for doing it as she did: she wanted to set up a space for knowledge sharing that would lend itself to collaboration not only among the knowledge services staff but, most important, among the various employees of the company. There was often – as in many organizations that require a considerable amount of research and background development – little time or space for collaborative interaction. Most research in the firm took place privately, either conducted by a single architect and his or her individual team members or among a particular group brought together for one purpose. When necessary a research assistant or specialist was called in but basically there was not much consideration in the firm's management structure given to collaboration. In this situation, the knowledge strategist specifically wanted to build a collaborative space and she did it because she had a private dream of how collaborative relationships among company employees would affect the work for which she was responsible.

"When we think about research," she told me, "most of the work isn't with other people, and once the work is completed, the research activity is soon forgotten. I had a very special goal. I wanted us to move in this direction for one reason. I called it marginalization avoidance. By doing it this way, we would remain an important and critical section of the firm in the minds of the people who knew about that."

Was the idea – or perhaps just the phrase – a little gimmick-y? After all, "marginalization avoidance" is not exactly a phrase that rolls off the tongue. Nonetheless, the term defines what this knowledge strategist and her organization needed to do. As they started to move forward with their knowledge strategy, she and her team (and corporate management, don't forget) had discovered that the well-managed, well-structured research and knowledge services business unit for which she had management responsibility might be in trouble. The number of service requests and products identified for delivery to the architects, their teams, and research associates were falling off, and their unit was not as busy as she thought it should be. Many people were getting their information elsewhere, and only when she or one of her staff stepped in and joined a project or team as the knowledge-sharing specialist did they recognize – and come to value – KD/KS/KU in the organization.

How did she do it? What unique steps did she take to avoid marginalization?

There were seven, as valid now as when she used them to re-focus her operation:

1. *Commit to collaboration.* Recognize from the beginning that people – even people who do not particularly enjoy coming to work – respond positively to a collaborative atmosphere. Because most people do work alone or in small groups within a scientific and research organization, they like having the opportunity to discuss what they are working on, what challenges they are dealing with, and – as important as anything else – they like having a strategic knowledge specialist on hand with whom they can discuss their knowledge development, knowledge sharing, and knowledge utilization issues. They like having a collaborative relationship with the company's knowledge experts.

2. *Integrate.* The next step is the easiest. Get out into the corporation, learn about what people are working on and join them. Identify where they need to share knowledge and help them figure out how to do it. Demonstrate to teams, working groups, CoPs, and anybody else, who needs to know how strategic knowledge transfer works in their particular situation.

3. *Live where your colleagues live.* Coming from the above, the strategic knowledge services manager gets out of the office. Indeed, in some companies and organizations the knowledge services team will not even have an office. The team will be called on to advise as required. Collaboration comes easily once people know what the strategic knowledge team can do.
4. *Use what the users use.* Forget about maintaining collections and building up resources. Once you and your team identify projects and working groups that need an embedded strategic knowledge professional, make it your business to learn – from the group – what tools, techniques, and dedicated resources generally support their work. Then, using your strategic knowledge expertise, transfer your own skills and those of your staff to managing and enabling your knowledge customers.
5. *Leverage organizational tools for knowledge creation.* At the same time, each of the strategic knowledge professionals and the knowledge strategist should acquire high levels of facility in identifying and working with organizational activities that advance their role in the company. If a committee needs another member and the subject is one you or one of your team knows something about, step up. Become the committee's knowledge specialist (and you'll probably end up chairing the committee!). Your fellow committee members will be very surprised – and very grateful.
6. *Form partnerships.* As part of your organizational networking (especially with committee assignments such as the situation just described), make it your business – or that of one of your team who has the assignment – to identify people from other departments who can use the expertise of strategic knowledge professionals, just as you can use some of their expertise in whatever field is their strength. Then team up on projects – official, informal, or simply recreational. You'll be surprised at how important strategic knowledge will become in the organization and how talked about you and your group as a knowledge services team will be.
7. *Merge information and knowledge, and bring in strategic learning.* Make it your business to ensure that colleagues and co-workers start to recognize that the so-called "distance" between information and knowledge is a myth (especially when you think of IT/ICT and KM as functions). Move on over to knowledge services by bringing strategic learning into the mix and you'll soon find you have many like-minded colleagues in the company. You'll be pleased to learn that focusing on knowledge services – merging information, knowledge, and strategic learning – is the way people want to work. Take advantage of that interest and bring collaboration into your organization's overall knowledge-sharing structure.

2.2 Critical Success Factors: The Knowledge Services Audit

Successful KD/KS/KU (knowledge development, knowledge sharing, and knowledge utilization) is the foundation of the organizational knowledge culture, and meaningful KD/KS/KU supports and leads to organizational effectiveness. To achieve KD/KS/KU success, organizational leaders turn to the knowledge strategist to develop knowledge strategy. The strategic framework for the successful knowledge strategy, as we have seen, is knowledge services, and our key word here is "successful." What is the quality of knowledge services practiced in the organization? As we develop the strategic framework for knowledge services – the knowledge strategy – what methodology do we use to measure the organization's success with its knowledge domain?

In organizations in which knowledge services is practiced as the organization's KD/KS/KU strategic framework, the knowledge strategist and his or her colleagues who share responsibility for the knowledge domain perform a knowledge services audit for that purpose. As a methodology for measurement capture, the knowledge services audit systematically examines and evaluates the organization's well-being with respect to the management of information, knowledge, and strategic learning. It is an activity which is *performed*, and that term is used to describe this activity (as in "the knowledge team *performs* the knowledge services audit). While the term "perform" is generally understood to apply to audits undertaken in financial services or for regulatory compliance purposes, I choose to bring the term to the evaluation of knowledge services for a single reason, a reason which relates to my determination to advocate for the understanding of and establish the *seriousness* of the activity. In doing so, I seek to raise awareness about the value of enterprise-wide knowledge sharing in the minds of managers and enterprise leaders, most of whom do not work with our profession's background and expertise and this early in the history of knowledge services do not have – and cannot be expected to have – a clear understanding of the value of knowledge services in the organization, business, or institution for which they are responsible.

An approach to developing and then performing the knowledge services audit is to identify the basic elements of organizational management that relate to the organization's knowledge domain and its performance (or, as one colleague puts it, "what keeps management up at night") and take a good hard look at the effectiveness of these management elements as they are being implemented – with respect to the knowledge domain – in the organization under discussion. All of these do not relate to every situation in which the knowledge services audit is being considered, but even if some of these are not specifically relevant, considering the list might be a useful beginning for thinking about the audit and enabling a determination for the relevance of each of the following and an evaluation of their effect – where they apply – on the KD/KS/KU process in the organization:

1. Knowledge services, as currently practiced. What does a snapshot of current knowledge services reveal?
2. The knowledge services audit or opportunity assessment. When was the organization's intellectual infrastructure last inventoried? Has the knowledge services environment changed since then?
3. Knowledge strategy. Is there an enterprise-wide knowledge strategy? For individual information-, knowledge- and strategic learning-focused departments or functional units? Are there strategic maps that demonstrate how to move from where knowledge services is today to where it should be in the future?
4. Strategic learning. How is enterprise-wide strategic learning managed? Does strategic learning as currently practiced have impact on organizational effectiveness?
5. Management, professional, and service delivery ethics. How is attention given to ethics throughout the organization? How would the enterprise-wide ethics structure affect the development of a knowledge culture?
6. Collaboration and cooperation. What hierarchical and collaborative management techniques determine the value of resource sharing? In the organization, what is the general feeling about KD/KS/KU? Is sharing something people are comfortable with?
7. Business development, customer services, and customer relationship management (CRM). Who are the people who would benefit from improved knowledge sharing? Can they be identified? What specific, measurable tools and milestones are adapted and implemented for establishing and/or increasing any knowledge-centric user base?
8. Measurement and metrics. What tools are used for measuring knowledge services success? Are benchmarking, added value, discussion tracking, customer satisfaction surveys, and the growth of intangible assets used to measure operational success?
9. Risk management. What is the connection between knowledge sharing (in all sections of the organizational structure) and organizational risk management?
10. Enterprise content management (ECM). What opportunities exist for utilizing knowledge services for developing and managing enterprise-wide content, particularly in terms of identifying solutions for dealing with both structured

and unstructured content that cannot be found through the services of any recognized or "usual" department or functional unit?
11. The relationship between technology management and knowledge/systems. Recognizing that technology is the tool that enables knowledge services and the knowledge culture, what is the critical enterprise-wide framework for determining and assessing the role of technology? Does the organization focus on application services, smart tools, organizational data management, and similar solutions while at the same time identifying issues that relate to the management of intellectual capital from the non-technical and interpersonal perspective?
12. Project management. How are projects managed enterprise-wide? Are there opportunities for incorporating KD/KS/KU into the project management function? Is attention given to KD/KS/KU in the overall process, including goal definition, planning the work required to achieve the goal, oversight of the total project and support teams, monitoring and measurement, and, as required, bringing the project to closure when completed or truncated?
13. Personal knowledge management (PKM). What techniques and tools are available for identifying knowledge services processes that colleagues can utilize for enhancing their own role in enterprise success? What is available for transitioning this into organization-wide opportunities?
14. Knowledge services ownership. What are the responsibilities of the organization's knowledge strategist, the corporate spokesperson with respect to knowledge services? Is there a description of organizational duties and expectations for knowledge services leadership with respect to management, organizational strategic learning?

Critical success factors. Measuring the success of an organization's knowledge services and the excellence of knowledge sharing within the organization begins with the identification of critical success factors. If they choose to undertake this approach, the task of the knowledge strategist and the knowledge services team or working group can be provided with a useful perspective about their measurement activities and what they are seeking to achieve. Often referred to simply as CSF, critical success factors are those activities and undertakings that must "go right" to ensure that the organization succeeds in any particular endeavor, including the activities specific to knowledge sharing. There are, not surprisingly, formal definitions and descriptions of the critical success factors idea, and I do not reject the more formal approach of some management experts in their thinking about CSFs. Nor do I misunderstand that as a term for business management, the critical success factor has specific approaches (with the number of CSFs usually limited, and the critical success factors generally described as something along the lines of elements or part of the organizational structure that are necessary to ensure success). And certainly according to some management experts, CSFs are simply a concept, so in seeking to identify and share thoughts about critical success factors, the organization's stakeholders focus attention on what's important in the larger enterprise.

As such, CSFs provide an outlet (because critical success factors are easy to communicate and easy to monitor) for keeping track of what is contributing to the organization's success and what isn't. Obviously critical success factors require that identified activities be successful; for long-term success, the same activities must achieve a level of excellence that goes beyond mere day-to-day success. For most managers, CSFs are an integral part of the strategic planning process. Often identified as "milestones" or other time-framed measures that must be met if the process is to be considered successful, it is not unusual for a strategic plan to include, under each proposed activity, a phrase such as "this activity will have succeeded if..." followed by specific criteria that can simply be checked off when the activity has met that criteria.

So I am drawn to the CSF idea and adapting it to the knowledge domain as a workplace. In establishing critical success factors for knowledge services, I have often found that most organizations use CSFs that can be categorized in three ways: some have to do with the mission of the larger enterprise, others relate to the management process in the larger organization, and the third group connects with good management practices for the specific functional unit with knowledge services responsibility. A possible fourth category, which might or might not have relevance in some organizations, has to do with the on-going viability of the knowledge services business unit and/or the knowledge workers and strategic knowledge professionals employed there.

For knowledge services, the first would seem to be the most important. Without question, the management and delivery of knowledge services tools, advisory services, and other user-focused activities must be designed and executed for the purpose of directly supporting the organization's work. When measurement results determine that some activity or service provided by the unit does not match that requirement, changes must be made. The most typical example in this situation – and easiest to document – is the ongoing maintenance of a particular knowledge services tool when the larger enterprise, perhaps through a merger with or acquisition by a company with a different focus, limits the benefits of the tool. A real-estate management firm, for example, taken over by a financial services company with plans to outsource the apartment-management operation, will have little use for a tool or tools that had been developed to support that management function. When the change in focus takes place, the knowledge services management team will probably extend the courtesy of providing the tool to the new colleagues in the company to which the work is outsourced (although that is not necessarily the case). Whatever the relationship between the two companies, though, the continued maintenance of the product by the re-focused knowledge services business unit would not support the company's new mission and would of necessity be eventually abandoned.

On the other hand, the change can result in better service and workplace functioning. One of the most pleasant consultancy assignments of my experience was a long project in Australia, focused in Melbourne and Canberra, when two federal agencies merged. The two had similar specializations for service delivery to citizens and despite the anticipation of the separate staffs of the two knowledge services functions in the two agencies that barriers and impediments would prevent the merging to go forward, it turned out that each to the two groups of knowledge workers – perhaps serendipitously or perhaps simply coincidentally – took it upon themselves to support the combined benefits of the merger and moved forward with special effort to make the change a positive collaborative interaction. Among the nay-sayers, with their expectations of disaster or, at least, a difficult time in the merger, several were happily proven wrong and the transition from two knowledge services functions in two separate agencies moved to a combined function that succeeded very well indeed.

Critical success factors in these two examples are the identified and stated connections between services provided by the knowledge services unit to the larger organizational purpose and the real, perceived, and anticipated value of knowledge in supporting strengthened decision making, accelerated innovation, and better research in the parent company, for the first example, and the merged agency in the second example. These connections are identified in a number of ways: through relationships with knowledge services sponsors, advocates, and champions, through functional relationships with parallel knowledge-focused functional units in the company or agency (HR, corporate communications, the company's organization development and/or organizational effectiveness unit, if there is one, and similar units or departments), and in the relationships with knowledge stakeholders and other information, knowledge, and/or strategic learning targets. In the examples described here, knowledge workers and strategic knowledge professionals employed in the knowledge services units work regularly with people who have specific service delivery needs. Through these interactions, they become attuned to those needs, responding to them with tools that are developed or acquired for that purpose. When the needs of the user base change, as when some of the employees go to the outsourced company or are

2.2 Critical Success Factors: The Knowledge Services Audit — 153

otherwise no longer affiliated with the now re-purposed organization, the knowledge services unit will no longer have reason to maintain the tools they required in the former situation.

An important consideration, and one which is as much personal as professional, has to do with the abilities and capacities of knowledge strategists and their staff members to monitor, control, and measure the usage of tools and services offered by the unit. It is not unusual for a tool developed and maintained in-house to take on a kind of "sacrosanct" aura, simply because it was developed in-house, and setting it aside or turning the tool over to another functional unit is difficult. Most people working in knowledge services, with its converged link to the successful management and dissemination of information, knowledge, and strategic learning content, are reluctant to give up a tool or a technique. Its very existence testifies to their basic KD/KS/KU expertise, and they obviously want to see the tool continue as a functioning resource. Good knowledge strategists – as good knowledge asset managers – recognize, however, that when a tool, technique, or service is no longer valid, as determined through appropriate measurement, they do their organizations a disservice if they determine to keep it in place.

Certain critical success factors relate directly to the role of knowledge services in the larger organizational management process, and it is here that the knowledge strategist has a fine opportunity for establishing rapport with enterprise leaders, as well as with managers with the same or similar responsibility throughout the larger organization. One useful CSF, for example, uses measurement to determine the extent to which the knowledge services function is integrated into the overall management process, particularly in identifying and articulating organizational structures that impact service delivery. All organizations have bureaucratic impediments, some minor and in today's management environment, mostly unintentional.

Nevertheless, they exist, and one of the best critical success factors is to establish where a knowledge services product or tool is impeded in providing the benefits it has been established to provide. A quick and easily recognized example is a chat room or wiki for colleagues working on a particular project. Having been built for their dedicated use, for exchanging notes, comments, document drafts, etc., among themselves, there seems to be – in the organization where they are employed – an almost perverse resistance to working with knowledge services staff to learn to use the tool and then, when they have reluctantly gained enough skill to use the tool for sharing their information and knowledge, to build the utilization of the tool into their workplace experience.

It is this type of impediment that often stops or "kills" a tool before it is fully functional, but it is also this type of situation that enables the knowledge strategist and strategic knowledge professionals working with him or her to experiment with metrics and measures from other functional activities in the organization, to determine how, say, the records and information management unit (now called RIM and formerly "records management") works with staff to engage them in using necessary tools and products. It is also the type of situation that enables the building of strong relationships with success partners or potential success partners, as managers in parallel knowledge-focused functional units also find themselves up against similar obstacles and will have developed techniques and direction for dealing with these situations. As solutions fall into place, natural and mutually beneficial relationships are created, increasing the opportunities for further shared solutions.

With respect to ensuring good management practices for the specific functional unit with knowledge services responsibility, critical success factors include determining whether the acquisition of certain information, knowledge, and strategic learning management tools are cost-effective (whether purchased externally or developed internally). If the benefits of having the tools available to identified users are provided at costs within the established range of costs for providing such tools, the knowledge strategist is meeting his or her fiscal responsibility to the larger organization. Likewise, in the opposite direction (as noted in the earlier example), when the cost to maintain certain knowledge assets becomes higher than the benefits, measures enable the knowledge services staff to take steps to retire or re-purpose knowledge assets. In both situations, these are critical success factors and provide useful information and direction for planning.

An important consideration with critical success factors is that, just as with the knowledge services audit itself (which might be considered the fundamental CSF for knowledge services management and delivery), critical success factors provide information for measuring *how well* knowledge assets support strengthened decision making, accelerated innovation, and improved research. As such, they provide the basics of opportunity assessment, identifying and ascertaining the viability of product development to meet newly recognized needs, as well as determining results capability, establishing what the knowledge services business unit is *capable of* providing and whether that unit is the best and most effective vehicle for provide the product or service.

Finally, although not applicable in all situations and organizations, a possible fourth category has to do with the continued presence (or even continued existence) of the knowledge services function. While no one – in management or amongst the knowledge stakeholders in the larger enterprise – has any doubt about the ongoing and critical place of knowledge in organizational success, the value of intellectual capital as an organizational asset, or the need for successful

KD/KS/KU as an organizational practice, for some enterprise leaders there continue to be questions about how to structure intellectual capital management.

Throughout the larger management community there continue to be on-going concerns about the viability of stand-alone functional units devoted to providing and/or managing one or another of the several types of research assets required by the larger enterprise. Many organizations operate without a specialized library or other knowledge, information, or research center, either having determined that such a functional unit is not a necessary business unit in that particular organization or having operated successfully without such a unit in the past.

Obviously knowledge stakeholders in these organizations have identified alternative methodologies for connecting themselves with the information, knowledge, and strategic learning content they require, and it could be argued that in each case critical success factors invoked were used to support the decision to do without the knowledge services operational function. Nevertheless, in those organizations that continue to have such functional units, many knowledge services professionals find it necessary to include among their unit's critical success factors measures that address the opportunity to enhance and strengthen the organizational position of the knowledge services professionals employed there. They must also, in many cases, include among their critical success factors measures that ensure the very survival of the knowledge services business unit itself.

The knowledge services audit. Having considered critical success factors and become comfortable with the idea of evaluating the success of knowledge sharing in the organization, the knowledge strategist and the knowledge services strategic framework development team moves forward with the knowledge services audit. The knowledge services audit grew out of another "audit" methodology (of the 1990s or so), the "information audit." At that time, many of us consulting with research organizations came to understand that it was necessary to codify the methodologies we used to determine the success of various research development and sharing activities. We had been using a needs analysis process, which was not strong enough for what our clients required, and in my first published comments about the information audit I described the needs analysis as primarily a "reactive" exercise. I then went on to describe the information audit – which our management consulting team was using frequently with clients – as providing a "more proactive approach, seeking as much to elicit trends and concepts from potential users as to determine specific requirements for success in the performance of specific tasks." And even then I was taking this methodology very seriously because, although it was a new (as far as I knew) evaluation tool, I cautioned research managers that it was not to be taken lightly, as I compared it with the needs analysis currently in vogue for information and research organizations.

The needs analysis can, if properly designed, be performed by the information services staff as part of current work, and the results will still be usable. The time required for the successful design, implemention, and presentation of results for an information audit is generally far too great for staff to undertake." Perhaps – although this was not the case at the time – I was falling back on my role as a management consultant and protecting my "turf" but I don't think this was the the reason why I urged caution. The information audit (now the knowledge services audit) really was not appropriate as a part-time or "add-on" staff activity (St. Clair, 1993).

In support of my assertion, I went on to become something of an advocate for the information audit, even going so far as to contribute three essays and a sample survey to an anthology on the subject (St. Clair, 1996).

I was not, of course, the only person doing work with the information audit for "information" was very much on our minds in the 1980s and 1990s. In fact, many companies and organizations changed the names of their specialized libraries and research departments, creating "information centers" and "information resource centers" and the idea of working *with* information as a point of view became very popular. Among those working with the information audit – and duly recognized at the time – was Elizabeth Orna, and much of her work influenced later information audit specialists. Working from Melbourne, Sue Henczel became the foremost protagonist for the information audit, wrote the definitive book on the subject, and traveled the world working with clients and corporate strategic learning groups on perfecting the information audit for their organizations.

So the "information audit" concept came into general use. It was not an unexpected step, and a number of the profession's leaders and scholars provided a variety of approaches to the subject. While it became apparent, as Henczel has pointed out, that "there is no one universally accepted definition for the information audit, nor is there a universally accepted methodology for conducting one," common to all of the efforts was the distinction that the information audit was designed to measure value, to focus in on the quality of the services being provided (Henczel, 2001).

As time passed, several of us working with knowledge management, knowledge services, and knowledge strategy quite naturally saw the principles of the information audit as applicable in our field and we were lucky to have the good work that had gone before with knowledge and strategic learning. In the process, we became convinced that the concept of the information audit not connected to knowledge and strategic learning was not strong enough, and my colleagues and I began working with the knowledge services audit, specifically designating the technique as such. Nevertheless, it was not a total move away from the format

and technique of the information audit, and in my consulting work and teaching I continued to combine all our work together. Indeed, it is extremely rewarding to take Henczel's seven-stage model for the information audit (described later in this section) and apply it to knowledge services. As we moved from the information audit to the knowledge services audit, the knowledge strategist and his or her knowledge services strategic framework development team can find useful and viable direction. As they use the knowledge services audit, they find that it will enable them and their colleagues throughout the organization to:
- identify how knowledge sharing affects the success of the organization in the achievement of its mission;
- establish what knowledge services provides (and *should*) provide for the organization;
- compare and contrast current information management, KM, and strategic learning tools and performance against future needs;
- determine strategic direction for KD/KS/KU;
- establish resource requirements to support KD/KS/KU;
- incorporate change management and change implementation into the operational function.

It is important, in my opinion, to give thought to the strategic role of the knowledge services audit in the organization. The emerging emphasis on the importance of intellectual capital and knowledge services has provided an opportunity for a normal transition from the information audit to the knowledge services audit. From where I sit, this transition has had a noticeable influence on management thinking about knowledge, providing an opportunity for attention to

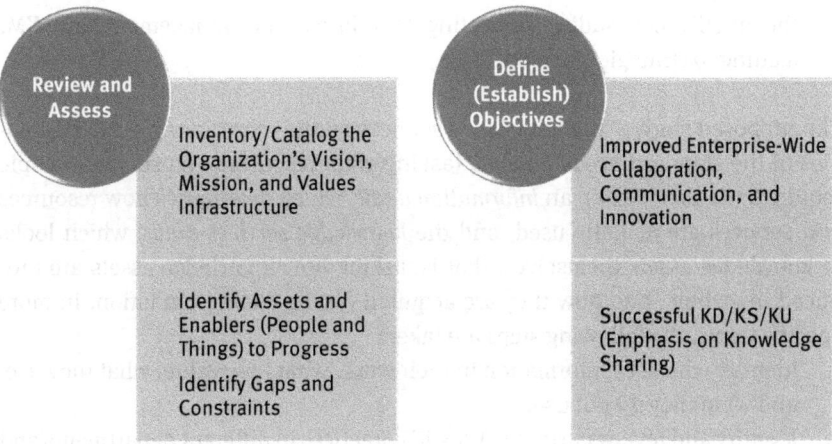

Figure 2.2: The knowledge services audit.

the value of knowledge in characterizing the larger organizational environment as a knowledge culture. There are probably many explanations why the value of knowledge has become important as a management topic as we move deeper into the twenty-first century, but whatever the reasons, establishing the value of the knowledge services audit has come along as a corresponding activity. For one thing, the knowledge services audit serves to raise awareness about the role of knowledge in the larger organization, as the knowledge services audit becomes the tool for establishing the role of working with knowledge and managing the knowledge eco-structure in achieving mission-critical success. At the same time, the audit serves to encourage buy-in about the value of knowledge (and, indeed, the development of an organizational knowledge culture) from critical stakeholders, from the highest levels of leadership to the knowledge workers who deal with information, knowledge, and strategic learning in their day-to-day activities.

From a slightly different angle, Botha and Boon provide a handy list that supports the strategic role of the knowledge services audit by positioning it as an evaluative tool in their list of a wide range of other information- and knowledge-connected audits:
1. the communications audit, looking at organizational information flow;
2. information mapping, looking at the identification and use of resources;
3. the information systems audit with its focus on technology management and technological tools;
4. the knowledge services audit with its connection to knowledge management, positioning this audit as the "highest" or last level of information management (according to the evolution of information management functions) and therefore logically follows on information management and information auditing;
5. the intelligence audit, connecting to information management and KM, leading to strategic learning.

The proposed study – the knowledge services audit – combines the methodologies of the standard *needs analysis* (asking what resources and services people require to do their work), an *information audit*, which determines how resources and services are actually used, and the *knowledge services audit*, which looks at knowledge assets themselves, that is, asking how knowledge assets are produced, by whom, and how they are acquired for the client population. In more specific terms, the following steps are taken:
1. Identify who uses information in their work, what they value, what they use, and what they do not use.
2. Identify and review current KD/KS/KU practices in different departments and sections of the company.

3. Identify personnel responsible for KD/KS/KU management.
4. Identify employees who use information in support of their work (contextual decision-making, knowledge asset management, etc.).
5. Identify best practices in knowledge services delivery and describe how these practices can be related to the company's KD/KS/KU framework.
6. Review current work patterns and responsibilities to determine KD/KS/KU needs and expectations.
7. Determine where a formal approach is required so staff can acquire information, knowledge, and learning to strengthen the quality of their work.
8. Review personal knowledge management (PKM) procedures and applications, informal and interpersonal KD/KS/KU communications, and interactive relationship practices.
9. Review formal and informal strategic learning and training activities.

In their approach, Botha and Boon emphasize the diagnostic and evaluative purpose of the audit. They conveniently offer a long list of functions which, with a little editorial assistance for transitioning the process from an information audit to a knowledge services audit, provide the knowledge strategist and his or her auditing team with valuable insight as they move forward with the knowledge services audit process. Devising four "levels" for ranking the extent to which the knowledge services audit contributes to successful knowledge management (or to "working with knowledge," in the now-accepted definition), Botha and Boon's methodology suggests that knowledge strategy might be built around personal knowledge management, operational knowledge management, organizational knowledge management, and corporate or strategic knowledge management. It is an interesting direction and brings a new approach to the effort to develop the knowledge services strategic framework (Botha and Boon, 2003).

So it becomes clear that there are many ways to describe the knowledge services audit. Sometimes the knowledge services audit is characterized as a "needs assessment," an "opportunity assessment," an information or knowledge "evaluation," or even – in some more methodical environments – as an "analytical framework" but as I'm sure is apparent by now the knowledge services audit (the term I use) is in many ways the very basis of the strategic framework development process for knowledge services. Indeed, when we think about what we are doing as a process or methodology, we generally don't think of the knowledge services audit and the knowledge strategy as separate entities. They are connected and the procedure most knowledge strategists follow is structured around both the audit and strategy development. Once we have dealt with the theories and principles of knowledge services, knowledge strategy, and the approach to the structuring of the organization as a knowledge culture, we move forward with the knowledge services audit and the knowledge strategy as the two pillars of the entire strategic framework development process for knowledge services.

Once the knowledge strategist has determined with his or her colleagues that there is a demand for a solution to a knowledge-related problem or an opening for an innovative knowledge services approach to a knowledge-related issue, we have a few immediate steps to think about. These steps are not complicated and they can be structured for almost any knowledge-related problem or innovative direction. I choose to think of the elements as a sort of "research project," as that concept gives me the opportunity to focus on a specific direction for the work.

If the project has a wide-ranging focus (as in the development of a strategic framework for knowledge), I set up a working outline which begins with an introduction to the project, setting out the reasons for undertaking the project and providing a brief outline of what we plan to address. In this case, our project objective begins with a description of the background and our expectations for the project. We recognize, as noted, that in the current organization (as in many organizations), knowledge sharing does not function well or, depending on the organization, not at all. That is our "driver," our reason for taking on the development of the strategic framework, the knowledge strategy. Information management, knowledge management, and strategic learning outcomes in support of organizational success are not shared as well as they should or could be shared. Our goal – which we often refer to as our "desired effect" for the knowledge services strategic framework – is to enable the organization to transition to a knowledge culture, a functional entity (company, organization, or institution) as we

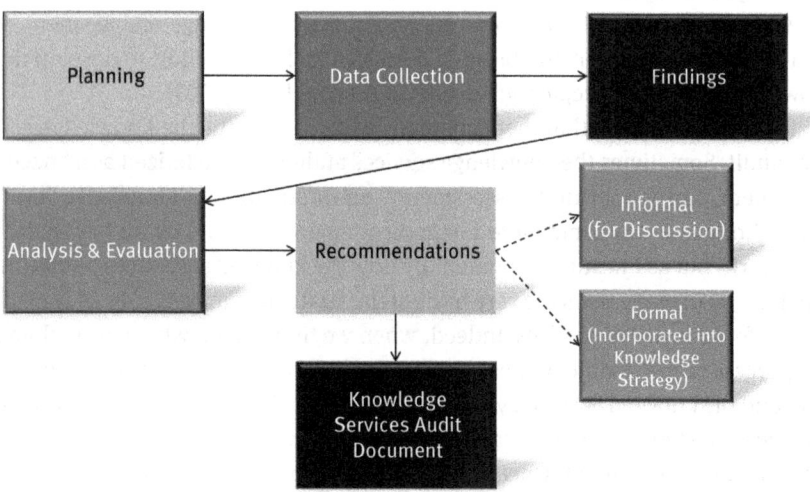

Figure 2.3: The knowledge services audit: Process overview.

2.2 Critical Success Factors: The Knowledge Services Audit — 161

discussed earlier. A summary of the attributes of the knowledge culture combining into our "desired effect" might be described as:
- leadership in information management, KM, and strategic learning;
- collaboration at all functional levels;
- breadth of scope with respect to knowledge services;
- technology and communications maturity;
- management enthusiasm and support for knowledge sharing in all information, knowledge, and strategic learning situations and opportunities (recognizing specific limitations for knowledge sharing, depending on organizational functional or mission-related requirements);
- value creation.

With this objective – this desired effect – in mind, we look again at our overarching driver for the exercise, emphasizing again that the knowledge culture is recognized as critical for success for achieving the corporate mission. In the knowledge culture, a working environment in which KD/KS/KU defines every activity, the effective re-use of knowledge and the creation of new knowledge are enabled and become the workplace standard. In turn, KD/KS/KU is enabled through the management and delivery of knowledge services, converging information management, knowledge management, and strategic learning for strengthened knowledge asset management, improved contextual decision making, and accelerated innovation.

With the knowledge services audit, one of the most important elements of the process is the statement of scope. This clearly stated description defines how "narrow" or "broad" the audit is to be (that is, whether it will be limited to one department or functional unit or whether it will encompass a group of departments, sections, divisions, or, indeed, the entire organization). Parallel information, knowledge, and strategic learning functions will also usually be targeted, and there will often be some expressions of interest about the role of knowledge (prior knowledge/corporate history/industry trends, etc.) at the leadership level, with additional or supplementary functional operations considered for inclusion in the knowledge services audit. In most cases the intention is to start small, with a named group or unit, but once the project begins, the knowledge services audit team can expect a considerable cross-functional operational exchange of information, knowledge, and strategic learning references, a situation that often requires a re-focus and a second look at resources committed to the audit.

In planning the knowledge services audit, attention is also given to the stakeholders, the people who will be participating in, contributing to, and, importantly, affected by the audit. Again, once news of the audit begins to move throughout the organization, considerable interest begins to be expressed and, as with the scope of the audit, important and viable "additions" will be brought into the activity (for this reason, it is advisable, when appropriate, to provide as much internal publicity and discussion about the up-coming audit as possible, to ensure that there are no "surprises" and restraints on resources when it is too late).

As for identifying the stakeholders for the audit, a clear statement of roles and responsibilities will be devised at some point – with the cooperation of the affected colleagues, of course, and their supervisors and managers – and their responsibility to participate in the knowledge services audit process will include committing time for participation at whatever level seems feasible. Linked to this participation is the importance of having senior management sponsorship for the knowledge services audit. With sponsorship, senior managers and enterprise leaders commit themselves to express their enthusiasm for the audit, provide model behavior by participating themselves, and reinforce their commitment to the audit by making clear their expectation that others participate with them in ensuring that the audit succeeds and is taken seriously in the organization or functional unit in which it is being conducted.

Naturally, and not to be casually dismissed (always a risk when dealing with colleagues who are in a position of influence but do not have much understanding of the organization's knowledge domain and its contribution), the development of knowledge services audit plans with respect to resource allocation, staff involvement, financial requirements, and metrics and evaluation processes is critically important. Determining how the knowledge services audit will be conducted and establishing, in effect, who will do the work can have a serious impact on the success or failure of the planning process for the audit. In considering resources and resource allocation, those with responsibility for moving the audit forward will determine whether the work can be done with in-house staff or if external staff, contractors or consultants, are required. Some companies and institutions automatically include such activities in their annual budgeting (particularly if there is a strategy-development function in the organization or a Chief Strategy Office in the executive suite – a circumstance to be highly desired but not often in place). Other managers expect departments and similar functional units to make use of in-house consultants already on staff and in some cases, management in some organizations expects the unit conducting the audit to provide staff to conduct the audit, or to include in its annual appropriation budgets funding for hiring auditors for the knowledge services audit.

Whether external participants are engaged or not, a knowledge services audit team will be developed, including the knowledge strategist as the team or working group's leader. Additionally, a representative or representatives from organizational leadership (perhaps for advice, sponsorship, and holding a nominal leadership role, instead of literal participation), a chair (team leader/facilitator/lead

2.2 Critical Success Factors: The Knowledge Services Audit — 163

auditor, probably the knowledge strategist unless he or she chooses to appoint someone else who will handle administrative work as a direct report to the knowledge strategist), a solid and, hopefully, experienced group of team members for taking on various activities and responsibilities in the effort (including – depending on the size of the knowledge services functional unit – knowledge workers and strategic knowledge professionals from that staff), and, as noted, external consultants/audit leaders if utilized. As with many other questions having to do with the knowledge services audit, decisions about who will participate will very much depend on what is customary in the parent organization in similar situations.

A final consideration, related to the above, is the development of the work plan, outlining clearly what the work breakdown structure and schedule will be, who will be responsible for each section of the work structure, and who will actually perform the tasks. Also included in planning the knowledge services audit is the requirement that the knowledge strategist and his or her team embark on a serious overview of procedures currently in place related to KD/KS/KU, identifying, analyzing, and assessing current KD/KS/KU policies and procedures. The work plan, often referred to as a Statement of Work (SoW) will call for several specifics, including such activities as:

- operational or management review, often including a planning review describing future expectations and the strategies (either in place or anticipated) for achieving them;
- research relating to the project, including what is commonly referred to as "desk research" – that is, research conducted by the consulting organization or in this case the working group or team charged with developing the knowledge services strategic framework; also usually conducted with the involvement and support of the client organization (that is, the organization in which the knowledge strategist and his or her team are employed);
- the knowledge services auditing or evaluation process itself (the subject of this chapter and, as indicated, one-half, we might say, of the central focus of the strategic framework development process), including data-gathering through focus groups, departmental and/or sectional meetings, and individual interviews, and usually incorporating a survey of company management, selected staff, and other stakeholders;
- framework development and report preparation;
- the organizational knowledge strategy (the subject of the Chapter 2, Section 2.4 and usually in a consulting situation referred to as the project "deliverable").

A work schedule is also organized at this point, with a careful and studied (and realistic) look at organizational calendars, staff availability, and similar elements that can influence the progress of the knowledge services audit.

When the work plan has been developed and discussed with appropriate management and staff, and agreed-upon terms are in place (preferably in a brief document made available to all participants), the knowledge strategist for the audit will then proceed to look at the audit methodology, a communications strategy, and a data collection and analysis framework.

In most cases, the development of the audit methodology will include a statement of the project purpose and a brief statement of attention to some of the terms and concepts that have been considered for the knowledge services audit. These might include attention to some of the goals of the audit, such as defining, for example, the kinds of information, knowledge, and strategic learning resources and services people require to do their work, how these resources and services are actually used, and how knowledge assets used in the organization are produced (and by whom).

A second statement might describe a strategic plan for the audit, noting that it is intended to review the current state of affairs with respect to the provision of information, knowledge, and strategic learning service delivery in the organization, to identify the desired state, and to determine the necessary elements for providing enhanced service delivery (the designation "world-class" is often used with respect to KM and knowledge services), to identify strategies for achieving this objective, and stating a timeline and resource requirements for accomplishing the plan's goals.

A quick synopsis or list of elements for the knowledge services audit is provided by Botha and Boon. As noted earlier, although their intention is to review the literature and provide analysis and synthesis for the information audit, the concepts and terms they use apply to the knowledge services audit. In their study, Botha and Boon offer a typical list of procedures required for audits:
- defining the organizational environment
- planning
- identifying knowledge needs
- designing the survey instrument
- scheduling appointments/meetings
- investigating technology
- analyzing the audit findings
- costing and valuing resources
- testing key control points (to identify failures, "weak links")
- generating alternative solutions and evaluating alternatives
- monitoring adherence to existing standards and regulations
- preparing the final report
- implementing monitoring mechanisms.

2.2 Critical Success Factors: The Knowledge Services Audit — 165

As indicated earlier, Henczel in her description of the information audit also provides a framework that works very effectively for the knowledge services audit. Henczel offers a seven-stage audit model, and her list, like that of Botha and Boon, provides a neat checklist. In Henczel's case, though, there is considerably more detail, since the list is specifically designed for providing direction in implementing the audit, instead of describing it. Henczel's work, described fully in her book which was published as part of the De Gruyter Information Services Management Series (disclosure: for which I was the series editor) has strongly influenced and provides a viable seven-stage approach for the knowledge services audit as well as for the information audit. Her list includes:
1. planning
2. data collection
3. data analysis
4. data evaluation
5. communicating recommendations
6. implementing recommendations
7. the Information Audit as a continuum (Henczel, 2001)

Of critical importance is an important point that should be kept at the forefront of the knowledge strategist's or team leader's work (and shared with others at every opportunity) is Henczel's last stage in her information audit, that the audit is recognized (and is expected to continue to be recognized) as a foundation or starting point. As is discussed more often in the consulting community than we would like, one of the great weaknesses of the profession is the tendency, in some organizations, to engage a consultant (either internal or external) to address a problem or study a proposed innovative process and – once the deliverables are received – nothing more is heard about the project or the implementation of any of the consultants' recommendations. Fortunately, because so many people become aware of and even often participate in the knowledge services audit during the process, there is far less likelihood that the effort will end up as only "a report on a shelf." One of the great advantages of the knowledge services audit is the willingness of those participating to look for actionable results, supporting Henczel's emphasis (with which I concur wholeheartedly) that the audit is but the beginning of an ongoing review of information and knowledge services in the organization.

Two additional considerations will be of value in the planning and execution of a knowledge services audit. In the first, attention to and conversation about (both with leaders and with line staff) what data collection and communication models are appropriate for the specific organizational need will yield valuable "bonus points" for the audit team. Such attention will eliminate awkward situations in which information about certain types of data or activities is inappropriate to the study, and for which going forward with requests about these subjects might result in damage to the process. In most project work with which I've been connected, we do not generally give enough attention to what might be thought of as the cultural or political environments (despite meaning to do so, as we state in our formal proposals), sometimes resulting in less than satisfactory results (especially from our own point of view).

Similarly, in implementing the knowledge services audit, it is important to recognize that – no matter how ambitious we or our immediate management might be about the value of a planned knowledge services audit – it is always wise to start small (to "take baby steps," as one professional auditor puts it). The early deliverables from a smaller project (our famous "low-hanging-fruit") can provide a sense of what the final product might be, often resulting in one or more "quick wins" which can be implemented without much disruption and described to the entire enterprise, raising awareness that in itself produces useful rewards for the audit process (and the knowledge services audit team). At the same time, such small projects can provide a useful preview of what might come with a larger project. Instead of attempting to conduct a knowledge services audit about, say, the knowledge resources of an entire organization or department, it is best to work with one unit or section, to conduct a pilot deployment and attempt to determine what direction an audit might take.

And as the auditing team begins to wrap up its work, we give attention to how the results of the knowledge services audit are communicated and, not to put too fine a point on it, the risks involved in undertaking the audit. When the findings of the audit result in weak conclusions, or there is no prospect of action, the situation might be worse than never having done the audit at all. At this point, recognition must be given to established practices and arrangements in the larger organization and to the benefits to the organization in reacting to the findings of the audit.

Thanks to new perspectives in organizational management and the technological advances of recent decades, the management and delivery of knowledge services (or the research and management support activities that in another era would have been the activities we now identify as knowledge services) are established as necessary functional roles. In this environment, the larger enterprise has the opportunity to take its quest for success to an even higher level of excellence.

Yet in this advanced and continually evolving knowledge domain workplace, understanding and dealing with the relationship between organizational management and knowledge services is a challenge, especially for enterprise leadership. Not that the organization's senior management is particularly concerned with the specifics of how the relationship plays out. There are established expectations for knowledge services in support of the organizational mission, and management assumes that those expectations are met through the efforts of the knowledge strategist and his or her team of knowledge professionals. For senior management, the costs of providing the necessary professional expertise for managing and delivering knowledge services and for the technical infrastructure supporting knowledge services are the items that demand attention. Other specifics having to do with connecting people to knowledge are subsumed into and are expected to be controlled and managed as part of the usual operational function for providing knowledge services, the responsibility of others in the organization and not the purview of senior management. As long as a viable case can be made for the required expenditures, paying for the expertise and technology become no more than a matter of making a case for supporting those requirements.

On the other hand, in terms of the successful functioning of the larger organization, there is interest (and often concern) amongst all stakeholders in how organizational assets are used and exploited to support the organization's stated mission, however that mission is defined. It is thus the responsibility of all managerial employees – including the organization's knowledge strategist – to incorporate performance measures relative to management and service delivery into their work. With respect to knowledge services, how the organization benefits from the management and delivery of knowledge services has for some years been a matter of considerable interest to those with responsibility for organization development (or, as this discipline is increasingly described, organizational effectiveness).

Understanding and assessing that connection and establishing the degree to which knowledge services supports the organizational mission constitute an essential element in the management and delivery of knowledge services, regardless of whether the measures relate strictly to financial performance or whether – painted with a broader brush – they enable stakeholders throughout the enterprise to determine the value of and exploit the role of knowledge in their work.

In the management process, the role of strategic planning necessarily depends on examining and preparing a value judgment on the success of the organization in meeting its objectives, and the review process supports and provides the constituent elements that define enterprise success. The same is true of knowledge services and the management and delivery of knowledge services through the organization's knowledge services business unit, regardless of how it is structured or what it is called. It may be a unit of a larger research management function, a specialized research library, a research and development functional unit, or any of the many other units that fall under the purview of the "knowledge domain." Whatever its name or its unique knowledge-related function in the particular organization or enterprise, the unit's standard over-arching assessment methodology for knowledge services management and delivery responsibility is the knowledge services audit.

The knowledge services audit includes an examination of the organization's knowledge needs, existing knowledge assets and resources, how knowledge flows throughout the enterprise, identifies knowledge needs not being addressed, and provides knowledge gap analysis. The knowledge services audit usually includes some attention to the behavior of people working with the KD/KS/KU process and seeks to match the organization's strength as a knowledge culture with organizational strategy, its leadership, its ambiance with respect to collaboration, its training, learning, and career development structure, and it intellectual asset and technology infrastructure.

The knowledge services audit examines what already exists and seeks to describe the current knowledge services situation as objectively as possible. Its goal is to identify usable information (using both subjective and objective information-gathering techniques), and it is recognized as a proactive exercise, attempting to elicit trends and concepts from potential users and to determine requirements for success. As an evaluation tool, the knowledge services audit determines if current methods for knowledge sharing – for managing and delivering information, knowledge, and strategic learning – are meeting the organization's needs and, in particular, the quality of those services as they are provided, delivered, and contributing to successful KD/KS/KU for the company, organization, or institution. In its utilization as a measurement tool, the audit combines, as described earlier, the processes of the needs analysis (asking what information resources and services people require to do their work), the information audit (which determines how information resources and services are actually used), and the knowledge services audit (which looks at knowledge assets, how they are produced, and by whom). Taken together, the several processes of the knowledge services audit provide an over-arching, enterprise-wide framework for working with knowledge in the organization and sets the stage for the various individual approaches to measuring knowledge services that are employed as required in whatever functional units have responsibility for them.

The result of taking these steps is a collection of findings that when transitioned into recommendations for the development of the knowledge strategy will lead to a definition and direction for establishing (or strengthening) the organization as a knowledge culture. In utilizing the knowledge services audit the organization's knowledge strategist and his or her knowledge services strategic framework development team can drill down into those activities, results, even relationships that connect with how knowledge services is managed. If the knowledge services audit is well designed, the audit additionally includes the analysis and evaluation of the many and varied knowledge elements that also affect knowledge performance throughout the enterprise; when gathered these are valuable components of the KD/KS/KU process. They provide the opportunity for ongoing investigation and analysis of the organizational knowledge environment, leading to a good, solid picture of the organization's "knowledge health" (as this larger analysis is sometimes called), especially in terms of the organization's knowledge value potential.

There are many situations in which audit findings may not match preconceptions about the outcome of the knowledge services audit, and those preconceptions, if not understood and recognized, can serious affect the implementation of the audit recommendations. For the knowledge services audit team, managing perceptions and expectations throughout the audit process and, particularly, at the conclusion of the audit when the recommendations are presented, can be a delicate undertaking, one in which a certain level of sensitivity to the larger organizational culture (not just its knowledge culture) is required.

Nevertheless, the value of the knowledge services audit will have been established in its execution, and as organizational leadership and the audit team begin to consider next steps in the process, it becomes important to recognize that the effort is, in fact, an ongoing one. The knowledge services audit, if it is successful, will be thought of as a "living" process, and the procedure will be reviewed on a regular basis, with updating as required, and treated as a standard management tool. With these considerations in mind, both enterprise leaders and the knowledge strategist and the staff of the knowledge services business unit who engaged in the knowledge services audit will continue to be positioned as essential and critical players in organizational success.

2.3 Measures and Metrics for Knowledge Services

Having completed the knowledge services audit and now well on the way to a first version of the knowledge service strategic framework – the organization's knowledge strategy – the knowledge strategist and the knowledge services team now turn to developing a knowledge services measurement strategy. The objective now is to ensure that the value of knowledge in the organization's operational and functional structure is quantified and, as a result, recognized. With the knowledge services audit now providing findings and recommendations for the organizational knowledge strategy, the knowledge services team will devise a measures and metrics plan in order to convey clearly the concept of the *value* of organizational knowledge – its intellectual capital – in the achievement of the organizational mission to the at-large organizational community. It is an activity generally referred to as *value creation*, and its development is not open to question for employees working in or otherwise affiliated with the organization's knowledge domain. Knowledge is an essential and critical organizational asset and the knowledge development, knowledge sharing, and knowledge utilization process is a legitimate functional operation in the organization. Yet because KD/KS/KU is ubiquitous in the pursuit of organizational success (whether acknowledged or not), the value of the process must be given specific attention as enterprise leadership begins to embrace the concept of the knowledge culture. Providing the means for that attention would seem to be a fairly straightforward process, but there often seems to be a somewhat negative attitude about how knowledge services – as an operational function – is valued. When asked to express his views on the subject, one colleague noted with sadness that it had been his experience that "when the accountants are looking for cost savings these departments are at the top of the list."

Is there a solution to this problem, a way to change this attitude on the part of those with authority in the organization, when this idea represents the way they think about knowledge services? For some it would be the solution, as this manager puts it, to "find a 'magic bullet' – to come up with an explanation that could demonstrate in accountant friendly terms just what value knowledge strategists bring to the organization." Other knowledge strategists have their own techniques and approaches, but like other managers in the organization, they are often surprised at how little financial value is put on the services they and their colleagues provide.

According to another knowledge strategist, there does seem to be one approach that can provide a slightly different perspective to this situation. This person writes, "The biggest challenge that I see here (and elsewhere) is that we are being asked to do more with less. The smart organizations (and I would like to think that there is still an abundance of those!) will not do away with KD/KS/KU – they can't do that and stay in business – but they might ask knowledge strategists to manage with smaller staff and increased responsibilities." In the situation he is describing, the knowledge strategist has responsibility for the organization's research operations, organizational archives, the organization's legacy content digitization project, and, since the organization includes a wide membership base, an information resource and clearinghouse for scholars and academics in the field in which the organization specializes. For this knowledge strategist, "The solutions to the challenge will be (and are currently) multi-level: we re-think our priorities and we question whether all of yesterday's services/tasks, etc., are relevant and necessary today. When required, job descriptions are modified and if the tasks are more than can be accommodated in the hours in the day, we look to what can be outsourced. These are the challenges relating to service delivery and staff capacities that we must confront, and on a daily basis."

For knowledge strategists, the value of services offered must be matched against the organization's success in accomplishing its strategic mission. This means, in the words of one colleague, moving "away from" defending the knowledge services unit as a place or function ("as we find ourselves doing too often") and "concentrating on the professional skills and values our knowledge workers and strategic knowledge professionals bring to the organization."

Another solution to the "value" challenge urges knowledge strategists to think of themselves as businessmen and businesswomen: "Metrics, metrics, metrics," another colleague pointed out in a meeting. "Measure, measure, measure. And deliver measurement results in business terms. Management has only one question it wants answered: Do the services provided by knowledge services save the organization money? Or, put another way, does the knowledge services unit bring in revenue? It's that simple. From the organizational management perspective, it's all about metrics and ROI. In our field we tend to roll our eyes when we hear about ROI but this is what management wants. It is very important to capture metrics, and they must be specific, actionable metrics."

Hearing these comments, the knowledge strategist finds himself or herself in an almost-ideal position to apply business principles and concepts to the development of the knowledge services strategic framework for the organization. In fact, using the word "ideal" intentionally, my strongest recommendation to the knowledge strategist and the knowledge workers and strategic knowledge professionals working with the strategist in the knowledge services unit would be to recommend that they become familiar with the Knowledge Value Chain®. Created by Timothy W. Powell, now President and CEO of The Knowledge Agency® and, well-known for his pioneering work in KVC studies, Powell writes about and defines the knowledge value chain for us:

> The KVC framework is easy to understand and apply because it builds on a simple insight: in a complex organization the people who produce information (producers) are fundamentally different from the people who use it to create results and value (users). This creates a *knowledge-value gap* between producers and users that is often vast – some call it a "gulf" – and includes many professional and cultural barriers.
>
> In short, information people don't typically understand the language of business, and business people don't typically understand the language of information. The connection between the two halves – *the knowledge value chain* – is broken.
>
> The net result is that information resources and the people who manage them fail to have the impact they could have, and fail to optimize their return on investment. Instead of being part of the organizational solution, information becomes part of the problem as people scurry to absorb and make sense of it.
>
> Understanding the knowledge value chain from both producer and use perspectives is a first step toward bridging this fundamental barrier. (Powell, 2014)

With this concept, the knowledge services team has the opportunity literally to make that transition described earlier. In doing so we re-state the terms in Powell's quotation by referring to information people (the producers, those who produce information) to the "producers" in knowledge services work, those employed in the KD/KS/KU process, our knowledge workers, strategic knowledge professionals, and of course referring to the knowledge strategist, the leader or knowledge executive.

Likewise, Powell's description of "business people" and the difficulties of business people (the users) to speak the language of information can help us bring the knowledge value chain construct smoothly into the knowledge domain and refer to the knowledge development, knowledge sharing, and knowledge utilization that takes place in the organization. And, of particular note in both iterations of the knowledge value chain, whether speaking of a company in the business world or of any other type of organization, the producers (whether of information or of knowledge) must seek to close the *knowledge-value gap* not only between the producers and the users but between the producers and a more specific group, those enterprise leaders with decision-making authority. These people must be made to understand that their agreement and commitment is required, to ensure not only that the gap is closed but that they will support knowledge services so that the gap stays closed. Again from Powell (and St. Clair is in total agreement): "When we speak of knowledge management and knowledge services, if we are going to be successful, we are required to be speaking at the board level, at the senior management level of the organization."

When knowledge strategy-focused activities are initiated and when benefits accrue, the knowledge strategist has attained a place in the organizational culture (not just the organization as a knowledge culture) that many knowledge workers aspire to but few achieve: adding value because of the identified and recognized output of the excellence of the KD/KS/KU process. Getting to that KD/KS/KU excellence is a goal Powell recognizes. Working with companies as they pursue knowledge value or seek to close the knowledge-value gap, Powell has frequent opportunities to observe what works and what doesn't, and his focus on KVC® is essential background for helping the knowledge strategist and the knowledge services team relate to how companies and organizations work with knowledge value.

Developing a knowledge services measurement strategy. As with any management function, expectations play a key role in the measurement of knowledge services. Not only must metrics be developed and used in order to keep organizational management informed about the financial performance of knowledge services, all workers affiliated with the organization's knowledge domain – knowledge workers, strategic knowledge professionals, and (particularly) the knowledge strategist – must develop and use measurement tools for very basic management tasks: to continually examine and analyze operations, to differentiate the knowledge services function in its larger organizational service sphere, and to reduce costs and improve productivity. Metrics tell us, with respect to our work, where we've been, where we are now, and provide us with the basic information we require to determine the direction we're going. Given the critical role of measures in the management of the knowledge domain and especially as the emphasis turns to both the knowledge services audit and how the findings of the audit are used in support of the business case for knowledge services, attention to measures is not an option. It is part of what the knowledge strategist and the knowledge services team do.

The first step in establishing the value of knowledge services is to state the objective and purpose of the measurement effort, and that is not a difficult activity to undertake. The organization's knowledge strategist and the team staffing the knowledge services unit understand the importance of measures. Their goal is direct: to develop a measurement strategy that will identify and codify the central value proposition for knowledge services within the larger enterprise in alignment with the vision, mission, and values of the organization. This strategy will link to the findings and recommendations of the knowledge services audit and the implementation and planning directions of the organization's knowledge services, its knowledge services strategic framework.

In taking on this task, the knowledge services team expects to determine organizational standards and expectations, thus enabling themselves to evaluate current operations and service delivery and to establish a baseline for managing and delivering knowledge services (and eventually, of course, for going beyond the baseline to establish standards of excellence for the management and delivery of knowledge services in the larger enterprise).

Once the purpose of the exercise has been established, the focus can move to the "how-to," to identify further steps that will enable the development of a measurement strategy for knowledge services. A typical situation is one in which team members looking at the measurement strategy discuss the process; "What do we do first?" is the usual opening question in their initial discussion. If some in the group have experience with metrics, an early step often involves identifying metrics tools and seeking to fit the recognized tools (or those with which some staff members have experience) into the present strategy planning.

There is more, though, to building a measurement strategy for knowledge services than simply identifying metrics tools; looking at the tools first is somewhat akin to putting the cart before the horse. To be safe, every metrics development activity should proceed by thinking about the two questions which always must to be asked:

1. Who will be receiving the information (and making decisions based on these metrics)?

    The success of the measurement effort depends on understanding the audience for whom the metrics are developed and to whom they will be delivered. Most of these people are not necessarily focused on the role of knowledge in the organization, except as a support mechanism. It is not patronizing them to note that for these people, metrics must be presented in language that makes sense to them as non-specialists (that is, in terms of knowledge services). For most situations, a well-used technique presents measurement results in terminology that is understandable and relevant to others in the organization, recognizing that information management, knowledge management, and strategic learning are but part of their daily work life, not their workplace focus. Some information and knowledge professionals get around this impediment by applying the "so what?" question to each metric presented (either literally or rhetorically), thus giving those who see the metrics a description that resonates with his or her own experience and expertise.

2. What do those people want (need) to know?

    So we clearly understand that any knowledge services measures must relate to business outcomes and to how the business will be favorably impacted or affected by the elements measured. Another key issue, particularly when developing metrics for knowledge services, is to think about how the metrics will be used. Thus the knowledge strategist and the knowledge services unit's staff are required to use care in not only deciding what to measure, but what measures to use. This can be a cumbersome and sometimes off-putting prospect, but the solution is easy to come by, and it has two parts. First, the knowledge strategist and his or her staff simply look around the organization and identify other functional units that are required to measure service delivery. Metrics development (and certainly the development of a metrics framework) does not take place in a vacuum, and since in managing and delivering knowledge services the knowledge strategist expects to take an enterprise-wide perspective anyway, it is a wise choice to look to others in the organization for conversation and advice, to learn about their previous experience, and to seek direction in planning a measurement activity.

In addition to looking at how other departments and functional units measure performance, a second important step is to address the topic with senior management. Whenever possible, selected enterprise leaders should be engaged, certainly in discussion, and occasionally (when there is an expression of interest), even in participation in the planning. Obviously such participation is usually at a strategic and not tactical level but that distinction is not really important. As is often desired with any organizational functional unit, the attention of senior management to the workings of the unit can lead to a better understanding of the role of the unit in the larger organizational picture and, when appropriate, lead to the development of a sponsorship relationship. While such a relationship is not necessarily required for the successful development of a measurement framework for knowledge services, when such engagement takes place with a management leader, the metrics effort is starting off on a sound footing. The classic sponsorship role is to say or speak about, model, and reward whatever effort is being undertaken, and if a member or group of members of the senior management team signs on to champion the development of metrics for knowledge services and becomes involved in the effort, the entire process moves forward more smoothly (and not unexpectedly the larger enterprise realizes even higher-level benefits).

As for the specifics of the effort, as described above it makes sense to look beyond the immediate discipline and identify tools and techniques from other service delivery functions related to the work done with knowledge services. An obvious relationship already exists with the organization's technology management unit (and especially since information management is one of the three elements of knowledge services), and a recent list of "essential" metrics for technology management can be transcribed for use with the knowledge services unit. In a white paper from Forrester Research, Craig Symons and his colleagues note that "the key to success is choosing a small number of metrics that are *relevant* to the business and have the most *impact* on business outcomes" (Symons et al., 2008, emphasis added).

Transitioning the Forrester recommendations into the knowledge services framework, with its emphasis on sustained knowledge development, knowledge sharing, and knowledge utilization (KD/KS/KU), criteria for determining the relevance and impact of knowledge services and the knowledge services operational function can be established. A first metric demonstrates the alignment of the organization's investment in knowledge services to its business strategy. How have organizational goals been described? Does the company's mission statement provide a thematic approach to achieving success? Probably not, and if that is the case, where does the knowledge strategist locate, say, the primary 3–5 organizational drivers for the next two or three budget periods? These must be identified before a measurement strategy can be developed, but once identified, the relationship between the services, products, and consultations offered by the knowledge services unit and the company's focus can be linked. Metrics can then be developed, for demonstrating how well the knowledge services function does (or does not) support that linkage.

Another of these identified essential metrics seeks to measure the business value of knowledge services investments, and as described in the discussion of return-on-investment (ROI) below, the relationship of knowledge services to the larger enterprise purpose, as identified through an analysis of projects throughout the organization affected by the presence of the knowledge services unit, enables the knowledge strategist to establish value. By looking at the maximum expected return on the organizational investment in projects and linking these to such measurable knowledge services elements as efficiency, the quality of service delivery, and the development of strategic partnerships throughout the organization, the knowledge services contribution to the success of the projects is established. An important caveat with respect to determining the business value of knowledge services naturally demands a recognition that the subject is not only knowledge services and that the knowledge services unit does not operate as a stand-alone office or business unit. The viability of knowledge services solutions depends on the level of integration of knowledge services throughout the organization, together with an understanding – despite the enterprise-wide focus – that no one solution applies for all situations in the larger organization, and that for each situation a distinction must be made between local, centralized, and enterprise-wide.

For most knowledge services operations, when looking at the relationship between balancing legacy service delivery with new initiatives and connecting these to budget activities, the pattern has generally been to rely on existing tools, information-gathering resources, and service delivery methodologies rather than to focus on new initiatives. Part of the reason for this has to do with the often typical assignment of support for the management and delivery of knowledge services to overhead; thankfully there are signs that this pattern is changing. In many organizations, knowledge services is increasingly recognized for its contribution to organizational success and knowledge strategists are embracing a more expansive role. For some of them, benchmarking – described later – provides a methodology for identifying how other organizations and disciplines connect new initiatives with established procedures, and they use ratios in their external benchmarks to describe a variety of measures. At the same time, these strategists make use of internal benchmarks, to determine how the knowledge services unit performs in comparison with other departments and separate functional units within the larger organization.

Both service level excellence and operational excellence (or "operational health," as this attribute is termed in some organizations, just as with the knowledge services audit) provide what is sometimes referred to as operational metrics (as opposed to mission-specific, value-focused metrics). There is a diversity of opinion about the interest of senior management in operational measures because in the ideal management situation it is understood that the individual departments and functional units are well-run and the delivery of operational metrics is not necessary and merely distracts senior management from the "big-picture" metrics. In reality, the finances of the overall organization, including those relating to operations, come under constant scrutiny and service level excellence is required, as well as metrics demonstrating levels of excellence. Both the knowledge services audit and customer satisfaction surveys and service-level agreements – if they are in place – provide specific metrics and play an important role in the knowledge services measurement strategy.

Types of measures. When we think about measuring knowledge services, what seems to work in most organizations is a three-way approach: establishing tools and techniques for identifying *types* of measures, for *capturing* measures, and *communicating* measurement results. In the first, ROI and effectiveness measures are *types* of measures, as are anecdotal measures when they are used, and we capture measures through such activities as benchmarking, customer satisfaction surveys, and of course the knowledge services audit, already described and probably already well under way for some readers. We communicate the results of our measurement activities through such vehicles as the balanced scorecard (developed by Robert Kaplan and David Norton), Karl-Erik Sveiby's Intangible Assets Monitor, anecdotal reporting and discussion, and the usual reporting mechanisms employed in all organizations (annual reports, monthly activity reports, internal newsletters and other awareness-raising activities, management team/committee participation, etc.).

Any number of efforts to establish standards for measures have become part of the management toolbox. While most managers recognize that coming up with formulas for measuring intangible assets is a sometimes elusive goal, other measurement tools have been developed within the larger management community. When these are applied to knowledge services and the development of the knowledge services strategic framework or to technology management and information management as practiced in the more commercial- or research-focused environments, the effort has resulted in a certain level of confusion about performance measures, and we have a seeming conglomeration of synonyms being applied to a number of different activities.

Because there are so many different ways to focus on metrics, it might be appropriate to attempt to clear up some of the confusion. In doing so, we go back to that initial question in the measurement team's first meeting: "How do we start?" A picture of different types of measures (and how metrics terms interact with one another) might look like the diagram in Figure 2.4:

Discussions about different measuring methodologies seem to move quickly into debate about the distinctions between "measures" and "metrics," together

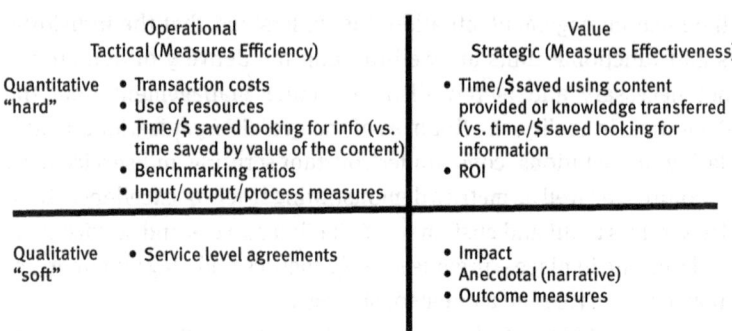

Figure 2.4: Types of measures (Dale Stanley, SMR International).

with some sort of attempt to identify how the two concepts are different. Practically speaking, the distinctions are probably more semantic than anything else, with practitioners in the non-profit or not-for-profit fields of work more inclined to prefer speaking about "measures," leaving the hard-sounding "metrics" for the business community. This is not an unreasonable way of looking at the two descriptors, since the use of "measures" would appear to be more "open," so to speak, to including reference to intangibles in the evaluation process and thus more appropriate to the inclusion of the anecdotal as a legitimate methodology for determining value.

In any case, regardless of whether knowledge strategists speak about how they "measure" success or whether they use "metrics," the discussion of the "hard" vs. the "soft" characteristic of the measure promptly becomes part of the conversation, with the one referring to the quantitative and the other, generally speaking, having to do with qualitative measurement as knowledge services staff seek to evaluate knowledge services performance in the larger enterprise.

At the same time, though, other semantic problems creep into the conversation, particularly with respect to the overlapping characteristics of some of the techniques that must be applied as we seek to measure knowledge services. As critical success factors for knowledge services are identified, a wide variety of measurement techniques and tools can be considered. For example, Joseph Matthews writes about the balanced scorecard (which in itself is not specifically a measurement technique but a structure for the utilization of various measurement methodologies, linking them to the organizational mission) and in doing so provides definitions for several different types of measures.

Matthews identifies the four variables utilized by organizations and describes how resources, capability, utilization, and impact or effect influence organizational success. These variables are equally applicable to the organization's knowledge services unit, and Matthews describes the four different classic assessment tools generally used in these environments:

Input measures: resources or inputs allocated to the unit (budget figures, resources, staff count, etc.), notably easy to quantify and gather.

Process measures: "focused on activities that transform resources into services" – time to perform a task, for example (such as materials processing, etc.). As Matthews notes, "process measures are ultimately about efficiency."

Output measures: used to establish the degree to which the functional unit and its services are being utilized, usually limited to volume counts (how many people e-mail queries received, etc.).

Outcome measures: generally characterized as "effectiveness measures," these measures indicate the impact or effect of the functional unit and its services on the people who utilize them. In most cases, as Matthews notes, these measures have an "outward" focus or thrust and do not emphasize process management or product counts. (Matthews, 2003)

The first three of these types of measures fit into the operational/quantitative measures shown in the "types of measures" chart in Figure 2.4, with the last ("outcome measures") being examples of both types of value/qualitative measures. For some authorities in the knowledge services industry, these measures make up the "soft" end of the "soft" vs. "hard" or the "measures" vs. "metrics" spectrum. Even though these include quantitative measures, they are not exclusively quantitative and the numbers collected are used to support what are, in fact, qualitative deliverables from the knowledge services unit. As such, they can be thought of as operational metrics, since they reflect primarily the overall management success of the functional unit and are primarily of interest to the managers of the unit and those to whom they report directly. These are the types of results that describe the internal workings of the unit ("this database was used X times during the past month") and provide the unit's knowledge services staff a snapshot of how their work is succeeding on their own terms. There are exceptions, of course ("the XYZ Department measured an increased productivity level of 15 % because the knowledge services team provided training for its staff members for using a particular tool on ABC project"), and tools such as effectiveness measures can transition from operations to the measurement-of-value side of the measurement scale, if the effects they report are indeed responsible for changed behavior, improved knowledge service delivery, and increased customer satisfaction.

At the other end of the measurement spectrum we have the "pure" metrics, with their focus on financial benefits from the knowledge services unit. These are the measures that are particularly strengthened when the "so what?" question is attached to the measure, stating that the particular information or knowledge provided matched what the recipient needed to know. The knowledge becomes usable – and hopefully actionable – when the follow-on to "so what?" permits the knowledge strategist to state something along the lines of "Knowing this, we can now assert/judge/understand that such-and-such a mission-specific activity can be implemented and its results brought to fruition."

Between these two ends of the measurement range, a wide variety of tools and techniques have been developed for measuring knowledge services, all contributing to the challenge that the knowledge strategist must confront. All have their advantages, and several are most useful when combined with other measurement techniques, yet taken together these measurement activities represent an ongoing and valuable tool for the organization's knowledge strategist and the audience to whom the measurement statement must be delivered.

Return-on-investment (ROI). Financial benefits provided to the parent organization through the management and delivery of knowledge services are usually expressed as return-on-investment (ROI). Any number of definitions can be found for this much-used methodology. In the accounting profession, ROI is generally thought of as the ratio of net income to total assets which includes, in our work, knowledge assets and the value we and our organization give to organizational intellectual capital. Simply put, ROI can be described as the financial benefit to the organization after the cost of the investment has been subtracted from that financial benefit. In the public sector and in organizations in which there is no specific quest for financial profit *per se*, ROI can include other values, such as cost reduction or avoiding the cost of some action which might have been taken, less the cost of whatever activity or task enables the development or enhancement being measured.

As we speak about ROI, Tim Powell, introduced earlier, has a quick description which works even in those situations in the knowledge domain in which the knowledge workers do not give much attention to the role of knowledge and knowledge sharing in the workplace:

> The math of ROI is easy. *Return on investment* literally means net return divided by net investment. Another way of saying it: benefit divided by cost (though it's usually written *cost/benefit*).
>
> Cash flow is often used as a measure of ROI, where the metrics are cash flow in and cash flow out. ... In the vernacular, ROI is spoken of as *value* – what you get for a given outlay. The American slang is "bang for the buck." (Powell, 2014)

The importance of ROI in managing knowledge services is unquestioned. As with any other functional unit of the organization, a financial value must be attached to the products and services provided by the knowledge services unit, as well as to the costs of maintaining the unit (overhead), simply because operational costs for all functional units determine whether the organization is going to continue as a viable entity or not. For knowledge services, measures must identify, in terms of the financial management of the larger organization, the unique value that the management and delivery of knowledge services brings to the enterprise. Is the impact of knowledge services of value to the organization? Is each expenditure considered (and reported) in terms of impact? Are these expenditure and impact results germane to the requirements of organizational management, as those senior staff members seek to ensure that operational funding specifically supports the achievement of the organization mission? These are the kinds of questions that are answered with a well-developed and implemented ROI process, and they resonate particularly with the provision of knowledge services.

The case for demonstrating the organizational value of knowledge services in financial terms has been addressed. In a survey of knowledge strategists and their direct reports, respondents were selected because they were known to be leaders in their organizations. These are people who have achieved a level of management expertise and experience in knowledge services, and they were asked two questions:

1. What do you think will be the top two or three challenges for knowledge services in the next few years (probably best to think short-term rather than long-term)?
2. As a knowledge strategist, knowledge worker, or strategic knowledge professional working in the field, how do you expect to deal with these challenges?

The responses to the questions and the identified challenges were not surprising, but the seriousness with which the respondents spoke about the two that ranked highest was remarkable. The challenge that was cited most by the respondents, demonstrating the highest concern of these professional leaders, was relevance, that the knowledge services unit must be relevant – and remain relevant – to the achievement of the mission of the organization, however that mission is defined and stated. The responses of those participating in the study made it clear that while the relevance of the unit (or any other information, knowledge, or strategic learning delivery function in the organization) is fairly well acknowledged in many organizations, particularly by colleagues in the organization who make regular use of the function, that relevance was not often known or acknowledged throughout the larger enterprise.

The second worrisome challenge had to do with financial value, and all respondents speaking to this issue seemed to be aware – even for some who were uncomfortable with the situation – that organizational management is required to look at quantitative measures. Such activities are part of the management discipline and, as one respondent said, "it's what executives are hired to do." Many respondents made it clear that they understand that the role of an executive is to control costs, and that the executive's success is itself judged by how well that manager performs that task. So regardless of how they themselves feel about this emphasis on the financial, these managers of knowledge services units made it clear that whatever methodologies they prefer for their own particular professional measurement, to be recognized and taken seriously in the larger enterprise they are required to look to quantitative measures, and especially to financial measures.

In seeking to manage and provide service delivery for information, knowledge, and strategic learning (even when limiting themselves to the management of strategic learning content alone, without considering the other functions connected with strategic learning), the knowledge strategist and his or her team are first restrained by the fact that the context and the results of these activities are generally thought of as intangible. People speak about information, knowledge, and learning in very lofty terms, but when we try to pin down what we get when a particular database is searched, or a colleague with experience in a project of the kind another worker is undertaking speaks with the person seeking to share in that knowledge, or the application of ideas and content picked up through attendance at a departmental brown-bag lunch program, we find that there is not a lot there to "count." No one is going to question the benefit of the activity, but to measure that benefit in quantitative terms is very difficult.

Similarly, the very people with whom knowledge services staff interact do not themselves understand the concepts of value, or if they do, they do not think much about the value of the interaction. With respect to information, knowledge, and strategic learning, most people do not have background or a professional affiliation with these disciplines, so the outcomes of the situations – like the examples just mentioned – are useful just because they happened, and because there was an outcome, actionable or otherwise. In these situations, the users and participants do not identify these activities as anything special or give a great deal of thought to what they come away with. If there is to be any recognition of perceived value, it is in many cases up to the knowledge services staff to establish the validity and value of the transaction (which is why, of course, there is so much emphasis on the development and sustenance of an enterprise-wide knowledge culture and why, in many situations, that emphasis must emanate from the knowledge services team).

Another challenge to managing the ROI process is often organizational, both within the knowledge services unit and in the larger enterprise. In many environments, particularly if the knowledge services function is limited to the provision of services through a specialized library or information center, the management structure categorizes the function as overhead, with the costs and expenses for operating the unit and supporting the services it provides considered ongoing expenses, necessary to the continued functioning of the organization (as long as knowledge services is perceived as contributing to the success of the organization). The knowledge services unit is not expected to generate profits or contribute in any direct way to the organizational bottom line however that bottom line is defined. In smaller organizations, the specialized library or information center – particularly if the unit is managed and operated by a single information professional – is not even carried as a budget item but is incorporated into the operational structure of whatever functional unit or division it is part of. As a result, ROI with respect to knowledge services is of little interest to management, and the single-staff information professional with responsibility for the management of the unit must look for opportunities to incorporate ROI into whatever other organizational measures are used. As with other challenges, the organization that does not have any particular measurement framework for knowledge services that can be translated into – or at least approach – a statement of the return-on-investment for the provision of knowledge services will require particular innovation skills from the knowledge strategist, since management must be kept apprised of how well the knowledge services unit serves the larger organization.

In most circumstances, though, it is through the expert deployment of return-on-investment documentation (usually in combination with another measurement tool or technique) that the knowledge strategist can make an impressive showing in how the delivery of knowledge services is perceived and valued in the organization. To reach that goal, we connect first with the formulas for ROI, and the formulas connect first and foremost with the users of the organization's knowledge services products. And while a great many variables are given consideration in calculating the contributions of the knowledge services function (dollars saved, revenue generated, decision support, cost avoidance, etc.), to most users how the product or services affect their own time is usually the primary concern.

This focus on measuring the benefit to the unit's users relates to establishing cost/benefit analysis, as mentioned in Powell's description. It is the comparison between the costs (time spent, for example, or ease of use) to the user and the costs of having the service provided by a knowledge services or other knowledge-sharing unit. In one example, a knowledge strategist describes for colleagues at a professional conference presentation a dramatic scenario in which some 3,000 knowledge workers subscribe to (or have access to) a particular information service. When surveys and other methodologies establish that the particular knowledge-sharing service saves employees two hours per week, the cost saving for the organization is calculated by multiplying the average hourly salary of those employees ($33.65) by 2 by 3,000 (number of employees) by 49 weeks (weeks worked per year) to arrive at a cost savings of more than nine million dollars. In a second scenario, a second knowledge strategist calculates cost savings on four projects, assuming that the average annual salary is $70,000, that the service provides a 10 % reduction in time on the four projects, and factoring in that the average project uses 50 employees. In this scenario (50 employees × 4 projects × $70,000 salary × 10 % cost saving), the calculation of cost savings is $1,400,000 per year.

Not included in the cost/benefit analysis, however, are other benefits. For example, such value-add during the search process as the interaction between the user and a strategic knowledge professional who has experience and expertise in the subject being searched and who can suggest alternative resources or, even better, connections to a prior user who has worked on the same topic. These cannot generally be factored into the cost-benefit analysis.

The purpose and value of using ROI as a measurement tool for knowledge services, and of including reference to cost-benefit analysis, relate naturally in our considerations of benchmarking as well. While ROI is a type of measure and benchmarking is a process or a vehicle for capturing measures, the two combine conceptually when knowledge strategists and knowledge services staff seek to evaluate the management and delivery of knowledge services. The power of using ratios in benchmarking is that they permit the comparison of seemingly disparate quantities, a technique which enables the management team putting together the metrics the opportunity to use a "snapshot"-type description that is not required to allude to specific dollar figures (which are not always appropriate in comparing performance in organizations of different sizes, for example, or with widely different purposes or objectives).

In thinking about return-on-investment for the management and delivery of knowledge services, a no-less-important concern is the consideration of the relationship between the knowledge services unit and organizational management, what we might think of as "measuring the distance." Some further attention is given to this subject as the audience for the report of any measurement is considered, but it is, nevertheless, a subject with particular resonance with respect to ROI. As implied in the responses of knowledge strategists about relevance and measurement, there is a "distance" between knowledge services staff – with their training and formal education linked to the larger research management field – and senior management. The knowledge strategist recognizes that the role of the latter is to focus on "wide-angle" matters (and results) with respect to the larger organization, yet the role of most knowledge services staff – even knowledge services staff with management responsibility – is service provision, to ensure that the management and delivery of knowledge services matches the needs of the knowledge services unit's specific sphere.

The two are not incompatible, but they are differently focused, and for success in measuring knowledge services, especially in terms of the value that knowledge services brings to the larger organization, it is necessary to identify carefully the distinctions between what is of interest and use to those to whom measures are reported and those who are responsible for knowledge services. In some organizations – perhaps most – the two are distinct, and not only is the knowledge strategist required to understand that the distance exists, he or she must also be prepared to "measure" that distance in terms of the larger relationships that exist between the knowledge services unit and the larger enterprise.

Effectiveness measures. In his list of the variables that influence the success of the knowledge services unit, Joseph Matthews (quoted earlier) refers to impact measures or, as they are often described, effectiveness measures. In measuring knowledge services, there are few measurement techniques more needed than these, yet most knowledge services staff with responsibility for the management and delivery of knowledge services find themselves caught up in quantitative measures and the impact of a particular resource or activity is often neglected.

With effectiveness measures, the service or product delivered is weighed in terms of how the recipient of the service or product has been affected by the having access to that service or product. For some knowledge strategists, effectiveness measures connect with values measures (as opposed to operations measures). In all cases, though, effectiveness or impact measures are studied to determine if a) the activity undertaken was successfully implemented and b) the impact or effect of the successful implementation of that activity was sufficiently realized. In most situations, the latter refers to the success of the knowledge services activity in terms of cost to the user, with cost being characterized as any expenditure made by the user, whether in resources (funding), the best mechanism for finding the solution, time spent approaching (and sometimes in learning) the tool or resources with the needed solution, convenience, speed of delivery, and similar factors which might or might not influence the user in participating in the knowledge services delivery activity. Such concerns are not, of course, included in effectiveness measures when the solution is delivered directly to the colleague or co-worker needing the information, knowledge, or strategic learning content without participating in the search (although the time and cost of professional services provided by a knowledge services unit can be calculated). In the modern organization, however, these types of "delivery services" are becoming less and less common, since most users expect to be engaged in the search, at least to some extent.

For many knowledge strategists, whether measurement efforts are enacted by the larger enterprise or through (and limited to) services provided by the knowledge services unit, success is not achieved until the effectiveness of the activity can be determined. The unit's primary focus becomes one of output or, as Joseph Matthews pointed out in his description of outcome measures described earlier, of having an outward focus, as opposed to the inward focus of efficiency or process measures. Effectiveness measures determine that the service provided relate to the success of the person seeking to take advantage of the knowledge services activity as he or she utilizes and implements the information, knowledge, or strategic learning content acquired in the transaction.

Like Matthews, Powell uses inputs, outputs, and outcomes in his ROI measurement recommendations, linking them to effectiveness measures. In his lectures

and writings, Powell has his own identification for three classes of metrics that can be applied to knowledge processes and assets:
- *Inputs* are (not surprisingly) what you put into the process – resources like money, people, time, and effort.
- *Outputs* are 'what you get' for the input – like web site pages produced, documents captured, users served, and reports produced. The ratio of Outputs to Inputs measures the *efficiency* of a process. Tim's examples are users served, reports prepared, portal hits.
- While these are all valid measures, they each fall short of measuring the impact of our investments and efforts on our organization's goals and strategies. These are *Outcomes* – benefits, value received, impact, and business results.

In Powell's description, he digs a little deeper, using these metrics to provide the knowledge strategist and the knowledge services team with a practical and viable definition of effectiveness measures, demonstrating that the closer the measure moves from inputs (through outputs) and to outcomes, the stronger the business case and return-on-investment claim. Powell then goes on to provide further guidance:

> Consequently, my advice is to – rather than create new metrics for knowledge – use those business metrics already in place. If for example a knowledge process supports sales-related decisions, its value derives from the incremental sales that result from its deployment. (Powell, 2013)

As we pay attention to Powell's knowledge value chain, which he defines in another useful description as "a structured methodology for understanding and accelerating the transformation of your data into knowledge and intelligence, and finally into outcomes and operating results," we see how this thinking supports the knowledge strategist and the staff in the knowledge services unit as they seek to provide convincing measurement results for their colleagues and managers. Indeed, Powell makes the effort even more attractive, noting that

> within your organization, this transformation typically happens in the form of knowledge-based processes – for example, business strategy, market research, corporate intelligence, knowledge management, special libraries, and even R&D and legal research. Those processes occur within a value context – that is, they produce both costs and benefits. While the costs are usually pretty clear, the benefits often are not – and consequently the opportunities for producing even greater value are often overlooked. (Powell, 2012)

Anecdotal measures. While the term is somewhat misleading, "anecdotal measures" has captured the imagination of many knowledge strategists and turns up often in discussions about metrics. The reason is not hard to find. When balanced against the "hard" facts of quantitative measures, relating stories about how one or another service provided by the knowledge services unit matched organizational priorities is a natural and quite satisfactory way to establish value. Particularly with respect to qualitative measures, a story is a measure of value and often is the most successful method for conveying a particular value. Typical examples can be seen when the delivered service or product enables the larger organization to save a great deal of money (as with the discovery – through research conducted by the knowledge services staff – that an initiative had been undertaken previously, with specific documentation readily available before the process was re-initiated). Or, similarly, when a discovery by the staff of the knowledge services unit positions the organization for mission-specific success that would not otherwise not have been possible or perhaps even recognized as an opportunity, as when the knowledge services staff identifies the growth potential of an organizational activity, performs due diligence about the background of the situation, and delivers evidence-based research supporting the undertaking. In these activities, the anecdotal provides a delivery mechanism and enhances the metric being provided.

We obviously work with anecdotal measures – often not called that – in the formal interviewing process of the knowledge services audit, described earlier. An important component of the knowledge services audit (or indeed, of any audit other than those that are limited to the quantitative) is the interaction between the audit team and knowledge services stakeholders. Whether conveyed in individual interviews, group discussions, or formal focus groups, the data gathering of the knowledge services audit will incorporate the sharing of a wide variety of situation descriptions, experiences, identified impediments to quality service delivery, and the like. In these meetings with users, typical open -ended questions like "Are you satisfied with the results obtained when you contact the specialized library?" or "Are documents retrieved for you in a timely manner?" are often "conversation starters" and result in responses in which specific incidents and/or the actions of specific personnel are conveyed, in order to demonstrate the performance of the measured activity. It is the role of the audit team and the compilers of the audit report (usually the same people) to cull through the many anecdotal responses and determine which can be used as measures as the audit result conclusions are prepared.

Not surprisingly, there are circumstances in which several measurement types are used together. In what might be a typical example, we have a knowledge strategist who has become aware of good performance from his knowledge services unit in the form of literature analysis. In one case, when the analysis was delivered, the requestor sent a note of thanks (which of course could have been proactively asked for but in this case was spontaneously provided by the user). As usual in these situations, the message was very brief "... thanks for the good work on...."

As it happened, the strategist had the opportunity to verbally provide his own "thanks for the thanks" comment, noting that his unit is always interested in the impact its work has on the company and the performance of its employees and wondering if, in this case, his unit's work saved the company any time or money. The requestor responded positively, even enthusiastically, commenting that if he had been looking for the information himself, the search "would have taken me hours." He even provided an estimate of the time he saved, enabling the strategist to perform a typical metrics calculation:

hours saved × user's salary (estimate) – actual search time × literature analyst's salary

The difference between the two figures is a quantitative or "operational" metric, measuring efficiency (money saved by the larger organization by having the services of the literature analyst available). And while there might be some debatable assumptions in the calculation (e.g., the searcher perhaps didn't find anything of more value than the requestor might have found, despite the fact that the searcher could find it faster), and while all the resources invested in support of the searcher's role were available and could have been used by the requestor, if he had the proper training, availability to the resources, etc., the general success of this metric is clear and this type of calculation works.

With this basic metric in hand (and with an obvious positive relationship having been built up between the requestor and the knowledge strategist), the next question turned the metric into a "value" or, as described by some specialists, metric: Did this work save the parent organization money or time, or make money for the company? The response was more of an anecdote or narrative instead of a calculated metric but no less valuable because it clearly demonstrated the value-add of the activity. If the searcher had not found the information delivered to the user, the company was prepared to create an entire research unit (including several scientists and a fully-equipped laboratory) to pursue continue research about a topic that the search of the literature had revealed to be an un-fruitful path. With that impressive result in hand, the strategist asked the requestor if it were possible to estimate how much time and money would have been invested in the effort, including the overall project, the people, and the laboratory. The estimate was in quantities of multiple years and millions of dollars, significantly more that the "time saved finding the information." Thus in one striking situation, the management and delivery of knowledge services is measured in three types of integrated metrics: the quantitative or "operational" in time saved searching for the information, the qualitative or "value" in the story of the proposed new research facility, and the combined quantitative/value when the user was asked to put a dollar figure on the "cost avoidance" realized by *not* moving forward with the work.

In the long list of measurement tools that can be put to use in developing the knowledge services strategic framework, many others can be studied and applied as circumstances require. In addition to ROI, effectiveness measures, and anecdotal measures, the specifics of the knowledge services audit, customer satisfaction surveys, and benchmarking have strong champions among knowledge strategists. For organizations and institutions more research-focused and for which there is an organizational interest in more in-depth and detailed background, the balanced scorecard and the intangible assets have value for measuring knowledge services.

The balanced scorecard. For many knowledge strategists and their knowledge services teams, who work with them in the organization's knowledge services unit, the measurement process comes together with the balanced scorecard. While not in and of itself a measurement methodology, the balanced scorecard is an approach to management that lends itself very well to knowledge services, primarily because the balanced scorecard is designed to work with and to incorporate measures and metrics already in place (or being put in place) in the larger organization. The Balanced Scorecard Institute in Washington, DC has described the concept:

> The balanced scorecard is a strategic planning and management system used to align business activities to the vision and strategy of the organization, improve internal and external communications, and monitor organizational performance against strategic goals. It was originated by Drs. Robert Kaplan (Harvard Business School) and David Norton as a performance measurement framework that added strategic non-financial performance measures to traditional financial metrics to give managers and executives a more 'balanced' view of organizational performance. While the phrase *balanced scorecard* was coined in the early 1990s, the roots of the this type of approach are deep, and include the pioneering work of General Electric on performance measurement reporting in the 1950s and the work of French process engineers (who created the *Tableau de Bord* – literally, a "dashboard" of performance measures) in the early part of the twentieth century. (Balanced Scorecard Institute, 2008)

According to specialists, the use of the balanced scorecard is characterized as much as a management methodology as a measurement system and it is in this approach to *balance* that the process provides the best results, particularly for knowledge services. Broadly speaking, the balanced scorecard is not another set of metrics. It is a way to arrange and communicate the metrics, connecting to the larger vision of the organization.

In fact, it is in that connection with the larger vision that the technique excels, for translating the corporate or organizational vision into an operational vision is the first process of the balanced scorecard (Kaplan and Norton, 1996). With respect to knowledge services, the balanced scorecard asks the questions, "Why are we seeking to manage knowledge services?" and "What are our visions for knowledge services in the organization?" In doing so, the knowledge strategist and the knowledge services staff must work with others in the organization to agree upon the purposes of knowledge services, as is advocated in the guidelines offered in this book. Following on to the other processes of the balanced scorecard, the knowledge services framework is described by how well the "idea" of knowledge services is accepted and KD/KS/KU is rewarded in the organization. This thinking then connects with a look at internal business processes, to determine how they match with the processes and objectives of knowledge services. In this process, goals are established, metrics aligned with organizational goals, and time and money allocated for the management and delivery of knowledge services in the organization. Finally, the balanced scorecard comes together in what practitioners refer to as learning and feedback (matching the knowledge services focus on strategic learning), asking such questions of knowledge services as "Is it working?" "Are there results?" and "Are there processes and practices that can be done better?" As this "balance" begins to take shape, we begin to see the need to review – and to continue reviewing – whatever strategies we have put in place for knowledge services.

The intangible assets monitor. In use a little longer than the balanced scorecard as a measurement tool, Karl-Erik Sveiby's intangible assets monitor is of particular value to what he refers to as "knowledge organizations" (which of course includes those in which the knowledge services framework supports the knowledge culture and enables the successful KD/KS/KU process). As such, the technique provides a good method for both measuring intangible assets and for delivering the results of the measures through a number of relevant indicators. Its claim to fame is its simplicity, and like the balanced scorecard, the intangible assets monitor links to the larger organizational picture, particularly its strategies for achieving the corporate mission. It is designed to be used with the organization's management information system and it is limited in scope to only a few indicators and a few comments. Sveiby notes that the most important areas to focus on have to do with growth and renewal, efficiency, and stability of the knowledge services function, providing – as with the knowledge services audit – a broad-based picture of the role of knowledge services in the larger enterprise (Sveiby, 2001).

By looking at three intangible assets as "real" assets (as explained in Sveiby's description), the methodology matches non-financial measures (the intangible) with financial measures (the tangible) and seeks to look at external structure, internal structure, and the competencies of the people who are involved in the KD/KS/KU process. These three are comparable to the customer perspective, the internal business processes perspective, and the learning and growth perspective of the balanced scorecard. As Sveiby has structured it, the intangible assets monitor does not focus on the operational but on values measures, which in this process are described as strategic. Notably, and particularly as we focus on knowledge services, both approaches are strengthened by their emphasis on change (to be discussed in depth in the following chapter) and the value of measuring change, with the measures to be used for strengthening strategic learning and knowledge exchange in the larger organization. Linked to the emphasis on change, however, is the focus in the intangible assets monitor on the knowledge stakeholders as the organization's "profit generators" (as Sveiby puts it) with "the profits generated from people's actions ... the signs of success but not the originator of the success." For knowledge strategists and their knowledge services teams, of course, the challenge of that focus is going to be re-phrasing the "profit" generators to whatever are categorized as "mission success" in the organization.

With their measures, metrics, and goals and objectives – their "profit" – established, the knowledge strategist and the knowledge services team can return to Timothy Powell's thoughts about how knowledge value affects organizational success. He and I speak often about his good work with the knowledge value chain and – unless I am mistaken – he likes the idea that just as I have achieved some recognition in my work with knowledge services he has become the acknowledged KVC guru. For both of us, we're aware that our separate specialties come together in supporting the company or organization's success, and to my way of thinking, Powell's point of view, re-iterated often in our conversations, sets up an almost-perfect scenario for describing how the knowledge strategist can perform when knowledge value comes into the picture:

> 'Value creation' is the fundamental keystone of our competitive economy – and one of the genuine Mysteries of the Universe. For me one of the best things about business school was the opportunity to think and talk about value for two intense years – both in an abstract theoretical sense, and in very applied sense as it relates to creating value in live casebook situations.
>
> You learn not to take value for granted, even to have a certain *reverence* for it – that it's transient, not to be treated carelessly – it can come and go. Much like other living organisms, products, business models, companies, even whole industries have life cycles – they're born, they grow, they thrive, they ebb, they die. (Powell, 2012)

For the knowledge strategist, knowledge value then becomes the vehicle, the structure, if you will, for that knowledge services strategic framework we are building and the case we are making for knowledge services. With knowledge valued across the organization the knowledge strategist serves as the enterprise-wide knowledge authority. In doing so, this KD/KS/KU manager-leader takes on one of the most respected roles in all of knowledge work, becoming the knowledge strategist for the entire company, firm, or organization. With all staff – at all management and functional levels – referring to the knowledge strategist for guidance in all matters having to do with the organization as a knowledge culture, with knowledge development, knowledge sharing, and knowledge utilization, the organization is positioned to succeed and thrive, and the organization's intellectual capital enables organizational effectiveness for the benefit of all stakeholders.

2.4 The Knowledge Services Strategic Framework: A Recommended Strategy ("A Strategy for a Strategy")

> There is no way to overestimate the critical importance of the connection between the knowledge services audit and developing measures and metrics for knowledge service, and the knowledge services strategic framework.

So says Anne Kershaw, Founder and Managing Director of Knowledge Strategy Solutions LLC. As a lawyer, knowledge strategy consultant, and educator, Kershaw does not hesitate when she describes the value of a knowledge services strategy in today's organizations and the connection between the knowledge services audit and establishing measures and metrics for knowledge services. Here's how Kershaw sees it:

> Every day I see movement in dealing with challenges in the knowledge domain, and it's happening in every type of organization. Much of my work has to do with legacy data management and disposition and, particularly, the development of sensible, cost-effective business records management programs that actually work.
>
> But it isn't just in business records management. We see this need in every type of organization, from the highest level, sophisticated multinational company to local art museums and historical societies working totally with volunteer staff. They all need to figure out how to deal with the knowledge that has been built up as their organizations grew, and they need a strategy for figuring out how to deal with it. That's their knowledge strategy.
>
> The development and maintenance of a mature and effective knowledge services strategy also has the potential to prevent and resolve a myriad of legal issues, with considerable cost savings along the way. After all, knowledge – comprehensive, shared knowledge – is what the lawyers, judges, and government regulators want, but they need some sort of verification, "defensibility" if you will, that the knowledge they are obtaining is complete and accurate. This is why the knowledge services audit and measuring knowledge services are critical: if done correctly, with preconceptions acknowledged and managed so results are embraced and implemented, they provide powerful evidence that the organization is, in fact, walking the walk, and not just talking the talk.

So before the knowledge strategist and the knowledge services team can develop and implement that knowledge strategy, they determine how well they are managing knowledge services. Once they know what the problems are – and happy situations when they establish that what they are doing is right – they can then go forward with developing and implementing their knowledge strategy, their knowledge services strategic framework. (Kershaw, 2016)

Proposing a recommended strategy for developing a knowledge services strategic framework (a strategy for a strategy?) begins with a few simple core actions. For these steps, our inspiration could be what Simon Sinek refers to as addressing the "why?" of our exercise, before we get to the "what?" and the "how?" By making use of Sinek's system, we ensure that we have an explanation – a reason – for what we propose to do.

Developing the knowledge services strategic framework is our purpose. That's what this effort is all about. It's why you are reading this book. It is the development of the knowledge services strategic framework – which when developed and implemented becomes in essence the organization's knowledge strategy – that drives our purpose, and the book is primarily targeted to people who are themselves employed as knowledge strategists, as well as others who aspire to this type of work. The book is also offered as a background and planning document for enterprise leaders who are interested in hiring knowledge strategists – described in Chapter 1, Section 1.4 – to provide leadership for addressing the organization's knowledge-sharing challenges.

Nevertheless, the strategic framework the knowledge strategist expects to develop is based on an even earlier step on which he or she must focus attention. The knowledge strategist must take the *idea* of the knowledge services strategic framework – the organization's knowledge strategy – forward before strategy development can begin. And what are the component parts of that idea? What is it we wish to think about, to examine before we start discussing knowledge services and the organizational knowledge culture with colleagues and managers? As I've indicated, to my way of thinking, preparing a knowledge services strategic framework begins with Simon Sinek's "golden circle," put forward in his 2009 book *Start with Why: How Great Leaders Inspire Everyone to Take Action*. Often referred to as "the golden circle" because of an image he uses effectively in the book, Sinek's concept is explained in what is often referred to as the third most-viewed video on TED Talk, *Simon Sinek: How Great Leaders Inspire Action* (Sinek, 2009).

Using this golden circle for building the knowledge services strategic framework, the knowledge strategist starts with "why?" Asking that basic question even before moving further into the process provides direction that an action is going to be taken, something is going to be done: Why are we doing this? Why, in this case, am I proposing a strategic framework for knowledge services, as an approach for managing intellectual capital in the organization where I am employed? Is there some driver or particular situation that needs to be addressed? Is there a knowledge-sharing problem that requires a solution? Or a knowledge-sharing innovation that can be undertaken, for the benefit of the organization?

I now put forward a suggestion I hope will be useful, that the knowledge strategist and his or her colleagues codify what they know about knowledge services and about how some of the ideas contained in the knowledge services approach might match what they have identified as a subject they need to address as they develop the knowledge services strategic framework. And in moving forward, a critical consideration requires understanding that there is probably no single proposal or framework that works for all companies and organizations. Indeed, it might even be said – since no two companies or organizations are exactly alike – that there is no way to prepare a single framework that can be guaranteed to work in all situations, and the unique attributes of each environment must be taken into consideration. So what the knowledge strategist has here is a guide, a planning tool to help the strategic development team as it investigates the the steps for building the knowledge services strategic framework for the organization.

To simplify the effort, remember that it is the knowledge strategist who is in charge of the process. To begin, give the team, working group, or community of practice a name ("Knowledge Services Working Group" will do for now) and move forward with the knowledge services strategic framework initiative. In management language, that is exactly what it is: a specific strategic initiative (defined in the management literature as a task or process managers – in this

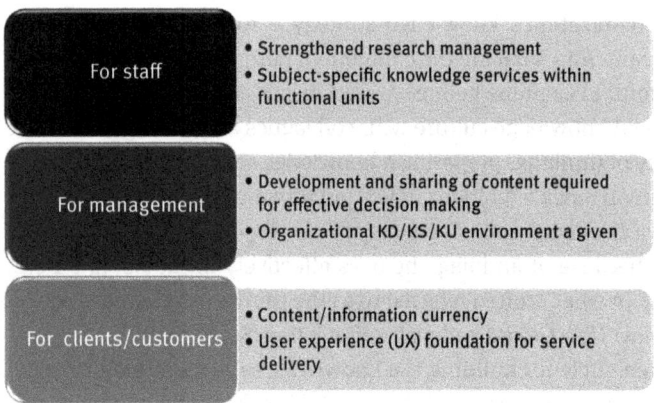

Figure 2.5: Strategy development: Purpose and implications.

case the knowledge strategist – use to transform a vision into practice). In many situations having to do with the methods teams use to determine the benefits of the strategy, a trio of steps has been identified in a paper about how strategists succeed in strategy development by working on a regular basis with senior executives. The steps to take:
1. Involve the top team, and the board, in periodically revisiting corporate aspirations and making any big, directional changes in strategy required by changes in the global forces at work on a company.
2. Create a rigorous, ongoing management process for formulating the specific strategic initiatives needed to close gaps between the current trajectory of the company and its aspirations.
3. Convert these initiatives into an operating reality by formally integrating the strategic-management process with your financial-planning processes (a change that usually requires also moving to more continuous, rolling forecasting and budgeting approaches) (Bradley et al. 2012).

These directions will fall into place as we move forward with studying the process for the development of the knowledge services strategic framework, but for an initial connection they can be addressed by the knowledge strategist and the strategic framework development team now. With the first, as has been suggested often in these pages, linking the knowledge services strategic framework – the organization's knowledge strategy – to the organization's specific management mission is critical, and the essential relationship for making this happen occurs when one (or more) of the senior enterprise leaders commits to the support of the strategy. The management process, too, under the good leadership of the knowledge strategist provides the operational and aspirational structure for the strategy's success as it is developed and implemented and directed in support of the organization as a knowledge culture. And the strategic-management process does indeed move to "more continuous, rolling forecasting and budgeting approaches" as these important changes in the organization's management of its intellectual capital and higher-level knowledge sharing are realized.

At this point, a useful first step for the knowledge strategist is to provide colleagues (and any other interested parties) with a simplified general description of knowledge services and the organizational knowledge strategy. Putting together a discussion document based on the following content can be an easy and convenient approach (and if it works better to put this content in language or phraseology more appropriate to the organization, feel free to re-work these steps to match what works in the organization). The following ideas should be sufficient to begin the conversation:

Who Knows What?
> Use Knowledge Services to Manage Intellectual Capital

Every business and organization runs into snags managing what its people know. It doesn't matter whether the enterprise is for-profit, not-for-profit, or non-profit. Identifying the organization's intellectual capital – the knowledge developed, shared, and used by the workers and all others affiliated with the organization – is an ongoing challenge. The best way to meet this challenge is to utilize knowledge services.

What is knowledge services? Knowledge services is the name given to a practical solution for knowledge sharing. It is made up of three elements:

- Information management: acquiring information, maintaining it, distributing it to those who need it, and ultimately disposing of the information, through archiving or deletion.
- Knowledge management (KM): working with the organization's intellectual capital – the combined knowledge of all organizational stakeholders – KM is the knowledge services element that enables the capture, development, sharing, and utilization of organizational knowledge for the benefit of the organization.
- Strategic learning: training and learning – in any format, formal or informal – that when acquired leads to better performance in the workplace, in support of the organizational mission.

How does knowledge services work? The process is relatively simple:
1. A knowledge-sharing problem or a proposed knowledge-sharing innovation is identified. Here's what you do:
    a. Define the problem or articulate the proposed innovation.
    b. Describe the background – how did the subject come up?
    c. Focus on the "why?" Why solve the problem or undertake the innovation? What will be the benefit?
2. Conduct a knowledge services audit/evaluation. Among the points you will address are:
    a. Whose work is affected by the problem or would be affected by the proposed innovation? How?
    b. Identify knowledge-sharing gaps.
    c. Identify related procedures (perhaps in other departments or business units) that are working well – can these be replicated or adapted to solve the problem? Or will the implementation of the proposed innovation be of benefit?
    d. Establish recommendations from the audit findings.
3. Develop a knowledge services strategy. Use these steps as your road map:
    a. Establish how each knowledge services element (information management, KM, and strategic learning) contributes to the solution or supports the proposed innovation.

b. Determine how each knowledge services element affects the removal (or lessens the impact) of identified barriers or impediments?
   c. Will change be required? If so, will change management be accepted so the change can be implemented?
   d. Likewise, determine if the solution to the problem or the implementation of the innovation requires training/strategic learning; if so, how will the training/strategic learning process be managed?
   e. Create a feedback loop by assigning metrics in order to measure the efficacy of the implemented knowledge services solution or the proposed innovation.
4. Devise an implementation plan for your knowledge services strategy. Your responses to these questions provide your deliverable:
   a. What recommended actions are proposed?
   b. What is a reasonable timeline?
   c. What resources will be required (staff time, new staff, financial resources, etc.)?
   d. Who owns the strategy? Who has implementation responsibility and oversight?

Examples. If you and your team wish to review situations in which a knowledge services strategy has provided an enterprise-wide knowledge-sharing solution, look at the following. Each of these describes an opportunity typical of the changes that can realized with a knowledge services strategic framework in place:

- In a multi-office public relations firm, the open-access (for all authorized employees) repository for project reports has no controlled, specific findability standards; tagging is informal and usually the responsibility of newer employees with limited knowledge-sharing experience and/or training.
- In a company active in petroleum exploration, knowledge sharing is seriously impacted by a rash of retirements and transfers; senior management has appointed a working group to devise an expertise database to be incorporated into the onboarding process for future employees, to capture skills, specific project contributions, etc. The database will be maintained throughout each employees' tenure, with the goal of providing a structured knowledge-sharing description of the employee's work, to be used when the employee leaves the company.
- A large multi-national development organization – responsible to a board of directors composed of political leaders of several countries – is required to operate with separate and free-standing research units in each field office; the research units are not connected and oversight is the responsibility of individual managers in the field offices.
- Enterprise leadership in a limited-partnership healthcare organization recently conducted an environmental scan focused on the role of knowledge use, KM, and knowledge services in the organization; the findings of the environmental scan are not available for the organization's chief strategy officer and the planning team's consideration.

For each situation, and probably any others under consideration, the "why?" is clear: there is a problem that needs to be solved or an innovation to be organized and implemented and, in our work, it is a situation that affects the quality of knowledge sharing in the organization (or in some specified part of the organization). The knowledge services business unit's own strategic plan for creating the knowledge services strategy framework (the "how?") is the knowledge services process described above, with supporting activities and exceptions relevant to each. The activity to be undertaken (the "what?") is the exploration and development of a plan for addressing the wide variety of methodologies that could be used for identifying and addressing the knowledge-sharing issues under discussion.

Knowledge services in practice: putting KM to work. With this background, we begin our transition from considering the fundamentals of knowledge services as a strategic approach to managing intellectual capital. We are now thinking about identifying how we can use knowledge services in our work, how we can move from the theoretical to the practical and build a strategic framework for knowledge services that supports and enables the organizational knowledge culture. In the process, we move through two useful steps, with each providing examples from the world of knowledge services that can illustrate ideas, concepts, and practices that can be used in creating or enhancing the management of knowledge services in our own organization. In the first, we consider some of the reasons why we must think about knowledge services in "real-world" terms. In the second, we look at the highest management standards for knowledge services, standards that have evolved into what we like to think of as "world-class" levels of management and service delivery for this important enterprise function.

In any discipline, theory is useful for providing the model, the standard, or the ideal for performance. While theory – generally agreed to be a body of rules, ideas, principles, and techniques that applies to the discipline – might capture the essence of the discipline and the goals of its practitioners, theory alone cannot take us to the desired effects we seek, particularly in the workplace. For many, since we think of "theory" in terms of how theory is distinct from actual practice, theoretical musings on a subject can be nothing more than setting the stage, providing an intellectual or conceptual snapshot of where we want to go or what we want to accomplish. It cannot work by itself or in a theoretical "vacuum," as we all know from experience as one or another of our good ideas crashes when taken "to the floor," as industrial managers describe the experience. We learn the hard way that we must test our theories before they become actionable.

Moving these thoughts into the knowledge-centric workplace, we also know – from experience and from many years of management science as a discipline

– that workers cannot (or perhaps are not inclined to) apply tools, techniques, or concepts unless they are directly applicable to work, so we must acknowledge that moving to a knowledge services framework will be a futile exercise unless the people affiliated with the larger enterprise, its employees and other stakeholders, can quickly recognize the advantages available to them – individually – if they begin to think about KD/KS/KU in their work.

Connected to this is a similar consideration. The move to the practical obviously requires a commitment to KD/KS/KU, but knowledge workers must be incentivized to develop and utilize a KD/KS/KU framework, a formidable challenge in any circumstance but when dealing with how people manage information, knowledge, and the strategic learning activities in their business lives, the challenge becomes considerably more difficult to overcome.

To meet such challenges, we must look to the value proposition for knowledge services, to build a business case for incorporating KD/KS/KU into the working lives of employees in the organization. Establishing the organizational or management value for knowledge requires giving attention to a number of special activities, such as identifying strategic opportunities for demonstrating how KD/KS/KU makes a difference in performance or impacts the bottom-line of an activity or undertaking. Similarly, focusing on projects with limited or short-term payoff gets the KD/KS/KU success story before organizational stakeholders quickly, providing them with the opportunity to think about how that same sort of effort or activity might impact some task or assignment in their business unit or their own work. Particularly important in meeting these challenges is the development of meaningful measures of progress and demonstrated results; nothing makes a greater impression than the relevance of a solution, and if any KD/KS/KU activity or product can be branded as "relevant" and its operational impact clearly and succinctly stated, there is no question but that the same activity or product will be looked at in other functional units to determine if it can provide equal success there.

How do these fortuitous circumstances come about? How are such desired effects realized in other functional units throughout the organization? Particularly important in this context, what role does the knowledge strategist play in establishing the knowledge culture, and what are the specifics of using knowledge services as the methodology for doing so? As we move from the theoretical of KM to the practical of knowledge services, a first example might look at the much-described embedded information specialist approach, a KD/KS/KU technique which in the early days of knowledge services was called "insourcing." First identified as a specific technique in the pharmaceutical and mass entertainment (read "theme parks") industries, insourcing happens when a specific product development team or other working group brings a member of the knowledge services staff into the group. The embedded knowledge strategist is identified as and performs as a regular member of the team, working as the team's information/knowledge/strategic learning specialist. He or she works with all team members and at all levels to ensure that they are using the best applications for managing the information they need to utilize, that they understand how to share that information and knowledge, and – bringing strategic learning into the picture – not only sharing the information and knowledge but working with fellow team members as the information transitions into practical, useful, and tangible knowledge for the success of the team in completing its work.

Another example takes us to the other end of the knowledge services spectrum, to a large multi-national organization that has, through a variety of iterations, evolved from the rather unsophisticated but well-meaning (and well-funded) organization it was sixty years ago, when it was created to support research in its field. As it happens, much of the organization's present work continues to require many of the same approaches that were required throughout the organization's history.

For this organization, it has been clearly established that without a combined structure for managing information and knowledge related to prior projects (without, for example, a single entry point for similar projects completed over the years), and without a commitment to strategic learning to ensure that prior knowledge is available, the organization is facing an unwieldy and awkward future. Whether that prior knowledge is structured knowledge (i.e., captured in published documents, project reports, organizational archives, and the like) or unstructured knowledge (i.e., informal documents, assorted files "born" digital, correspondence, the memories of people who worked on the projects, and so forth), it is an important organizational asset and it needs to be available for the future. In this situation, the convergence of the three elements of knowledge services – working together as an over-arching management methodology and service delivery framework enterprise-wide – positions the organization for providing a single approach that will, in fact, enable the company to avoid a difficult future and continue its work within its markets, and possibly beyond them to new markets as they are identified.

In a third example, we have a very different organization, a medium-sized specialty chemical firm that has taken advantage of a structural re-organization to create an operational function that combines the company's specialized library, a knowledge sharing group, a strategic learning group, and a function devoted to internal communications. While still new, this combined function is finding opportunities for integrated approaches, with "integrated" in this case having two distinct aspects.

First, the combined efforts of the company's specialized library staff's expertise with external information and its very good customer approach were linked with the organization's knowledge-sharing technology expertise. Then, in a second integration, that combined activity was further matched up with knowledge delivery expertise in the learning and graphics production groups. Together, this integration activity results in a comprehensive and high quality application for the knowledge customer. And there are even more benefits, for in this case the integration was structured to connect this knowledge-sharing expertise with the business processes of the client group, resulting in the design of a knowledge-sharing system for process development that involved recommendations for changes in the actual workflow of individuals.

Thanks to the commitment and enthusiasm of senior management sponsorship, the changes were actually undertaken and not simply talked about, with the inherent synergies of the combination of functions – integrated together in a package that provides high-value realization and quality – ensuring adoption with the customer.

In all three examples, we see the value of an enterprise-wide approach to a knowledge culture. When the role of knowledge as an organizational asset is recognized and exploited and the successful implementation of a knowledge services solution leads to the success enterprise management is seeking, we are in that desired state Kenneth Hatten and Stephen R. Rosenthal refer to with their version of the knowledge culture (which they describe with a slight semantic twist as the "knowing culture"). Hatten and Rosenthal urge individual knowledge workers – among whom we include knowledge strategists, particularly those with knowledge services management responsibility – to "prepare for change by increasing our awareness of what we do or do not know." In doing so, knowledge workers and knowledge strategists learn to deal with the two types of knowledge that enable that preparation: "the knowledge you need to boost your performance when you know your organizational objectives [and] the knowledge that will help you define new objectives and the strategies to pursue them" (Hatten and Rosenthal, 2001).

As these examples demonstrate, in the embedding of knowledge workers into specific projects, in the development of single points of entry for enterprise-wide access, and in the integration of information, knowledge, and strategic learning delivery for higher-value service delivery, it was recognized in each parent organization that in the larger scheme of things, there was a need to "do something" about knowledge transfer, that KD/KS/KU as an operational function was not performing at its best. As various discussions among the several stakeholders were initiated, and with everyone understanding that the solution would of necessity be context-specific, the intellectual explorations began to unfold. In most cases, the discussions would have suggested a number of practical, "real-world" ideas, goals, objectives, solutions (even, perhaps, a few desiderata: "wouldn't it be nice if we could...?"). As these were winnowed down, and as resource allocation, staff time, and other enablers and/or barriers were identified, it would have become clear that there were solutions that could be pursued, solutions which would involve attention to how information, knowledge, and strategic learning are converged and how, in that convergence, practical and workable solutions could be sought.

What happens, of course, is that when there is concern that the KD/KS/KU process is not functioning at its best, organizational knowledge workers (often the company's specialist librarians or other senior knowledge strategists) talk about the problems and look for opportunities to resolve the issues related to finding a knowledge services solution. They then recognize that there is a list of subjects that must be addressed, and as they pursue the knowledge services idea or solution, they identify specific management tools and techniques that work in other management environments and can be expected to work in the knowledge-centric enterprise as well:

1. *The knowledge services audit/opportunity assessment* is a systematic examination of an organization's knowledge resources. Despite the term "audit," it is not dealing with these resources in a purely financial way, though this certainly will be considered (see #5 below). Often referred to as a catalog or inventory of a company's intellectual infrastructure, the knowledge services audit – as an audit – actually goes beyond identifying knowledge assets to evaluating those assets and how they are used in support of the organizational mission.
2. *Strategic planning* has been variously defined, and in the knowledge services environment refers most often to developing vision, mission, and values statements for aligning knowledge services with organizational priorities. With strategic planning, we identify critical steps – including change management and change implementation – for launching or enhancing service delivery for the benefit of the larger organization.
3. *Strategic learning* as an element of the knowledge services discipline is usually thought of as the critical foundation for KD/KS/KU, since the way people interact with one another and understand their work environment as a learning/teaching organization affects how knowledge is used in support of the organizational mission.
4. *Awareness-raising, client relationship management (CRM), customer service, and marketing* provide the necessary entrepreneurial perspective for the successful management of knowledge services and ensure that all affiliated persons know about and understand the KD/KS/KU purpose and the business value of knowledge in their work.

5. *Return-on-investment (ROI), metrics, and measurement* constitute one of the most valuable elements of the knowledge services construct, with relevance and effectiveness measures providing a direct correlation with the parent organization's other constituent functions and determining enterprise-wide success.
6. *The relationship between technology and knowledge* and establishing how technology is used to connect people with knowledge have become critical components in determining the success of knowledge services management in the larger organization. KD/KS/KU and its connection with workplace success is seriously impacted by how well knowledge services addresses increasingly digital and electronic information formats.
7. *The evolution of the collaborative workplace* affects organizational management in many ways, and the role of KD/KS/KU, resource sharing, and the management of knowledge services continues to provide enterprise leadership with useful and measurable success opportunities for meeting organizational mission-critical goals.
8. *Strategic project management* is no longer thought of as something "extra" or to be looked at "when needed." In today's knowledge-centric workplace, project management and a commitment to understanding and relating to new structures and frameworks requires those with management responsibility for knowledge services to take on important enterprise-wide leadership roles.
9. *Personal knowledge management (PKM)* continues to bring forward demands from organizational colleagues for guidance in learning about (and utilizing) new products and services. In the knowledge services environment, the ever-growing presence of social networking and other Web 2.0 tools offers challenging opportunities for service delivery.
10. *Competencies, skills, and qualifications for knowledge leaders* in the organizations (and specifically for managing knowledge services for the larger enterprise) all require greater and continuous attention to strategic learning, to ensure that classic management and executive skills keep in step with the demands of the knowledge-centric workplace.

All of these constituent elements come together in support of the knowledge culture. By understanding and alluding to their role in the development of the strategic framework for knowledge services, the organization's leaders are able to ensure that the knowledge services function they seek to establish (or strengthen) will meet the KD/KS/KU requirements of the larger enterprise.

World-class knowledge services. Examining knowledge services management processes in different types of settings and with a number of different projects, emerging trends in the management of the modern, "world-class" knowledge services function have been identified (Harriston et al. 2003). Using interviews, observations, and research conducted in connection with a variety of consultancy projects for strategic planning, management reviews, information and knowledge management audits, learning audits, content management/collection development studies, information sharing and analysis projects, physical access and space-planning studies, and similar activities, this group of attributes has been characterized as describing the fundamental qualities for world-class knowledge services management.

In the study, an assortment of knowledge services business units were examined, including operations in commercial research and development organizations, public scientific institutions (including those in the academic R&D environment), journalism and editorial offices, international financial organizations, scientific and research organizations in the defense community, professional associations and trade groups, philanthropic organizations, and research organizations ("think tanks") that exist to conduct research and provide reports and documents to influence or, in some cases, aid in the implementation of policies developed for the larger societal common good. The list is impressive, and when connected with examples from some of these organizations provides guidelines for the development of a strategic knowledge services framework for the organization:

1. The world-class knowledge services business unit is understood within its organization to be *managed from a holistic perspective*, and its work is integrated into the larger business purpose of the parent organization. *Example*: In a large research and publishing organization located in Cambridge, MA the former specialized library has transitioned to a central knowledge nexus or focus, serving as an enterprise-wide knowledge services business unit. The products and services offered include identifying knowledge needed in the organization, building project teams to work with other divisions, constructing databases and corporate intranet resources, and developing other tools that enable the library (now the "Knowledge Center") to publish directories, guides to research resource collections, and similar products for the company's entire workforce.
2. *Cross-functional collaboration* (with no disincentives for collaboration) is a critical feature of the knowledge services unit's operation. *Example*: In a research and development organization in Pretoria, South Africa the staff of the IT department has teamed up with members of the research asset management unit to work together on a project to enable staff to access all organizational content – structured and unstructured – through a common, single-access entry point. From the users' perspectives, the location of the

content is irrelevant, but the research asset management staff, most of whom are research librarians, understand the content and how it is used in this particular research environment. In working with IT, the expertise of both units is put to work in a collaborative exercise that benefits all staff.

3. *The knowledge services unit is recognized as the central information/knowledge connection for the organization.* *Example*: In Northern Virginia, in one of the Washington suburbs, a large GSE – government sponsored enterprise – was created by the U.S. Congress to work with the home financing industry. With the whole-hearted support of senior management, the knowledge services staff has built a knowledge services "hub" for the company. The company is a large organization with a multi-faceted operational framework, and having established one functional unit as the preferred (and first-thought-of) source for information, knowledge, and strategic learning enables everyone in the company to reap the benefits.

4. The service ethos in the knowledge services unit builds on *higher value services*. Queries brought to the knowledge services staff demand highly intensive approaches to research. There are few "simple" queries, as users generally find this type of information for themselves. *Example*: At an energy utility in California, the research management staff uses a knowledge services template to provide clients with information about a wide range of documents, complete with full-text search capability, providing links for customers so they can get to websites, documents residing in other websites (at the Department of Energy, for example), internal reports, project profiles, energy benchmarks, and the like. An important capability – recognized by the librarian and incorporated into the catalog database – is a group of fields for linking to specific experts or past employees or consultants who have worked on or otherwise been part of a project. This capability gives the knowledge customer the opportunity to interact with someone who has had past experience in the subject of the research, but it is designed to be used carefully. The template has a built-in "privacy-factor," as it might be called, and does not permit the searcher to contact the other person directly. It merely identifies the person and describes their connection with the subject being researched, but requires a "pass-along" from one of the research management staff.

5. *Adding value* to information services, products, and consultations is standard practice in the knowledge services unit. *Example*: In a large membership organization devoted to a special-interest activities group, located in the American Mid-West, the organization sought to strengthen its archives by asking its older members to contribute their memories to the organization's historical record, for incorporation into the organization's recognized archives on the specific subject. The knowledge services staff developed a

member participation survey which was distributed to all members through the organization's website, its magazines and other publications, and through the membership mailing system. Members were invited to key their thoughts into a user-friendly database, in order to provide their own content and deliver first-hand information for the organizational archives. The organization is thus enabled to serve as the "archives of record" for the institution's specific subject. The project could have been facilitated through various other departments and units of the organization, but with the knowledge services staff skills and competencies in working with reference queries, varying user expertise levels, and similar background experiences, the knowledge services unit not only enabled the activity to go forward but strengthened its own visibility and value with the larger organization.

6. *Awareness building* within the constituent user base is a given, as is marketing. There is no assumption that everyone who can use the organization's knowledge assets knows about them or knows and understands all the services that are available through the knowledge services business unit. *Example*: At one of the world's foremost cancer research centers, the research library has developed a tool which provides clients with a listing of internally produced publications, which clients can then browse, print, export, or connect to the full text. Having identified the different elements customers need to see, which includes not only external information but documentation about research conducted in the cancer center, the tool is an example of how KD/KS/KU enables connections. As such, it is fundamental to knowledge services delivery, linking together what the customers themselves have created, and in doing so enabling the research library staff to meet its goal of functioning literally as the connecting point for the entire organization.

7. *Customer needs are tracked on an on-going basis*, as is their satisfaction with service delivery. Customer service and CRM are key elements of the management picture in the knowledge services business unit. *Example*: In the Pacific Northwest, knowledge services is provided in an engineering firm through the facilities of the firm's Knowledge Resources Division. The division incorporates the firm's IT function, the technical library, records and archives management, and a presentations and visual resources department. During the past five years, the division has sought to keep track of customer needs, and a recent activity was to devise a member satisfaction survey for distribution to all identified knowledge services customers. The survey was designed to provide quantifiable data about how customers use the information, knowledge, and strategic learning content obtained through the Knowledge Resources Division. A key element of the survey was to determine cost effectiveness for knowledge services customers (from their own perspective) and to identify customers' preferences in types and formats of service delivery.

To this end, the working group responsible for the project included several members of the customer group, to ensure that the customer perspective was included in the study. With the survey results, the knowledge services management team has been able to re-direct certain activities to other operational functions and to eliminate other activities altogether, thus freeing up resources for the provision of new services required by knowledge services customers.

8. *Strategic learning is recognized as a critical organizational function,* and continuous efforts are made to review training and learning needs and to provide opportunities for organizational employees to gain new skills and competencies to help them with their work. *Example*: At an international financial services company in Houston, TX the manager of the knowledge services unit identified a need to orient new hires, particularly in terms of their understanding and their potential utilization of the company's knowledge services products and tools. At the same time, there were indications that usage of the company's enterprise-wide knowledge bank was decreasing, and an abbreviated knowledge services audit determined that employees other than new hires needed additional learning opportunities. Working with the company's internal training unit located in the human capital department, the manager of the knowledge services operation was able to not only structure a strategic learning framework for the specific goal (basic training for new hires and enhanced learning for regular staff), but the level of strategic learning overall was enhanced and the knowledge services business unit was eventually given full responsibility for all strategic training and learning for the company.

9. *New paradigms of service delivery* (including the development of specific products and services by internal staff, as well as those purchased or subscribed to from external vendors) are *recognized as opportunities* for enhancing knowledge services for the parent organization with which the knowledge services unit is affiliated. *Example*: In a large company in upstate New York, the manager of the knowledge services unit works with clients as they advise retailers and manufacturers about quality assurance in their products, to assist them in meeting regulatory, quality, and performance requirements, and to help them assess manufacturing facilities to ensure social and legal compliance, review processes, and audit capabilities. With this wide range of products and services, the company takes knowledge services seriously and to meet the demand, the knowledge services unit created a suite of tools that specifically support KD/KS/KU. The first project was an enterprise-wide search engine. After that, the unit developed a yellow pages-type solution so people can connect with other people, and this is linked to a collection of CVs because much of the company's work has to do with identifying inspectors,

experts, and technical contractors, both from within the company and externally. Together, these products create an experts' database that brings important benefits to everyone in the company.
10. *Advocates and users recognize the value of the knowledge services unit* and make efforts to see that it is supported and that sponsors are recruited to demonstrate their commitment to the role of knowledge services in achieving the organizational mission. *Example*: At a multinational technology services company with headquarters in North Carolina, the director with management responsibility for knowledge services became aware of continuing interest by some of the top executives in the organization, noting that several of them were sending staff to conduct research which was then utilized in executive level reports, public statements, and similar non-scientific products. Contacting all of the senior management staff via an internal e-mail message, the director invited them to "apply" to sponsor the knowledge services unit and in the application to demonstrate how they would say or speak about, model, and reward their (and their staff's) use of corporate knowledge services. To everyone's surprise, all of the executives "applied" and the company now has an annual rotation of corporate sponsors for knowledge services who have, among other responsibilities, the obligation to demonstrate to other senior managers in the company how knowledge services impacts the work of his or her office.

The knowledge services strategic framework: a recommended strategy. As the organization moves to develop a knowledge culture for facilitating enterprise-wide KD/KS/KU, fundamental questions must be asked of organizational leaders, including management at all levels and knowledge strategists with (or who would be designated to have) management responsibility for knowledge services. First and foremost, enterprise leadership must establish (or agree to look into, if the issue has not been raised before at the senior management level) the value of the transformation effort. Whether the objective is to transition an existing functional unit with knowledge services responsibility (such as a specialized library, research department, information center, etc.) into a knowledge services unit with enterprise-wide responsibility or to create a wholly new business unit to manage and deliver knowledge services, the following questions must be addressed:

– Is there an organizational (read: enterprise leadership) desire for a knowledge culture? What is the level of support and enthusiasm for such an activity, especially among senior managers?
– In the larger organization, what is the philosophical approach to service delivery? Regardless of the type of service, how is service delivery managed

in various departments and functional units (especially units not necessarily connected with "research" or "knowledge")?
– Is there a leadership team (ideally made up of experienced knowledge workers in the larger enterprise, regardless of their department or functional affiliation) for undertaking a major change in the management of knowledge services throughout the organization?
– Will it be possible to build an enterprise-wide knowledge services strategic framework in order to incorporate KD/KS/KU into the larger organizational culture?
– As information management, knowledge management, and strategic learning take on the defining characteristics of the twenty-first century, is there a willingness in the larger organization to move to an integrated digital environment in which collaboration and KD/KS/KU are the norm?
– Finally, can enterprise leadership commit to the support of a knowledge-centric opportunity-focused and results-focused structure?

The effort begins with a review of the current organizational picture and the management of knowledge services in the larger enterprise. Usually informal and built on conversation and anecdotal descriptions, the review captures ideas about how knowledge is thought about in the organization and, particularly, how the broader subject of knowledge and knowledge services is perceived as affecting enterprise success. The result is an organizational snapshot of knowledge services in this particular enterprise, with its particular environment and larger organizational culture.

First steps
1. Build a leadership team. Even early discussions will require the support and enthusiasm of people who are well-versed and understand the role of knowledge in the larger organizational environment. Identify and seek participation from knowledge workers who are comfortable with organization development, strategic planning, strategic partnership development, strategic learning, and KD/KS/KU.
2. Learn about and confirm the culture and values of the organization. Nothing kills a project more effectively than one that is misaligned with the user community's culture and values. Learning and discussing this topic and then incorporating the language and concepts learned in the early proposal stages of the project will ensure alignment and the best possible user uptake and value.
3. Related to the above, give some attention to developing a "conversational" knowledge culture in the larger organization through identifying and engaging

knowledge workers who can be effective advocates and champions and, if at the senior level, are willing to sign on as knowledge services sponsors. Bring organizational politics into the process and use political skills to achieve your objectives.

4. Learn about your environment and engage your potential user base. Obviously your team is starting with considerable anecdotal information and probably more than enough information based on the team members' own observations. Talk about what you know.
5. Move on to more formal studies. A knowledge services audit (or the same tool with a more positive and optimistic point of view, if referred to as an "opportunity assessment"), surveys, interviews with executives, and the use of benchmarking studies are tools that will be used, probably with other tools as well, at this stage. Make use of MBWA (Management-by-Walking-Around), identifying and then listening to people who are interested in knowledge services.
6. Challenge your mission. The opportunity to implement knowledge services will likely cause you to stretch or propose stretching the very mission or purpose of your role or function in the larger enterprise. This is an essential exercise because it forces you to think of the largest possible impact of your initiatives. Be prepared to recognize that this enterprise mindset can be at once energizing and threatening, and keep in mind that relying on solid values, good research, and strong sponsorship will help ensure success.
7. Create an enterprise vision for knowledge services. Incorporate your knowledge of the culture, the enterprise needs, and the changing mission and values of the enterprise to create a compelling and clear future vision for the larger organization – and your role and that of all parallel information-, knowledge-, or strategic learning-focused business units in the organization. This step will be a critical foundation to creating relevant and innovative enterprise goals.

Develop your activities

8. Find a sponsor. Before you get much further along with your planning, identify and seek commitment from a senior-level manager to support your efforts, even if you are still only in the "thinking-about-it" stage. Get to know that senior manager (it probably is someone with whom you already have relationship of one sort or another, and you recognize one another in the workplace). Encourage that person to come along, and explain to them how important it is to say, model, and reward employees and fellow executives who support the value of the initiative you are thinking about pursuing.
9. Put together a knowledge services strategic framework planning team or working group and to make the effort easier, use your experience with the development and implementation of the knowledge services audit. Begin to Identify people in your leadership team (see Item # 1, above) who have

either expressed interest in the subject or who can be pressed into service because of their particular skills and expertise. Recognize that this activity is going to require time, commitment, and much hard work, and it is the type of exercise that will often (indeed, can be expected to) require a level of commitment beyond the usual tasks associated with people's work. There are people who are willing to go "the extra mile." For this process, the planning team members must understand that they will be required to do so.

10. In addition to bringing actual "workers" into your working group or planning team, you and they should make special efforts to identify people who are accustomed to working with information, knowledge, and strategic learning. (That may be the person in charge of training activities in human resources, if that is the function in which training and strategic learning activities "reside.") Bring these people in as advocates or "interested parties," people to whom you and your working group can go for questions that are best discussed "on the floor" rather than in theory or in a management office.

11. Set specific goals. The SMART (Specific-Measurable-Achievable-Relevant-Time-bound) method – one of the most popular techniques for goal-setting – can assist the planning team as it develops tangible and realistic proposals.

12. Prepare the Statement of Work (SoW), again, based on your experience in setting up the same process when you and your team designed and implemented the knowledge services audit. Before you get too far along in thinking about knowledge services in the larger organization, it is helpful to attempt to specify the scope and details of your projected effort and describe any conditions or particular or unique environmental situations that might affect the work. Later attention to a more formal terms of reference document will define the work and include schedules, timelines, etc., but at this point you need a brief (and flexible) background document in place, just to ensure that all stakeholders are in agreement and have a shared understanding of the value of the effort.

13. Propose plans. With the input and engagement of strong sponsors and champions, devise and propose plans that are in alignment with the culture, methods, and procedures in your enterprise, using the implementation framework described above or, if your organization has its own planning framework, use those concepts as a guide and incorporate them concepts into the corporate framework.

Implement, execute, and control your activities

14. With one or two of the organization's recognized knowledge leaders serving as a team lead (or leads), the planning group will begin to coalesce into subgroups or focus teams, with specific areas of responsibility and established collaborative and cooperative links. Communities of practice (probably

but not necessarily informal) will be set up, and a central group will seek to capture the results of the different mapping exercises undertaken to give attention to identified "pain points," ensuring that these are included in the larger planning focus.
15. Invite interested observers (those advocates mentioned above) to attend – as visitors – meetings of the working group. Manage the meetings well and be very specific about staying with the agenda but give the visitors the opportunity to form opinions from their observations about the group's work.
16. Once the effort is underway, the different teams and groups will begin to establish baseline schedules and progress milestones. Documentation standards will be developed next, to ensure that all participants continue to have a clear picture of steps taken and that evaluation methodologies, when appropriate, can be utilized.

Moving forward
17. As the idea of the strategic framework for knowledge services begins to take shape, review goals and expectations developed in early conversations, to determine if everyone is still "speaking the same language." If some of the earlier concepts require adjustment, due to the organizational environment or external forces, make the adjustment and determine whether such changes will seriously alter the direction of your effort. At the same time, carefully monitor participation levels, departmental (or personal) agendas, and other variations that might impact the progress of the move toward a knowledge services framework.
18. At this stage, begin to raise awareness in the organization (or in some parts of the organization) about looking into the development of a knowledge services strategy. Talk about what the benefits might be: staff works better and smarter; there is less frustration from searching for "lost" information, knowledge, and strategic learning content; there will be a healthier, more enabling work environment, with less competition and more collaboration (we like to say moving from "information power" to "relationship power").
19. As plans begin to come together, take the time to develop an implementation program and, when appropriate, initiate efforts to incorporate recommendations and possible changes into formal plans (marketing, business, strategic), to have them in process when they are required.
20. Develop a post-implementation strategy and identify opportunities for organizational re-structuring when required, and for establishing activity patterns that support and strengthen the move toward the development of the strategic framework for knowledge services.

As these efforts begin to show results (even tentative results this early in the work), all staff – and not just knowledge workers – will begin to express interest in what the group is doing and be curious to be kept informed (and invited to participate in bringing knowledge services to their own business units and function). As this happens, these steps will come together in workplace roles that help to establish a straightforward and productive direction for the organization, for bringing the qualities of the knowledge culture, enabled through an enterprise-wide knowledge services strategy – built on knowledge services – into the working lives of its employees, stakeholders, and affiliates.

As stated throughout, our purpose in this book, and particularly in this section, is to provide the knowledge strategist, knowledge workers, strategic knowledge professionals, and all other organizational stakeholders who share their interest in successful knowledge sharing in the organization with guidelines for developing the knowledge services strategic framework, the organizational knowledge strategy. For their review, the following outline can serve as a checklist.

Knowledge Services: A Strategic Framework for the Twenty-First Century Organization – A Guide for Knowledge Strategist. Organizational effectiveness begins with an enterprise-wide knowledge culture, built on a knowledge strategy supported by a knowledge services strategic framework for knowledge development, knowledge sharing, and knowledge utilization (KD/KS/KU). The knowledge strategy matches the organization's business management strategy.

To achieve KD/KS/KU success and to ensure the development of a meaningful knowledge strategy, corporate leaders turn to knowledge strategists.

The knowledge strategist and the knowledge services strategic framework development team begin with the knowledge services audit, developing the knowledge strategy by applying their own background of experiences and expertise to the knowledge services audit findings. These are then incorporated into the knowledge strategy.

The main objectives of the knowledge strategy are:
- To empower staff and increase corporate and organizational efficiency, effectiveness, and accountability by providing easy access to accurate, timely, and relevant information and knowledge and strategic learning content, including procedures that enable all organizational stakeholders to carry out their work effectively, make informed decisions, and promote an organizational culture of learning
- To strengthen internal collaboration and harness the organizational network in order to document and synthesize knowledge, experiences, best practices, and lessons learned
- To establish cost-effective organizational frameworks and systems to support priority knowledge needs, in order to improve evidence-based KD/KS/KU.

1. Why a Knowledge Strategy?
    1.1. Organizational success – however defined – requires an established supportive environment for managing intellectual capital.
    1.2. The knowledge domain is the environment in which intellectual capital is managed, the knowledge; the knowledge strategy provides the blueprint/guidelines for its management.

- 1.3. Understanding the data/information/knowledge/learning background enables collaboration and the application of knowledge for organizational success ("organizational effectiveness").
- 1.4. The knowledge services/knowledge strategy operational function exists as one critical element of the larger, enterprise-wide corporate or organizational structure.
- 1.5. Highest-level professional support in the knowledge domain creates an environment for innovation, contextual decision-making, strengthened research, and knowledge asset management.
2. It's all about *knowledge* and managing the organization's knowledge, its intellectual capital.
    - 2.1. Knowledge
        - 2.1.1. "What is known"
        - 2.1.2. Information ("practical and utilitarian") for action based on insight and experience ("knowledge is information that is used")
        - 2.1.3. Can – and often does – refer to both tacit and explicit knowledge
    - 2.2. Knowledge management (KM)
        - 2.2.1. Usually defined as "working with knowledge"
        - 2.2.2. Also often thought of as managing the knowledge eco-structure
        - 2.2.3. For some knowledge workers, KM focuses on knowledge access through the utilization of an inventory or catalog (formal and/or informal) of the organization's intellectual infrastructure, available to and shared by all stakeholders
    - 2.3. Knowledge services
        - 2.3.1. The *practical* side of KM ("putting KM to work")
        - 2.3.2. Converges information management, KM, and strategic learning
        - 2.3.3. Combines people, processes, and technology for managing information and knowledge assets at all functional levels
3. Why a "Strategy"?
    - 3.1. Strategy – a group of actions or activities that produces an established or agreed-upon goal
        - 3.1.1. Requires focus on the organization's vision, mission, and values
        - 3.1.2. Serves as a blueprint ("road map") for action
        - 3.1.3. Includes milestones for monitoring achievements and assessing results
    - 3.2. Strategic issues (for knowledge strategy): anything in the KD/KS/KU context that causes concern or impacts organizational performance or effectiveness – the level of urgency depends on leadership perspective about each issue
    - 3.3. Strategic issues probably include (but are not limited to):
        - 3.3.1. Organizational structure
        - 3.3.2. Financial planning/management
        - 3.3.3. Information management and information technology
        - 3.3.4. Knowledge services management and delivery
        - 3.3.5. Infrastructure planning/future services
4. Knowledge Strategy *vis-à-vis* Organizational Business Management Strategy
    - 4.1. Knowledge strategy (Drucker *et al.*)

4.1.1. Opportunity focused and results focused
4.1.2. Supports enterprise-wide emphasis on knowledge needs and service-delivery successes for the larger organization
4.1.3. Enables decision making about KD/KS/KU that balances objectives and needs against possible returns for the larger organization
4.2. Separate knowledge strategy? Or knowledge-domain concepts incorporated into the organization business management strategy (Zack: knowledge strategy: "organizational business strategy that takes into account its intellectual resources and capabilities")
5. Preparing the Knowledge Strategy: Establish the Perspective
    5.1. Identify the perspective or point-of-view of the parent or client organization with respect to the development of the knowledge services audit (sometimes referred to as the analytical context)
        5.1.1. Carefully describe how the knowledge strategy is structured on the same basis for both the knowledge services strategic framework development team and management staff with responsibility for the audit (this point-of-view is usually evident in the results of the knowledge services audit)
        5.1.2. Categorize the reason or reasons for the development of the knowledge services strategic framework
            – Solve a problem?
            – Seek an innovative approach to a new product, concept, or activity?
            – Conduct a management review for a group of functional units all focused on knowledge work?
            – Other
    5.2. Identify sponsors, advocates, and champions who have some affiliation with the knowledge-related situation under study; cultivate their understanding of the purpose and goals of the knowledge strategy (their support and enthusiasm will be required to ensure implementation success for the knowledge strategy)
6. Describe the Results of the Knowledge Services Audit
    6.1. Demonstrate the direct connection between the organization's overall business management strategy and the knowledge strategy. Is it clearly established? If not, make it so.
        6.1.1. Company, institution, or organization overview (if not included in the knowledge services audit; if included provide a brief summary)
        6.1.2. Descriptive statement of the company, institution, or organization business management strategy
    6.2. Describe the knowledge services audit findings, in as much detail as required
    6.3. List and explicate recommendations based on the audit findings
    6.4. Use the findings and recommendations of the knowledge services audit to demonstrate how the organization's knowledge strategy will

       6.4.1. Foster a knowledge culture in the larger organization by:
- Establishing the organization as a learning organization
- Providing guidance for establishing enterprise-wide policies and procedures that support knowledge sharing

7. Propose a Core Strategy, including but not limited to such topics as:
    7.1. Enterprise leadership expectations
    7.2. Knowledge services value proposition
    7.3. Employee engagement/knowledge services strategic framework team development
    7.4. Communication and reflection
    7.5. Situational/environmental analysis
    7.6. Priorities and requirements evaluation
    7.7. Organizational strengths (especially relating to knowledge services)
    7.8. Key performance indicators
    7.9. Untapped resources (missed opportunitites?)
    7.10. Technology issues
    7.11. Analysis and evaluation
    7.12. Strategic learning and continuous improvement
8. Propose a Knowledge Strategy Implementation Plan
    8.1. Change management preparation – early in the process, create a change management/strategic learning plan (to ensure buy-in from all affected stakeholders)
    8.2. Identify what's been done already (management needs to know if there has been an earlier approach to the situation under study)
    8.3. Provide a statement of recommended activities, the knowledge services "road map" for the organization or institution
    8.4. Identify required resources for implementing the knowledge strategy
    8.5. Describe required awareness-building and marketing activities
    8.6. Timeline – what will happen when?
    8.7. Describe responsibility assignments – what are the staff requirements for which parts of the knowledge services?
    8.8. Milestones and metrics – establish procedures for monitoring and measuring success along the way; for each milestone ask these questions:
        8.8.1. Who will be receiving the information and making judgments based on the metrics?
        8.8.2. What do these people want (or need) to know?
        8.8.3. How will the metrics be used? Are decisions made based on these metrics?
9. Identify Risks – Does the Knowledge Strategy Involve Risk?
    9.1. What kind of risk?
    9.2. Who is affected?
10. Threats to the Proposed Knowledge Strategy
    10.1. What barriers/impediments are or might be in place

     10.1.1. Environmental scan – if undertaken as part of the knowledge services audit – might reveal possible anticipated threats or barriers; if that content is pertinent it should be summarized and included
     10.1.2. Unanticipated threats or impediments (financial crisis, natural or other disasters, etc. – generally not included in a knowledge strategy)
   10.2. Is there a contingency plan and/or exit strategy, in case the knowledge strategy cannot be implemented or if implemented, does not succeed?
11. Make Your Case and Conclude the Knowledge Services Strategic Framework – The Organizational Knowledge Strategy
   11.1. Collaboration is critical
     11.1.1. Ensure that the entire knowledge strategy development process includes all affiliates (or their representatives) whose work in the corporate or organizational knowledge domain will be affected with the implemented of the knowledge strategy
     11.1.2. Offer a preliminary or draft/interim report for commentary from critical enterprise management or leadership and, if appropriate, from other stakeholders as well
     11.1.3. Review comments submitted and establish a process for incorporating or rejecting specific concerns, strengthening recommendation and/or procedures if required, and publishing and delivering the final strategy document (usually with a presentation to selected leaders or organizational knowledge domain stakeholders)
   11.2. Knowledge strategy
     11.2.1. Is the strategy an end in itself or part of a larger KM/knowledge services function?
     11.2.2. How is the strategy positioned within the company, institution, or organization as a knowledge culture?

2.5 Knowledge Services in Context: Enterprise Content Management (ECM) and Knowledge Asset Management (with Barrie M. Schessler)

In the twenty-first century, the attributes of Alvin Toffler's famously predicted "Third Wave" have become as pervasive and influential as he anticipated (Toffler, 1980). At this point in time, there is no question but that information management has rapidly developed from crude attempts to manage overwhelming amounts of data to an entire industry, with impact on nearly every individual on the planet, even to the genesis of something with even deeper impact, that of "knowledge cultures" in the organizations and businesses where knowledge workers are employed.

It has been an evolution in parallel, a simultaneous development of technology and philosophy, each influencing the other. Over and over, technology opens up new vistas of capability and then culture rushes in to react and exploit and mold the markets and establish uses for that very innovation. Technologically enhanced social networking didn't really boom until applications such as Face Book, Twitter, and LinkedIn became pervasive in the Web 2.1 world; now these applications are essentially just part of life for many people, accessed and used without any particular attention to their existence as an application or tool.

While technology has been the more dramatic and visible element in this parallel development, moving from room-sized computers to fully functional knowledge processors that can be carried in one's hand, cultural and business process shifts have also played an important role, often driving the technology. Indeed, when we speak of the advantages of KD/KS/KU, there is a growing realization in organizations that the messy process of sharing knowledge is more valuable than had been the neat, restricted, and "silo'd" data repositories of yesterday. No one doubts that large-scale, enterprise wide intellectual capital is important to the organization and Prusak and Davenport's characterization of managing knowledge as working with knowledge has opened enormous possibilities for strengthening knowledge value in all organizations.

Knowledge services excels in this modern work environment. The idea of three existing disciplines (information management, knowledge management, and strategic learning) converging and being utilized simultaneously has garnered recognition as a management concept offering a more practical and applicable model that any of the disciplines implemented alone. Through the synergistic combination of strategies relating to these disciplines, organizations can obtain a single point of access for the organization's information, knowledge, and learning infrastructure, providing a number of tangible and measurable benefits.

Such activities naturally capture the attention of organizational leadership because they are efficient and have practical application. An organization's most desired state requires a change in culture, moving to an organizational culture that values and uses shared information and knowledge. This, in turn, can drive enterprise leaders to create actual organizational structures to support the concept and the possibility of creating a "knowledge culture," supported by a "knowledge nexus." It is a pattern that now resonates among many enterprise leaders.

2.5 Knowledge Services in Context: Enterprise Content Management (ECM) — 219

In the usual organizational structure, and in those organizations for which the guidelines of this book are prepared, the organization's knowledge nexus is thought of as something along the lines of "the knowledge services unit" or "the knowledge services center" (my preference is the former). As noted in the section about the duties and responsibilities of the knowledge strategist in Chapter 1, Section 1.4, the work might be service-based (that is, providing a service that is knowledge-focused) and the knowledge strategist responsible for the unit's management should be a managerial or leadership role, perhaps departmental or having to do with one or more functional unit.

In an ideal situation, the work connects to an enterprise-wide knowledge function or activity. Indeed, in the ideal situation which I envision, there is not a particular "place" or knowledge services unit, but a senior management officer (with the title of something along the lines of Chief Knowledge Strategist) with enterprise-wide responsibility, authority, and of course accountability for excellence in knowledge sharing across the organization. In this circumstance, the job description, in supplementing that offered in Chapter 1, Section 1.4, reads more along these lines:

> The Chief Knowledge Strategist owns and leads the strategic development of knowledge services practice at [the organization]. The Chief Knowledge Strategist is responsible for the enterprise-wide management of knowledge services (the convergence of information management, knowledge management, and strategic learning) and in this role has oversight for leveraging internal knowledge, external knowledge and secondary research, and [the organization]'s corporate intranet and the knowledge services management system, including the implementation of [the organization]'s knowledge services strategic framework – [the organization]'s knowledge strategy – to enable depth of analysis for the organization's research and development staff and clients, drive innovation for knowledge-related initiatives, support business strategies, manage organizational learning and development initiatives, and provide guidance, processes, and training relating to knowledge services in support of the organization as a knowledge culture.

In either case, the work of the knowledge strategist represents the new emphasis on the role of knowledge in the operational environment, one in which each organization has embarked on a different way of looking at its intellectual assets, its collective knowledge.

KD/KS/KU is now clearly desired and valued in organizations that are operationalizing the knowledge services concept. Enterprise leaders recognize that the knowledge-centric organization is one in which success at all levels is supported by a willingness to share information, knowledge, and strategic learning. The ability to leverage institutional knowledge for improved research and asset management, for enhanced decision-making, and for accelerated innovation is apparent, with the value proposition resulting from these critical organizational effectiveness factors providing tremendous opportunity for knowledge services leaders.

Technology, especially with technology management facilitating access to and the sharing of content, plays an essential role in the emerging knowledge-centric organization. What is clear is that in order to address the many challenges of the new information age and the now-recognized "knowledge society" (thank you, Peter Drucker), we cannot – and as our organization's knowledge strategists should not – ignore the continuing revolutionary and inevitable impact of IT in the workplace. There is great opportunity for the knowledge strategist to enhance and exploit IT solutions in pursuit of – and in alignment with – leadership's desires for a more knowledge-centric organization.

So if knowledge services and the desire for a knowledge-centric culture provide the impetus and drive, and IT provides the technology, how do the knowledge strategist and enterprise leadership actually put these disciplines to work? The answer for many organizations is Enterprise Content Management (ECM) and, for some organizations, an extension of ECM that has come to be known as knowledge asset management (KAM).

After some evolution over the past ten years, it is now generally agreed that ECM/knowledge asset management is applicable to a wide range of KD/KS/KU issues and opportunities within nearly every type of enterprise. If knowledge services can be considered "putting KM to work" then ECM can be considered, "putting knowledge services to work," placing tools and processes in the hands

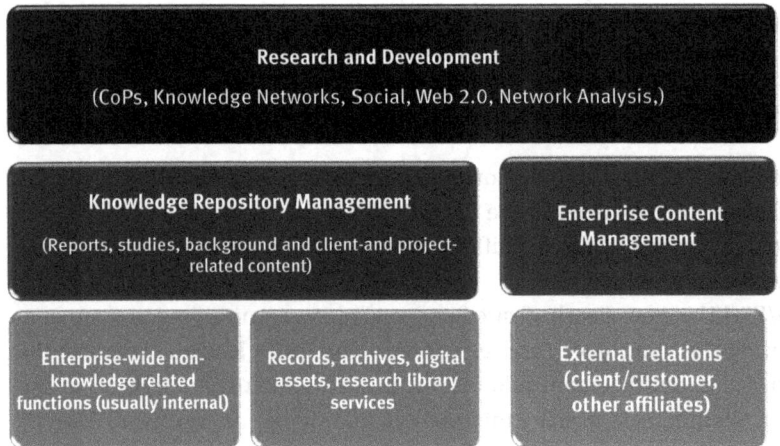

Figure 2.6: Knowledge services in context: ECM and knowledge asset management.

of knowledge workers to enable them to effectively manage information and knowledge (i.e., content) and, as knowledge asset management is integrated into the management process, strategic learning as well.

Just as it is important to understand the concepts of knowledge services in order to develop a strategic framework in support of an organizational knowledge strategy, it is equally essential that we understand the IT constructs of planning and implementation as they relate to successful KAM. This traditional IT framework is discussed below. For now, we will simply note that in the knowledge-centric enterprise, understanding ECM and, as appropriate, KAM, provides a critical link between strategy (that is, the organization's knowledge services strategic framework, designed to serve as the organization's knowledge strategy) and its implementation through tools used on a day-to-day basis by individual participants.

ECM defined. Enterprise Content Management (ECM) is an amalgamation of business strategies, processes, and tools that comprises a number of IT solutions in the knowledge services realm. In all organizations, the goal of ECM is quite simple, the lifecycle management of all structured and unstructured content across all constituent organizational elements of the enterprise.

As would be expected in a highly-charged and fluid environment, strict and stable definitions are difficult to find. For our purposes in this chapter, we can begin by discussing each of the component terms separately.

Enterprise: The term generally refers to the entire organization within which the content is intended to be shared. Since content (be it data, information, or knowledge) can only provide value when it is actually shared and used, the ideal and proposed scope of an ECM system would be as wide as possible, hopefully including the entire organization and occasionally even beyond the traditional boundaries associated with the organization.

Content: Content is traditionally divided into two types: "structured" and "unstructured." In seeking to define the two, the easiest route is simply to describe how they contrast. Structured content is generally accepted to be information or content that has been classified using metadata, arriving at a tagging or classification that describes the data elements. Its purpose is to ensure that the content can be reused and builds on clear, structured content guidelines. Ann Rockley offers a useful description of structured content:

> Structured content adheres to principles of cognitive psychology and is based on how people read and comprehend information. Structured writing also assumes that "not all information is created equally." In other words, information differs according to its type and should be consistently structured in a way best suited to its type. For example, a procedure is different than a process, or a concept, and should use a structure best suited to procedural information. (Rockley, 2003)

Rockley also defines the arrangement of content, providing useful criteria for identifying whether content is structured or unstructured. These include recognizing that content is identified for different audiences, product lines, and platforms, understanding how content will be reused, and establishing whether the content is structured and how (by type, potential audience, etc.).

Unstructured content is the opposite, content that has not been classified and is not built on formal content standards. This includes data or information that is not curated and/or formatted, and thus, could be rendered useless or not findable to a knowledge worker unfamiliar with the data set. Unstructured content can be just about anything, from a photograph or other picture, to a hand-written document or archive, to a list of personal passwords that the owner wants organized in some manner. Designing a database for developing and capturing metadata for these unstructured content elements moves the designation of the content from unstructured to structured.

Management: In IT terms, we speak of "management" to refer to the manipulation of the content itself, as well as to designate the systems and potential oversight that help make the content useful and available. The Association for Image and Information Management (AIIM) includes four components as important for managing content: capturing, storing, preserving, and delivering. In planning an ECM strategic framework within the knowledge services context, the authors expand the last ("delivering") to include knowledge sharing since, in our opinion, this management component brings so much value to the enterprise that it should be explicit in any knowledge services-related ECM definition.

In addition, there are various domains in which the actual management of content typically occurs, among which are content management (both internal and external and as an official operational function), records and information management (RIM) or, document lifecycle management (DLM), Web content management (via a Content Management System), and rich media and digital asset management.

Now to put enterprise, content, and management together into an enterprise-wide deployment is easier said than done, despite the visionary intentions of many organizational leaders, the knowledge workers and knowledge specialists within the enterprise, and the software vendor/partners who work with them. Sometimes so difficult, in fact, that the situation has recently led at least one respected practitioner and writer to characterize ECM as being "… at a critical turning point where it must prove itself or be lost altogether." Another industry observer has even labeled ECM a "myth," saying that attempting to implement enterprise-wide solutions is like "trying to boil the ocean."

Does this mean that a well-intentioned ECM advocate should not attempt large scale or enterprise-wide ECM projects? No. It is entirely possible – and even recommended – that within a ready culture with a high-level sponsorship and other recognized and successful change implementation elements in place, an enterprise-wide ECM strategy can be developed and implemented with success. Of course, it is also possible for a large-scale strategy to begin its implementation small and grow, which in many cases is exactly what happens. In some environments, this approach is preferable and more in line with the organization's culture. Still, regardless of the ambitions of the organization's knowledge leaders or the size of the project once initiated, it is important to include an enterprise-wide vision in the development of the knowledge services strategic framework from the outset, to enable the growth of the knowledge-sharing benefits of ECM.

This point of necessitating an enterprise-wide ECM vision can be depicted during an ECM deployment Barrie Schessler – my co-author for this chapter – managed for the company where she is employed. The strategy agreed upon and supported by management was such that the ECM deployment was going to be implemented is phases based on department. By establishing the ultimate goal as complete enterprise adoption and keeping that goal paramount, each department migration utilized the same best practices with regard to ECM components such as information architecture, taxonomy, search functionality, and governance structure. Thus, when the ECM deployments for all departments had been rolled out, the enterprise-wide vision remained intact and could be effectively managed going forward.

So given that there have actually been successful enterprise-wide initiatives, and given that there is value in visioning and planning for enterprise-wide implementation, we offer that the term "enterprise" remains in our vocabulary and represents, at minimum, a vision or an ideal to be achieved.

Whether an organization decides to implement ECM enterprise-wide, all at once, in a single department or unit (or a group of departments or units), or incrementally depends on a number of factors which can be explored. All of them come together as we put the elements of these definitions together, as Lynn Blumenstein has done.

Focusing on the far-reaching and inclusive role that ECM can play in the organization, Blumenstein described ECM as "... a comprehensive information management and retrieval strategy that addresses internal documents and records, digital assets, and Web content." Noting that organizations want more control over all their corporate information, Blumenstein describes how knowledge workers are leading the effort, providing companies with an ECM strategy "driven by a knowledge of business processes, metadata, taxonomy classification, and technology skills, all leading to the effective capture, retrieval, and repurposing of content" (Blumenstein, 2005).

To summarize, we offer this working definition of ECM: An organizational application which uses business processes and automated tools to assist the organization in capturing, storing, preserving, and delivering its knowledge and information.

ECM-plus: knowledge asset management. Yet more is needed in the knowledge services environment, particularly as the knowledge strategist and his or her team of knowledge workers and strategic knowledge professionals seek to develop a knowledge services strategic framework – an enterprise-wide knowledge strategy – designed to structure the organization as a knowledge culture. While ECM as a practical management and service-delivery methodology has well-known applications and benefits, the company's knowledge services strategy requires that the elements of the knowledge services construct be incorporated into the enterprise content management picture. ECM helps us deal with the organization's internal content, the many documents, policies, procedures, and other materials generated and intended for internal use, a point supported by *KMWorld* journalist Jim Murphy when he describes how the most successful and influential providers of enterprise content management are grouped around document management and Web content management (Murphy, 2008). This management of internal content is the activity that most closely appropriates the second of the three component elements of knowledge services – knowledge management – and thus fits naturally into the knowledge services construct.

For dealing with external content, the management process must be expanded, and it is here that knowledge workers seek a broader framework, a step that takes them into information management, the first of the three elements that make up knowledge services. Likewise, if the management process is to be successful, giving attention to and connecting with knowledge sharing will be required. This productive step – which usually comes after the knowledge has been developed from whatever information- or data-gathering activity has taken place – is the basis of strategic learning, the third of the three component elements of knowledge services and the one that by definition matches that much sought-after KD/KS/KU that drives the management of an organization or company's intellectual capital.

To bring knowledge management and strategic learning into enterprise content management, we expand ECM into knowledge asset management, an approach to enterprise content that incorporates the knowledge services audit,

2.5 Knowledge Services in Context: Enterprise Content Management (ECM) — 225

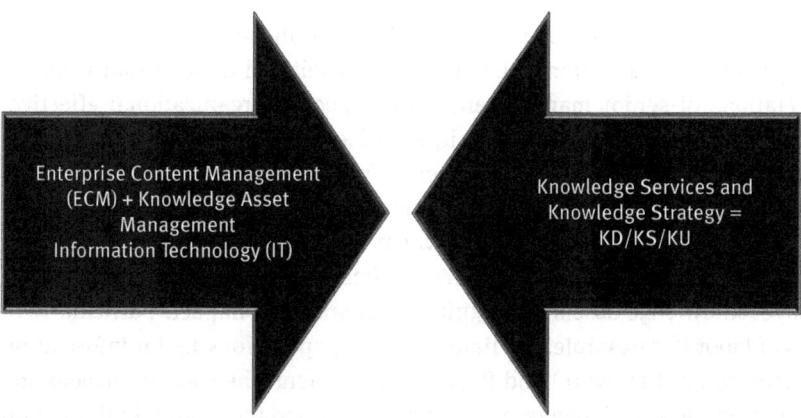

Figure 2.7: The knowledge domain workplace.

knowledge strategy development, and (when required) restructuring and change management – all described in detail elsewhere in this book – to ensure that the widest possible attention is given to identifying, managing, and utilizing enterprise content.

As a management methodology, knowledge asset management requires a slightly different assessment of organizational content and can be looked at from three different points of view, from what we might refer to as the functional focus, from an enterprise focus, and from the perspective of the knowledge worker. The functional focus identifies a knowledge asset as any collected information or knowledge held by the larger enterprise and used by anyone affiliated with the organization to help the organization achieve its goals. Often thought of as organized content to get something done, we might also think of a knowledge asset as anything we are able to refer to as we make decisions, attempt to accelerate innovation, and/or conduct research.

From the enterprise perspective, the knowledge asset is seen as any collected information or knowledge within the larger enterprise which can be used to help the organization achieve its goals, as with the functional focus. In this iteration, however, we recognize that all operational units create and retain knowledge assets and include in that recognition an understanding that, as an operational function, knowledge asset management strengthens all units and all departments of the enterprise. Not surprisingly, the reasonable follow-on is the knowledge worker's definition of a knowledge asset, thinking of a knowledge asset as any information, knowledge, or strategic learning content saved in a form that makes it accessible and usable.

With little effort, we can establish that the significance of knowledge asset management emanates from the organization itself and in particular from the expectations of senior management with respect to organizational effectiveness. Not to put too fine a point on it, knowledge asset management is essential if employees are going to perform effectively and efficiently. Getting to that goal, though, requires that enterprise leaders evaluate their approaches to knowledge asset management and, where necessary, take steps to improve the management of the organization's intellectual capital. How an enterprise manages knowledge assets has significant operational impact, particularly in terms of labor (for example, the time employees spend looking for information they require for their work) and financial investment (the costs for developing or acquiring the knowledge resource that will contain the required information or knowledge base).

Thus every company has by default a knowledge strategy, even if it is unacknowledged and simply built-in as part of the larger organizational business strategy. Ideally the company's knowledge strategy links to the larger organizational purpose and includes attention to the role and value of knowledge content, as well as emphasizing the enterprise-wide sharing of knowledge through collaboration. All of these knowledge strategy elements build on the recognition that the organization's intellectual capital is one of its most valuable assets and that the management of those assets contributes to organizational success.

Why focus on knowledge asset management? We recommend that in terms of its application for knowledge services ECM be expanded to incorporate attention to external content and strategic learning, and that this be accomplished through the integration of knowledge asset management into the ECM process. The viability of knowledge asset management is quickly established and matches that of ECM: economic accountability, service delivery, and value all come together to support a robust ECM/knowledge asset management initiative. In the well-managed enterprise, there is no room in organizational budgets for any process or activity that does not provide direct and verifiable return on investment. Determining ROI for the development, acquisition, and maintenance of knowledge assets is simply required in today's management picture, and there is no choice for the knowledge strategist with responsibility for the management and delivery of knowledge services but to meet that requirement.

Service delivery, too, is structured to match financial circumstances. Fortunately, for most people who need to "look something up" (as most people who use knowledge assets describe the activity they are undertaking), it is no longer particularly essential that another person – colleague or information professional – be brought into the process. For much of the information, knowledge, and strategic learning content required by workers, processes have been developed and total dependence on the interventions of others in fact-finding, researching legacy documents, and similar information-gathering activities are past. Contributing to this welcome scenario is technology, since today's technology offers vast opportunities for self-service and locating what the worker concludes is "good enough." Programs now have efficiencies built in (such as taxonomy and metadata tagging), making information even more successfully and quickly searched.

Nevertheless, there are plenty of situations requiring intervention, and the role of the knowledge strategist and the team in the knowledge services unit continues to be naturally required in many situations, either for further guidance in refining the search or in seeking advice and consultation about the quality of the search results, and it is in this context that the connection with strategic learning in knowledge asset management is made.

Connected to this new thinking about service delivery is considerable deliberation about the consolidation of related functions and functional units, with some organizational managers reviewing the contributions of each of the units that provide some information- or knowledge-focused service. From the larger organizational perspective, it is not unlikely that there will be opportunities for merging the operations of some of these units, with, for example, records and information management (RIM) combining with the organization's knowledge services unit, or certain IT activities merging with some content-focused units (HR or human capital management systems with, say, a company's training and development unit). Indeed, such combinations can be expected to proliferate in the future, and fortunately technology solutions are available, requiring only that the managers in these areas recognize the advantages of cross-functional KD/KS/KU and its implementation into the workplace areas for which they have management and service delivery responsibility.

In creating value from knowledge assets, knowledge strategists can give their attention to providing service delivery and operational support for what they have established as required and mission specific to the support and growth of the larger enterprise.

The ECM/knowledge asset management process. Beginning with the recognition that knowledge assets are in place (even if these assets are not clearly identified or ideally categorized) leads into focusing on enterprise leadership's responsibility to reduce costs and generate income. The next step in the process is to conduct a knowledge services audit. That activity will lead to planning for an enhanced knowledge strategy for the larger enterprise, directing the organization toward the development and continuation of a sustained knowledge culture. Built into the process is a final step, although it is one that in no way is expected to culminate or conclude and it will, in fact, lead to ongoing and (hopefully) regularly scheduled oversight and monitoring. This is the move – following agreement on the recommendations of the knowledge services strategic framework – toward implementing the recommendations and, if required, restructuring and the establishment of change management and change implementation procedures.

Once the audit is concluded, the knowledge asset management process moves forward, with the knowledge services strategic framework planning team engaged in developing enterprise-wide knowledge strategy (or revising or enhancing a strategy already in place). Obviously strategic planning is not a recent addition to the knowledge services management toolbox, and information and knowledge services professionals long ago became expert in adapting techniques applied in the larger management environment to the management of knowledge services.

Thus the knowledge services strategic framework itself is not necessarily the primary objective in developing knowledge strategy, especially if the planning focus does not veer away from mission-specific content and KD/KS/KU. As with all strategic planning, the goal is to use collaboration and sharing techniques to enable colleagues to come together to focus on how the enterprise, as a knowledge-centric organization, can develop a knowledge culture (or strengthen a knowledge culture that is in place). When they do so, they identify and implement tools, techniques, and processes for ensuring that the organization is positioned to take best advantage of its knowledge assets for the benefit of the larger enterprise. The strength of the process is that strategic planning brings together the best planning minds in the organization, detailing them to focus on the future and how the enterprise can be expected – using its knowledge assets – to function in that future.

Finally, the effort moves into change management, again a recognized methodology in the larger management community and one regularly appropriated in the management of knowledge services (and a topic explored further in the next chapter). Having developed an audit "package" listing collections and repositories or storehouses of the organization's information and knowledge content (and in as much detail as the perimeters of the audit permit), and with the knowledge strategy in hand, recommendations for enterprise content management – incorporating knowledge asset management – can be implemented. Responsibility for this activity is usually assigned to a senior-level information or knowledge services professional – a knowledge strategist, perhaps, or a CIO or CKO – who then puts together a knowledge strategy implementation team. Whether attempting to organize a full-scale enterprise-wide knowledge services restructuring or simply to focus on carefully chosen elements of a strategy already in place, the focus again will be on knowledge content and on establishing the highest levels of service delivery through an organizational and boundaryless KD/KS/KU process. With a thorough understanding of the overall organizational culture, and of how stakeholders are likely to react to the changes for a new or enhanced knowledge strategy, the team moves forward to manage and implement a change framework that best serves the needs of the organization and matches its business goals.

Thus we identify three main steps of The ECM/KAM process (conducting a knowledge services audit, developing a knowledge services strategic framework, and determining the change management methodology); in doing so, we come to learn that keeping these steps in mind is essential in deploying an ECM, as evidenced by the intranet creation at Barrie's financial services company. Concurrent with adding business information and knowledge to a central ECM, Barrie was in the process of developing an internal intranet site to be the top-level portal to access the ECM. Here it was determined, based on the knowledge services audit findings, that management and stakeholders across the firm needed a central location to house all the non-sensitive and non-departmental specific information – for example human resources documentation and policies. These audit findings helped determine a framework for which the content manager/knowledge strategist could use going forward, in order to know where and how various types of knowledge should be stored. Additionally, this framework helped solidify the company culture, as all stakeholders now have places to house knowledge around brand management, communities of practice, or internal rich media. This framework was supported by the change management methodology used, and in this case the sense of urgency around implementing an ECM was very high. With audit findings and recommendations having been very transparent to the staff at large, buy-in was largely in place. There was, however, a large need for proper communication and training around the agreed-upon ECM implementation implications, and here again, with change management activities identified early on and kept at priority throughout the project, high user acceptance was created with little resistance.

Planning a strategic framework for ECM/knowledge asset management. This book has a specific purpose, to assist knowledge strategists as they seek to enhance (or create) a corporate culture supporting KD/KS/KU for the larger enterprise. It is our premise that an organizational knowledge culture is essential for the achievement of the organizational mission, whatever that mission is or however it is expressed.

KD/KS/KU succeeds when all people affiliated with the parent organizations or workplace are able to find, create, and share the information, knowledge, and strategic learning required for their work. To do that, an enterprise-wide tool or collection of tools, behaviors, and other vehicles for KD/KS/KU is critical. And with that statement there is an obvious caveat: even if an enterprise content management (ECM) application is utilized only locally, the concept of ECM/knowledge asset management as a universal goal strongly affects the organization's success.

So the motivation for planning a strategic framework for ECM in the knowledge services context seems clear, but it must be acknowledged that all industry leaders are not in agreement. Nav Chakravarti, writing in a KMWorld publication, makes the case that content management systems (what we might refer to as a public or external "ECM") were "not designed for knowledge management and because of several gaps in product capabilities, many organizations are failing in their efforts to foster greater collaboration" (Chakravarti, 2008).

Among the differences or, as Chakravarti puts it, "elements of KM vs. CM," Chakravarti identifies the fact that "daily life depends on granular snippets of knowledge" and content management (CM) is generally designed to manage information that is typically not granular in nature. He also notes that "people don't and won't take the time to document what they know." In order to capture this tacit information, Chakravarti asserts, knowledge capture must be easy and it must be done as part of the work process and "not as a separate document or content publishing task that an employee might engage in one day."

It was a lesson Barrie was ready to take to heart in her work, for she made it her business not to relegate the ECM/content management system (CMS) to take place "one day" or "some day." Recognizing that most often when one is implementing ECM for the organization, it is thought of as an internal system to store information and data and/or as a workflow tool to streamline processes, Barrie decided to take a different approach. Internet of Things reaches a much wider audience than only the organization's people and its servers, and she felt that a natural expansion to this ECM concept would be a content management system (CMS) for an organization's external website. So that's exactly what Barrie did, creating at the financial services company in which she is employed a CMS that works with ECM. Concurrently as she was deploying a phased ECM solution for the various departments at her company (which story comes later), she was helping to update the website from simple HTML and CSS files that had little-to-no analytical functionality. Once the project was complete with the CMS built into the site, Barrie implemented features such as a strong information architecture in order to leverage a more robust template and breadcrumb usage. Additionally, with clear content guidelines, Barrie was able to enhance the site's search engine optimization (SEO), applying best practices such as defined title and page descriptions, meta-data tagging and asset management functionalities. With this tiered knowledge management strategy in place, Barrie – as the company's knowledge strategist – continues to be positioned to influence a holistic KD/KS/KU strategy.

Nevertheless, Chakravarti's comments point of view is common in many organizations, and his recognition that the most important difference between CMS and knowledge management and knowledge services has to do with measurement, we can think about what he has to offer with respect to the ECM/CMS connection. Noting that "the ability to holistically monitor and measure critical elements of the entire workflow process is a fundamental difference between ECM and CMS," Chakravarti offers these core elements to measure:

> *Capture effectiveness.* Tracking contributions of authors, and the value of those contributions for rewards and recognition is critical, so that authors have an incentive to divulge the tacit knowledge in their heads and take the time and effort to document it. This also helps discourage information hoarding since, in the old model, information is power. Given that there is widespread authorship, it becomes critical to distinguish the more expert authors from the beginners. This is especially true in self-publishing environments such as blogs and forums.
>
> *Route efficiencies.* In the route process it is necessary to measure time in the workflow process and identify approval bottlenecks. Given that knowledge has a shelf-life, it also becomes critical to measure the speed of knowledge updates and ensure timely flow.
>
> *Conversion success.* In the convert process, the whole objective is to drive the user to the best solution for his or her needs. This is only possible by providing ways to capture feedback from users and customers, such as ratings and comments, discussion on content, or surveys. Further, document ratings need to be captured, and automated review tasks need to be initiated for documents that receive poor ratings.

With Chakravarti's guidance at hand, the question for managers seeking to develop a strategic framework for ECM becomes one of making it easy for the user to find the required information, knowledge, or strategic learning content and to differentiate "content-driven websites from conversion-focused, knowledge-based Web applications."

Certainly the subject of how well content is managed is being given attention. Mary Lee Kennedy and Angela Abell write about the changing roles of the knowledge professionals and give very strong advice about how those roles – if incumbent knowledge professionals are willing – can drive the knowledge management and knowledge services process in the larger organization. But first, they note, there are challenges, including the "major" challenge of managing growing volumes of content. "As more decentralized behavior emerges on intranets," Kennedy and Abell write, "infrastructure (i.e., team spaces and project collaboration spaces) and the amount of duplication and redundant content will grow exponentially" (Kennedy and Abell, 2008).

Kennedy and Abell suggest that avoiding these pitfalls is going to be difficult, and solutions, including ECM/knowledge asset management, will necessarily be "largely driven by a perceived recognition of their immediate value." They agree that there will continue to be much attention to technology solutions that (as they quote Andrew McAfee's suggestion) "make visible the practices and outputs of knowledge workers." It is here, it seems, that the influential role of the organization's knowledge strategists, knowledge workers, and strategic knowledge professionals, both in the knowledge services unit and in all sections of the organization must be brought into play.

The roles of the knowledge professionals thus relate to an important enterprise-wide function which establishes a valuable relationship in the development of a strategic framework for ECM. Kennedy and Abell recommend six "clusters of responsibilities" for knowledge workers and strategic knowledge professionals, each with an important function in ECM and establishing work that needs to be done. Kennedy and Abell's clusters are:
- information and knowledge strategy
- enterprise information architecture
- information governance
- content creation and acquisition
- communication and publication
- information exploitation and use.

Thus the running important theme throughout both of these resources is that companies and organizations must focus on business needs as the ECM/ knowledge asset management strategic framework moves forward. It is a point of view with which Janice Anderson would agree. In her work, Anderson has long made the connection between records and information management (RIM) and KM/ knowledge services. In her article on best practices in the RIM environment, she connects ECM and RIM with logical and practical steps. Describing the value of combining RIM and ECM, Anderson writes that in the present organizational environment, "companies that are identifying their business requirements and organizing their information are several steps ahead of their peers" (Anderson, 2006). Anderson's recommended first steps are:
- Assess the needs of the organization.
- Develop policies and procedures for managing information.
- Define and document business practices.
- Discover information being created and received within the organization.
- Create and populate information management tools.

Offering "three things to remember as you consider an ECM system implementation," Anderson advises managers with knowledge services responsibility to note that:
- Buying and implementing an ECM system does not guarantee compliance or adherence to best practice.
- All ECM systems require a significant up-front investment of time, effort, and money.
- Well-designed and deployed ECM systems are worth the effort and provide significant return on investment.

Anderson concludes with six "tips" for implementing an "ECM system that will endure:"
1. Identify the right team for ECM product selection, implementation, and maintenance.
2. Prepare for the complexity of implementing an ECM system with your taxonomy, file plans, and retention schedules.
3. Choose an ECM system that will allow you to be flexible.
4. Develop an implementation plan that will allow you to prioritize according to highest risk/need.
5. Create policies and procedures for your ECM system based on the RIM policies and procedures that you have already developed.
6. Address organizational change and communication within your design/build process (Anderson, 2006).

While some might disagree with Anderson's implementation tip relating to creating policies and procedures based on RIM policies and procedures, such distinctions would typically spring up in environments in which the holistic approach to knowledge management and knowledge services is not yet instilled as an organizational characteristic. Regardless of the model chosen (after all, we all have to start somewhere, and alluding to a previous model is generally much more palatable – and more likely to result in an achievable plan – than starting with a totally new pattern), the purpose is, as Anderson puts it, "to incorporate industry best practices for search and retrieval and lifecycle management as reflected in an ideal program."

Putting ECM to work. With this guidance and now with an understanding of ECM/knowledge asset management and its place in the organization, we can turn to examples of how ECM is actually implemented and demonstrate how ECM planning helps to put knowledge services to work. We begin by thinking about two approaches. We call them best practices, and we recommend a focus on using ECM as a business process improvement and integration method, and using a portfolio approach to content offered as a service (searchable databases).

Best Practice (1): Use ECM as a business process improvement and integration method. We make two points:

When possible, incorporate business process reengineering (BPR) into your ECM program. BPR involves (usually) first mapping the existing processes and then re-designing the processes and procedures to better match the business need and, concurrently, to achieve increased efficiencies. In general, the planning and implementation of any automated system should include, at minimum, an evaluation of the business processes involved.

When we seek to bring ECM into the knowledge services context, we examine how both structured and unstructured content is dispersed across different repositories, how the information, knowledge, and learning content is used as it is dispensed from those repositories, and the effectiveness of the system in delivering content, particularly in terms of workflow and operational function. It is senseless to implement an automated system intended to facilitate or speed an inadequate, out-dated, or otherwise irrelevant set of work processes. Implementing such a system would, at best, merely speed up the wrong activities! An ideal plan begins with a review of the existing processes (the formal methods) and human behaviors (informal ways of getting work done). We then engage the people actually doing the work and come up with a "desired state," a better business process including attention to workflow and roles. With these steps, the design and workflow of the new ECM system will best match the purposes and goals of the enterprise.

The following example describes how one organization matched BPR utilization with its ECM goals. A large pharmaceutical company had a manual process for obtaining approvals for external scientific publications. The existing process had been in existence for many years through a time of tremendous growth. The old system required many levels of approvals, such as the entire reporting chain from scientist to President of Research. In addition, it required approvals from the chief patent legal council, copyright agreement clearances from the library function, and even a reprints ordering feature. When the company's research function consisted of 2,000 scientists, the manual system (hardcopy sent via inter-office mail) worked fine, but when the research division ballooned to nearly 12,000 employees and included six major sites on four continents, there was an clear need for a viable ECM system.

In consultation with stakeholders and the executive sponsor of the project, process maps were created for the existing and desired states during the planning stages. It was quickly determined that the chain of approvals should be shortened and made more flexible according to location. Reprints ordering was also eliminated, and the process would now include a local legal sign-offs responsibility instead of referring to the US-based chief patent counsel. In addition, it became obvious that there were multiple chains of approval and if electronic copies of the articles were routed and tracked, the chains (such as reporting-chain, library, and legal) could be done in parallel.

Some experts in the field contend that the BPR approach is outdated, that initiatives should be aligned with the existing informal channels and agreements since this is where "real" knowledge interchange occurs. Despite these differences in opinion, the BPR approach continues to be valid and effective, as can be seen in this example (which addresses Chakravarti's reference to route efficiencies in the measurement process). In addressing the dilemma of where the knowledge interchange occurs, we recommend that knowledge professionals and knowledge managers learn about and pick whichever business processes (formal, informal, or combined) that seem have the most uptake and participation in your own organization. Then, learn as much as you can about this social-process construct and design your ECM system and implementation accordingly. Experience has shown that most successful implementations take into account both formal work processes (which set the context, timing and rationale for knowledge transfer) and flexible, incentivized, "volunteer-based" information sharing opportunities. Whatever the approach (or terminology used to describe it), the human element cannot be ignored. We now recognize that KD/KS/KU cannot be forced and can only exist in a culture in which people desire to share the knowledge they develop. As the knowledge professional's role has expanded to include skills, attitudes, and values relating to partnerships and alliances, mutual respect and trust, and communications, that role also now requires leadership strengths for influencing colleagues to want to share what they know.

Our second point has to do with the scope of the ECM effort. If the project has wide scope and might be considered more fully "enterprise" in the ambitions of organizational leaders, it will overlay so many work functions and processes that it would be impossible to re-engineer in either manner described above. Our recommendation here is to, at minimum, inventory the various roles played by departments (or individuals, in small organizations) by conducting a thorough knowledge services audit which would likely involve representatives from the various roles in the inventory process – that is, stakeholders in the ECM process – and to have them provide advice and guidance from their specific perspective to the project team early on in the planning. This practice serves two purposes, to identify hurdles or pitfalls in the planning that can be headed off in the planning phase (as opposed to taking this step during the executing phase when changes are much more difficult to incorporate), and to engage a population of potential users (and hopefully "change agents" or "champions"). This latter is extremely important to your ECM strategic framework development project because even the best system will fail (and many do) if the individual users are not engaged or motivated to change their behaviors by using your new ECM system, as noted in an example from the life insurance industry. In this example, a company was experiencing "astronomical growth" in new policy applications. The company decided to design an ECM system aligned with a corporate strategy to manage the growth while improving customer service. After reviewing their organizational structure from a functional standpoint, management decided that an automated system of routing, retrieval, and storage of applications would reduce processing time of policy applications without having to increase headcount.

As a result of surveying the roles, functions, and workflow of the involved departments and involving representatives from all levels, the company decided to create a new department called the "Digital Mailroom" which was implemented in conjunction with an ECM/ workflow system. The new system has been well-accepted and realized impressive productivity and improved customer care. The company states that "process transparency" and "workload redistribution" capabilities have been critical success factors.

Best Practice (2): Use a portfolio approach to enterprise content management, with searchable databases to include the following:
- subscription databases (external)
- operational databases (internal)
- historical/archival
- information-based (unstructured text-based)

Some types of content are necessarily presented as large databases (variously called "databases", "info-bases", "knowledge bases", etc.) that contain information for to a wide audience and for a variety of needs. Many times, this type of content is presented as a service, usually in the form of a searchable database. The content is searched on demand (usually by the end-user or sometimes by an intermediary expert searcher) and applied by the user to fulfill business needs for research, decision-making, or pursuing innovation. The content may be externally generated and purchased or licensed or it may be compiled and maintained within the enterprise.

There are multiple challenges with these types of content and the business model, including the constant need to match the database's content with the user's needs. Many times, especially with external purchased content, there are competing resources, differing interfaces, changing needs, needs for training and expert evaluation, and the like. In other situations, this calls for a subject matter expert or knowledge content manager to help the enterprise select, deploy, train, and monitor these resources.

In most situations, this step too is part of the knowledge services audit, reviewing resources of all three knowledge services disciplines (and is not limited to those typically thought of as knowledge resources). The purpose is to identify the various knowledge assets in the larger organization since, as noted in the earlier description of the various ECM domains, there can be a large contingent of "items" in the ECM portfolio.

It is in developing the portfolio – beginning with a list of its constituent parts – that the strength of the portfolio approach comes into play. With an inventory of knowledge assets in place, knowledge asset management has a place on which to build. Without it, both management and staff are left to wonder what the specifics of KM/knowledge management are, or might be.

A good example of the portfolio approach took place in a medium-size research and service-delivery organization in which senior leadership had identified the need for an integrated information/knowledge/strategic learning management system. Management expectations were that the system would not be limited to the management of information but would also incorporate captured knowledge ("intellectual capital") and strategic learning content.

The stated vision and purpose of the system was chosen: to provide a unified format for access to corporate information, knowledge, and strategic learning content, in order to enable company stakeholders to make better business decisions.

Following a knowledge services audit in which the ECM Planning Task Force compiled – to its and management's satisfaction – a comprehensive list of resources, each was analyzed for its contribution to the corporate business purpose. As the list included both formal knowledge repositories and informal arrangements (communities of practice, social network tools, committees, groups, and other knowledge-sharing elements), the knowledge services audit required a large outlay of resources but the commitment was offset by the recognition by all task force members – and corporate leadership – that the directory of resources would provide critical content for building the ECM strategic framework.

The next step was to evaluate each content repository and/or element according to the following criteria:
- capacity to perform as part of an integrated process and operating system (i.e., does the repository "fit" as part of a "one-stop shop" or portal?);
- level of tactical vs. strategic content;
- linkage to users, with specific reference to how users actually (and easily) access resources, how the accessed content is used, and how that usage matches the organization's strategic purpose;

- user acceptance, ease of use, and speed of response;
- ability to bring together data from disparate sources (both formal and informal);
- integrated report tools, required for summary and analysis.

When the ECM Planning Task Force delivered its implementation plan, it described the company as positioned to move to a strong ECM system and recommendations were made to take the plan forward.

Two critical elements in the success of the program were first, a recommendation for a senior management employee to join the task force as an "interested" party. A second critical element was the recommendation for an all-hands learning initiative, to set up an enterprise-wide learning program emphasizing the overall benefits (both individual and corporate) of the ECM plan with – an important consideration – change management principles incorporated into the learning program (as discussed in Chapter 3, Section 3.1).

A closer look at ECM domains. As described earlier, enterprise content management (ECM) is an amalgamation of different domains. As information professionals with management responsibility for content management assess the organization's KD/KS/KU needs, it is important to consider these domain aspects of ECM and consider their applicability in the workplace:

Content management: This domain can include either internally generated or externally acquired content or both. These business functions create significantly added value for the enterprise. By connecting "what the enterprise knows" with "what the world knows" on a subject from the same place and time to a decision-maker, innovator, inventor, or other product/service developer can by definition create enhanced strategic value.

Records Management (Document Lifecycle Management): The world of Enron scandals, Sarbanes-Oxley, US Code of Federal Regulations 21CFR, Part 11, and the relentless pursuit of corporate litigation has made organizations acutely aware of the need for good records management practices. Physical records may be sorted into types, each with rules as to retention schedules, archiving, and access. For obvious business reasons – and in their own defense – enterprise leaders now require the same of electronic records (especially e mail). This new awareness now brings considerable attention to the value of organized and retrievable information.

Web Content Management: In today's organizations every function or department wants a web presence. Human capital departments want to advertise job vacancies, investor relations wants to attract and inform investors, sales wants products advertised, and the organization's fund-raising or revenue development function wants its activities widely known. Complicating the picture, global companies may want the same information in different languages, and the time-sensitive nature of much information also plays a role in determining the extent to which web content is brought into the content management system (CMS) structure. All of these requirements can overwhelm a dedicated webmaster, and the solution is to make CMS tools available to content owners who can manage it themselves (at the same time, of course, providing the strategic learning framework that will enable them to do so).

Rich Media and Digital Asset Management: High speed Internet connections, wide-bandwidth networks, and fast personal computers are now taking content management far beyond text. Since these types of content can be expensive to put together, there can be huge cost drivers to create ECM or DAM ("Digital Asset Management") systems that enable re-use and lifecycle management of information in this domain.

Enterprise architecture and change management. No matter which domain, technology, applications, or business processes are involved, every successful implementation needs to be tightly linked to the larger organization's strategies and culture. If we fail to make this a strong and early connection, our efforts will not succeed, and large commitments of resources will have been wasted. To avoid this scenario, the knowledge strategist makes use of two disciplines:
– An enterprise architecture framework for linking ECM to strategy, planning, and communications.
– Change management principles to ensure that the ECM solution connects with the organizational culture and to ensure the highest likelihood for user uptake of resources and work behaviors required by the new systems.

Enterprise architecture. The IT world has long recognized that even the best implementation of the best software is a huge waste of resources unless there is a robust and logical rationale between chosen IT solutions and business strategy. In enterprises in which multiple software platforms, strategies, and security profiles occur, making this connection requires constant and significant effort. In support of this, most large organizations create a logical construct called an "enterprise architecture." Indeed, many larger organizations employ "enterprise architects" whose role it is to design and constantly monitor these activities. The purpose of enterprise architecture is to align IT investments with the business or management strategy, particularly in terms of standardization and governance and to ensure long-term support for that strategy. In practice, this enterprise-wide framework has evolved to include a host of activities designed to understand, justify, optimize, and communicate the linkages between the various applications and the organizational strategy.

Many of these activities connect, quite naturally, with the various "levels" that make up the general structure of the enterprise architecture concept. As such, these levels (or another firm-specific term) provide the knowledge strategist with terminology and practical concepts for use in working with IT professionals, a point worth remembering since the specialist language of IT professionals and that of knowledge services professionals is often not the same. Thus understanding and being able to incorporate some of the ideas of enterprise architecture provides knowledge professionals with the opportunity to "speak the language" of IT as they seek to describe the needs that they have identified for strengthening the KD/KS/KU process.

These "levels" of enterprise architecture first came to the attention of the information community in the work of John Zachman, first described in a 1987 paper published by IBM. Called "categories" in Zachman's work (now referred to as "the Zachman Framework", these descriptions have been much written about and discussed in the IT community since 1987 and provide convenient points of reference for the knowledge strategist (Zachman, 1987). Generally speaking, the levels of enterprise architecture are thought of as

- business processes and activities
- applications (such as custom or off-the-shelf software tools)
- data that must be collected, organized, safeguarded, and distributed
- technology as hardware (e.g., computer systems and telephone networks).

In thinking about these levels as they apply to planning ECM for knowledge services, the knowledge strategist is thus able to link KD/KS/KU strategy with the information and knowledge seeking efforts of organizational employees. As this process moves forward, we strongly recommend consulting the organization's enterprise architecture (and "architects," if there are employees in the organization with these responsibilities) during the planning and design of any ECM effort.

Doing so will accomplish at least three very important goals:
- Provide an outline of the entire effort and allow the important analysis and discussion of the linkages between content and technology. This is the optimum path to a solid technical and business justification of investments in ECM programs.
- Provide a communications platform for essential and efficient discussion between the business owners (sometimes called "initiators" or "advocates") and IT and the business strategy. If the leaders of the ECM initiative are not in IT, credibility can be enhanced or maintained by the use of this standard strategy method and language.

2.5 Knowledge Services in Context: Enterprise Content Management (ECM) — 241

– Set the stage for additional planning and implementation. More time spent on a solid architecture early on will result in more efficient implementation and ensure the adoption and carrying out of change management practices later on.

Basically, the creation and organization of an enterprise architecture begins with documenting the organization's strategy and high-level operating model, which the knowledge strategist has already documented within the findings of the knowledge services audit. It then becomes more and more tactical and detailed, describing which applications (the computer programs and interfaces) support the strategy and operations, that is, managing the business of the firm. Enterprise architecture then moves to descriptions of the actual data and information used by the applications, and finally describes the underlying technology or infrastructure needed to support the other elements.

Typical elements supporting this structure include those for both business management and for information management. For the former – managing the business – these include:
– Road maps, goals, corporate policies
– Functional decompositions (e.g., ways of expressing inputs, processes, and outputs or flowchart models), capabilities and organizational models
– Business processes and procedures
– Organization cycles, periods, and timing
– Suppliers of hardware, software, and services
– Applications software inventories and diagrams
– Interfaces between applications (that is: events, messages, and data flows)
– Intranet, Extranet, Internet, e-Commerce, EDI links, with parties within and external to the organization.

For the latter – dealing with the management of the organization's information, knowledge, and strategic learning content – attention is given to
– findability: Metadata, taxonomy, search
– data models: conceptual, logical, and physical
– technology:
    – hardware, platforms, and hosting
    – software (in house and cloud-based)
– local and wide area networks, Internet connectivity diagrams
– operating System
– infrastructure software: application servers, DBMS
– programming languages, etc.

In the development of any proposals for an ECM solution, an investigation of prior work done with respect to enterprise architecture should be considered. Once these have been given attention, proposals for an ECM solution should address how and where the integration of the architecture with the needs of the content by end-users will occur.

Change Management: Also referred to as "organizational change management" or "human change management," change management is generally described as a set of principles that take into account the human element of any implementation or organizational change. Even the best conceived goals, the best designed processes, greatest software and most detailed planning will fail if change management principles are ignored. As these principles are given detailed attention in Chapter 3, Section 3.1, it is only necessary at this point to describe some of the principles of change management as they relate to planning the strategic framework for ECM. In addition, for our purposes here, we highlight a few of the critical junctures within a project's lifecycle where change management may be effectively applied.

Probably the most effective change management principle that can be put to work in planning a strategic framework for ECM is sponsorship. For the effort to succeed and contribute to organizational effectiveness, it is critical that those initiating (or assigned) the responsibility identify an influential leader who will agree to say (i.e., speak about), model and reward the use of the new ECM application or the changed behaviors that will result.

Related, of course, is the principle in which champions and change agents are enjoined to help influence the change and the move to a new ECM system. These champions and change agents are influential people who can speak about the benefits of the new program and encourage uptake and usage. Champions are good for speaking as early-adopter users who have seen and realized improved performance from the benefits of the change, and change agents are simply individuals who have been identified and indoctrinated to speak about ("say"), model, and reward to new behaviors to a population of users.

A similar consideration has to do with targeting readiness and surfacing resistance. Realizing that everyone goes through a drop in productivity and may even resist the changeover to a new or different way of managing work-related activities, this change management principle can prepare managers for handling situations that, while not inevitable, come up frequently enough in the change implementation process to inhibit progress. Engaging users early on and taking the time to look for and address resistance will help individuals (and organizations) go through the change curve faster and with considerably less anxiety for all stakeholders.

All of the above have to do with communications, and the development of an effective and comprehensive communication plan that engages users at the outset and recognizes these elements in a coordinated and consistent manner is recommended. At its simplest level, a calendar of expected events/milestones or a project plan that incorporates elements of a consistent "message" accommodating the audience and using appropriate organization media will be effective and lead to wider acceptance for and implementation of the ECM strategic framework.

As knowledge management has matured and as knowledge services as a management and services delivery methodology has emerged, the demand for knowledge development, knowledge sharing, and knowledge services (KD/KS/KU) programs and activities has also matured and grown. This is not due solely to an academic or theoretical re-conceptualization of the KM models (although that, no doubt, has happened as well). Organizations have begun to realize that embracing KD/KS/KU has strategic and operational value, and opportunities for organizational impact come to light when one examines some of the causes of this shift in thinking:

- The demand for knowledge sharing, especially tacit knowledge, has increased. Globalization of nearly every industry on earth has created competition for resources (human, capital, energy, etc.). Indeed, as Drucker expert Bruce Rosenstein notes, the knowledge strategist seeking a brighter future will build a "Drucker-like mindset" and learn to "think and act globally" (Rosenstein, 2013). As a result, the demand for "how to" knowledge, for knowledge that enables faster innovation, faster processes, faster decision-making and higher quality products at a lower cost has experienced a commensurate increase, opening a whole new world (no pun intended) for the knowledge strategist.
- The urgency to do something about the much-talked about information overload. The concept of information overload, now commonly referred to as "big data" is an established reality, not an imagined difficulty of a helpless population. The exponential increase of e-mail alone has reached a breaking point for many workers, particularly knowledge workers, and when e-mail is matched to the billions of added web pages and the demand for faster and more informed decisions that knowledge workers are expected to handle, it is no surprise that the term "overload" is invoked. Some organizations are recognizing that the situation is not merely an individual productivity or effectiveness issue and are seriously interested in identifying and implementing coping mechanisms.

Implementing ECM/knowledge asset management: the IT connection. In today's technical workplace structured as a knowledge culture, KM is inherently bound to technology. All parties seek to strengthen the relationship between technology and knowledge, with particular emphasis on KD/KS/KU in the workplace. Extremely sophisticated tools are now available for capturing, storing, and retrieving rich content that – when retrieved by knowledge workers – is processed into knowledge. Indeed, technology not only provides the pipes or conduits for conveying the content back and forth. Now with the development of social networking technology and tools for value network analysis, real-time KD/KS/KU is not only possible but, in many situations, is being established as a requirement of the workplace.

Thus the essential role of IT and the development of information management (including technology management) as one of the three components of knowledge services is no surprise. In most organizations, it seems, management is now beginning to observe a welcome blurring of responsibility with respect to technology and knowledge, radically altering the separations so prevalent in the earlier days of electronic content capture and dissemination. In that not-very-distant past, the "pipes-vs.-content" distinction was accepted as the convention, with the people who managed information technology expected to have little or no interest in content management, service delivery, and least of all, in providing advice or interpretation with respect to the user's needs and particular usage requirements. And vice versa. People who dealt with content and its interpretation on a regular basis were generally not expected to be well-versed in IT matters, resulting naturally in a certain distance between those with IT responsibility and those who dealt with the information, knowledge, and strategic learning content provided by and accessed through the IT system.

That picture is dramatically changed now, and the IT professional is as likely to be referred to as an "information professional" or "content specialist" as other experts claiming those job titles. A healthy collaboration has been taking place over the past decade or so, and it is not unusual in today's workplace to find the information specialist or enterprise content manager and his or her staff as part of the functional unit labeled "Information Services," reporting to the organization's Chief Information Officer (CIO). Likewise, in other businesses "Knowledge Services" falls under the aegis of the Chief Knowledge Officer (CKO) or a Knowledge strategist (or even, as recommended earlier, the Chief Knowledge Strategist), with this functional unit shown on the company's organization chart with responsibility not only for the management and delivery of knowledge services, but with organizational IT responsibility as well. Further demonstrating the merging of this formerly discreet configuration, much of today's combined IT and knowledge services function is structured around identifying structures and management frameworks that enable the focus on content and KD/KS/KU, giving managers and HR (or, as in some organizations, human capital) managers the

2.5 Knowledge Services in Context: Enterprise Content Management (ECM) — 245

opportunity to add "expertise in knowledge services" to the job description of every employee. Or the new approach might go the other way; the recent growth in corporate acceptance of software-as-a-service (SaaS) is a sure sign that when a company can outsource some of its technology management responsibilities, benefits accrue. Indeed, by making use of such innovative management methodologies as SaaS, and taking advantage of the cloud, the organization's knowledge services staff and selected members of the IT staff are then positioned to direct their attention to responding to internal service delivery needs relating to the company's larger business strategy.

As noted, connecting to these higher-level benefits is an attention to more formal collaboration, now mandated in some organizations. Obviously the development of – and acceptance in using – social networking tools has contributed greatly to the success of management's collaborative goals, and these links between IT professionals and other knowledge-focused staff are resulting in "location-neutral" workplaces for many teams and communities of practice. These can be expected to continue and increase in number, resulting in benefits for knowledge workers and for the larger enterprise as well.

A recommended structure for planning and terminology is offered here. It is based on the internationally recognized standard (PMBOK – the Project Management Book of Knowledge) that is used directly or with some modifications in most IT development organizations. The standard incorporates the "life cycle" model that assumes that any implementation has the following major stages:

- Initiation
- Planning
- Execution
- Controlling and monitoring
- Closing

As knowledge professionals with responsibility for initiating and/or implementing planning for an ECM strategic framework begin their work, we recommend that these terms be used. Alternatively, if variations are used by IT partners, those terms should be determined and matched to these, so that they are used exactly as they are used in the management of the IT function. Particularly when putting forward proposals and communicating with senior management and with IT partners, this "same page" communication level is essential.

Initiation: This stage includes preparatory research, needs analysis, and a formal proposal for the project. It is critically important not to be sparing with this stage. In fact, one of the major achievements of the PMPOK methodology has been to institute better and more comprehensive pre-planning into IT projects. Typical sub-components of this stage are:

Audit/Needs Assessment: Ideally, this is in the form of a comprehensive "knowledge services audit" or needs assessment of the target audience or enterprise. The methods and rationale for the knowledge services audit – described in detailed terms earlier – will include several specific stages:
- planning
- data collection data analysis data evaluation
- communicating recommendations implementing recommendations
- the knowledge services audit as a continuum or continuing process.

A typical and powerful result of such an analysis can be the identification of a "serious business problem" for which a compelling business case can be articulated.

Considerations: The overall scope of the project and the rationale for the proposed scope of the project are described in this component. Typical scope parameters involve descriptions of the user population and organizational structures, general budgetary restrictions, and technology limits or imposed standards. The scope description should also consider and describe linkages to the existing portfolio of IT strategies and applications. Also important are statements that demonstrate harmony with the organization's enterprise architecture (as discussed earlier). Planners should also consider the user population's culture, and if there are any strong political "ownership" opportunities or challenges.

Change management begins here. Traditionally, concern about end-user uptake begins near the end of the execution phase with rollout announcements and training. We recommend that change management efforts to engage users, change agents, and sponsors begin as early as possible. Among the reasons for this are the fact since ECM has the potential to directly impact user's personal workflow and productivity, and the success of the program is highly dependant on the user's uptake of the new system and procedures. Admitting that there will be some disruption immediately and understanding that the program can be challenging – even threatening – to the individual users, engaging change management principles can be highly effective at this point.

Planning: Once *preliminary* approval is obtained (usually, this involves some level of management approval for individuals to spend their time and a limited amount of money on investigating the feasibility of the project), plans and research for a formal proposal of the project are put into place. This step usually involves further needs analysis, including pilot programs, resource planning, vendor and software selection, preliminary negotiations, and engagement with additional partners (internally and externally to the enterprise). The result is a formal proposal to management articulating the business benefits, risks, risks of not doing the project, resource needs, and a high-level timeline. By this time, a sponsor and project champions have also been engaged and given opportunities to express their support.

Execution: Once the project is approved, the work of building the system begins. Usually the roles of a business owner, technical leader, project manager, and other roles are established. Sub-projects and timelines are established and monitored by the project leader and reported to the team. Pilots are completed and their results incorporated early in the project, and events such as testing and quality checks take place during the latter phases. At this stage, the change management best practice of developing a communications plan is well under way, for keeping all stakeholders engaged and informed as to the progress of the project. This is especially important if (and probably when) timelines and deliverables change. Documentation of coding, configurations, version controls, and a host of other elements become very important in this phase. The end result of this phase, though, is three-fold: the rollout of the new product, communication and training of users in the use of the application, and a recognition of (and codification of, if required) changes in associated work processes. Careful monitoring of user uptake and resistance to the changes is a recommended change management best practice in this stage, and leads to the larger and critical role of controlling and monitoring in the process.

Controlling and monitoring: It is important to plan for and monitor usage, value, and other metrics during the ongoing life of the application and business processes, and these steps become especially important in planning the ECM strategic framework. Many times adjustments in the applications and procedures must be modified to accommodate changes in the work environment, software upgrades, and other changes. "Application Owners" should be established to monitor and control these changes, typically re-constituting small teams for this purpose. Often referred to as the "sustain" phase because there is recognition that it takes resources for the ongoing support of training, software upgrades, bug fixes, minor modifications of code and settings, and the like, this stage provides another opportunity for all players to agree on their future objectives.

At this point, there is a natural tendency for the portfolio of products and services to become heavy, and sustaining these can become an inhibitor of the organization's ability to be flexible and innovative. If this turns out to be the case, good IT and knowledge services managers and portfolio managers will periodically look at an enterprise's sustained operations and question the ongoing value of older applications, looking for redundancies and studying usage metrics. The knowledge strategist and other information and knowledge professionals with responsibility for initiating ECM planning can do the same. The business owner of an application in this phase should be proactively monitoring the same metrics and engaging tools as advisory boards, champions, user groups, and value metrics in order to avoid arbitrary or un-informed portfolio decisions to close still-useful applications.

Closing. This phase typically involves much more than merely shutting down the software. It likely involves transitions in business processes, data migration, possibly the archiving of some data into alternative systems, and communications with existing user communities. Best practices include good documentation of data disposition and lessons learned.

Suggested strategic approach. The following are our recommendations for how the knowledge strategist can define and implement an ECM program:

1. Learn about and engage your environment and potential user base. A knowledge services audit, surveys, interviews with executives, and the use of benchmarking studies are tools that can be used.
2. Understand and confirm the culture and values of the organization. Nothing kills a project more effectively than one that is misaligned with the user community's culture and values. Learning and discussing this topic and then incorporating the language and concepts learned in the early proposal stages of the project will ensure alignment and the best possible user uptake and value. It will also help smooth your change management efforts.
3. Challenge your mission. The opportunity to implement knowledge services will likely cause you – as the knowledge strategist – to stretch or propose stretching the very mission or purpose of your role or function in the larger enterprise. This is an essential exercise because it forces you to think of the largest possible impact of your initiatives. This enterprise mindset can be at once energizing and threatening. Relying on solid values, good research, and strong sponsorship will help ensure success.
4. Create an enterprise vision for knowledge services. Incorporate your knowledge of the culture, the enterprise needs, and the changing mission and values of the enterprise to create a compelling and clear future vision for the larger organization – and your role and that of all parallel information-, knowledge-, or strategic learning-focused business units in the organization. This will be a critical foundation to creating relevant and innovative enterprise goals.
5. Set specific goals. The SMART (Specific – Measurable – Achievable – Relevant – Time-bound) method can assist the ECM strategic framework planning team as it develops tangible and realistic proposals. This will also help you determine what parameters will affect your ROI.
6. Propose plans. With the input and engagement of strong sponsors and champions, propose plans that are in alignment with the culture, methods, and procedures in your enterprise, using the implementation framework

described above or, if your organization has its own planning framework, use these concepts as a guide and incorporate these concepts into the organizational framework.
7. Monitor ongoing success. Just because the ECM was implemented does not mean it was successful. You must monitor end user acceptance and be flexible and nimble enough to adjust the system as new business requirements arise.

3 The Way Forward

3.1 Change Management and Change Implementation: The Fundamental Knowledge Services Competency (with Dale R. Stanley)

Evident throughout these pages is the fact that one of the knowledge strategist's critical roles is to serve as the organization's change agent, change architect, or as Dale Stanley – my co-author for this chapter – refers to this serious duty, as the organization's *change leader* for knowledge services, knowledge strategy, and the development of the organization as a knowledge culture. As stated in this chapter's title, change is fundamental to the successful management of the organization's intellectual capital. We must also emphasize that change is essential. As organizational management, workplace staff, educators in the professions represented in the workplace, and even society at large take on a new understanding of the value of knowledge, so too must they experience change in order to identify methodologies and actions for handling this new understanding of knowledge and its value.

Nevertheless, as all of us have experienced in our personal and professional lives, change does not happen accidentally or without some attention to *how* change is to come about. As with everything else having to do with knowledge services and knowledge strategy, plans must be made and change management guidelines incorporated into the knowledge services strategic framework. The knowledge strategist – now the knowledge change leader – will use these guidelines to manage the organizational move to the knowledge culture.

Managing change. In 1994, writing about the "age of social transformation," Peter F. Drucker described what the editors of *Atlantic Monthly* called "an economic order in which knowledge, not labor or raw material or capital, is the key resource." In the essay, as he wrote about the rise of the knowledge worker, Drucker made it clear that the move toward a "knowledge economy" is more than simply a rearranging of the workforce:

> The rise of the class succeeding industrial workers is not an opportunity for industrial workers. It is a challenge. The newly emerging dominant group is "knowledge workers".... the great majority of the new jobs require qualifications the industrial worker does not possess and is poorly equipped to acquire. They require a good deal of formal education and the ability to acquire and to apply theoretical and analytical knowledge. They require a different approach to work and a different mind-set. Above all, they require a habit of continuous learning. (Drucker, 1994)

As Drucker was helping us understand the basic differences between what was expected of workers in earlier societies and today's knowledge-centric environment, an additional and critical attribute of the new workplace was being identified. During that same last decade of the previous century, John P. Kotter – one of the most respected of the change management specialists of the late twentieth century – and other influential management leaders were stating that those same knowledge workers, in order to take on those different approaches, would need not only to identify the changed work environment in which they were expected to perform but to adapt to the requirements of change.

As a fundamental component of leadership and management, change is now recognized as constant and inevitable, indeed, so constant and inevitable that it is referred to often in these pages, with specific attention to the particular focus of the topic being written about at various points in the book. Change, change management, and change implementation – there's no getting away from it – are all part of the KD/KS/KU process. If managed properly and with an eye toward long-term improvement, also as noted in these pages, change is desirable as well. This recognition continues and will continue to be vital to how the organization's knowledge strategists – and the people for whom knowledge services are delivered – succeed in their work.

In our work at SMR International, both as knowledge services consultants and as teachers, webinar leaders, and, in particular, strategic learning advisors to clients, Dale and I often characterize knowledge services as putting knowledge management to work, the practical side of KM. Managing change in that context was connected, perhaps unwittingly, by Drucker in his *Managing in a Time of Great Change*. In the book, Drucker described change management and entrepreneurial thinking in a quotation that is almost custom-made for knowledge strategists and the knowledge workers and strategic knowledge professionals who work with them in developing the knowledge services strategic framework:

> An organization must be organized for constant change. It will no longer be possible to consider entrepreneurial innovation as lying outside of management or even as peripheral to management. Entrepreneurial innovation will have to become the very heart and core of management. The organization's function is entrepreneurial, to put knowledge to work – on tools, products, and processes, on the design of work, on knowledge itself. (Drucker, 1997)

For individuals, the ability to adapt to change is as fundamental as it is to organizations although, truth to tell, anyone through simple observation soon comes to understand that many people – as individuals – are not particularly careful about dealing with change, and some have learned (or been taught) to resist change. For organizations there is no choice. Change it is essential. And for organizations, the primary change requirement is leadership. Successful organizations not only adapt to change, but also anticipate it, drive it, and even make the point of requiring it, of themselves and of their enterprise leaders. They must become, in the words of Rosabeth Moss Kanter, "change adept." Kanter's influential works, such as *The Change Masters* and *When Giants Learn to Dance*, emphasize and illustrate this essential need as well as the hard work it takes to keep organizations vital throughout their natural lifecycles. Kanter states that "change-adept organizations share three attributes: the imagination to innovate, the professionalism to perform, and the openness to collaborate." These are attributes – given much attention in this book – that are very much aligned with the precepts and basic tenets of knowledge services. In putting them forward Kanter challenges knowledge strategists to consider that such as state cannot be attained without strong leadership. She states that leaders must deliver confidence, set high standards, and encourage "connections" with human and knowledge resources (Kanter, 1985). Successful knowledge organizations have, indeed, thought about these concepts. Programs and projects that implement the KD/KS/KU process and are understood to "work" within the organization are those that not only recognize the behaviors of change, but use them to support and strengthen their success.

Change management principles. Smart knowledge strategists and enterprise leaders turn to change management with the confidence that managing and implementing change is required; they embrace the challenge. At this point in the history of management as a science and as an art – and as a profession – there are many approaches to dealing with change, change management, and change implementation. For many managers (including knowledge strategists with management responsibility for organizational knowledge sharing), the best place to begin is with established change management principles.

In doing so, the knowledge leader also becomes the "change leader." He or she, in his or her role as a knowledge strategist, will help the organization take the "different approach to work," attain that "different mind-set," and help the organization and all those affiliated with it move through their own "change curves" to become the more productive, more innovative, and more responsive knowledge workers that Drucker challenges them to be.

Based on our experience and our observations over many years of working together, Dale and I identify four fundamental principles for successfully managing change. While recognizing that there are inevitably any number of subconcepts that support and enhance successful change, the focus in the knowledge services environment is generally on the following:
1. Change readiness: A manager of any initiative needs an assessment of the environment, any significant issues, and the "readiness" of the individuals and the organization as a whole for the impending change.

2. Dealing with resistance: Resistance to change is natural and always present. It must be dealt with, and can often be turned to a positive advantage for the change initiative.
3. Sponsorship: While the knowledge strategist/change leader is the recognized authority with respect to knowledge services, commitment to organizational change for recognizing the value of knowledge services and incorporating the KD/KS/KU process into the managerial structure requires the support of one (occasionally more than one) influential leader. It will be an enterprise-leader, preferably a C-suite officer who commits to a critical role in the change process. In our discussions of sponsorship, Dale and I choose to use the S/M/R acronym, matching to our business's own acronym (SMR International) as a quick reference for codifying the sponsor's commitment for supporting knowledge services. Thus we state that for successful change management, the sponsor is willing to **S**ay (or perhaps, **S**peak about), **M**odel, and **R**eward those who agree with his or her own commitment to the desired change. As described later, we have come to understand that sponsorship is probably the change leader's most powerful lever for acquiring support for knowledge services and implementing change in the organization.
4. Communications planning: During change, nothing is as important as communications. While it is best constant and fluid, it also must be planned, coordinated, and delivered through multiple channels and media types.

With that introduction, we look at each of these principles.

Change readiness. Before change management can begin, good intentions must be tempered with a strong dose of reality, with asking a fundamental question: is the organization (or its knowledge services unit) ready for change? It is all well and good to want to seek to transition the enterprise to a knowledge culture; it is quite another thing to take on such responsibility without a good understanding of the degree of "change readiness," as the subject is generally described.

As noted already, it is clearly recognized in all lines of work that change is inevitable and if implementing knowledge services is the objective, the organization must be "made ready" to change to the knowledge services environment, using recognized change management principles. Rosabeth Moss Kanter and Rick Maurer have separately taken on the study of organizational change readiness since, as each of them emphasizes, the success of any change process depends on the outcome of this determination. Maurer offers a list of guidelines that continue to relate well, especially for knowledge services, as he advises organizational thought leaders to:
– Build a foundation. The knowledge strategist/change leader must ask how he or she can cultivate a strong relationship with those affected by

the change, and how to use the change to build relationships with other stakeholders.
- Communicate with constituents. Simultaneously, the knowledge strategist/change leader will provide a context and a compelling business case for the change and, whenever possible, engage in face-to-face conversation about the change and its implications. At the same time, the change leader will find ways to communicate informally with people at all levels in the organization about the change, throughout the life-cycle of the change.
- Encourage participation. To what extent is the knowledge strategist/change leader able to identify all the individuals and groups that have a stake in the outcome? Is there a way to involve them in the planning making decisions?
- Expect resistance. No matter how well change is planned, resistance will occur, so one of the most important considerations the knowledge strategist must think about is how to make special efforts to monitor people's acceptance or resistance to the proposed change. And ask at the same time how people can be engaged in dialogue so their concerns can be heard and understood.
- Create rewards and benefits for stakeholders. Are there ways to demonstrate that the change will be mutually beneficial for all stakeholders? How do the affected people know that the change will benefit them?
- Lead the change skillfully. Finally, the knowledge strategist/change leader must take special steps to ensure that he or she – and the knowledge services strategic framework development team – have created alignment among diverse interests, making it clear that critical feedback is invited and will be given serious attention, that the compelling vision that change leaders have created is articulated to all stakeholders, and that people are informed about the change as it moves forward. In our opinion, when Maurer says "skillfully" he means that the knowledge strategist/knowledge services change leader will apply the communication, facilitation, and flexibility skills that good, interactive leaders employ (Maurer, 2010).

Kanter, when asked how organizational leaders get past "the rhetoric of change," replied with characteristic directness, describing three key steps taken by knowledge strategists and enterprise managers when they expect to move forward with the change management/change implementation process:
- They put actions behind their words; talk is cheap. Leaders that do the best job of leading change – first of all, they have a vision of where they want to go that's well-articulated, communicated wisely, and communicated repeatedly. That way, everyone has a sense of the destination. There's no point in talking about change if you don't know where you want to go.

- Second, they look for exemplary practices – innovations – that are already occurring in the company that reflect the new way that they want to operate. Leaders put those in front of people as tangible models of what can be done.
- Third, they organize to manage a change process in which projects help move the company to a new state of being. And they put real resources into it. Leaders give people responsibility. They set in place new measures that tell people what the standards are and measure progress toward the goals. They give feedback to an organization. They look to see whether policies, practices, systems, and structures support the change goals (Kanter, 1998).

Kanter's advice is particularly appropriate as knowledge strategists turn their attention to the specifics of change required in the workplace. In moving to an organizational knowledge culture, particular attention must be given to ensuring that the relevance of the function continues and is not dissipated by external and non-essential distractions. At the same time, staffing for a knowledge-centric organization requires new and specifically developed skills and competencies which naturally include the ability to adapt to change. This sometimes over-whelming picture is all part of the transformation of the service delivery focus for knowledge services, and knowledge strategists, knowledge workers, and strategic knowledge professionals in the knowledge services unit (or however they are deployed to meet their responsibilities throughout the organization) are required to recognize the enormous role of the larger and over-arching organizational culture and its influence in determining success or failure in managing change.

Leaders wishing to implement any change, and particularly large "organizational change" may therefore wish to do an assessment of "change readiness." A change readiness assessment is analogous to the "surfacing resistance" ideas discussed below, but in this case the assessment has a different purpose and hence uses different questions and probes. The best change readiness assessments require input from the target audience on:
- Perceptions of the organization's experiences and degrees of success in implementing change (i.e., how has change been managed in other situations?)
- The current overall level of stress and capacity for the addition of a new initiative
- The existence of compelling drivers of change or urgency to solve issues to which the change initiative may be linked
- The existence of strong leaders and potential sponsors of the change, including the rationale they might use to compel the target audience to comply with the needed changes.

As for finding answers to these questions, the usual types of broad surveys can be created with the above questions in mind, asking the target respondents to rate the organization on how well it dealt with change in the past and to what degree they think they and their organization may be "change ready" under the current circumstances. In our experience, these instruments are helpful to ascertain the general temperament, but not entirely adequate. Additionally, often as a follow-on to the broad surveys, small group meetings or focus groups are helpful, meetings in which the audience (and/or key representative individuals) are coached to tell stories of change in the history of the organization. Typical discussion topics or questions might be:
- Tell me about a time when our organization underwent great change.
- How successful was that change?
- What were the factors that helped or hindered the change?
- How well do you think this organization is ready for (this type of) change?
- What do you think would need to happen in order for this type of change to be successful?

The responses to these types of questions will give the knowledge strategist/change leader much-needed insight as to the magnitude of change readiness and ideas as to some of the root-causes and reasons for past failures or sources of resistance.

As part of this conversation, it is important to keep in mind is that a good assessment should give sufficient insight as to the overall change approach or "tone," a tone related, of course, to the overall perspective about change in the larger organization. The knowledge strategist/change leader, the senior manager who has agreed to sponsor the change, and all other change agents involved in the process are required to be consistent in the "telling" portions of the endeavor, and messaging must be consistent with the current culture and values of the organization. This requirement can be acted upon in a variety of ways, and this change approach can range from the very authoritarian ("This is going to happen whether you like it or not") to the more transitional ("We're all in this together and if we work together, we'll get through it"). Deciding on this "change approach" should depend on both the drivers of the change, especially identifying and being prepared to react to the need for the change – its urgency – the culture of the organization, and the organization's readiness for such change.

Dealing with resistance. Many of the barriers to innovation, to the sustainment of bureaucracy and "silos" in organizations and, indeed, to the realization of an effective knowledge organization may be attributed to resistance to change. For our purposes, it is helpful to understand the two most common and powerful species of resistance.

The first of these has to do with the the "indispensable expert." The idea here that in an organization consisting of experts, each with his or her own specialty and who can somehow be reliably found, consulted, and given credit is, indeed, not only old fashioned. Such a scenario is simply impossible in today's organization, given the drive for increased speed of innovation and the expanding realization of what Drucker early on characterized as our "knowledge economy." To many in the workplace (especially experts or leaders in their subject specialization), it may still seem counter-intuitive that knowledge workers must share or "give away" their knowledge, the essential commodity in this new KD/KS/KU world. These experts may feel they must maintain some sort of mysterious aura of the "authority" and that by sharing freely what they actually know, their own indispensability will be diminished. This form of resistance to change may be the most pervasive and the highest threat to the success of any modern, innovation-driven, and knowledge-driven organization; it shows up all too common in research and development and in intensive organizations that draw heavily from academia (where, of course, the paradigm of the "expert" is very much alive and rewarded).

The other type of change resistance is even more common and just as powerful: it is the natural tendency of all of us to resist recommended (or required) change in the ways we actually do our work and "get things done." We are all just human beings, after all, and we spend a lot of time and energy at work. In the workplace, we devote much energy into thinking and learning about the "how" of our work, and as we think and learn, modifying our personal productivity processes to make them efficient, personalized, and as painless as possible. Our workflows and our relationships with our coworkers, clients, customers, and even to our tools are a part of our personal and professional identity. When someone (especially those in leadership roles or employees from another department who don't really understand, "what it is that I really do") come in with a "better way," it's no surprise that we question and resist. Our rational mind may acknowledge that we must embrace change in order to adapt and survive, but in this situation such "interference" nevertheless looks and feels threatening. We react to this type of intrusion as a threat to our identity and to the way we do things every single day! Thus we see it as threatening failure or requiring a lack of productivity to portions of our work day that we have already "mastered." Furthermore, these "better ways" almost always promise easy and faster ways of doing the work, which sounds rational, but to the knowledge worker who is being asked to change the way he or she does something, the idea is frequently translated as, ". . . and they'll expect me to work even faster while not giving me any time to learn or adapt."

This level of attention to our individual work processes brings out our biological "fight or flight" responses, and the rational arguments are not always

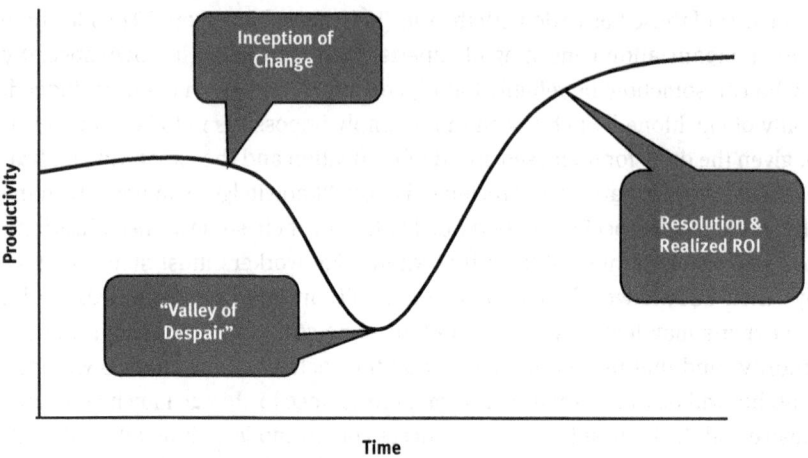

Figure 3.1: The change curve (adapted from William Bridges: Managing Transitions, 2003).

heard. On the personal level, this drives us deeper into the "valley of despair," described below and demonstrated in Figure 3.1. At the organizational level, it will slow or even stall the momentum needed to drive the organization through the change curve and sufficiently alter the collective behaviors of the affected knowledge workers, in order for them to implement or cooperate effectively with the required change. Resistance is often responsible for the failure of projects, particularly in structural changes such as mergers, sales campaign objectives, and the like. It is frequently attributed to such reasons as "insufficient training," "poor user-interfaces," "poor project management," "communication issues," etc. Whatever it is called or however blame is place (many CIOs have lost their jobs due to failed large-scale projects such as ERP or financial systems and a large proportion of these failures can be attributed to poor resistance management or in attempting to ignore it altogether), resistance is real and must be dealt with. Ideally, it is dealt with early and proactively rather than too late or reactively and as a result, we continue to hear plenty of negative stories. Organizational leaders, including knowledge strategists, have learned that the most relevant vision, the best software, even the most talented project managers are no match for a population of users who resist the change in their roles or work. In fact, that description of the difficulties with change management can be taken a little further, as Ron Ashkenas has done:

> As a recognized discipline, change management has been in existence for over half a century. Yet despite the huge investment that companies have made in tools, training, and thousands of books, most studies still show a 60–70 % failure rate for organizational

change projects, a statistic that has stayed constant from the 1970s to the present. Given this evidence, is it possible that everything we know about change management is wrong and that we need to go back to the drawing board? (Ashkenas, 2013)

Ashkenas thinks we might, indeed, have been looking in the wrong direction, and he has a suggestion for us as we go back to the drawing board. He offers his own alternative suggestion, one that gives the knowledge strategist/knowledge services change leader a welcome opportunity for establishing how change management and change implementation might be dealt with as the knowledge services strategic framework is developed. Ashkenas asserts that "the content of change management is reasonably correct, but the managerial capacity to implement it has been woefully underdeveloped. In fact, instead of strengthening managers' ability to manage change, we've instead allowed managers to outsource change management to HR specialists and consultants instead of taking accountability themselves – an approach that often doesn't work."

That, it seems to us, is what takes the knowledge strategist – in his or her role as the organization's knowledge services change leader – to a new "place" with respect to the management of the organization's intellectual capital. "Putting knowledge to work" cannot happen if knowledge is not freely shared (the "KS" of our KD/KS/KU process as well as Kanter's "collaboration" theme – and ours as we saw in Chapter 2, Section 2.1). And if knowledge cannot be freely shared, how will it be "utilized," our KU? Helping the knowledge worker get beyond the fear of sharing his or her knowledge – whether voluntarily or proactively – is beyond a mere enabling concept: it is central to the success of any knowledge services initiative. This is why managing change and helping people change is central to successful knowledge services and, indeed, to the success of this new age of knowledge work. Knowledge workers are confronted with a fear that is real, and the idea of somehow becoming dispensable or less valued is frightening to all knowledge workers. As such, it represents the major change management challenge in the knowledge domain and for today's knowledge leader.

The psychological and even the physiological phenomenon of change management has been often observed and can be described in this "change curve" (shown in Figure 3.1), adapted from William Bridges (Bridges, 2009). Bridges describes the human and organizational change phenomenon as one in which productivity or one's sense of well-being is depressed while individuals deal with the need to "let go" of past ways and embrace the new. The curve describes the natural human reaction to any change event over time (the x-axis of the curve) while "productivity" (or, if there were measures, the mood or sense of well-being of a person, or the "morale" of an organization) varies during the time of change. When the inception of the change occurs there is always a significant drop in productivity. It has much to do with the human response to threats and change, and also indirectly to the fact the humans need to communicate, commiserate, speculate, and otherwise spend time that takes away from their usual work tasks. In some environments, especially when the stakes are high (e.g., pending layoffs) and prolonged with inadequate communication, the trough of productivity can be severe. This phase has thus led many of us to characterize this time as the "valley of despair." With time and adaptation, people and organizations are usually able to climb out of the valley, establish some resolution to move forward and begin to reap the benefits of the proposed change.

As the discussion moves into how the knowledge strategist/knowledge services change leader moves into working with staff when change is required, for some it might be useful to think about how this phenomenon could be analogous to the Kübler-Ross model of the stages of grief, which also involve initial resistance, a more rational stage of "negotiating" and eventual acceptance (Kübler-Ross, 2005). Understanding this natural process is helpful to the change leader, as we see when we refer to the change curve. Skillful change management will not eliminate the change curve, but there is no doubt that the mere recognition of this universal phenomenon is helpful in itself. Good change management helps individuals and organizations shorten the timeframe towards resolution, and it will also help decrease the amplitude of the curve (i.e., make the "valley of despair" not so deep). This challenge of addressing the human side of changing to the knowledge culture takes on then the characteristic of an essential knowledge services principle and skill set for the knowledge workers, the strategic knowledge professionals, and of course the knowledge strategist.

From our experience, we have learned that effectively dealing with resistance should occur in three distinct actions: "surfacing" the resistance, "acknowledging" it, and "responding" to it. Leaders are typically accustomed to "telling," and too many of them forget to ask, listen, and acknowledge what their constituents are saying before telling them what to do about something and how to do it. The bulk of the "telling" should occur after the asking, listening, and acknowledging. It should also employ the role of the sponsor and good communications planning as described in the remainder of this chapter.

Surfacing resistance involves asking and listening. And, as Kotter puts it, ". . . a lot of it." Too many managers or implementers don't want to hear about problems or resistance. For them, there is often a tendency to interpret resistance as disloyalty or lack of respect for their authority or competence as leaders. As a result of these attitudes, these leaders are always the fastest to go through the change curve. In their enthusiasm and their optimism, they tend to forget that there are others who may be slower, or still be struggling with denial in the "valley of despair" and yet to see and embrace the benefits or hard work it takes to make the transition. And the leaders, as project managers or project sponsors, are often motivated to move forward with implementation quickly to stay on time and on budget. But if ignored, resistance can easily cause delays, cost increases and even total failure of the desired change initiative.

We have our advice for the knowledge strategist, now (as we have surely made clear) working also as the organization's change leader in bringing the knowledge services strategic framework into play:
- Engage those affected by the change, early-on, asking about potential "roadblocks", "challenges", "issues" or "problems." Listen to what they say, implement any changes if possible, and then tell them that you heard them and that you did something about it.
- For the implementation stage, build in time in your project planning in order to listen to what is being asked or said (and then to respond).

Note that the above advice entails the three aspects of surfacing, acknowledging, and responding. To expand on these, we turn to Sharon Penfold, who wrote one of the classic books on change management as part of the Information Services Management Series (disclosure: as noted earlier, Guy was the series editor). In the book, Penfold shares useful and commonsense advice provided by experts in the human resources/human capital field:
- Identify the type of resistance (expected as well as in evidence).
- Analyze (based on the factors of intensity, source, and focus).
- Look for behavior (emotional) and rational (system) factors.
- View resistance as rational, not irrational.
- Ask what useful purpose the resistance is serving.
- Identify real or perceived negative consequences of the change.
- Weaken the apparent link between the change and the negative consequences.
- Reduce rather than eliminate resistance (e.g., avoid surprises, ensure participation).
- Work directly with individuals affected to deal with their personal concerns.
- Use a mix of push and pull styles to influence individuals, dependent on each situation and individual (Penfold, 2013).

This is helpful advice, and especially useful for interpreting resistance and in deciding how to respond. Building on Penfold's concepts, additional thoughts, such as these, for responding to resistance can follow:
- It's okay to say, "I don't know, but I'll find out." Or, "I don't know, but we will consider that and get back to you."

- It's okay to indicate that you will not solve all the existing problems or issues in the first phase of a project (or ever, for that matter). You can say that the solving of a particular problem or shortcoming is "not presently being considered" or is "presently out-of-scope in the up-coming rollout."
- You can acknowledge an emotional response without conceding a planned activity. It's okay to say, "I hear what you are saying . . . . and we are going ahead." In this regard, note that we recommend you say "and" and not "but" (there is something about the word, "but" that is interpreted as negating everything that was said beforehand).
- On a strategic note, Dale and Guy in their work have often observed that, in anticipating resistance to a particular project, the project leaders/sponsors find opportunities to reference an overall knowledge strategy in their responses. We have often been asked to help with change management for projects and find that most responses to resistance can be answered with something to the effect of, "Thanks for asking. We have a long-range knowledge strategy that addresses that and we will devote the time and resources to make appropriate accommodations." Of course, the more specific the plans are that can be referred to, the more specific, credible, and acceptable the responses will be.

We should mention that it is often the case that the organization has been so intent at implementing projects that they do not have an up-to-date knowledge strategy. Anticipating resistance to the implementation of a project, realizing that the best response to that resistance would be to reference a knowledge strategy has, more than once, compelled an organization to "take a step back" and create that strategy. We should also mention that the likelihood of this "step-back" effort being considered a viable alternative is directly related to how early in the project the change management planning and questions of how to respond to resistance is brought up.

As the knowledge strategist/change leader asks, probes and listens, a pattern of responders and their reactions will be revealed. The responders can be easily categorized as:

1. The "resisters." These are typically the staff members (or managers) who are actively – and usually vocally – either resisting the change or saying it doesn't matter and soon everything will be back to "normal."
2. The "early adopters." These are the staff members who quickly see the benefits of the change or are otherwise motivated (sometimes through loyalty or high trust in the leadership) to embrace the change and move on. Often enthusiastic about the change they many times have quickly done the internal calculus of weighing the benefits of the new versus losing the old, plus the work involved in the transition.

3. The "fence-sitters." In early stages of implementation, this can be the largest group. They are either passively waiting to see whether the initiative will succeed and how exactly it will affect them, or they will be actively questioning the specifics of what, when, and how.

In any population undergoing change, the proportions of these subpopulations will vary. Early-on, the proportions will likely be driven by the current culture and its change-readiness. An organization with recent or frequent changes, and particularly ones in which change initiatives have been perceived as painful or failed, will naturally have larger numbers of initial "resisters."

As the initiative continues, it will be important to observe the shifts in patterns by continuing to ask, acknowledge, and respond. Where they have been identified and invited by the knowledge strategist/knowledge services change leader to participate in the process, embedded change agents can be key sources of intelligence in this regard, as we discuss a bit more below. The patterns and the shifting are easily explained by referring to the change curve. Different people move through the change curve at different rates. The early adopters (which always include the change leaders) have moved quickly, while the resisters and fence-sitters have either moved more slowly or have gotten stuck in one of the stages.

A skillful knowledge services change leader will be able to recognize these subpopulations and focus their communications and responses accordingly. We recommend the following general approaches:
– Use the early adopters as your champions and change agents. Identify them, make them feel special, reward their behaviors and attitudes, and recruit them to help build support and momentum for driving the rest of the population through the change curve
– Focus most of your communication and influencing efforts on the fence sitters. Probe for resistance, respond, and reward adoption
– Ignore the resisters. Some vocal individuals may have to be dealt with, but for the most part, the change leader's energies should be focused on creating momentum by rewarding the adopters and moving the fence-sitters.

Resistance is inevitable and real. The knowledge strategist/knowledge services change leader who tries to ignore it does so at the project's peril. Surfacing, acknowledging, and responding to the resistance, while uncomfortable for many leaders, is essential for helping an organization and its individuals change. The key here is momentum. Recognizing, helping, and even rewarding people for moving through the change curve – even for "acting as if they are moving" – is imperative. Here are additional suggestions, this time focusing on maintaining momentum:

- Create "quick wins" and easily-attained milestones early on and publicize them
- Find and communicate success stories and testimonials from your early adopters, champions and change agents
- Do surveys, polls and use any additional data to both publicize movement and success as well as to understand who and where the fence-sitters are. Many times there are sub-populations of fence-sitters that are distributed along other naturally occurring strata such as organizational divisions, geography, and hierarchy. Once identified, targeted and tailored approaches can be devised. For example, a common set of fence sitters are supervisors or middle management. These individuals are not, as a group, resistant to change, but due to their job function, they do not always have the long-range vision or engagement of upper leadership, or the specific focus on tasks and job duties as those below them.

Sponsorship: Mentioned throughout this book, we now move on to looking at this critical change management principle with a specific definition of sponsorship, along with specific behaviors that are considered to be the most powerful "lever" in attaining organizational change. In establishing a sponsorship arrangement, the knowledge strategist identifies an organizational leader – a leader with influence – who is willing to commit to a critical role in the change process and agrees to say or speak about, model, and reward others about their commitment to the desired change. Sponsorship is the change leader's powerful handle for obtaining support and implementing change in the organization and, in fact, could very well be considered the knowledge strategist's most-powerful tool in the change-management process.

As it happens, effective sponsors communicate in a specific manner, for these people have direct authority and influence over all who will be affected by the change and they are open in performing the primary function of the sponsor, to – as we like to phrase their role – Speak about, Model, and Reward the desired behavioral changes. They are considered to be a specific type of change agent or champion of the cause. Sponsors have the following attributes:
- They have direct organizational authority over those whose behaviors need to change. Despite the various models and experiments in self-managed teams, matrix management, and the like, one can always find someone in authority. Because of their position, these sponsors have a unique power and influence that must be leveraged by the change leader. While sometimes it is the organizational leader him/herself who is also the change leader, most of the time this involves finding and recruiting someone else for this role.

With respect to sponsors, the "message" is direct. Think of the desired behavior or message you want your sponsor to help change and support, and get your sponsor to:

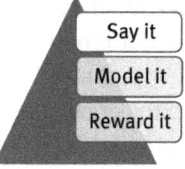

Figure 3.2: Sponsorship in change management.

- They are committed to the objectives of the change initiative. Importantly, they have the ability to connect the change goals to the larger organization's vision, mission, values, or other highly visible goals.
- They are committed to acting and communicating as a sponsor.

The role of the sponsor: It is the sponsor who helps the organization move through the change curve and embrace the needed behavioral changes. The sponsor can most effectively accomplish these by using specific modes of reinforcement along with a recognized model of communication. Using our quick recommended acronym, the modes of sponsorship communication are:
- *Say*, speak with, or tell their constituents that they, the sponsor, support the initiatives and the specific desired behavioral changes that will result from the initiative. When the sponsor says something, the constituents generally listen. When he or she is specific, the changes are much more likely to happen.
- *Model* the desired changes. When the sponsor not only says but actually demonstrates that he or she is engaged and will also be complying with the recommended changes supporting the initiative, we have a hugely powerful driver. When the sponsor is prompted, coached, or even ghost-authored, to say something to the effect of, "This is a good thing that's aligned with the organization's goals, and I am going to do/use it along with you," the result can be transformative in moving the fence-sitters and driving momentum. And as a slight aside, the "model-ing" works best when the sponsors (or a group of "cascaded sponsors," as noted below) engage literally in the act of serving as a model the change. Guy tells the story of a client situation in which a planned change would result in a more efficient and less time-consuming response effort for various forms required for the organization's work (it was a large international development organization, with many layers of form reviews for many internal activities). As it happened, as the change was being proposed to the organization's Deputy Executive

Director, she said, with no hesitation, that it was exactly what was needed in the executive offices. She and her staff – she made it clear – would be the first group to support the change management study and effort and when it was completed, her team would be the first group to take up the new way of doing things. Needless to say, her support and enthusiasm – and her not-so-subtle way of letting everyone in the organization know that she supported the effort – had great effect in changing the minds of some of the resisters.

- *Reward* or reinforce the desired changes. The most powerful and unfortunately least-used method is the creation of reward systems for the desired behavioral changes. When the sponsor is perceived as the author or supporter of the rewards or reinforcement, the incentives become much more powerful. What the reward is does not particularly matter; the point is that the participants must have the sense that their participation is recognized by the sponsor as providing a benefit, however defined. Indeed, in most organizations we have found in our experience that the actual value of the reward (or degree of disincentives) doesn't need to be exceedingly high. The mere visibility of such systems seems sufficiently effective. A current trend is the current trend in "gamification" of many social media and networking programs, a testament to this powerful motivational tool.

We can also describe the importance of the sponsor by looking at another critical role the sponsor takes on, often unwittingly. This has to do with his or her position in the organization, recognizing again that sponsors are often as valuable for their influence as for their actual participation. Indeed, in change management and change implementation that influence can be almost as critical as their cooperative leadership with the knowledge strategist/knowledge services change leader. In connection with the sponsors' influence we can share a few specific guidelines.

The first of these simply recognizes that – as we hope we have made clear – sponsors are the bedrock of successful change in any organization, and in moving toward a knowledge culture, with the enormous requirement for changed thinking and behavior that is required, sponsors are identified and invited to engage in the development process.

It is not surprising that the effectiveness of sponsors in change management is greatest when there is a critical mass of involved participants, as W. Chan Kim and Renée Mauborgne describe. "In any organization," they write, "fundamental change can occur quickly when the beliefs and energy of a critical mass of people create an 'epidemic' movement toward an idea." The example they use, the technique of which they refer to as "tipping point leadership" comes from

William Bratton's success in bringing about massive change in the New York Police Department. Bratton employed four change management tools:
1. He put managers face-to-face with operational problems.
2. He identified change implementation opportunities in areas that would result in the biggest payoffs and high-visibility.
3. He identified and exploited key influencers who (as Kim and Mauborgne describe) have "disproportionate power because of their connections or persuasive abilities."
4. He was consistent and would not allow his change effort to be lured "off message" (Kim and Mauborgne, 2003).

With this story, we have a clear example of what is expected of the sponsors in the knowledge services strategic framework development project and in dealing with the changes required for implementing that strategy. In simplest terms, we simply advise both the knowledge strategist/knowledge services change leader and the sponsor to remember and keep at hand the acronym we propose: *SMR: "Say"/"Model"/ "Reward."* It can be the key to effective sponsorship and communications.

Sponsorship recruitment: Once the sponsor has been identified, the next challenge is usually finding the time on an executive's busy calendar to solidify the partnership. And make no mistake about it – this phase of "partnering" with the sponsor is critical; the sponsor must "co-own" the project with the knowledge strategist/change leader. Otherwise, all the work of saying, modeling, and rewarding can easily come across as disingenuous. The face-to-face interaction is very highly recommended.

And the knowledge strategist/knowledge services change leader should not be satisfied with simply a tacit expression of support. Once he or she has the attention of the sponsor and the sponsor expresses interest and a willingness to join in the activity, the change leader might be inclined to make a quick and humble exit, but such a gesture could ruin the entire process. It is imperative at this juncture to stand one's ground and assume cooperative partnering with the respective sponsor. To get to that stage, the knowledge leader should say something along the lines of, "Thanks for your support. And now your help is needed on *our* project: We need you to speak about, model and reward the following messages and behaviors in support of our project . . . ." If there is any executive pushback at this point, the knowledge leader – as politely as possible – goes into the second stage of the message: "Is there some way I can help you with this? I know you and your team are specially busy, so I'm wondering: would it help if I write the emails, the speeches, or give the background materials to your staff? I can personally train you on the system (or give you background materials on our strategy) so you can model the new ways; I can help design the appropriate reward systems." And if there is still a little sigh of "Hmmm," you push on: "When can we start?"

With the support of your sponsor, there is now another concept to consider, what we like to think of as the sponsorship cascade and overcoming the middle-management gap. In our opinion – we are adamant about this – the sponsor must be at as high a level in the organization as is appropriate for the change initiative. Generally, the higher the status of the sponsor, the better. As mentioned above, however, a common problem is the lack of accessibility and the huge time-demands of a high-level executive. It is many times impossible to get sufficiently frequent meetings with these people, or have messages from them. This situation is remedied by the concept of cascading sponsorship, which works like this: The high-level sponsor is engaged, and to the extent possible, is asked to speak about, model, and reward the changed behaviors. Initial communications from the primary sponsor are critical but then, as a part of the partnering agreement with the change leader, the executive appoints multiple subordinates to carry on the sponsorship commission. The original sponsor may still have his or her own (assigned) communication plans, but he or she also authorizes subordinates to speak about, model, and reward the behaviors and programs throughout their own sub-organizations. This pattern serves at least two purposes: it allows for additional reinforcing voices of authority that are closer to the constituents, and it helps eliminates the gap of communication that happens all too often in middle management.

The emphasis here is on identifying and obtaining commitments from influential people willing to speak about the benefits of change, people who will encourage adoption (champions are usually thought of as early adopters and change agents as individuals who will speak about, model, and reward the new behaviors to a population of users). In practice, "change agents" are not only enthusiastic about the initiatives, they are skilled in surfacing and responding to resistance. In large or longer-term change initiatives, it is helpful to not only identify potential change agents, but to create a change-agent map and strategy. Such a strategy typically involves at least the following elements:
- Identifying potential change agents
- Mapping the organization and naming the known change agents and their spheres of influence
- Recruiting and grooming potential change agents where there are gaps in the map
- Training the change agents in:
  - Well-articulated benefit statements of the changes
  - The skills of facilitating, surfacing, and responding to resistance

– The principles of change management, creating an understanding of what individuals and organizations go through, especially the change curve for individuals and organizations.
– These individuals are important to recruit and reward because – while they lack the influence that comes from formal authority – they have earned a high degree of credibility and informal influence. They are nearly as powerful as sponsors in supporting change initiatives.

Communications Planning: Of almost equal importance, this change management principle enables the engagement of users early in the process and connects with the above principles in a coordinated and consistent manner. As an example of an effective application of this principle is the development of a calendar of events or project plan that incorporates elements of a consistent message in language that matches that of the organizational culture in which the affected stakeholders are employees.

When looking to enter into the change management process for knowledge services, good background directions can be found in Susan Curzon's list, provided a generation ago. She referred to it as "The Basic Steps of Change Management":

1. Conceptualize.
2. Prepare the organization.
3. Organize the planning group.
4. Plan.
5. Decide.
6. Manage the individual.
7. Surface and address resistance.
8. Implement.
9. Evaluate (Curzon, 1989).

Of course, the first step is conceptualization, and in any organizational effort, moving toward a new or different management framework requires those with management responsibility to begin their thinking and their discussions with their colleagues.

In today's organizations with their multi-media forms of communication, and in recognition of today's variety of learning and engagement styles, it is essential that the communication plan span the breadth of the media that are commonly used in the organization. An analysis of what media are used for which kinds of communications and for which audiences is a good place to begin. Then, tailoring the communication plans to entail a wide variety of appropriate media, timing, and "channels" can be achieved. Creating a simple planning table such as drafted below can help, and the knowledge strategist and the knowledge services team can begin by identifying the "messages" they wish to send. As we always emphasize, the messages must be transmitted early and often, and we recognize that it is perfectly permissible in most organizations to send the same "message" in a variety of media (e.g., emails, memos, speeches, video, posts), modes (i.e., lengths, tone, etc.), and timings (e.g., "It's coming," "It's almost here," "Now's the time," "Don't forget," "It's not too late," "It's still not too late," "If you haven't yet..." etc.)

Message	Audience	Medium	Timing	Who's Responsible	Follow-up

So in most communication plans, there are many repeated rows in this table where the same "message" is communicated through multiple media, to multiple audiences, each tailored to ensure the targets of the messages hear it multiple times and in multiple ways.

Building on the critical necessity of communications planning for knowledge services, we recognized that no discussion on change management is complete without describing in some detail the work of John P. Kotter, who published his "eight-stage process for creating major change" some years ago (and re-published it in 2012, with a new Preface for the book). As Kotter sees it, organizational change must be "anchored" in the culture, which means that the knowledge strategist/knowledge leader and others with responsibility for moving the organization to a knowledge culture must make every effort to understand the larger organizational culture before they attempt to make the change. In his book on the subject, Kotter suggests that successful change management has four particular characteristics which we can see relate specifically to change management in the knowledge services environment:

- Successful change depends on results, since new approaches usually sink into a culture only after it is very clear that they work and are superior to old methods
- Successful change requires a lot of talk, for without verbal instruction and support, people are often reluctant to admit the validity of new practices
- Successful change may involve turnover, since sometimes the only way to change a culture is to change key people
- Successful change makes decisions on succession crucial, since if promotion processes are not changed to be compatible with the new practices, the old culture will reassert itself (Kotter, 1995)

Kotter then puts forward his eight-stage process. While less of a step-by-step "process" and more of a set of guiding principles, they provide solid advice to knowledge leaders embarking on organizational change:
1. Establish a sense of urgency.
2. Create the guiding coalition.
3. Develop a vision and a strategy.
4. Communicate the change vision.
5. Empower broad-based action.
6. Generate short-term wins.
7. Consolidate gains and producing more change.
8. Anchor new approaches to culture (Kotter, 2012).

Obviously the transformation of any knowledge-centric organization into an enterprise built on a knowledge culture, with its broader and more demanding knowledge services responsibilities directed to a larger marketplace, is essentially an operational restructuring. At the same time – and surprisingly still posing a challenge to the successful development of a knowledge services structure – connections with information technology continue to come into play, as can be seen in the description of change management from Ann Rockley, introduced earlier. It is a definition that can – with a little imagination – be transferred to a definition of change management for knowledge services:

> Change management is managing the process of implementing major changes in IT, business processes, organizational structures, and job assignments to reduce the risks and costs of change, and to optimize its benefits. Change management is focused on the issues of managing the resistance and discomfort experienced by people in an organization when new processes or technology are introduced. (Rockley, 2003)

As Rockley makes clear, for many people the tasks associated with change are difficult. In dealing with (or at least attempting to deal with) that resistance and discomfort, organizational leadership has a responsibility to recognize and attempt to understand the various barriers that inhibit change.

From the perspective of many managers, change and change-related activities are traditionally considered – and are expected to be – disruptive and painful in the workplace, but that does not necessarily have to be the case. With a clear understanding of the elements of the change management process that supports and enhances knowledge services, change can proceed for the common good. Indeed, for many leaders in the field, a focus on resistance is less productive than an emphasis on the benefits, and, as Lyndon Pugh (2007) accurately describes, "managers have already at hand the tools to do this, in addition to their skills in understanding the psychology of the people they work with."

The key motivational structures, for Pugh, are job enrichment, job enlargement, and team structures. With them, Pugh connects successful change management (as do the present authors, as noted below) with Maslow's recognition that an essential higher order need is self-esteem, coming from, as Pugh puts it, "a belief in one's own ability and also in one's value to the organization" and involving self-analysis and the achievement of "a realistic and honest view of one's capabilities." Such success also means that for managers, there is an obligation to encourage people to understand what they can accomplish and to provide support for them to do so. At the same time, change management, in Pugh's assessment, "involves that most difficult of things, particularly for managers, that of seeking and accepting feedback from others."

Pugh also gives a generous and surprising nod to R.H. Cox, who writes about self-esteem in sports: "Learning and development," Pugh writes, "... play a part in increasing self-belief," and he notes that – from the change management perspective – self-esteem is important for the long-term, an "essential pre-requisite for sustaining motivation. Once [self-esteem] is weakened, high-achievers become risk-avoiders."

Pugh then provides his own lists for success with change management, for ensuring that – as we would frame it – the fear of "imposing" a knowledge culture is offset by a willingness and a desire to work with change management and change implementation principles to bring about a knowledge culture. In his list, Pugh describes how managers bring about change success, to make the enterprise an interesting place to work.

Pugh follows this advice with a good list of specific managerial actions that will, he states, lay the foundation for a well-motivated workforce. Pugh's guidelines for accomplishing this important goal urges managers to:
- Convince people what they can achieve in the new environment.
- Design jobs to permit development and learning.
- Engage in real and ongoing structural change.
- Foster cultural change.
- Develop and sell a vision.
- Give people responsibility.
- Communicate.
- Change themselves (and take a good look at their own management patterns).
- Dispense with bureaucratic behavior.

When change management for knowledge services works, there is no better time to be the knowledge strategist for the organization. A fine example was published in Linda Stoddart's description of the development of a knowledge sharing strategic framework at the United Nations. The changes put in place resulted in many solid accomplishments, but of particular importance was the success of the change management process in creating a sense of community with respect to knowledge services. As described by Stoddart (2007), "A sense of community has been fostered by the creation of a network of local points providing content across the organization worldwide.... This community approach has helped encourage knowledge sharing and a transition toward a more collaborative organizational culture."

Notably, in this work the capture of the incremental steps Stoddart and her team undertook provide a strong model that, not surprisingly, incorporates important directions and reinforces their validity:
- Articulate the goal and establish focal point community.
- Conduct a knowledge services audit.
- Create an internal communications working group.
- Reach out to all stakeholders.
- Conduct planning and strategy focus training workshops.

For an example, we might look back at an earlier approach to change management. Many remember an advertising campaign of several years ago, one which asserted that "change imposed is change opposed." Today, in some circles, the same is said about knowledge services, that the development of a knowledge culture cannot be imposed upon a group of workers or made obligatory, at any level. No one disputes this but some even posit that there is no advantage to be gained in attempting to create a knowledge culture for an organization, institution, or enterprise. Dale and I beg to differ. While we agree that imposed change is quite naturally wrong, if the goal is important enough, as we believe it is when we speak about the value of organizational success in an enterprise managed as a knowledge culture, the organization's leaders can – and indeed have an obligation to – identify how the principles of change, change management, and change implementation will lead to the desired effect they envision for the larger organization.

Which leads us to offer our change management strategy for knowledge services. When preparing the organization for developing and sustaining an enterprise-wide knowledge culture (and implementing the principles of knowledge services to do so), change management takes on a different cast. As the knowledge strategist/knowledge services change leader and the team working with him or her pursue the knowledge services strategic framework – the organizational knowledge strategy – discussions naturally turn to how enterprise leaders they will lead the change. These are very appealing situations because they enable the change leader and his or her colleagues to envision just how good they can make the workplace. On the printed page or computer screen and in conversations with their colleagues, it all looks very nice. The apparent ease of transition from idealized and theoretical KM to the practical, day-to-day workings in each situation appeal to the tidy and methodical perspective that many bring to their work in the knowledge domain.

But there is a different side to the story. Organizational change is hard, and while it is often not too difficult to articulate a new strategy or a re-structuring, or to demonstrate the potential value of a desired result (as described earlier in those references to the pleasant intellectual discussions that take place), bringing any change into an organization is going to be difficult. Hopefully concepts and ideas like those described here are helpful, but even when they are, all the players involved in the change management effort are forced to wrestle with dealing with change management and change implementation in their specific organizational environments.

What is hard – indeed, the hardest part – is getting the larger organization to understand the value of the change and to then accept the change as it becomes part of the organizational effort. As we speak about so often – and not only the authors of this section but almost unendingly by almost everyone in the management community – people and organizations just naturally seem to resist change.

Nevertheless, if knowledge workers, strategic knowledge professionals, and all others having any affiliation with the organization's knowledge domain truly desire to participate in the process of moving the organization to a knowledge culture, and indeed, to lead the process (which they all should do, at one level or another, even if that leadership role is no more than giving voice to their support for the effort), there are steps that can be taken:

– Define the change. If the knowledge strategist/change leader and the knowledge services team are not sufficiently clear and precise about what will be required (not just the desired end result but the activities that will be needed to achieve that result), it will be far too easy to resist or passively avoid any desired change. In terms of moving to a knowledge culture, to establishing a KD/KS/KU framework for the knowledge transfer process in the organization, all participants should familiarize themselves with the concepts and specific roles described here, taking them as talking points, a basis for articulating the specific changes to the people who can help you initiate change. This leads to . . . .
– Find a knowledge services/change management sponsor. Before the project begins, the knowledge strategists/change leader must establish strong sponsorship for whatever change will be required. Despite the verbiage that supports "grass roots" ideas and discussions about "demonstrating feasibility,"

there is a strong need for an advocate or champion (or several) to take a stand. Additionally, that person or group of people is going to be required to move from simply championing the change ("that's a good idea") to actual participation ("what you're proposing will impact my work – I'll support it, I'll tell people how this helps me and the company, and I'll reinforce and reward the change"). Usually there is a point in the change process where behaviors and decisions need to be influenced on a substantial scale. That can't happen unless there is leadership buy-in and a commitment to buy-in that is expressed in the words and actions of enterprise leaders.
- Create alliances and identify change agents. The organizational shift to a knowledge culture is initially the result of an alliance (or in many cases a group of alliances). The knowledge strategist/change leader and all of his or her supporters must utilize the various elements of the many definitions of KM that fit the immediate situation, match them with information management and strategic learning in knowledge services, and work to establish a KD/KS/KU environment with knowledge services as the organization's management methodology and service-delivery focus tool. Then all of the team will work to integrate those alliances, starting with like-minded functional leaders and thought leaders in the organization and joining with them, with everyone working as change agents and identifying areas where everyone shares concerns related to the full range of information/ knowledge/strategic learning interests. A key step will be to look for areas where knowledge sharing is needed but is not taking place or not working well; the change leader (now plural: change leaders) will meet with and engage with these colleagues to come up with integrated solutions. The end result will benefit all business units in the organization, realizing an enterprise-wide holistic solution.
- Use caution. For everyone taking part, a certain level of wariness is called for, looking to avoid quick fixes and reactive responses. When there is an established desire for improvements in the knowledge transfer process within the organization, leading, hopefully, to the beginnings of a knowledge culture, many of the players (including sponsors) naturally start to look for mere tools or techniques. The song is often the same: "Ah, hah! Now we are ready for KM/knowledge services. Find me the best software application and let's make this happen!" We must all be careful. It's not just about software.

Drucker's "social transformation" to the knowledge society is upon us, but moving into it is hard. It is not an easy transition, and as Kanter reminds us again and again, change also requires leadership, and in the process, the knowledge strategist has now become organization's primary change leader, its knowledge services change leader.

The knowledge strategist must keep in mind that at this juncture in the knowledge services process, he or she is going to be required to reiterate – often – to colleagues and organization leaders that culture shifts require new ways of doing work and new ways of relating to enterprise stakeholders. In addition to strong reinforcement from sponsors, all involved in the change management process will require a variety of approaches and tools. The tools of knowledge services implementation must now include change management and change implementation methods. In organizations, whether the change is happening on the broad scale of a knowledge strategy or at the tactical level of rolling out the latest ECM or collaboration application, the methods still apply and are equally important in successful implementation.

With the broad knowledge services strategy in mind, and with good execution in managing the required changes, the knowledge strategist will position himself or herself to ensure higher value realization and smoother change management, resulting in real, sustainable change for the larger organization.

This is the hard work of knowledge services. Putting knowledge management to work and using your knowledge services strategic framework – the organization's knowledge strategy – to enable practical solutions is hard. But we can also say that witnessing the knowledge services strategic framework move into action is the most rewarding part of the entire effort.

3.2 Knowledge Strategist to Knowledge Thought Leader

Throughout this book, the term "knowledge strategist" has been used to describe the senior management employee with responsibility, authority, and accountability for the organization's knowledge domain. We have seen the knowledge strategist come to understand the connection between KM and knowledge services, to recognize the role of management and leadership in establishing the authority of the knowledge strategist, and the steps that the knowledge strategist can take to lead the organization toward its valued purpose, its structuring as a knowledge culture (or to strengthening the knowledge culture if it is already in place). We have explored the role of collaboration in the knowledge domain and taken up learning specific steps for applying knowledge services in the organization (performing the knowledge services audit, exploring measures and metrics for knowledge services, and developing the knowledge services strategic framework, the organization's knowledge strategy). With Barrie Schessler we have given attention to the specific work – ECM and knowledge asset management – of the knowledge strategist and his or her team of knowledge workers and strategic knowledge professionals in the organization's knowledge service unit (or, if the knowledge strategist is among the organization's C-suite enterprise leaders, knowledge-focused work of the enterprise-wide staff of the larger organization). Finally, moving forward, we have taken advantage of Dale Stanley's expertise in change management and change implementation as he shared his ideas about change management tools and techniques for the knowledge domain.

All of these activities lead up to and include the development and implementation of the knowledge services strategic framework – the subject of this book – with the expectation that this organizational knowledge strategy will enable the achievement of the highest levels of knowledge sharing among its leaders, staff, stakeholders, and all others affiliated with the organization. By transitioning information, knowledge, and strategic learning to *strategic* knowledge, knowledge strategy enables contextual decision-making, accelerated innovation, strengthened research, and excellence in knowledge asset management for the organization.

As the preparation the book progressed, we saw an evolution in the role of the knowledge strategist, and this closing section addresses the culmination of this process, the transformation of the knowledge strategist into the knowledge thought leader. From my point of view, it is important to recognize that the knowledge strategist – as important as the work of that leader-manager is in the knowledge domain – has now the opportunity to go further, to be the inspirational knowledge leader of the organization, what I choose to refer to as the organization's knowledge thought leader.

Of course the two terms ("knowledge strategist" and "knowledge thought leader") can naturally refer to the same employee. Now, though, my reference to

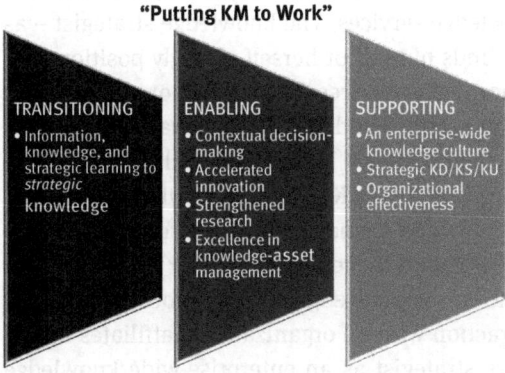

Figure 3.3: Knowledge services: The *practical* side of KM.

the knowledge strategist will incorporate what I hope is the desire of each knowledge strategist, to serve also in a position that builds on but is essentially a far more influential role for the person who does this work, the organization's knowledge thought leader.

The "new" knowledge strategist. So while the knowledge strategist and the knowledge thought leader might be two different management employees, I am positing that to be truly successful the knowledge strategist must seek and assume this second – and strengthening – role. In this section, we explore the knowledge thought leader's influential role and his or her expected direction of the knowledge-sharing process, how he or she can use knowledge services and the KD/KS/KU process to ensure that knowledge sharing is achieved at its highest level. Hopefully this chapter demonstrates that as the knowledge thought leader, this leader-manager (with leadership attributes more in the ascendency than before) will be able to shape the organization's knowledge services strategic framework in support of the organization as a knowledge culture, creating an organizational knowledge services "personality," (*à la*, perhaps, Marvin Bower's "firm personality" at McKinsey?), an empowering quality that will be recognized for the good it brings to the organization.

The transformation begins with thinking about the knowledge thought leader and how that person's influence in the organization can be established and sustained. As the knowledge thought leader, the knowledge strategist is not only working with and expanding the parameters of knowledge services and the KD/KS/KU process. This senior management employee is now beyond the mere application of knowledge services that leads to enabling the total acceptance of knowledge sharing, so much so that the organization becomes positioned – with all the attendant benefits – as a knowledge culture. As a knowledge thought leader, the knowledge strategist becomes a leader-manager whose performance is grounded on and matches philosophically the organization's value proposition for knowledge services. The knowledge strategist – as the knowledge thought leader – finds himself or herself strongly positioned to move the effort for applying knowledge services forward. He or she now has a clear understanding of the organization and of the organizational culture, of how information, knowledge, and strategic learning are valued within the organization, and of the functioning of the KD/KS/KU process within the organization. And, regardless of one's individual management or personal leadership style, integrated into the work of the knowledge thought leader is a passionate and high-level enthusiasm for the entire knowledge-transfer process, a passion that carries over into every interaction with all organizational affiliates and in fact distinguishes the knowledge strategist as an enterprise-wide knowledge thought leader.

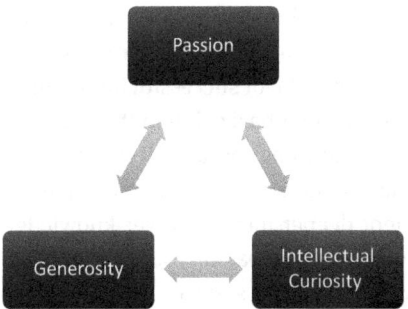

Figure 3.4: The knowledge thought leader.

This passion for knowledge work in the organization carries over and matches two other personal characteristics that come into play for the knowledge thought leader.

The first of these is what I like to think of as "a generosity of spirit," a way of looking at one's work that connects with an almost-automatic interest in sharing what one learns and knows. This is, to me (particularly for the person specifically charged with the authority to manage the organization's intellectual capital), the baseline supporting all work in the knowledge domain. Attached to this passion for one's work and generosity of spirit is an almost equal characteristic: intellectual curiosity. The knowledge thought leader is not only satisfied to understand and have mastered the management and leadership principles required for raising knowledge work in the organization to its highest standards; he or she is constantly on the look-out for doing better and better and more and more, always asking "is this the best way we can do this?" or "can we go beyond the minimal standards or the basics?" In other words, the knowledge thought leader is always asking the big "why?" – always aiming to find a "bigger" solution to the situation than just fixing what needs to be fixed. In any given situation, the knowledge thought leader probes, asking questions that get to the basic concepts for solving whatever problem must be solved or need be met.

With that almost idealistic idea of the knowledge thought leader in mind, though, perhaps a touch of skepticism can be brought in at this point. Is it possible to distinguish between the knowledge strategist's managerial and administrative responsibilities and his or her leadership role – the basics, if you will, of knowledge strategy – and the characteristics and contribution of the knowledge thought leader? I think it is, and I begin by looking at some of what I observe when the topic of a "thought leader" comes into the conversation. An almost immediate observation is what appears to be – in some organizations – a fairly weak link between knowledge leadership and the practice of knowledge services. As a matter of fact, some who work with knowledge services feel uncomfortable with speaking about thought leadership because in their organizations the "process" and "technology" components of the now-accepted formula for successful information management, KM, and strategic learning are more emphasized than the "people" side of the principle. That is not necessarily a bad thing, because it means there is a place for new thinking in the knowledge services workplace, and if part of that new thinking pulls the "people" element deeper into the larger knowledge services construct, all knowledge workers (and their colleagues) stand to benefit. And it makes sense anyway as we incorporate knowledge services into the organization's knowledge-sharing structure and recognize knowledge services for what it is – and which is alluded to often – the practical side of KM, the methodology we use to ensure that the management of intellectual capital works in our organizations. So I respond to that skepticism and that concern by stating that the knowledge thought leader does, indeed, bring in and emphasize the "people" element of the three-part process/technology/people knowledge services construct.

The knowledge thought leader is particularly qualified for the task of bringing the humanistic side of management into the formula for success. For one thing, due to his or her leadership in the development of the knowledge services strategic framework – the organization's knowledge strategy – this management employee is already recognized as the primary advocate or champion supporting the organization's knowledge domain. The reputation has already been acquired, and the knowledge strategist is already the oft-described "go-to" person for any question relating to the organization's knowledge-related issues. What has happened is that the knowledge thought leader has in effect built up an enterprise-wide "brand" for knowledge services, knowledge strategy, and the role of the organization as a knowledge culture. While we generally do not think of "branding" as part of awareness raising with respect to a particular aspect or element of a management discipline or the organizational context for a particular activity, as the work of the knowledge thought leader begins to affect the success of organizational operations and the achievement of the organizational mission, that is what is happening. A brand is nothing more than the establishment of a way of thinking (an impression) about a particular person, activity, or a product within the minds of those who hear about it. With the success of the knowledge thought leader – and the recognition of that leader-manager's role in the success of intellectual capital management in the organization – the brand for the organization's management of knowledge services falls into place. It defines knowledge services and how knowledge is thought about within the organization and determines its position, if you will, in the hierarchy of topics that are considered by enterprise leaders and organizational stakeholders as important to the organization's success.

And is that "brand" – such as it is in the overall organizational context – permanent and never changing? Obviously not, for throughout our discussion of knowledge services as a strategic framework for the twenty-first century organization we have referred time and time again to how the organizational environment (and hence our perceptions about the value of knowledge within the organization) will change, along with that of others within the organization. And the "brand" disseminated through the efforts of the knowledge thought leader will likewise change as required. How so? We answer that with a point made about branding by another Columbia University faculty member. In a totally different context about the role of a brand, Bernd Schmitt, a Columbia Business School professor and "brand-marketing guru" (as described by the author of an article in *Opera News*, of all places), notes that when considering any brand, "like every brand, there has to be change, but there also has to be continuity" (Cohn, 2016).

That change will not be bad, not from the perspective of the knowledge thought leader, for it is this knowledge leader-manager who brings continuity to the management of intellectual capital, performing his or her leader-manager duties in an uninterrupted chain of knowledge-focused tasks and activities that keep the organization moving forward. The knowledge thought leader is very naturally being a knowledge services champion or advocate, but there is more to the role of the knowledge thought leader than that. If he or she has been doing a good job as the organization's knowledge strategist, that relationship with the work is already in place. Additionally, though, other attributes are identified in people we know as knowledge thought leaders. When I ask colleagues how they describe the knowledge thought leader, to tell me what characteristics come to mind, the themes I hear identify these fellow colleagues as people who:

1. recognize – and understand – the role and value of knowledge services in the success of the larger organization;
2. connect knowledge services to the organizational mission, vision, and values;
3. listen to employees and subordinates and take their advice – or at least consider what they have to say – with respect to enterprise-wide knowledge services;
4. connect the role of psychology, human relations, and human interactions with knowledge development, knowledge sharing, and knowledge utilization (KD/KS/KU);
5. perform – usually without even thinking about it – as leaders;
6. have no use for complacency and what some think of as "lazy" thinking in the workplace;
7. are committed to continuous improvement;

8. go beyond just the practical (knowledge thought leaders are recognized for their innovative thinking and they have the confidence to turn innovative thinking into actionable opportunities);
9. combine – again usually without thinking about it – professional ethics with understanding and recognizing when subordinate team members require development and undertake a developmental role without castigating the staff member;
10. practice integrity (the knowledge thought leader does what he or she says he or she will do).

As can be seen from the list, these people also, it can be noted, take on an almost inspirational role among their colleagues (especially their direct reports and others who work with them in the knowledge services unit or the enterprise-wide knowledge services function of the larger organization). From that experience comes a "following," one might say, a group of people who understand the role of enterprise-wide KD/KS/KU, perhaps even as a community of practice or something like a society of knowledge-focused individuals, people who share in the passion, generosity, and intellectual curiosity of being involved with knowledge work. This is one of the fundamental elements of the knowledge thought leader's role of influence in the department or division in which he or she is employed. There is an aspirational quality in the products and services of the knowledge domain, and the people who work in knowledge services – and particularly with the group's leader-manager – are expected to understand this and bring this idea into his or her thinking about the knowledge domain and its results.

These thoughts take the knowledge strategist – hopefully soon to be the knowledge thought leader – to a slightly more demanding workplace situation than he or she might have thought about before. This management employee now moves from the organization-focused principles of managing and leading as the knowledge strategist to giving attention to a new perspective on knowledge sharing. It is a move to a more influential role and with this move, he or she now gives consideration to a number of concepts that might be a little different from what he or she has been accustomed to, a move to a level of professionalism that might not have been experienced prior to the expectations for the knowledge thought leader.

As often happens in the workplace, such a move to different levels and activities in one's profession requires thinking about one's personal qualities, to determine if there is a "fit," as we usually say. A first question has to do with the prospective knowledge thought leader's ambition, asking himself or herself about personal and professional goals. For example, what workplace rewards is this leader-manager looking for? Is the interest in the work based mostly on receiving a salary, or does the employee expect to contribute to enterprise success? It is a necessary consideration, and even though the employee might have done an excellent job as knowledge strategist, does his or her understanding of the work of the knowledge domain encourage working in a more influential role in the organization? Related to this question, naturally, is the employee's own personality; does the knowledge thought leader see himself or herself as a leader (especially after having learned principles of leadership and applying them as the organization's knowledge strategist)? Along those lines, another question has to do with his or her willingness to take on an entrepreneurial/intrapreneurial role in the organization's knowledge domain, with product development and new approaches that enable better knowledge services delivery. Or is this leader-manager's inclination simply to "leave things alone," and permit others in the organization to use these skills for the benefit of the organization?

Another important element in the transition to knowledge thought leader has to do with the importance of looking around the organization and learning to identify and interact with other leader-managers who in their areas of specialty or practice – like the knowledge thought leader himself or herself – are in a position to influence the success of knowledge services in the organization. Why is this important? Because (unless the knowledge thought leader works for a very well-enlightened organization and happens to occupy a position of Chief Knowledge Strategy Officer or hold a similar C-suite position), he or she is looking for that proverbial "seat at the table" when important corporate management decisions are made, to represent the point of view of the organization's knowledge domain. The knowledge thought leader expects to use his or her professional skills, education, and expertise to ensure that the growth of the organization as a knowledge culture moves forward. That success is more assured if he or she is part of the decision-making process. And for true success, its quest is not limited to simply being part of the process. For those of us who were fortunate to be in the audience in 2012 when President Barack Obama gave the commencement address for Barnard College in New York (a women's college affiliated with Columbia University), we heard the president advise Barnard graduates, as he spoke to them about their career paths: "Don't just fight for a seat at the table," he said. "You want to sit at the head of the table" (Obama, 2012). If the knowledge thought leader is willing to move in that direction professionally, of course he or she should be the organization's Chief Knowledge Strategy Officer. After all, he or she was the leader-manager who made possible the organization's knowledge services strategic framework, its knowledge strategy.

That experience in itself is enough to match the knowledge thought leader with thoughts about his or her expectations with respect to a career in knowledge services. For example, Dale Stanley points out that as knowledge strategists move into broadened positions as knowledge thought leaders for the employing organization, their roles enable them to "mature" their careers. When that happens, their contributions to the organization's successful achievement of its corporate mission change the perceptions of others in the organization about them (including the perceptions of enterprise leaders). The knowledge thought leader becomes established as an invaluable and indispensable contributor, and is recognized as such (Stanley, 2016).

That's what the knowledge thought leader must strive for, that level of influence in the organization. And even if that exalted position is not part of the (current) organizational structure, as the knowledge thought leader this management employee is now in a position to strengthen his or her role in the organization. What this means for us is that the knowledge thought leader is ambitious to occupy a leadership role in the organization. This manager must lead, not just in the knowledge domain but throughout the entire organization, engaging with the organization and its leaders and stakeholders and affiliates in a proactive and participative way (and sometimes even provocatively if provocation is required for unlocking the ideas, skills, and motivation of the employees in the knowledge services unit and other knowledge-focused employees throughout the organization, and gathering the attention of enterprise leaders). This leadership is a major part of the knowledge thought leader's work, and it is required because, when you get right down to it, cutting through the layers, the job of the knowledge thought leader – in the classic understanding of the thought leader – is to innovate and to manage change.

And how does the knowledge strategist do that? What steps must he or she take to move into "the way forward" as a knowledge thought leader?

For the answers to these questions, I went to another of the special Drucker experts I've come to know, Bruce Rosenstein. Rosenstein is the Managing Editor of *Leader to Leader*, published by the Frances Hesselbein Leadership Institute. Having written two books on Drucker and shared his insights about Drucker through many lectures, films, presentations, and much academic teaching, Rosenstein was definitely the person to ask.

In response to my query, Rosenstein offered two insightful concepts for us as think about as the knowledge strategist transitions toward a new distinction, a new role as the organization's knowledge thought leader. The first is a concept we have already thought about, that the knowledge strategist will benefit by building a "Drucker-like mindset" about the future, noting that the future "must be created rather than left to chance or fate."

> We must figure out ways to differentiate ourselves from peers and those we serve, so our work around knowledge is not thought of as a commodity that can be purchased elsewhere, or obtained for free. We can start by realizing that we are creating the future for ourselves and our organizations in the present moment, by today's thoughts, actions, decisions, and commitments.

A second Drucker insight, also via Bruce Rosenstein, has to do with what we have just been reading in the last section as we explored thoughts about change management with Dale Stanley:

> In addition, Drucker contended that change is normal, inevitable and not to be feared. He advocated making peace with uncertainty and becoming organized for change, particularly for what he called systematic or planned abandonment. If you were not already engaged in a particular activity, or offering a particular service or product, would you start now? And if not, what would be your next step in either eliminating or scaling it back?
>
> In preparing for the future, Drucker advocated pairing this activity with *kaizen*, the art and practice of continuous improvement. In other words, once you have decided on the activities, products, processes or services you will keep, relentlessly improve them and they will eventually turn into something new and innovative. (Rosenstein, 2013)

So as the knowledge thought leader moves forward in bringing the knowledge services strategic framework – the organization's knowledge strategy – to the organization, he or she has the opportunity to embrace this special work as a new focus in his or her career. The knowledge thought leader already exhibits those criteria described earlier, and with continuing passion for the work, an ever-present intellectual curiosity, and a generosity of spirit that lifts every colleague, co-worker, or client who comes to the knowledge thought leader for knowledge direction, all those qualities come together in his or her professional persona and define that person's excellent qualifications for the work he or she undertakes. And as the knowledge domain moves beyond the cutting edge into a new and emerging collaborative way to work – and offering yet more of a leadership opportunity for the knowledge thought leader – there is further good advice from President Obama. Moving forward in that address, he said (almost, it might be suggested, embracing Drucker's reference to change as being "normal, inevitable, and not to be feared."):

> "Look forward," the President said, with emphasis. "Don't look back."

As the knowledge strategist thought leader now finds himself or herself beyond the role of the organization's knowledge strategist, he or she is in the good position for moving beyond his or her personal and professional ideas to thinking about the organization, the workplace environment itself. The knowledge thought leader does this in order to determine what the chances of success are and how he or she can work within the organization to achieve success for its knowledge domain, already spelled out through this book.

Again, specific questions can be asked, beginning with one of the most important: Does the workplace need a knowledge thought leader? If there are signs that things are going well with knowledge sharing, the knowledge thought leader – having identified any issues or difficulties through the findings and recommendations of the knowledge services audit and having built a working measurement and metrics strategy for knowledge sharing – is positioned to describe whether KD/KS/KU is well practiced. With respect to collaboration, is there evidence that the workplace is a collaborative environment (and not – hopefully – a workplace in which it is "every man for himself")? Or, addressing a situation this management employee does not want to find (but which sometimes happens), are some – or perhaps many – of the knowledge services activities having to do with information management, knowledge management, and strategic learning taking place in silos and isolated business units? Is there inconsistency in how results are obtained, shared, and used?

Another approach to identifying whether the work of the knowledge thought leader can be successful is – as some would describe it – to "scope out" the organization. More than likely some of the answers to this sort of query, such as asking how things "work" in the organization, probably were identified in the knowledge services audit or the development of the knowledge services measurement plan, but these are situations the knowledge thought leader needs to know about because, as much as anything else, they identify how successful he or she will be as this new position evolves (either formally or informally). Similarly, there needs to be information about whether some departments or sections assign information or knowledge "gatekeepers," specifically charged to ensure that knowledge sharing is not part of the management structure in those areas.

Enterprise leaders now recognize that organizational success and organizational effectiveness relate directly to how well KD/KS/KU (knowledge development, knowledge sharing, and knowledge utilization) is managed and led. Indeed, while it might not yet be true in every organization, company, or institution, knowledge value is now understood; in today's well-managed organization, enterprise leaders connect knowledge services as the driver for a new management emphasis in the company. With the knowledge services staff working with them, making that connection is the first step in the organization's re-organization as a knowledge culture, the development of a workplace environment in which knowledge services is practiced as well as it can be practiced.

How that connection is made and the organization structured as a knowledge culture makes use of a number of important organizational characteristics without which the connection to knowledge services would be difficult. One situation that brought three of these characteristics to mind came about in a conversation at Citicorp with some of the company's knowledge leadership team. It was in 2012, the year in which Citicorp was celebrating the company's 200th anniversary and in a group of people with whom, as it happened, I found myself in conversation. While we spoke, I began to realize that I was impressed that the company was in the position of celebrating such an anniversary, despite (as I knew, just from understanding a little about business history) many critical "ups-and-downs." I began to wonder how such an organization had managed to survive for so long, so I asked the group in the conversation. Speaking to the group, I asked what attributes in the company's history contributed to its success. Without missing a beat, one of our hosts replied quite simply: "Transparency, collaboration, and collegiality."

I heard what was being said, accepted it with thanks, and we continued our conversation. It was only later, and particularly in conversation with other friends, that I came to understand what a remarkable trilogy of attributes had been presented to me that day, particularly in terms of a multi-national financial institution but – to my way of thinking – absolutely applicable in any situation for which the knowledge thought leader seeks to put forward plans for the implementation of the knowledge services strategic framework. Transparency I knew about of course, and had in earlier studies come to recognize the importance of transparency and, indeed, to use what I learned in an organizational history I wrote several years ago. In this book, I asserted that transparency is one of the characteristics of the knowledge culture:

> The organization that has built a knowledge culture displays a respect for and supports the integrity of the knowledge process, in an environment that incorporates the highest moral and professional standards of service delivery. In a knowledge culture, that integrity connects with a workplace ambiance that expects and supports transparency (except in clearly defined situations requiring the highest levels of proprietary discretion or security), honesty, and trust in all interactions between individuals and groups. (St Clair, 2009)

Collaboration – to which we gave considerable attention in Chapter 2, Section 2.1 – is a natural in the knowledge culture and if the organization's knowledge culture has developed from a knowledge services strategic framework designed in support the organization as a knowledge culture, that attribute will be fixed in the organizational management structure.

The reference to collegiality came from somewhere else (I don't know where) and completely surprised me. In all my interactions with many people over the years, in many discussion of management, leadership, and the critical positioning of knowledge services as an enterprise-wide organizational component, the reference to collegiality had not, in my memory, come up as something to be discussed. Those of us interested in management, leadership, organizational growth, indeed in organizational success in any situation turn to many different elements in organization development to be sure that we are making the best use of the tools and concepts available to us. To the best of my knowledge, though, collegiality had not before in my experience been one of these stated attributes. So while collegiality is not discussed often as a management or leadership principle, giving the idea some thought tells us that collegiality cannot help but be a beneficial quality in the organization and, in particular, to its growth and effectiveness. The term, of course, refers to the relationship among people who have something in common (they are "colleagues" and they are "collegial" by almost any definition), and while being affiliated in one sense or another with the enterprise in which knowledge services is practiced, that connection could (or should) create a collegial relationship. It doesn't always happen, of course, but it seems clear that when collegiality is part of the communal environment of an organization – as described at Citicorp in the example offered here – it leads to a level of respect for one another among those who make up the population of the knowledge domain.

The knowledge services/strategic communications connection. Having come this far, the knowledge strategist *cum* knowledge thought leader requires a game plan, a solution for how to make the transition take place. While it is probable that this change will occur after the steps described in the preceding chapters have been taken, with (hopefully) many of these practices and principles established and put in place, planning for the position of knowledge thought leader can also be incorporated into the work of the knowledge strategist and undertaken simultaneously, a rewarding process when that arrangement is followed. More than likely, however, the "shift" from one role to a broader and more influential position in the organization on the part of this senior management employee will happen as the knowledge strategist is recognized for his or her success and finds opportunities to move into a new way of thinking about what his or her accomplishments in the organization's knowledge domain can be.

From my perspective, the most attractive next step for the knowledge strategist is a well-thought-out strategic communications plan, giving the knowledge strategist the opportunity to put together a two-part opportunity. With the knowledge services strategic framework in hand, together with an understanding that with knowledge services ECM and knowledge asset management happen at all levels of the knowledge domain throughout the organization (as Barrie Schessler asserts), and with a change management and change implementation plan in place or under consideration (with Dale Stanley's guidance), achieving two more goals is required. First, the knowledge services team must communicate the principles and objectives outlined the the knowledge services strategic framework plan for building a business case for knowledge services. Second, the team must raise awareness for all organization stakeholders, ensuring that everyone understands that knowledge services supports the growth of the organization as a knowledge culture. The strategic communications plan will be structured around these two goals.

One of the first things the knowledge thought leader has to work with is that he or she and the team of knowledge workers and strategic knowledge professionals on the knowledge services team are at a very good point for moving forward with this work. They are now well on the way to success with the findings and recommendations of the knowledge services audit, they have established measures and metrics to be used (or at least considered) to quantify success for KD/KS/KU, and they have put in place and made ready for implementation the components of the knowledge services strategic framework – the knowledge strategy – throughout the organization (although it should be noted that in most such situations some elements of the strategy's implementation have been moving forward throughout the process – this type of work seldom takes place as one specific, single-step activity). Now the knowledge services team must bring their work to the wider organization to have enterprise leadership and other management staff join them and support them in moving the organization's knowledge services strategic framework into place – i.e., sharing (and obtaining support for) the business case for knowledge services and, at the same time, joining the team in raising awareness about the team's work throughout the enterprise. Embarking on these two activities will create an enterprise-wide ambiance that not only understands and commits to the value of knowledge services for strengthening the organization in its purpose, but builds enthusiasm for the KD/KS/KU process. Using the strategic communications plan, the two-part effort of building the business case for knowledge services and raising awareness about how knowledge services will bring the knowledge services strategic framework effort to the attention of all organizational parties will lead to their participation, leading to further development, implementation, and utilization. It will be the knowledge thought leader who will lead this effort, with the result that the organization will be structured (or re-structured) as a knowledge culture.

Clearly a wide range of communication activities is required for achieving these two objectives, and would have been required whether they were sought individually or, as recommended here, advanced together. The practical plan for meeting both goals is to put them together as the expected results of a specific strategic communications activity undertaken for this purpose. The process will be fairly simple, with the knowledge thought leader beginning the process by falling back on the generally accepted methodology for "building the business case" for a project or activity (in this case, of course, a totally new approach to managing information, knowledge, and strategic learning enterprise-wide). Working with the principles for building a business case for knowledge services is a good plan to follow, for incorporated into the business process is creating an awareness of what is involved in the activity, what resources are required, and what the "pay-off" will be – a description of how the organization will benefit if others in the organization (especially decision makers and senior management) come into the process with their support. So aiming to both raise awareness and build the business case is a direction and a combination that makes sense.

As it happens, the knowledge services team already has a step up in terms of building the business case and raising awareness, for to a certain extent awareness has naturally been raised with the activities relating to the knowledge services audit, the measurement plan, and the development of the knowledge strategy. Since many of the team's organizational affiliates have already participated in these activities and they (and others) know of the objectives and activities of the knowledge services strategic framework planning team, they are already aware of what is taking place with the organizational knowledge domain.

The corporate strategic communications plan. An initial effort in this direction – just as was done in transferring the general model of critical success factors to the knowledge services audit – are the matched management ideas addressed in this section, building the business case for knowledge services and raising corporate awareness about knowledge services. The latter (with which we are circling back to remember that we are using the term "corporate" in its classic sense, referring to the corpus or the corporate body of the organization, not – necessarily – to a business corporation) is probably better thought about from the point of view of corporate communications, and specifically as internal or employee communications as this management activity is practiced in the organization. Having the commitment, support, and enthusiasm of all affiliates and stakeholders, including not just enterprise leaders but all staff, is required for an effort as powerful as bringing knowledge strategy to the entire organization.

Since it is often the responsibility of the corporate communications business unit to deal with employee communications activities as well as to work with external audiences, the activities of that unit's staff probably already includes dealing with a wide variety of tools for carrying required messages to the internal staff. Internal or employee communications can be as inclusive as managing design and production efforts for forms and similar documentation regularly required, all the way to working with groups to identify what staff issues most need addressing or working with enterprise leaders and senior management as they attempt to tackle situations having to do with staff relationships and human capital matters. These internal communications activities – as with almost every other form of communication requiring attention as the digital age continues to grow and improve – can include moving away from adherence to the old what-used-to-be-done communications structure. The structure can be re-framed to giving attention, in this case, to how a wide range of products can be shared to ensure that staff members have the information, knowledge, and strategic learning they require, not so much with respect to the actual work they do (that is a different "version" of knowledge services) but with how they perform in the workplace. So we have internal communications sections of corporate communications relating to such wide-ranging topics as mobile device management, using video for meetings and strategic learning, adapting social media in the workplace (and almost always adapted specifically within the specific corporate or organizational structural framework), images and image sharing for internal operational purposes, digital signage, and many others too numerous to list here, and with many newer methods and types of communication media coming into the management marketplace every day.

Both building the business case for knowledge services and raising awareness about the organization's new approach to managing intellectual capital are products from the general management background that can be adopted with much success by the knowledge strategist and the knowledge services strategic framework development team. If we look at how the organization's strategic communications planning is designed and used, we can see opportunities for using strategic communications for both building the business case and for raising awareness enterprise-wide for knowledge services.

While strategic communications planning is generally thought of as having to do with advertising, marketing, public relations, and similar external-facing activities, as we have noted here it is also seriously recognized as a management tool and part of the management communication framework. Kjerstin Thorson makes this point about strategic communication, that the work

> explores the capacity of all organizations – not only corporations, but also not-for-profit organizations (including advocacy and activist groups) and government – for engaging in *purposeful* communication. The strength of the approach is its emphasis on strategy rather than on specific tactics as well as its focus on communications understood holistically. This approach is particularly valuable given the increasing difficulty faced by organizations in differentiating among communication activities (and results) appropriately "owned" by various functional groups. (Thorson, 2013)

For the knowledge thought leader, that description matches what the two-part strategic communications plan will do. It will be combined in a package that can be used not only for targeting the organization's decision makers, in order to get their buy-in for what is happening with the knowledge services strategic framework, but work as an internal communications medium to ensure that all staff learn about knowledge services and come to recognize how a solid knowledge strategy supports their work.

Developing the strategic communications plan, as with other plans described in this book, begins with an established group of items to consider, and for each a decision must be made by the knowledge thought leader and his or her planning team. In many cases, the steps to be taken can serve as both elements for building the business case and for raising awareness about knowledge services. Speaking very simplistically the only difference might be in identifying the audience for each section, since most other elements will work for both. This list can give the knowledge thought leader an idea of some of the things he or she should consider:

1. Background: The knowledge thought leader and the knowledge services communications planning team will review the requirements for the plan. If I were the knowledge thought leader for the organization, a first step would be to use the findings and recommendations of the knowledge services audit, the results of the measurement and metrics program (or anticipated results, if actual results are not yet available), and the knowledge services strategic framework to prepare a simple background document, outlining what the team expects to accomplish (building the business plan and raising enterprise-wide awareness about knowledge services). As a "getting-started" promotional "piece," this one-pager will be distributed wherever appropriate, to trigger as quickly as possible a groundswell of interest in the whole knowledge services activity. As with other planning activities described throughout this book, this brief document outlines the "why?" of the proposed activity, with particular emphasis on the desired results, a specific description of what is expected from this effort.

2. Networking: Building on the response to the brief background document, the knowledge thought leader connects with the organization's corporate communications staff, particularly with the department head for corporate communications. These people are clearly experienced with internal communications, and the department head, if approached about the idea of the combined business plan/awareness campaign, can provide a wealth of advice and direction and, if so inclined (or encouraged), can become a strong advocate or champion for the project.

3. Capacity: A next task is to determine – probably with the help of the corporate communications director and some staff from that business unit – what staff and resources are required for implementing such a plan, a determination that there are people available to do the work, and that funding for their services has been provided in the knowledge services budgeting process. If any of these is not in place, the development of the knowledge services communications plan must be delayed until staff and resources have been allocated.

4. Target and Target Audience: It is here that, as noted, the knowledge strategy communication plan might split, or in preparation be designed in such a way that the value of the proposed knowledge services strategic framework – the organizational knowledge culture – is laid out in terms that the organization's decision makers can understand, relate to, and visualize integrating into the overall organizational management strategy. Again, along with everything else in the plan, the focus is on the benefits to the organization but in offering content to the decision makers, the knowledge thought leader and his or her planning team will want to focus on what it is they need to know and what they will do with the information once they have it. To make the process easier for all the participants, if the overall knowledge services strategic framework – the organization's knowledge strategy – is supported by a sponsor from senior management, as described in various places throughout the book – that person can be encouraged to participate at this level.

At this point, the knowledge thought leader can turn to the communications plan described by Dale Stanley in the previous section, detailing the steps for implementing the plan and, if it fits within the arrangements usually followed by the communications team, using the table of activities listed in that particular plan.

With the "news" of the business plan for knowledge services delivered throughout the organization, all organizational staff, affiliates, and stakeholders learn that the structuring of the organization as a knowledge culture is on the horizon. Indeed, for some readers that structuring (or re-structuring, in some cases) has probably already started in some organizations, or in some parts of other organizations. In any case, in these organizations the knowledge thought leaders and knowledge strategists – that is, those who have chosen not to take on the added leadership role of knowledge thought leader – have already been responsible for leading the organization toward the knowledge culture, and they can take much pride in how far they have been able to bring the organization.

Everyone now understands (as with all other implementation steps taken in building a business case for and raising awareness about any activity in the enterprise) that moving the organization toward the knowledge culture started with the development of the knowledge services strategic framework. Now using that framework as the organization's knowledge strategy, the process will continue and knowledge services, knowledge strategy, and the move toward organizational functioning as a knowledge culture will go forward. In that progression, all those involved can celebrate the changes they see, changes measured not only in how well everyone in the organization now works together, in sharing knowledge as not done before, but also in realizing growing knowledge services success. Now all employees, leaders, affiliates, and stakeholders are enabled for developing, sharing, and using the organization's intellectual capital. The knowledge thought leader has built on what came before and has put down the foundation for taking the organization even further, taking it on a journey no one associated with the organization will ever regret.

Epilogue: Knowledge Services. The Critical Management Discipline for the Twenty-First Century Organization

The last chapter of this book ends with a reference to our journey. For many readers, the journey is well underway. Knowledge strategists and knowledge thought leaders are using the prescriptive directions of the book to guide them as they undertake the development of the organization's knowledge services strategic framework, its knowledge strategy. Others are just beginning their journey, still contemplating just how far they want to delve into this business of re-shaping the established patterns of knowledge development, knowledge sharing, and knowledge utilization that have been in place, built upon, and structured and re-structured over time. Still others are comfortably building on much of what they were doing before Guy came along with his concepts and directions about how knowledge could be better shared in *any* organization. (Throughout the development of this book one colleague has all along referred to it as "Guy's Guidebook"!) Or perhaps these knowledge specialists are using these pages as a refresher or for thinking about new concepts and ideas relating to the management of the organization's intellectual capital.

So the journey is happening, in various ways, and it is currently moving along at different stages for different kinds of knowledge specialists, knowledge strategists, and knowledge thought leaders. If I have succeeded, we all have our road map now and we can go forward. At the same time, though, as we unfold the road map, we want to keep in mind what's behind it, where it came from, all this information and knowledge and learning we bring to the KD/KS/KU process. We want to consider what brought the development of the road map, the guidelines (the chart if you're a sailor) to where we could put it to use.

When I was a young man, it was often made clear to me that if I were going to succeed in life – in whatever I wanted to take on as a career or as a profession – I could make all the plans I wanted on my own. I could think about what I wanted to be or to do, but I was often reminded that to be truly successful I would need to remember that I would have to "stand on the shoulders of giants." I would discover what I was looking for – in whatever I was thinking about – only by being aware of what had been done before, by those who had been successful in doing what I wanted to do, and then by not only applying what I learned from them, but building on what I learned by moving forward with my own discoveries and truths. That's exactly what happened, and as I became active in (actually rather swallowed up by) concepts having to do with managing information, knowledge, and strategic learning – only I didn't refer to it as *strategic* learning then – I realized that I was indeed paying attention to what those who came before me had to say.

So it has been as this book developed (and with other things I have written, too). There is so much out there in the world of information, knowledge, learning, management, and leadership to influence me; I'm very pleased (and humbled) to have been able to acquaint myself with people like Drucker and Lilienthal and Hesselbein and the people Gleick and Isaacson and their like have written about. There is much for us to learn about the world of information, knowledge, and learning from all of these people, and about the background, history, and philosophy of these subjects. And we are doing that. But the real progress and excitement come as we attempt to figure out how to apply what we have learned from these giants (and there are so many, many more – not just the few named in this book) and apply what they have taught us as we think about what is coming. We have to combine what they have taught us with what we have learned, and then to use what we have learned in order to take on the challenges that are waiting for us.

I use the word "challenges" purposely. Among the people I tend to spend time with, we talk a lot about challenges for knowledge work in the organizations where we are employed, and we are pretty well agreed about what some of the *current* challenges might be. We talk about these six a lot, things like knowledge asset management, information/knowledge governance, e-discovery, privacy and security, data analytics, and big data strategy. And we're very aware that these six are just what *we* are talking about. Any other group of colleagues would surely come up with a different list, and probably a longer one.

Some of the challenges our group talks about are given attention in this book, but all of these topics – and so many more – will need to be dealt with in the up-coming months and years. And it will be the the knowledge thought leaders who will be dealing with these challenges. Which is why, when I'm asked, I respond that knowledge strategy, knowledge thought leadership, and enterprise-wide intellectual capital management are wide-open career fields. More and more educated and qualified people are going to be required to work with organizations as these challenges (the current ones or the new ones, the ones we have not even articulated yet) come to the fore.

We can see it happening, and that is why this book is ending on such an optimistic note. I didn't use "The Way Forward" as the title for Chapter Three as a gimmick. I firmly and sincerely believe that the proper management of knowledge services is the way forward. We're seeing it in our organizations, both in the corporate world and in not-for-profit and non-profit organizations. Within the past few years, there has been a critical turnaround in the management community. Knowledge services (sometimes still referred to as "KM" – which is fine, if that's the language used in the organization) is now part of the management agenda. The people who do the managing in our companies, organizations, and institutions now understand that good management means good knowledge services.

It has, indeed, been a radical change, a real break with the past. Just a few short years ago those of us dealing with knowledge workers found ourselves leading, cajoling, persuading, and doing everything we could to get senior management to pay attention to knowledge value. We worked very hard to get them to listen to what we had to say about KD/KS/KU. In those days sometimes we were successful but most of the time (if we are truly honest with ourselves), it didn't work. Enterprise-leaders just were not very interested. Today the opposite seems to be the case.

We all remember the scenario: Not that long ago, to be called in to meet with management about some knowledge services project (or even just a concept – forget about something as mature as a project) meant days of preparation. Most of the preparation had to do with coming up with definitions, case studies, examples, and just plain old story-telling to make sure the people you were meeting were on the same wave length you were on. Of course you had to do a lot of simplification, or "dumbing down," if you will, because you learned – early on – that anything that smacked of "knowledge" or "learning" was thought to be too *academic* for many of those enterprise leadership positions (read: decision-making authority for project resource allocation). Or if they had learned something about knowledge management or knowledge services – from reading *McKinsey Quarterly* or *Forbes* or *Fortune* or some such, these organizational leaders were well armed with reasons why they could *not* undertake any new initiatives having to do with knowledge sharing. So you went into the meeting knowing good and well that the people you were meeting with would not have any idea of what "knowledge management" meant – to say nothing of "knowledge services"—as a concept. And you had been through this often enough that you could hear it coming – and usually not far into the conversation: "What's this about managing knowledge? Knowledge can't be managed. You can't buy and sell knowledge." And you replied dutifully, "Well yes, that's true, but let me explain . . . ."

And off you went, you and the team that wanted to move forward. You took tiny steps in those days. You didn't want to get things too confused. And step by step, all the way along you and your team worked very hard to make sure that you were getting through, that the organization's leaders – the people who were going to authorize the funding for the initiative, no matter how small – understood that there would be value in managing knowledge (with *value* being defined in terms that were explicitly understood by management).

It's not that way now. We can't (yet) understand exactly how the change came about, but nowadays we are living in a very different world of organizational management. Today when someone in senior management opines "We're not taking advantage of what our people know," we bring up knowledge services. We talk about knowledge strategy and the organization as a knowledge culture, and we have the advantage of pointing out that knowledge services is now well embraced in the larger organizational management community. Leading organizations and institutions are now using the term to describe the research facilities in their institutions (as, for example, at Harvard University where the library at the Harvard Kennedy School is now known as "Harvard Kennedy School Library and Knowledge Services").

And here's the best part: these institutions and their managers are not interested in taking cautious, "tiny steps." They've figured out that it's not all about managing IT (which used to be the case with many of the people moving into management positions). It's not even about having the technology management leaders turn themselves into "knowledge managers." It's about – these enterprise leaders tell us – how people *use* information and communications technology to work better, more efficiently, and not to put too fine a point on it, to work together more collaboratively. To work, in fact, as knowledge strategists and knowledge thought leaders are showing them how to work with information, knowledge, and strategic learning.

Senior management knows this now and knows that high-end, high-quality knowledge services means that the whole organization is now more effective, leading to success with that over-arching goal so clearly sought in modern management terms: organizational effectiveness. However defined in any particular organization, effectiveness is today's management mantra and organizational effectiveness comes from one source and one source only: the competencies and the energies of company staff in developing and sharing knowledge. Management knows it, knowledge strategists and knowledge thought leaders know it, and the organization's employees know it. This is the time.

I am not the only person who thinks so. As the writing of this book began to move towards its conclusion, I went to six special people (I call them my favorite knowledge-services colleagues and partners) and asked them if they agreed with me, with the title I gave to this epilogue in which I state that knowledge services is the critical management discipline for the twenty-first century organization. These people have been referenced in the book, and it seems appropriate to wrap up our historical and philosophical exploration of information management, knowledge management, and strategic learning, together with my advice for the knowledge services strategic framework development team, by including their thoughts on this question.

Dale Stanley started us off. At SMR International, Dale is SMR's Senior Consultant and Marketing and Operations Manager. He is also responsible for SMR's various strategic learning activities, both for client organizations and for the company's own professional development offerings. He, as much as anyone, understands knowledge services and the role of knowledge services in the KD/KS/KU process. He has become the company's expert in change management, as was demonstrated in Chapter 3, Section 3.1, which he co-authored. Here are Dale's thoughts about knowledge services as the critical management discipline for the twenty-first century organization:

> As predicted in the past century, Toffler's information age and Drucker's knowledge worker were born, struggled through adolescence, and have begun to mature into the knowledge- and technology-based economy and society we are now experiencing. The theory and practice of developing, sharing, and utilizing knowledge for the benefit of organizations and society has also matured into what we call knowledge services. This parallel development has not been accidental. The development of this discipline has been a helpful response to the tremendous and pervasive changes of the past quarter century. Naturally, the next level of maturity demands focus and an identity. Whether it's a teenager "finding herself," a young adult discovering his career passion, or a new corporation executing its IPO, there comes a time for stepping out, defining one's mission, and mustering the courage and resources in order to focus on making a difference. Organizations are now ready to focus on being the knowledge-centric organizations they must be in this new age, and knowledge services is no longer a mere helpful response. Knowledge services has become the critical management discipline for the twenty-first century because the theory provides the identity and framework while the skills provide the ability to focus on creating and executing a vision for the knowledge culture so critically needed in these times.

Barrie Schessler, another chapter co-author, is content management and knowledge strategist for a strategic financial advisory and wealth management firm in New York, NY. Barrie also works with me at Columbia University, as the Faculty Facilitator for the courses I teach. To Barrie's way of thinking, knowledge services applies as the critical management discipline for the twenty-first century organization for this reason:

> Knowledge services, in its most simple definition, is the intersection between people and information, the two components in any organization that will either lead to the success of the organization, or the failure thereof. It is at this intersection where words (written or conceptual) are turned into, for example, useful processes or know-how, which leads to strategy development for future re-use and ultimately (hopefully), goal realization. To actively manage this exchange between information and people is not only critical in driving the desired culture to bring about a successful exchange, but, I would argue, essential.

Lee Igel, one of my personal Drucker experts (Elizabeth Edersheim and Frances Hesselbein are the others) was brief, focusing on what he teaches his students about the role of knowledge services as they learn from him in his consulting strategies courses in the graduate programs at New York University:

> It is understandable why people and organizations are excited over "big data" and "analytics." Yes, they are topics of conversation and they must be addressed in the twenty-first century organization. But big data and analytics are not the building. They are the scaffolding. Big data and analytics and similar topics are what we work from. They are the elements

that drive our inclination to explore, manage, and exploit available chords of knowledge. In the twenty-first century, the imperative is for us, as management teacher Peter Drucker (citing novelist E.M. Forster) wrote, to "only connect."

Anne Kershaw is a lawyer, founder and managing director of a consulting firm specializing in knowledge strategy, and a faculty member in the M.S. in Information and Knowledge Strategy program at Columbia University in the City of New York. Kershaw probably has more experience and expertise in knowledge services strategy than almost anyone else working in the field. Kershaw's ideas about the role of knowledge services in the twenty-first century organization begin with a question:

> How do we move from the old closeted-knowledge world to the new, critical-to-success, shared-knowledge world? Knowledge services, knowledge strategy, management and leadership, thank you. We listen to the teaching and learnings of those who are leading us (even within our client organizations) and when we share from their – sometimes brilliant – insights, we can make knowledge services and knowledge strategy work in the twenty-first century organization. We have learned and we now understand well that people dislike change. Knowledge services as a management discipline is critical for helping them get to where they need to be for developing and sharing the knowledge they are required to use.

Tim Powell, President and CEO of The Knowledge Agency®, created the concept of the knowledge value chain and is recognized for his success with KVC as he applies it for clients and students (he, too, is a Faculty Facilitator at Columbia University in the City of New York). Tim joins with me in acknowledging the value of our historical precedents in information, knowledge, and strategic learning studies:

> Classical economists defined the three essential productive resources of an economy as: LAND (natural resources), LABOR (human resources), and CAPITAL (financial resources.) Today we recognize a fourth productive resource, KNOWLEDGE ("epistemic" resources, also including data, information, and intelligence).
>
> Each of these sets of resources has benefitted from intensive development and pre-eminence during a specific time frame. During the nineteenth century, we achieved mastery of natural resources (mining, manufacturing, materials, etc.). During the early twentieth century, we began to understand human resources (thanks to the work of Frederick Taylor, Henry Ford, and others). In the latter part of the twentieth century, financial principles and technologies became more widely understood and practiced.
>
> During the twenty-first century we must (and we will) achieve greater understanding and mastery of epistemic resources – a science of knowledge, accompanied by rapid development of knowledge practices and technologies to help our enterprises perform effectively in the "knowledge economy."

> The pioneering work of knowledge strategists and knowledge thought leaders – and those they learn from – has paved the way for these developments. To those starting on your journey of exploration and discovery in the "knowledge domain," behold and benefit from those who came before you. They did not produce all the answers – in that, they have left plenty for you to accomplish. But they did – spurred on by the needs of their clients, their colleagues, and their consciences – begin to ask the questions: how can knowledge do more for people, for organizations, for civil society – indeed, for the world? Knowledge services and knowledge strategy are leading the way. Listen to those who came before, learn from them, use their insights – and be richly rewarded.

Andrew Berner is the Library Director and Curator of Collections of what is probably the world's largest private club library (I am qualified to describe it as such, as I once had the job he now holds). Like most of us, Andrew also places much value on the influences of the past that have brought us to where we are now. Originally a historian (and still a historian in his view of society), Andrew is able to see clearly the place of knowledge services in the twenty-first century organization:

> It was coal and oil that fueled the advances of the Industrial Revolution of the nineteenth and early twentieth centuries. Computers and microprocessors fueled the advances of the Technology Revolution of the second half of the twentieth century. It is knowledge that will fuel the advances of our own time, a time that may – when looked back on from a future vantage point – be seen as the Knowledge Revolution. Knowledge services – and the knowledge strategists and knowledge thought leaders who know how best to put it to work – will play an integral part in assuring that the Knowledge Revolution is every bit as significant as its predecessors.

So, where does this bring us? It brings us to the proverbial fork in the road. Down one road lies the long-established view that knowledge is an elusive commodity that is impossible to manage. Here lie the disincentives to knowledge sharing, through individual rewards for being "the first" or "the best." Down the other road are those who see the benefits of working together on the development, sharing, and utilization of knowledge in support of a common goal. Here companies and organizations move from knowledge management to knowledge services and individuals evolve from knowledge workers to knowledge strategists to knowledge thought leaders. Which road should you take? To me, the choice is clear.

Works Cited

Allee, Verna. "Value Network Analysis and Value Conversion of Tangible and Intangible Assets." *Journal of Intellectual Capital*. 9.1, p. 5 (2008).
Allio, Robert. "Mintzberg on Management." *Forbes*. 8 April 2011.
Allison, Michael, and Jude Kaye. *Strategic Planning for Nonprofit Organizations: A Practical Guide and Workbook*. Hoboken, NJ: Wiley, 2005.
Anderson, Janice. "ECM:RIM – Programs That Matter Programs That Last." *KMWorld* (2006).
Ashkenas, Ron. "Change Management Needs to Change." *Harvard Business Review* (2013).
Bachman, John A. "A Framework for Information Systems Architecture." *IBM Systems Journal* 26.3 (1987).
Bennis, Warren G. *On Becoming a Leader*. New York: Basic, 2009.
Berner, Andrew. "On Knowledge." *Personal interview*. 15 August 2010.
Blumenstein, Lynn. "Librarian as CM Leader." *Library Journal* 130.15, p. 38 (2005).
Botha, Hanneri, and J. A. Boon. "The Information Audit: Principles and Guidelines." *Libri* 53.1, p. 23 (2003).
Bradley, Chris, Lowell Bryan, and Sven Smith. "Managing the Strategy Journey." *McKinsey Quarterly* (2012).
Bridges, William. *Managing Transitions: Making the Most of Change*. N.p.: Da Capo Lifelong, 2009.
Brindley, Lynne. "Challenges for Great Libraries in the Age of the Digital Native." National Federation of Advanced Information Services (NFAIS). 2009.
Callahan, Shawn. "Crafting a Knowledge Strategy." (2002), *Academia.edu*. 24 Jan. 2016.
Cave, Andrew. "Milton Friedman Got It Wrong." *The Telegraph*, 7 July 2010.
Chakravarti, Nav. "Content Management vs. Knowledge Management." *KMWorld* (2008).
Clare, Mark, and Arthur Decore. *Knowledge Assets: Professional's Guide to Valuation and Financial Management*. New York: Harcourt, 2000.
Cohen, Alex. "Libraries, Knowledge Management, and Communities of Practice." *Information Outlook* 10.1, p. 23 (2005).
Cohn, Fred. "The Salzburg Connection." *Opera News* (2016).
Covey, Stephen R. *The 7 Habits of Highly Effective People*. New York: Simon & Schuster, 2013.
Curzon, Susan. *Managing Change*. New York: Neal-Schuman, 1989.
Davenport, Thomas H. "Saving IT's Soul: Human Centered Information Management." *Harvard Business Review* (1994).
De Cagna, Jeff. "Keeping Good Company: A Conversation with Larry Prusak." *Information Outlook* 2.5, p. 36 (2001).
De Silva, Nishan. "On Knowledge Strategists." Message to the author. 4 September 2012.
Dearstyne, Bruce W. "Records Management of the Future." *Information Management Journal*, 33 (4), p. 4 (1999).
Dempsey, Michael. "A Way to Stop Drowning in Data – KM for Small Business." *Financial Times* 25 January 2006.
Drucker, Peter F. *Age of Discontinuity*. New York: Harper and Row, 1969.
Drucker, Peter F. "Age of Social Transformation." *Atlantic Monthly* (1994).
Drucker, Peter F. *The Daily Drucker*. New York: Harper Business, 2004.
Drucker, Peter F. "Discipline of Innovation." *Leader to Leader* 9, p. 13 (1998).
Drucker, Peter F. *Effective Executive*. New York: Harper and Row, 1966.
Drucker, Peter F. *The End of Economic Man: The Origins of Totalitarianism*. New Brunswick, NJ, 1992. (originally published by The John Day Company, New York NY 1939)

Drucker, Peter F. *Essential Drucker.* New York: HarperCollins, 2001.
Drucker, Peter F. *Five Most Important Questions You Will Ever Ask about Your Organization.* San Francisco: Jossey-Bass, 1993.
Drucker, Peter F. *The Future of Industrial Man.* New York: The John Day Company, 1942.
Drucker, Peter F. *Landmarks of Tomorrow.* New York: Harper, 1959.
Drucker, Peter F. *Management: Tasks, Responsibilities, Practices.* "Introduction. The Alternative to Tyranny," New York: Truman Talley – E.P. Dutton, 1986.
Drucker, Peter F. *Management Challenges for the 21st Century.* New York: HarperCollins, 1999.
Drucker, Peter F. *Managing in a Time of Great Change.* New York: Elsevier, 1997.
Drucker, Peter F. "The Next Society." *Economist,* p. S3 (1 November 2001).
Drucker, Peter F. Preface. *Management: Tasks, Responsibilities, Practices.* New York: Harper and Row, 1973.
Edersheim, Elizabeth Haas. *The Definitive Drucker.* New York: McGraw-Hill, 2007.
Edersheim, Elizabeth Haas. *McKinsey's Marvin Bower: Vision, Leadership, and the Creation of Management Consulting.* Hoboken, NJ: John Wiley, 2004.
Ferrero, David, and Thomas L. Wilding. "Scanning the Environment in Strategic Planning." Proc. of Special Libraries Association, San Antonio TX USA. Washington DC: Special Libraries Association, 1991.
Gleick, James. *The Information – A History, a Theory, a Flood.* New York: Pantheon, 2011.
Goleman, Daniel, Richard Boyatwzis, and Annie McKee. *Primal Leadership: Realizing the Power of Emotional Intelligence.* Cambridge, MA: Harvard Business School, 2001.
Harriston, Victoria, Thomas Pellizzi, and Guy St. Clair. "Toward World-Class Knowledge Services: Emerging Trends in Specialized Research Libraries." *Information Outlook* 7.6–7, p. 10 (2003).
Harriston, Victoria. "Victoria Harriston at the National Academies: Collaboration and Knowledge Sharing Are Key Drivers to Success." Personal interview. 15 January 2006.
Hatten, Kenneth J., and Stephen R. Rosenthal. *Reaching for the Knowledge Edge:How the Knowing Corporation Seeks, Shares, and Uses Knowledge for Strategic Advantage.* New York: AMACOM/American Management Association, 2001.
Heifetz, Donald A., and Donald L. Laurie. "The Work of Leadership." *Harvard Business Review* (1997).
Henczel, Susan. *The Information Audit.* Munich: De Gruyter, 2001.
Hesselbein, Frances. "On Leadership." Personal interview. 7 March 2016.
Hesselbein, Frances. "Transformational Leadership." *Peter Drucker's Five Most Important Questions: Enduring Wisdom for Today's Leaders,* edited by Peter Economy. Hoboken, NJ: John Wiley and Sons, 2015.
Hislop, Donald. *Knowledge Management in Organizations.* Oxford and New York: Oxford University Press, 2009.
Hunt, Deborah. "On Leadership." Telephone interview. 19 February 2016.
Hydock, Jim. "SLA–Standing at the Crossroads." Web log post. *Outsell inc.* 14 July 2015.
Igel, Lee H. "On Drucker and Management." Personal interview. 21 August 2011.
Igel, Lee H. "Six Core Principles for Creating Strong Physician Leaders." *Physician Executive Journal* 36.3, p. 42 (2012).
Isaacson, Walter. *The Innovators – How a Group of Hackers, Geniuses, and Geeks Created the Digital Revolution.* New York: Simon and Schuster, 2014.
Jacobson, Alvin L., and JoAnne Sparks. "Creating Value: Building the Strategy-Focused Library." *Information Outlook* 5.9, p. 14 (2001).

Kanter, Rosabeth Moss. *Change Masters*. New York: Touchstone, 1985.
Kanter, Rosabeth Moss. "A Conversation with Rosabeth Moss Kanter about Leadership." Interview. *Training and Development*, 52.7, p. 44 (July 1998).
Kanter, Rosabeth Moss. "Evolve (Again)." *Harvard Business Review* (2011).
Kanter, Rosabeth Moss. *Evolve! Succeeding in the Digital Culture of Tomorrow*. Cambridge, MA: Harvard Business School, 2001.
Kaplan, Robert S. and David P. Morton. *The Balanced Scorecard: Translating Strategy into Action*. Boston: Harvard Business School Press, 1996.
Kennedy, Mary Lee, and Angela Abell. "New Roles for Info Pros." *Information Outlook* 12.1, p. 25 (2008).
Kershaw, Anne. "On Knowledge Strategy." *Telephone interview*. 18 March 2016.
Kim, W. Chen, and Renée Maugorgne. "Tipping Point Leadership." *Harvard Business Review* (2003).
Koenig, Michael E.D. "What Is KM? Knowledge Management Explained." *KMWorld* (2012).
Kotter, John P. *Leading Change*. Cambridge, MA: Harvard Business Review, 2012.
Kotter, John P. "Why Transformation Efforts Fail." *Harvard Business Review* (1995).
Kouzes, James M., and Barry Z. Posner. *The Leadership Challenge*. San Francisco, CA: Jossey-Bass, 2002.
Kübler-Ross, Elisabeth. *On Grief and Grieving: Finding the Meaning of Grief Through the Five Stages of Loss*. New York: Simon & Schuster, 2005.
Lilienthal, David E. *Management: A Humanist Art*. New York: Columbia University Press, 1967.
Matthews, Joseph. "Determining and Communicating the Value of the Special Library: Valuing the Balanced Library Scorecard." *Information Outlook* 7.3, p. 16 (2003).
Marshall, Edward. *Transforming the Way We Work: The Power of the Collaborative Workplace*. New York: AMACOM (American Management Association), 1995.
Maulitz, Russell. "Other Voices: Dr. Russell Maulitz Shares His Thoughts about the Intersection of Medical Informatics and Knowledge Services." Web log post. *Knowledge Services Notes*. SMR International. 20 May 2015.
Maurer, Rick. "Change Readiness Assessment." Web log post. *Change without Migraines*. 30 December 2010.
Mintzberg, Henry. *The Nature of Managerial Work*. New York: Harper and Row, 1973.
Montgomery, Cynthia A. "How Strategists Lead." *McKinsey Quarterly* (2012).
Montgomery, Cynthia A. *The Strategist: Be the Leader Your Business Needs*. New York: HarperCollins, 2012.
Murphy, Jim. "The Deep and Delicate Art of EM." *KMWorld* (2008).
Murray, Art. "The Future of the Future: Good-bye, Knowledge Worker ... Hello, Knowledge Entrepreneur." *KMWorld* 17.6 (2008).
Naisbitt, John. *Megatrends: Ten New Directions Transforming Our Lives*. Warner Books, 1982.
North, Mary Anne. "Seven Ways to Improve Your Resource Bank." *Information Outlook* 22.2, p. 11 (2002).
Obama, Barack. Keynote Address. Barnard College Commencement, May 14, 2012.
Organisation for Economic Co-operation and Development (OECD). *The Well-Being of Nations: The Role of Human and Social Capital*. Paris: OECD, 2001.
Oxbow, Nigel, and Angela Able. *Putting Knowledge to Work: What Skills and Competencies Are Required? Knowledge Management: The New Competitive Asset*. Washington, DC: Special Libraries Association, 1997.
Penfold, Sharon. *Change Management in Information Services*. Munich: De Gruyter, 2013.

Perdue, Mitzi. "Other Voices: Mitzi Perdue Talks about How – For Frank Perdue – Knowledge Sharing Was Simply Part of Sharing – It's What He Did." Web log post. *Knowledge Services Notes.* SMR International. 26 Jan. 2015.

Powell, Timothy W. "On the Knowledge Value Chain." Personal interview. 14 May 2013.

Powell, Timothy W. *The Knowledge Value Chain Handbook (Version 4.0).* New York: Knowledge Agency, 2014.

Powell, Timothy W. "The Knowledge Value Chain." Web log post. *Competing in the Knowledge Economy.* The Knowledge Agency, 27 March 2016.

Powell, Timothy W. "Metrics That Matter." Web log post. *Competing in the Knowledge Economy.* The Knowledge Agency, 22 October 2013.

Powell, Timothy W. "Value for Dummeze." Weblog post. *Competing in the Knowledge Economy.* The Knowledge Agency, 5 August 2012.

Prusak, Laurence, and Thomas H. Davenport. *Working Knowledge: How Organizations Manage What They Know.* Cambridge, MA: Harvard Business School, 1998.

Pugh, Lyndon. *Change Management in Information Services.* Hampshire: Ashgate, 2007.

Reczek, Karen. "KM Migrates: Info Pros Leverage the Network to Become KM Pros." *Inside Knowledge* 12.2, p. 14 (2008).

Rockley, Ann, Pamela Kostur, and Steve Manning. *Managing Enterprise Content: A Unified Content Strategy.* Indianapolis, IN: New Riders, 2003.

Rosenstein, Bruce. "Other Voices: Bruce Rosenstein on Peter Drucker and the Future of Knowledge Workers." Web log post. *Knowledge Services Notes.* SMR International. 12 November 2013.

Rosenthal, Evan. "Every Worker Is a Knowledge Worker." *Bloomberg Business.* 11 January 2011.

Rothmans, Joshua. "Shut Up and Sit Down." *New Yorker.* 29 February 2016.

Schein, Edgar H. *Organizational Culture and Leadership.* San Francisco, CA: Jossey-Bass, 1992.

Scrivens, K., and C. Smith. "Four Interpretations of Social Capital: An Agenda for Measurement." *OECD Statistics Working Papers* 6 (2013).

Seidel, Robert W. *Seeing Organizational Patterns: A New Theory and Language of Organizational Design.* San Francisco, CA: Berrett-Koehler, 1996.

Senge, Peter. "The Practice of Innovation." *Leader to Leader* 9, p. 16 (1998).

Sinek, Simon. *How Great Leaders Inspire Action.* TEDxTalks, September 28, 2009, TEDxPuget Sound (YouTube).

Sinek, Simon. *Start with Why: How Great Leaders Inspire Everyone to Take Action.* New York: Portfolio, 2009.

Smith, Megan. "Other Voices: Megan Smith on Knowledge Services in Associations"" Web log post. *Knowledge Services Notes.* SMR International. 14 March 2014.

Stanley, Dale. "Knowledge Strategy and Organizational Performance." Personal interview. 24 May 2011.

Stanley, Dale. "Knowledge Strategy Framework." Personal interview. 14 December 2009.

Stanley, Dale. "Knowledge Services = Catalysis." Personal interview. 12 October 2008.

Stanley, Dale. "The Knowledge Thought Leader's Contribution." Personal interview. 12 January 2016.

St. Clair, Guy. *Ask the Customers (I) (II) (III): You've Got the Data – What Does It Mean?* Washington, DC: Special Libraries Association, 1996.

St. Clair, Guy. *Beyond Degrees: Professional Learning for Knowledge Services.* Munich: De Gruyter, 2005.

St. Clair, Guy. *Customer Service in the Information Environment.* Munich: De Gruyter, 1993.

St. Clair, Guy. "Knowledge Management." *Encyclopedia of Library and Information Science.* New York: Dekker, 2003.

St. Clair, Guy. "Knowledge Services: Your Company's Key to Performance Excellence." *Information Outlook* 5.6, p. 6 (2001).

St. Clair, Guy. "The New Knowledge Services: Next Steps for Career Professionals – Specialist Librarians as Knowledge Strategists." *SMR International Special Report* (2012), July 2012.

St. Clair, Guy. Preface. *Bibliothekswissenschaft – quo Vadis? Library Science – quo Vadis? A Discipline between Challenges and Opportunities.* Munich: De Gruyter, 2005. N. pag.

St. Clair, Guy. "Qualification Management: My Grand Design." *Information Outlook* 4.6, p. 32 (2000).

St. Clair, Guy. *SLA at 100: From Putting Knowledge to Work to Building the Knowledge Culture: The Special Libraries Association 1909–2009.* Alexandria, VA: Special Libraries Association, 2009.

St. Clair, Guy. "Victoria Harriston at the National Academies: Collaboration and Knowledge Sharing Are Key Drivers to Success." *SMR International E-Profiles* (2006).

Stewart, Thomas A. *Intellectual Capital: The New Wealth of Organizations.* New York: Doubleday, 1997.

Stoddart, Linda. "Organizational Culture and Knowledge Sharing at The United Nations: Using an Intranet to Create a Sense of Community." *Knowledge and Process Management*, p. 182 (2007).

Surowiecki, James. "The Financial Page: A Fair Day's Wage." *The New Yorker* (2015).

Surowiecki, James. *The Wisdom of Crowds.* New York: Anchor, 2005.

Sveiby, Karl-Erik. "Methods for Measuring Intangible Assets." 2001 (updated 2010). Web.

Symons, Craig, Alexander Peters, Alex Cullen, and Brandy Worthington. "The Five Essential Metrics for Managing IT." *CIO Zone: Network for IT Leadership* (2008).

Thorson, Kjerstin. "Strategic Communication." *Oxford Bibliographies* (2013).

Tirana, Amrit. *The Knowledge Management Toolkit.* Upper Saddle River, NJ: Prentice-Hall, 2000.

Toffler, Alvin. *The Third Wave.* New York: Bantam, 1980.

Tripp-Melby, Pamela. "On Knowledge Strategy." Personal interviews. 27 August 2012 and 4 September 2012.

US Army. Army Knowledge Management Principles. 2008.

US KM Working Group. Federal Knowledge Management Initiative Roadmap (2008).

van der Linden, Geert. "Transforming Institutional Knowledge into Organizational Effectiveness: The Challenge of Becoming a Learning Organization." Presentation to the ARTDO International Management and HRD Conference, 25 September 2004. Penang, Malaysia.

Wenger-Trayner, Etienne, Richard McDermott, and William Snyder. "Cultivating Communities of Practice: A Guide to Managing Knowledge." *Harvard Business School Press* (2002).

Wenger-Trayner, Etienne. "Introduction to Communities of Practice," 2015. Web.

Zachman, Robert. "A Framework for Information Systems Architecture." *IBM Systems Journal.* 26.3, 1987. IBM Publication G321-5298. Web (pdf).

Zack, Michael F. "Developing a Knowledge Strategy." *California Management Review* 43.3 (1999), 24 January 2016.

Zaleznik, Abraham. "Managers and Leaders: Are They Different?" *Harvard Business Review* (1992).

Index

Abell, Angela 16, 231–232
Allee, Verna 143–144
allegiance, professional 102, 107
Allison, Michael 23–24, 39
Anderson, Janice 233–234
anecdotal measures 177, 186
anti-collaboration 132
Ashkenas, Ron 258
Association for Image and Information Management (AIIM) 222
Atlantic Monthly 250

Babbage, Charles 30–31
balanced scorecard 177–178, 189
Barnard College in New York 283
Barnard, Chester 27
benchmarking 184
Bennett, Charles 31
Bennis, Warren 63
– leadership vs. management 31
Berner, Andrew 94, 301
Bertolini, Mark 44
Billmyer, Kristine 7
Blumenstein, Lynn 224
Boon, J.A. 158
Botha, Hanneri 158
Bower, Marvin 278
– "The Bower Reach" 70–71
– on management consulting 69
– on the firm's "personality" 69
Bradley, Chris 195
Bridges, William
– change curve 259
Brindley, Lynne 12
Bush, Vannevar 31
business case for knowledge services 32
business process reengineering (BPR) 234

Callahan, Shawn 92
Carroll, Lewis 28
Cave, Andrew 75
Chakravarti, Nav 230
change
– desirable and inevitable 104–105
change leader 250

change management 104, 239
– definition (Rockley) 271
– ECM focus 228–229, 242
– readiness assessment 253
– steps for knowledge workers 274
change management principles 41–42, 252
– change readiness 252, 255
– communications planning 253
– communications plannning 253
– dealing with resistance 252, 253
– sponsorship 253, 264
– sponsorship recruitment 267
change resistance 257
– "valley of despair" 257–258
– acknowledging resistance 260
– responding to resistance 260
– surfacing resistance 260
Chief Knowledge Strategist 219, 244–245
– job description 221
Churchill, Winston 28
Citicorp
– 200th anniversary 286–287
– success attributes 286–287
Clare, Mark 115
Clinton, Bill (U.S. President) 66
Cohen, Alex 141–142
Cohn, Fred 281
collaboration 102, 119, 286–287
– "information power" vs. "relationship power" 138–139
– "silos" impediment 129
– approaches to 119–120
– as management methodology 119
– critical and fundamental component of knowledge services 119
– formal 135
– impediments to 132–133
– included in business model 136
– knowledge services focal points 136–137
– knowledge strategist leadership role 287
– mandated 135
– operational driver for KD/KS/KU 146
– respect for individual contribution 73
– three critical elements 133
– unwillingness-to-share impediment 129

Index

collaboration vs. transparency 128
collaborative environment
 – in organizational management 121–122
 – purpose 122
collaborative leadership
 – includes shared owndership 287
collaborative workplace 119
collegiality 286–287, 286
Columbia University in the City of New York 7–8, 95, 281–283
command-and-control management framework
 – knowledge services leads away from 101
communication 40–41
communications plan 288–289, 292
communities of practice 139–140
 – three elements 140
content
 – structured 222
 – unstructured 222
content management system (CMS) 230–231
Coolidge, Calvin 27
Core Principles of Collaboration
 – with respect to knowledge services 122–123
corporate social responsibility 43
corporate strategic communications plan 290
Covey, Stephen R.
 – "scarcity" mentality 130–131
Cox, R.H.
 – quoted by Lyndon Pugh 272
critical success factors 150–151
 – as part of strategic planning 151
 – attributes 150–151
 – categories for knowledge services 151
 – connection between knowledge services provided and knowledge value 152
 – connection with staff competencies and abilities 152
 – defined 150–151
 – determining quality of knowledge services 154
CSR 43
Curzon, Susan 269
customer satisfaction surveys 149

Davenport, Tom 14, 218
Dearstyne, Bruce 16
Dempsey, Michael 15
DeSilva, Nishan
 – on knowledge strategy 52
Detore, Arthur 115
doctrine of collaboration 122–123
document lifecycle management (DLM) 222–223
Drucker, Peter F. 27–28, 220–221, 296
 – "knowledge worker" defined 88
 – "knowledge worker" term introduced 88
 – *Adventures of a Bystander* 4
 – age of social transformation 250
 – knowledge worker as executive 88–89
 – management philosophy 62–63
 – *Managing in a Time of Great Change* 251
 – on change (normal, inevitable, and not to be feared) 285
 – on executive salaries 45
 – on kaizen (continuous improvement) 285
 – on management 37
 – on responsible management 43
 – on strategic learning 36
 – on the organization as an organ of society 45
 – *The Effective Executive* 88–89
 – *The End of Economic Man—The Origins of Totalitarianism* 4–5
 – *The Future of Industrial Man* 5
 – *The Landmarks of Tomorrow* 88–89

ECM
 – defined 224
 – portfolio approach 236
 – scope 236
ECM domains 238
ECM planning
 – three goals 240
ECM strategic framework (AIIM) 245–246
ECM/CMS measures
 – conversion success 231
 – effectiveness 231
 – route efficiencies 231
ECM/KAM strategic planning framework 245–246
 – terminology 245–246
Edersheim, Elizabeth Haas
 – on Marvin Bower at McKinsey 69
 – on visionary leadership 69

- *McKinsey's Marvin Bower: Vision, Leadership, and the Creation of Management Consulting* 69
- *The Definitive Drucker* 35
effectiveness measures 184
- defined 185
enterprise architecture 239
enterprise architecture levels 240
Enterprise Content Management 221
Enterprise Content Management (ECM)
- ECM defined 221
enterprise leadership
- desire for KD/KS/KU 108
epistemic resources
- defined 300

fact-based visioning 71
faux-collaboration 132–133
Fayol, Henri 26–27
Ferriero, David S. 104–105
Follett, Mary Parker 26–27
Forster, E.M. 299–300
Frances Hesselbein Leadership Institute 66
Friedman, Milton 303

Girl Scouts of the U.S.A. 66
Gleick, James 296
- *The Information—A history, A theory, A flood* 30–31
Goleman, Daniel
- leadership categories 64–65
Green, Stephen 44

Hardy, G.H. 31
Harriston, Victoria 203–204
- on embedded knowledge services 56
Hatten, Kenneth J. 55, 201
Hawking, Stephen 30–31
Heifitz, Ronald A.
- on "adaptive work" 53
Henczel, Susan 156
- information audit seven-stage model 156–157
- seven-stage model 165
Hesselbein Leadership Institute. *See* Frances Hesselbein Leadership Institute
Hesselbein, Frances 27, 296, 299
- on transformational leadership 67

Hislop, Donald 35
- on transformational leadership 67
Hopper, Grace 31
Hunt, Deborah 65
- on leadership 63–64
Hydock, Jim 2

Igel, Lee H. 32, 299
- core leadership principles 73
- on Drucker 32
impact measures. *See* effectiveness measures
information and communication technology 21
information audit 155
- no universally accepted definition 156
information overload 243–244
input measures 178–179
intangible assets monitor 177, 190
integrity 72, 102
intellectual capital 1
- legitimacy of 102
- value measurement 169–170
intellectual capital, defined 1
Internet of Things 230–231
Isaacson, Walter 296
- *The Innovators—How a Group of Hackers, Geniuses, and Geeks Created the Digital Revolution* 30–31

Jacobson, Alvin L. 103–104

Kanter, Rosabeth Moss
- change-adept organizations 251–252
- on change readiness 253
- *The Change Masters* 251–252
- *When Giants Learn to Dance* 251–252
Kaplan, Robert 177
Kaye, Jude 23–24, 39
KD/KS/KU 1, 101
- ignorance of purpose 128–129
- ignorance of value 128–129
- sharing skills 57
KD/KS/KU process
- includes change, change management, and change implementation 251
KD/KS/KU value
- why important to the organization 128
Kennedy, Mary Lee 231–232

Kershaw, Anne 192, 300
knowing culture 201
knowledge
– new organizational emphasis 107
knowledge asset management 107, 221, 226–227
– enterprise focus 225
– functional focus 225
– knowledge worker perspective 225
knowledge audit 112–113, 160
knowledge change leader 250
knowledge culture 25, 52, 69–70, 101, 276–277
– attributes 102, 160–161
– begins with knowledge services 105–106, 117–118
– built by knowledge workers 107
– challenge to building 54
– defined 101–102, 286
– development elements 106
– as "firm personality" 69–70, 278
– key players 108
– management or organizational barriers 108
– political ownership 108
– purpose 110
– value of enterprise-wide approach 201
knowledge culture vision
– defined 109
knowledge culture-building 53–54
knowledge culture-building process
– relevance of 110–111
knowledge development 1
knowledge development and knowledge sharing
– "golden age" 107
knowledge development, knowledge sharing, and knowledge utilization 101
knowledge domain 276–277
– defined 80
knowledge economy 250
knowledge integration
– leading to knowledge culture 104–105
knowledge leadership 52–53
– defined 54–55
knowledge management 1
– defined 115
– definition conundrum 103

knowledge nexus 25, 98
knowledge process
– integrity of 102
knowledge services 1, 3, 101
– "guru" 60–61
– "humanist" strength of KM 82–83
– "real-world" terms 198
– "strategy-focused" functional unit 103–104
– "world-class" standards 198
– advocates 133–134
– as catalysis 103
– as management and service-delivery methodology 102
– benefits of excellence in 119
– brand 280
– champions 133–134
– classical knowledge services tasks or workplace activities 90
– consolidated related functions and functional units 227
– constituent elements 202
– defined 1, 299
– defined as curating and managing content 107
– early stages discussion group 86–87
– elements of an organizational "snapshot" 209
– embedded 60–61
– employee types (three) 87–88
– human capital focus 85
– impediments to sharing 131
– importance in the organization 57–58
– in the collaborative environment 129
– in the workplace 198
– informal practitioners 87–88
– initiative 86
– insourced 60–61
– knowledge strategists 88
– knowledge workers 88
– measuring financial value 170
– organizational value proposition for 278
– ownership responsibility 117–118
– people, process, and technology 279–280
– premise 84–85
– purpose 1, 101
– reasons for 129

- relationship to organizational effectiveness 107
- respect for intellectual foundation of 102
- strategic knowledge professionals 88
- supports KD/KS/KU 106
- theoretical vs. practical 198
- underpins organization's larger focus 105–106
- value proposition 199
- value proposition, connects to knowledge culture 109–110
- why, instead of KM? 83–84
- workplace 98

knowledge services ambition 56
knowledge services audit 112–113, 148, 177
- as foundation or starting point 165
- departmental participants 236
- desired effect 160–161
- diagnostic and evaluative purpose 159
- ECM focus 227
- identify elements of knowledge domain 149
- influence on management thinking 157–158
- internal or external auditors 162–163

KVC
- knowledge topics examined 168
- performed by current staff 156
- purpose 148
- results and value 156–157
- stakeholders (participants) 161–162
- Statement of Work 163
- steps 158–159
- strategic purpose 157–158
- synopsis of elements 164
- team or working group 162–163
- topics for consideration 149
- transitioning findings to recommendations 168–169
- work plan 163

knowledge services charter 113–114
knowledge services continuity 281
knowledge services focal point
- role and definition 137
knowledge services focus
- themes 105

knowledge services functional unit. See knowledge services unit
Knowledge services in practice 198
knowledge services management strategy
- determine organizational standards 173
knowledge services marginalization avoidance
- seven steps (example) 146–147
knowledge services measurement strategy 169–170
- expectations 172–173
- goal 173
- objective and purpose 173
- purpose 267
- senior management involvement 169–170
- three-way approach 177
- two essential questions 173
knowledge services sponsors
- defined 134
knowledge services strategic framework 7, 20, 193, 277, 283
- built through collaboration 119
- discussion points 195
- ECM focus 227–228
- implementation responsibility 86
- outline 213–218
- ownership 86
- potential 192
- three essential steps 194–195
knowledge services strategic framework (organizational knowledge strategy) 213–214
knowledge services strategic framework development group 194–195
knowledge services strategic framework objectives 213–214
knowledge services strategic framework: a recommended strategy 208–209
knowledge services strategy framework
- benefits of 81–82
knowledge services thought leader 277
- aspirational role 282
- attributes 281
- followers of 282
- influence 278
- influential role 283
- innovate and manage change 284
- inspirational role 282

knowledge services unit 95–96, 98
knowledge sharing 1, 11
knowledge strategist 1, 91, 276–277
– as "go-to" person for knowledge issues 280
– as knowledge authority 41
– as manager 95–96
– as manager-as-leader 51–52
– as meaning maker 41
– as operator 41–42
– as voice of reason 41–42
– attributes, professional 102–103
– defined 91
– description of tasks 92
– in the organizational culture 102–103
– job description (example) 99
– knowledge services leadership role 103
– office-management responsibiities 99
– operational responsibilities 97–98
– strategic position 57
knowledge strategists
– as businessmen and businesswomen 171
– prior professional experiences 93
– typical demographic background 93
knowledge strategy 7, 21, 39, 192, 283
– as a new management discipline 91
– default 226
– defined 91
– discussion points 195
– no "one-size-fits-all" 194
– objectives 213
– outline 214
– three additional elements 92
– why needed 80
knowledge strategy (knowledge services strategic framework) 213–218
knowledge strategy implementation team 228–229
knowledge strategy objectives 213
Knowledge Strategy Solutions 192
knowledge thought leader
– generosity of spirit 279
– intellectual curiosity 279
– passion for knowledge work 279
knowledge utilization 1
knowledge value 12
– created through KD/KS/KU 103
Knowledge Value Chain 171

knowledge value chain construct 172
knowledge workers 2, 250
– non knowledge-focused workers 90, 90–91
knowledge-centric enterprise
– constituent elements 202
knowledge-*centric* organization
– defined 81–82
knowledge-value gap 172
Koenig, Michael E.D. 17–18
Kotter, John P. 251, 260
– eight-stage process 270
Kouzes and Posner
– five leadership practices 58–59
Kouzes, James 57–58
Kübler-Ross, Elisabeth 260
KVC 171
– on "adaptive work" 53

Laurie, Donald L. 53
Leader to Leader 284
leader-manager
– role in knowledge services 77–78
leadership
– and knowledge services 53
– defined 53–54
– integrity in . . . 52
– the "work" of leadership 53
– transformational 65
Lewin, Kurt
– leadership attributes 65
library and information science 5–6
Lilienthal, David E. 28–29, 29–30, 38–39, 123–124, 296
– *Management—A Liberal Art* 28–29
Lovelace, Augusta Ada, Countess of Lovelace 30–31

Machiavelli, Niccolò 26
management (IT) 222
management essentials 49
management, humanistic 83, 280
management, responsible 42
manager-as-leader 51
March, James G.
– quoted by Surowiecki 121
Matthews, Joseph 178–179
– four measurement variables 178–179
Maulitz, Russell 116–117

Maurer, Rick
- change readiness 253
- change readiness guidelines 253
measurement capture 148
measurement results communicated 177
measurement types 177
measures vs. metrics 177–178
measures, anecdotal 177
measures, effectiveness 177
metrics vs. measures 177–178
Mill, John Stuart 26
Mintzberg, Henry 30
Montgomery, Cynthia A. 41–42
Mumford, Lewis 31
Murphy, Jim 224
Murray, Art 64

Naisbitt, John 12
needs analysis process 155
network analysis 139
networking 59, 112, 139
Norton, David 177, 189

Obama, President Barack 283, 285
operational metrics 176–177
organizational effectiveness 213
organizational knowledge strategy 193
organizational leadership
- desire for KD/KS/KU 108
organizational learning. *See* strategic learning
Orna, Elizabeth 156
outcome measures 179, 186
output measures 179
Oxbrow, Nigel 16

partners
- value of 111
Penfold, Sharon 261
Perdue, Mitzi 117
Piketty, Thomas
- *Capital in the Twenty-First Century* 45
Posner, Barry 58–59
Powell, Timothy W. 39, 171, 172, 180, 183, 185–186, 191, 300
process measures 179
Project Management Book of Knowledge (PMBOK) 245

Prusak, Larry 15
Pugh, Lyndon 271
- guidelines for well-motivated workforce 272
putting KM to work 198

raise awareness for knowledge services 290
records and information management (RIM) 223
Reczek, Karen 115
research associates
- as knowledge workers 90
research managers
- as knowledge workers 90
research specialists
- as knowledge workers 90
return-on-investment 177, 180
rich media and digital asset management 239
Rockley, Ann 222, 271
ROI 177, 180
Roosevelt, Theodore 26
Rosen, Evan
- on "the knowledge worker" 89
Rosenstein, Bruce 243, 284–285
Rosenthal, Stephen R. 55, 201
Rothman, Joshua 78–79

Schein, Edgar H.
- on leader as "creator of culture" 53
Schessler, Barrie M. 218, 223, 276, 288, 299
Schmitt, Bernd 281
search engine optimization (SEO) 231
Senge, Peter 24
Shannon, Claude 31
Sinek, Simon 193
- "golden circle" 193
- *Start with Why: How Great Leaders Inspire Everyone to Take Action* 193
Smith, Adam 26
Smith, Megan 116
Snow, C.P. 31
Social responsibility 43
Sparks, JoAnne 103–104
specialized librarianship
- connecting with KM 115
- connecting with knowledge services 115

sponsors
– value of 111
sponsorship 112, 201
St. Onge, Hubert 139
Stanley, Dale 50, 81, 94, 97, 103, 112, 134, 178, 250, 277, 283–285, 288, 293, 298
Stewart, Thomas 13–14
Stoddart, Linda 272–273
– knowledge-sharing framework 272–273
Stoppard, Thomas 31
strategic knowledge professional
– defined 90
strategic learning 1, 19, 21
– defined 83
– purpose 83
strategy
– defined 92
Sun Tzu 26
Surowiecki, James 44, 120–121
Sveiby, Karl-Erik 190
Symons, Craig 175

Taylor, Frederick Winslow 27
technology and content
– mutually beneficial 83
technology management
– enthusiasm in knowledge culture 102
Tiwana, Amrit 16
Toffler, Alvin 218

transparency 102, 287
transparency vs. collaboration 128
Tripp-Melby, Pamela 94
Turing, Alan 31

United States Army
– "Knowledge Management Principles" 122
United States KM Working Group
– Federal Knowledge Management Initiative Roadmap 123

value creation 170
Value Network Analysis 139, 143, 240
value proposition for knowledge services 110
van der Linden, Geert 121–122
visionary leadership 109

Web Content Management 239
Web Content Management System 234
Wenger-Trayner, Etienne 139–140
Wheeler, John Archibald 31
Wilding, Thomas S. 105–405
World-class knowledge services 203–204

Zachman Framework 240
Zachman, John 240
Zack, Michael
– on knowledge strategy 92
Zaleznik Abraham 55

About Guy St. Clair

Guy St. Clair's academic specialty is knowledge services, the management methodology that converges information management, knowledge management (KM), and strategic learning for cross-functional organizational success. He is President and Consulting Specialist for Knowledge Services for SMR International, a management consulting practice in New York City.

Recognized as a knowledge services "evangelist," St. Clair has been affiliated with Columbia University in the City of New York since 2010, when he joined the School of Professional Studies as one of the founders of the M.S. in Information and Knowledge Strategy program. In 2015 he moved to the Postbaccalaureate Studies Program, where he now teaches *Managing Information and Knowledge: Applied Knowledge Services*. He also guest lectures for New York University's Consulting Strategies program and frequently conducts webinars and in-house seminars about knowledge services for client organizations.

St. Clair has written or coauthored numerous books relating to information management, knowledge management, and strategic learning, as well as articles about knowledge services and knowledge strategy. He is a graduate of the University of Virginia, where he earned his A.B. in Liberal Arts. St. Clair's graduate degree is from the University of Illinois (M.S. in Library and Information Science).